THE GROWTH OF THE MEDIEVAL CITY

A History of Urban Society in Europe
General Editor: Robert Tittler

This major series investigates the variety, functions and character of the cities of Europe, and the changing lifestyles of their inhabitants, since early medieval times. Strong in outline and rich in detail, each volume will synthesise the present state of scholarship on the often controversial issues involved; and each will offer interpretations based on the author's own research. The books will be necessary reading for students of urban and social history, and enjoyable and informative for non-specialists as well.

The Growth of the Medieval City

From Late Antiquity to the Early Fourteenth Century

DAVID NICHOLAS

Longman
London and New York

Addison Wesley Longman Limited
Edinburgh Gate
Harlow
Essex CM20 2JE
United Kingdom
and Associated Companies throughout the world

Published in the United States of America
by Addison Wesley Longman Inc., New York

© Addison Wesley Longman Limited 1997

First published 1997

ISBN   0 582 29907 1   CSD
ISBN   0 582 29906 3   PPR

British Library Cataloguing-in-Publication Data

A catalogue record for this book is available from the British Library

Library of Congress Cataloging-in-Publication Data

Nicholas, David, 1939–
    The growth of the medieval city : from late antiquity to the early
fourteenth century / David Nicholas.
       p.   cm. — (A history of urban society in Europe)
    Includes bibliographical references and index.
    ISBN 0–582–29907–1 (CSD). — ISBN 0–582–29906–3 (PPR)
    1. Cities and towns, Medieval.   2. Cities and towns, Ancient.
I. Title.   II. Series.
HT115.N53   1997
307.76'09'02—DC20   96–27185
                                            CIP

Set by 35 in 10.5/12pt Bembo
Produced by Longman Singapore Publishers (Pte) Ltd.
Printed in Singapore

Contents

Contents

Contents

List of Maps and Plans

MAPS

CITY PLANS

Editor's Preface

The five volumes of this series are designed to provide a descriptive and interpretive introduction to European Urban Society from the Middle Ages to the present century. The series emerged from a concern that the rapidly burgeoning interest in European Urban History had begun to outstrip the materials available to teach it effectively. It is my hope that these volumes will provide the best possible resource for that purpose, for the serious general reader, and for the historian or history student who requires a scholarly and accessible guide to the issues at hand. Every effort has been made to ensure volumes which are well-written and clear as well as scholarly: authors were selected on the basis of their writing ability as well as their scholarship.

If there is a bias to the project, it is that some considerable degree of comprehension be achieved in geographic coverage as well as subject matter, and that comparisons to non-European urban societies be incorporated where appropriate. The series will thus not simply dwell on the familiar examples of urban life in the great cities of Europe, but also in the less familiar and more remote. Though we aim to consider the wide and general themes implicit in the subject at hand, we also hope not to lose sight of the common men and women who occupied the dwellings, plied their trades and walked the streets.

This undertaking did not come about by random chance, nor was it by any means conceived solely by the series editor. Well before individual authors were commissioned, extensive efforts were undertaken to survey the requirements of scholars active in research and teaching European Urban History in all periods. I am grateful to Charles Tilly, Miriam Chrisman, William Hubbard, Janet Roebuck, Maryanne Kowaleski, Derk Visser, Josef Konvitz, Michael P. Weber, Laurie Nussdorfer, Penelope Corfield and Tony Sutcliffe, as well as of the authors themselves, whose comments and concerns have been extremely valuable in shaping the series.

Robert Tittler, Montreal

Preface

The physiognomy and spatial distribution of urban life in modern Europe were fixed essentially during the Middle Ages. Recent decades have witnessed an immense growth in scholarly literature that has weakened older classic interpretations. Archaeological finds and the social analyses made possible by archival investigations and computer-assisted studies have enriched our understanding while complicating our perspective. I have written these books to provide a framework that students of medieval urbanisation in the English-speaking world can use as a starting point for more detailed research. My focus is on the core regions of 'Latin Christendom': England, France, the Low Countries, Germany, the Iberian Peninsula and Italy.

I have dealt with 'cities', not 'towns' except for pre-urban settlements that eventually evolved into cities. English is the only west European language that distinguishes 'town' from 'city' functionally, although 'city' in French may refer only to the area enclosed by the late Roman wall while the rest of the settlement is the 'town'. German scholars in particular have used an all-embracing definition of urbanisation that lumps together as 'towns' everything from the great metropolises to the tiniest settlements that had charters of privilege. The geographer Robert Dickinson, attributing the specific characteristics of the city peculiarities to the centralisation of services, insisted that 'there was, and still is, no real difference in essential functions between the urban settlement in the country with 1,000 inhabitants and the urban agglomeration with several millions'. Dickinson did, however, admit that a central business district becomes more pronounced in cities than in smaller places, and the occupational distribution by regions within the city is sharper.[1]

1 Dickinson, *West European City*, 252.

The city–town distinction is admittedly arbitrary and depends to a great degree on the level of regional urbanisation. Places that were large enough to be cities in England would have been considered small towns in Italy, where most specifically urban functions were usually pre-empted by the enormous metropolis. Both cities and towns in the Middle Ages had permanent markets where goods and services were exchanged. Townspeople did produce some subsistence goods for local consumption, but most of what they exported, and the services that they provided, contributed to the quality of its life but were not absolutely necessary for survival. The extent of occupational heterogeneity also differentiated city from town and town from village. Both market towns and cities contained artisans and merchants; but the social structure of the cities had 'professional' elements not usually present in the market towns, and thus they had more complex functions and social structures. The small towns rarely had craft organisations. The larger centres also had numerous transients, who were a minor element in the small places.[2]

Henri Pirenne's classic works,[3] which were the first significant summaries of their topics to appear in English, have conditioned generations of British and American students to think of the medieval city as rigidly separated from the countryside. The city for Pirenne was a purely economic entity based on long-distance trade, originating after the Muslims allegedly closed the Mediterranean to trade in the seventh century. He saw the late medieval cities as increasingly industrial, dominated by craftsmen who, by controlling governments through their guilds, institutionalised a narrow focus that compromised the cities' prosperity by self-defeating industrial protectionism. Pirenne's typology of the medieval city was based largely on the enormous cities of Flanders. Many readers of *The Growth of the Medieval City* will know that the Flemish cities are also my speciality, but I hope to avoid the pitfalls of extrapolating local viewpoints into contexts where they have only a comparative relevance.

Pirenne and his early followers considered the cities to be islands of capitalism in a 'feudal' world. More recent students of medieval urbanisation, including many Marxists, have emphasised the essential linkage of the cities and the rural areas.[4] Yves Barel, insisting that the 'urban system is allied with feudalism', maintains against the weight of recent opinion that the urban patriciate was a commercial group from the beginning, with its 'own productive base in urban industry'. Craft goods that were manufactured in small shops, often in the home, and sold to the merchant

---

2   Hilton, *English and French Towns*, 6–7; Nicholas, 'Medieval urban origins', 58–9.
3   Pirenne, *Medieval Cities* and *Early Democracies in the Low Countries*.
4   Mumford, *The Culture of Cities*, 24–7.

patricians were thus the 'specific mode of production of the medieval urban system'. Cities originated out of feudal society, and their very existence depended on bourgeois exploitation of the workers.[5]

The German sociologist Max Weber saw the city as fundamentally economic in character, with a high degree of occupational differentiation. The city is not demarcated from the town by size alone. A regularly held market is fundamental, for it permits goods to be exchanged continuously rather than only occasionally. The largest cities attracted capital by providing services and eventually by exporting surplus raw materials and manufactured goods. But the demand generated by the local market, where city dwellers could satisfy virtually all their needs and wants, also helps to explain the permanence of the city. The medieval cities usually had an elite of wealthy consumers, political rulers or landowners who controlled capital through rent. They provided demand for the goods of long-distance traders, whose wares in turn became available to the less affluent and brought about an amelioration of the standard of living and a more fluid exchange of goods. Most cities were also political centres and above all fortifications; the city thus linked defence and market. Weber also saw the cities of western Europe as a distinct type, distinguished from those of other regions by their independent territorial base and at least quasi-autonomy in administration.[6]

Gideon Sjoberg has also suggested distinctions that are especially germane for the early medieval city, although the late medieval city became a catalyst for breaking down these barriers. When compared to the modern city, that of the early Middle Ages had a lower population and a central area that was more important for government and religion and for residences of the elite than for commerce. Facilities for credit and capital formation were poor. Ethnic and occupational groups were clustered in their own streets or quarters, and a powerful sense of social status made upward mobility difficult. Extended families were critically important for the elite, but the social relations and business dealings of the lower orders tended to be based on the nuclear family or even to have little basis in family ties. The family was patriarchal, but while upper-class women were isolated, poor women were more economically active.[7]

In a sense the medieval city was simply a town writ large. The two began similarly, then diverged. While a town might have a charter, it normally had fewer rights of self-government than a city. While the town

5   Rodney Hilton, *English and French Towns*, 8–9, 18; Barel, *Ville médiévale*, 11, 75–6.
6   A convenient summary of translated extracts from Weber's works, illustrating his essential theses, is Weber, *The City*, translated and edited by Don Martindale and Gertrud Neuwirth; see esp. 65–80.
7   Sjoberg, *Preindustrial City*, 321–8.

had both merchant and artisan elements, its economic radius was narrower than the city's, often causing it to be little more than a farm market. The town had a higher degree of occupational differentiation and special-isation than the villages but less in turn than the city. Accordingly, most towns were oriented toward services and basic manufactures. This was also true of many cities, but the services were more varied, involving capital-generating interaction with areas farther from the home settlement than was true of most towns. Although the extent of industrial production in the medieval city has been exaggerated, most cities did have a larger industrial component than towns. While most manufactured goods except textiles and metals did not reach a large export market, and accordingly the economic base even of most large cities was more in commerce than in industry, the cities came closer than did the towns to producing a large enough variety of manufactured consumer goods to satisfy their residents' needs. Commerce dominated over industry in city and town alike; but the commerce of the city involved marketing a wider range of goods, and the industry of the city produced more staple items needed locally, than was true of the towns.

We must understand the city in its social and spacial context. What caused it to appear in given places and at particular times? What did it look like? How did its residents make their livings? Who ruled the cit-ies, and how did those ruling elites change? We shall see important varia-tions and contrasts in social structure and governance between cities of the early and late Middle Ages; between those with a large industrial com-ponent and those lacking it; between cities whose trade was mainly local and those with interregional connections; between cities in the same economic region and those in different economic regions; and between those that managed to dominate their rural environs economically and politically and those that did not.

Acknowledgements

This book owes much to the support and encouragement of my long-suffering wife and to past and present professional colleagues, particularly Beth Carney, Richard Golden, Alan Grubb, Pam Mack, Steve Marks, Ed Moïse, Denis Paz and Bob Waller. The debt is especially great to Tom Kuehn, who read the entire manuscript and suggested emendations from the perspective of a profound student of urbanisation in medieval Italy. I am also grateful to the University of Georgia Library for permitting me the unrestricted use of collections there. The manuscript also owes a great deal to the careful critique that it received from Professor Robert Tittler, the general editor of the series in which it appears.

Dedication

The Growth of the Medieval City and its sequel, The Later Medieval City, are dedicated in affection and esteem to Bryce Lyon, who suggested in 1964 that I write a comparative history of urbanisation in the Middle Ages and has been waiting patiently ever since.

PART ONE

Antiquity and the Early Middle Ages

CHAPTER ONE

The Urban Legacy of Antiquity

The Roman and the medieval city

Although many medieval cities developed on sites previously inhabited by the Romans, 'continuity' is often more apparent than real. Important functional differences distinguish the Roman city from its medieval successor. Most large Roman cities were political and military capitals, more consumers than producers of goods and services that exploited the rural environs to which they were linked juridically and socially. The Roman urban elites lived mainly off the rental income of their rural estates rather than trade or industry. As late as the sixth century the emperor Justinian imported enough Egyptian grain to Constantinople to feed 600,000 people.[1]

The medieval city, by contrast, was a marketplace for its hinterland and produced manufactured goods. The distinction is overdrawn, for the Roman cities produced manufactured items and re-exported goods that were not sold on its own local market, while only the greatest medieval cities developed much export manufacturing. Industrial activity was centring increasingly in the cities by the fourth century, as government regulation increased and the rural areas became dangerous. Furthermore, although the Roman cities were consumers, they were not parasitic, for all provided important functions of demand, manufacture, governance and protection in exchange for the goods that they used. Although long-distance trade was dominated by luxury raw materials such as precious stones, spices, metals and particularly fine cloth, even such utilitarian items as pottery were sold far from their place of manufacture. The

---

1   Bairoch, *Cities*, 85. This thesis received its classic formulation from Werner Sombart. See discussion supporting the Sombart thesis by Hopkins, 'Economic growth and towns', 72–3.

long-distance trade of the Roman Empire was voluminous and varied enough to help support the large number of small cities.[2]

Throughout the Middle Ages the cities of the Mediterranean basin had closer ties to their rural environs than did most in the north. The Greek and Roman cities were actually city-states, but the Romans, following Greek practice, separated the central area (*urbs*) from the rest of the city by a tiny wall, which delimited a *pomerium* that was sacred to the gods. Full Roman citizenship was initially enjoyed only by residents of the *urbs*, which was the ceremonial, religious and governmental city, while military assemblies were held outside it in the *fora*.[3]

Organic and planned cities

The cities of antiquity, like those of the Middle Ages, developed in two basic but not mutually exclusive forms. Older settlements developed gradually and organically, often on hilltops, with curved streets that sometimes did not intersect. Both Athens and Rome (Plan 1) were easily defended hilltop fortifications surrounded by farm villages that eventually merged. The Athenian *agora* and the Roman *forum* were at the foot of the main hill and between the hills repectively. The *forum* began as a cemetery in a swampy valley, but it had been drained and converted to a field for assemblies by the seventh century BC. Both *agora* and *forum* quickly became the major markets of the city. While the *agora* was usually triangular, a characteristic that it shared with some early medieval markets that developed just outside fortifications, most Roman *fora* were rectangular, with a temple and a covered basilica at opposite ends. While the acropolis (high city), the famous hilltop citadel of Athens, became peripheral as the city developed at its base, the seven hills of Rome remained the centre of the ancient city.[4]

But the ancients also became sophisticated city planners. The Etruscans probably learned planning from the Greeks, who were founding settlements with rectangular street plans in Sicily by the seventh century BC.

2 Bairoch, *Cities*, 84–7; Kolb, *Stadt im Altertum*, 248; Claude, *Byzantinische Stadt*, 167; Hopkins, 'Economic growth and towns', 37–47, 54–5, 75. For a dissenting view see Vance, *Continuing City*, 84, which contrasts the parasitic Roman city with the medieval city, whose growth was based on the interaction of urban and rural areas rather than overt exploitation.

3 Rykwert, *Idea of a Town*, 27–9, 44–9; Kolb, *Stadt im Altertum*, 84, 150–1; Owens, *City*, 184 n. 21.

4 Vance, *Continuing City*, 77; Kolb, *Stadt im Altertum*, 142 ff.; Owens, *City*, 153–4; Ward-Perkins, *Cities of Ancient Greece and Italy*, 31; Benevolo, *City*, 56, 142–3; Morris, *Urban Form*, 25.

They passed their knowledge on to the Romans.[5] Like the Etruscans, the Romans used two main streets: an east–west axis (the *decumanus*) and a secondary north–south artery (the *cardo*), that intersected at the centrally located *forum*. This gave their foundations a nucleus that the often square Greek plans lacked. While the Greeks normally destroyed pre-existing settlements before building new cities, the Romans preferred to reconstruct older cities, always making the plans more rectangular. A planned newer area was characteristically linked by rectangular streets to an unplanned older core that gradually became more regular as the Romans built *fora* and aqueducts and paved streets. Thus the original settlement was frequently not at the centre of the Roman city; Pompeii is a famous example. The Romans divided their cities into quarters that began at the intersection of the two main streets. The intersection of side streets created rectangular blocks called 'islands' (*insulae*).[6]

Virtually all Roman cities had schools, and the larger ones had libraries. Streets were generally paved after Julius Caesar's time, and the large centres had pavements. The central government built aqueducts. The public baths and the *fora* were places of meeting and exchange. The cities had police and regulated the supply and price of food. The amphitheatres provided entertainments for the masses, but they were generally built outside the walls for security reasons and linked to the central city by a main street.[7] Even in the fourth century, when Rome had long passed its peak, the city had at least twenty-eight libraries, eight bridges, eleven public baths and 856 private baths, 290 granaries and warehouses and forty-six brothels. Although Rome had fewer than 1,800 single-family houses this late, it had more than 44,000 tenements that were dispersed in all parts of the city except in the Palatine and imperial *forum* areas, intermingled with the mansions of the aristocrats. They ranged from tiny shacks to solidly constructed buildings four and more storeys high. Most had businesses on the ground floor and residences above.[8]

Augustan Rome (Plan 1), with a population estimated at between

5 Ward-Perkins, *Cities of Ancient Greece and Italy*, 24–5. The notion that the Greeks did not plan cities before the career of Hippodamus in the fifth century BC is a myth. Owens, *City*, 95–6.

6 Rykwert, *Idea of a Town*, 72–88, 96–9; Kolb, *Stadt im Altertum*, 153, 195; Claude, *Byzantinische Stadt*, 41–3; Vance, *Continuing City*, 60–2; Owens, *City*, 100–7, 117–18; MacMullen, *Roman Social Relations*, 86; Morris, *Urban Form*, 40.

7 Rome itself and Arles were exceptions in having the theatres in the city centre. Jones, *Later Roman Empire* 1, 721; Jones, *Decline of the Ancient World*, 249–50; MacMullen, *Roman Social Relations*, 58–69; Krautheimer, *Rome*, 9; Kolb, *Stadt im Altertum*, 84; Ward-Perkins, *Cities of Ancient Greece and Rome*, 33–4.

8 Ward-Perkins, *Cities of Ancient Greece and Rome*, 36; Krautheimer, *Rome*, 9–15; Krautheimer, *Three Christian Capitals*, 12; Jones, *Later Roman Empire* 1: 689.

700,000 and one million, was the only megalopolis in the west. Its street plan, which at its greatest extent had 85 km of road, was an irregular maze. Most streets were footpaths or could accommodate only one cart at a time. The central city had only two *viae* (streets on which two carts could pass each other), on opposite sides of the main *forum*, although the outlying areas had twenty. All streets ended at the complex of public buildings and temples on the Capitoline and Palatine hills. Augustus (27 BC–AD 14) did considerable building, and succeeding emperors enlarged the main *forum* and added mausolea, theatres, temples and *fora* in their own honour. Nero reconstructed much of the central city after the fire of AD 64, widening streets and standardising building heights. Rome reached its maximum development in the second century. Later emperors embellished but made no fundamental changes until Constantine's reconstruction in the fourth century.[9]

An imperial 'prefect of the city' administered the capital, which was formally divided into fourteen administrative districts. Smaller neighbourhood associations based on streets were the scene of family feuds that presaged the vicious fighting of medieval Rome. Streets were named after prominent families, buildings or the trades practised in them. As in the medieval city, the central areas generally had the greatest wealth and the highest prestige, while the outlying areas and suburbs were poorer. Thus while basic necessities were available in neighbourhoods, power was concentrated at the city centre.[10]

ROMAN URBANISATION IN THE EARLY EMPIRE

City types and public administration

The Romans had various terms that we translate as 'city'. Colonies for army veterans were at the top of the administrative hierarchy, followed by *municipia*, which came directly under the provincial governments. The *civitas* was originally third in status. In the Mediterranean regions of the Empire *civitates* amounted to subdivisions of provinces, but in Gaul and Britain they were tribal capitals that became nuclei of Roman administration. But the colonies were predicated on the Roman practice of giving bonuses in land to veterans, which Augustus replaced with cash payments. Thus except in Britain, where the four colonies remained military in nature, the Romans began designating some existing communities

---

9 Benevolo, *City*, 143–7, 192.
10 MacMullen, *Roman Social Relations*, 69–80; Jones, *Later Roman Empire* 1: 687.

The Urban Legacy of Antiquity

as 'colonies', particularly those with a large number of Roman settlers. By the third century the original distinctions were completely blurred, and *civitas* became the normal term for the city and its rural environs. The *urbs* was the densely populated chief place of the *civitas*.[11]

The imperial government tried to standardise urban administration. Virtually all cities were ruled by councils, usually of one hundred *curiales* or decurions who served for life. So little was the economy of the Roman city based on trade that until the fifth century all *civitates* required decurions to own a large amount of land. Thus the city rulers actually spent much of their time on country estates. The chief administrators were 'two men' (*duoviri*), assisted by aediles, who administered markets and public services, and quaestors, who handled finances. The most serious problem of the Roman cities was their lack of a stable financial base. Some owned public land and realised a small income from ground rents on it, but few had the authority to levy direct taxes. Some collected customs at the borders of the *civitas*. The cities raised most of their revenue from market tolls, licence fees, sales taxes, and monopolies on strategic commodities, especially salt, which they leased to tax farmers called 'publicans'. The publicans were so corrupt that the decurions collected most taxes by Augustus' period. During the second century the central government appointed 'curators of the city' to supervise finances. They soon became the chief magistrates.[12]

The beginnings of urbanisation in Roman Gaul

The enormous demand market of Rome drew much of the productive capacity of the Empire toward Italy. Although there were several large cities in the east, Rome stifled the growth of provincial urban centres in western Europe, few of which ever had populations as high as 20,000.[13]

Except for Cologne, most Roman colonies for veterans were on or near the Rhône river south of its junction with the Saône. Farther north and east Augustus established a frontier along the Rhine and Danube rivers, studded with military centres that doubled as trading posts. The Romans frequently built on Celtic or even Greek sites. The Celts seem to have favoured rectangular streets but within an oval rather

---

11 Mitterauer, *Markt und Stadt*, 56; Andersson, *Urbanisierte Ortschaften*, 20–2; Kolb, *Stadt im Altertum*, 169; Merrifield, *London*, 42; Goudineau, Février and Fixot, 'Réseau urbain', 88–90; Nicholas, 'Urban origins', 60–1; Morris, *Urban Form*, 40.
12 Jones, *Decline of the Ancient World*, 243, 239–40; Jones, *Later Roman Empire* 1: 724–5; Hammond, *Ancient City*, 289–90; Kolb, *Stadt im Altertum*, 226.
13 Hammond, *City in the Ancient World*, 281–7; MacMullen, *Roman Social Relations*, 57.

than orthogonal area. Huesca in Spain and particularly Bourges in France are the best surviving examples of Celtic street plans.[14]

The Romans did not disturb the Greek cities in Gaul but usually moved Celtic hilltop settlements into the plains, probably because it was hard to incorporate hill forts into their road and hydrographic networks. The security provided by hilltops was also a less pressing concern during the early Empire. When they fortified cities later, however, the Romans often diverted the sacred streams into moats and thus from the Celts' perspective polluted them. Some *civitates* were slightly displaced existing settlements, but others were totally new foundations. The Romans founded Autun as a provincial capital in preference to five existing Celtic sites nearby. Moving into the plain permitted the Romans to build cities with regular plans. In this way Arles, Vienne and Toulouse were joined to Celtic forts in a manner prefiguring the classic medieval pre-urban nucleus: a largely unplanned area inside the fortification, inhabited mainly by soldiers, officials and eventually priests, which was loosely attached to a civilian settlement outside. Even when the Romans did not move Celtic settlements, as at Fréjus, Arles and Poitiers, they tried to regularise their previously organic street plans, forcing native proprietors to change their property boundaries. The Roman cities in Gaul tended to have mixed neighbourhoods, with little specialisation of quarters except for the *forum* and temple areas.[15]

The tribal *civitates* in Gaul and Britain were considerably larger than those in the Mediterranean and the east. The smallest *civitates* in Gaul were in the Rhône-Saône area, where most cities were larger but were colonies. In the late first century AD the province of Belgica in northern Gaul had only sixty-four *civitates* with an average area of 8,300 sq km, while the several hundred *civitates* in northern Africa averaged 100 sq km. Curiously, however, the extreme northwest, in modern terms northwestern France and the western Low Countries, had small *civitates*, virtually all of them tribal capitals. Thus while in southern Europe the *civitates* normally became catchment areas of cities, those of Gaul, particularly in the extreme north, were too large and were subdivided into districts. Thus, while some *civitas* capitals became important cities, several district capitals such as Bruges and Ghent also developed into centres of economic regions.[16]

14 Claude, *Bourges und Poitiers*, 47–9; Goudineau, Février and Fixot, 'Réseau urbain', 88–90.

15 Goudineau, Février and Fixot, 'Réseau urbain', 93–8; Kolb, *Stadt im Altertum*, 222–3; Hopkins, 'Economic growth and towns', 68; Guillerme, *Age of Water*, 4.

16 Jones, *Later Roman Empire* 1: 715–18; Kolb, *Stadt im Altertum*, 224; Vercauteren, 'Spätantike *civitas*', 123; Goudineau, 'Les villes de la paix romaine', 386, plan, 325 with commentary.

Roman urbanisation in Britain

Britain, the most exposed Roman province, is a special case. Virtually all Roman cities there had a military origin, including four colonies (Colchester, Lincoln, Gloucester and York) by AD 100. As on the continent, the colonies began with a single military nucleus but quickly included civilian settlements. The walls of the hilltop fort at Lincoln were extended to protect a single-street settlement extending down the hill, roughly doubling the area of the original agglomeration. At York the garrison was on the east bank of the Ouse, while a civilian settlement developed across the river.[17]

But the Romans governed Britain more through military *civitates* than through colonies. Canterbury and Verulamium (St Albans) were the earliest *civitates*, followed by Chelmsford, Caistor-by-Norwich, Chichester, Winchester and Silchester. As the legions moved north and west in the 80s, Cirencester, Dorchester, Exeter, Leicester and Wroxeter were added, followed in the second century by several in Wales and Scotland. Except for Verulamium, Silchester and Winchester, none was fortified at the beginning. Some were tribal capitals, but strategic concerns caused the Romans to move others away from the Celtic settlement. The alignment of Watling Street, their main north–south road, caused the Romans to establish Verulamium alongside a Celtic site, and Chichester succeeded a Celtic settlement at Selsey. Exeter became the *civitas* of the Dumnoni but is two modern counties away from Penwith, their capital.[18]

London was the largest place in Britain even in the first century, at a ford across the Thames at the last point where it could be bridged, at the terminus of the Roman road network and at the border between the territories of several Celtic tribes. Yet London only became a colony in the early fourth century and was never a *civitas*. London's street plan was less regular than most, particularly on the less developed west end. The wall, south of the east–west road paralleling the Thames, dates from the late second century, nearly a century earlier than most city walls in Britain. With an area of 330 sq ha, this was the largest Roman fortress in Britain and larger than most on the continent. It fixed the contours of medieval London; in the late eleventh century William I added castles at each end of it and strengthened the bastions, but the Tower of London, on the eastern edge of the city, was not part of the Roman fort. The six main gates of the medieval wall were all on the sites of Roman gates and led to a major market. As on the continent, the Romans

---

17 Rivet, *Town and Country*, 63–4, 138–9; Wacher, *Roman Britain*, 66.
18 Rivet, *Town and Country*, 74; Barley, *European Towns*, 9; Owens, *City*, 124.

did not initially build this fortress directly along the river but did so in 369, by which time the port of London had so little traffic that a wall would not interfere seriously.[19]

THE THIRD-CENTURY CRISIS AND ITS AFTERMATH

The walled city as an urban type

Although virtually all Roman cities in the eastern Empire were walled, most in Gaul were unfortified before the third century, for the Romans saw dangers in making the cities into bastions. Before then all fortified towns except Lyon and Autun were either on a frontier or along the Mediterranean. Cologne, Trier, Tournai, Tongeren and some smaller garrisons had walls. But after the Germans temporarily broke the Rhine frontier around 260 and burned most of the leading frontier centres, the physiognomy of Roman urbanisation changed fundamentally. The Romans did not re-establish the Rhine frontier north of Xanten, near Cologne, and the more exposed *civitates* east and north of it went into a precipitate decline. Although Mainz, on the west shore of the Rhine, recovered, its neighbour on the east bank, Wiesbaden, had only a small population left by the end of the third century.[20]

Celtic hilltop sites that the Romans occupied directly rather than moving them into the valleys, their normal practice, could be defended against the invaders but could not grow. The Celtic fort at Besançon had been on the crest of a hill that jutted into a bend into the river Doubs, which nearly surrounded it. The fort was at the neck of the isthmus, and the only route into the unfortified civilian town, downhill toward the river, was through the citadel. After the disaster the civilian population moved back into the Celtic hilltop fort, which, rather than the Roman civilian centre, became the nucleus of medieval Besançon. The lack of a settlement on the landward side of the citadel was a fatal obstruction to the development of Besançon.[21] Yet Limoges, the largest Celtic hill fort in Gaul, suffered because the Romans moved their *civitas* into the plain to link it to their road network. The central part of the agglomeration was rewalled in the fourth century, but the lower slope of the

19 Wacher, *Roman Britain*, 66–7; Merrifield, *London*, 18, 23–4, 42, 128–9, 213–16; Rivet, *Town and Country*, 138; Schofield, *Medieval London Houses*, 7.
20 Owens, *City*, 121; Kolb, *Stadt im Altertum*, 235; Renkhoff, *Wiesbaden*, 1–2.
21 Fohlen, *Basançon* 1: 35–9, 54–7, 71–6, 109, 123–8, 147–58.

hill was gradually deserted. The poles of the medieval city became the hill fort and the suburban tomb of St Martial.[22]

The Romans thus responded to the crisis by undertaking an empire-wide programme of walling the cities behind the much-reduced frontier, probably from the time of the emperor Aurelian (270–75). Many of the new fortifications used material recovered from the ruins of civilian buildings of the town. Except in Britain, where the walls were well constructed and evidently not built in an emergency, many fortifications were sometimes hasty and haphazard, suggesting 'panic building'.[23] Although the occupied surface of most Italian cities declined, there are fewer examples in Italy than in Gaul of late ancient walls of reduced size. Some Italian cities actually expanded. Baths and granaries in the eastern suburbs of Brescia were brought into the wall circuit. The suburbs of Naples, whose Greek wall was inadequate for defence, were fortified in the fifth century. Pavia and Milan grew in the late Empire. The grid plan was preserved almost unaltered in the centre of Pavia, and the wall of the late third and fourth centuries enclosed the entire city as it had been in Augustus' time and was still in use in the ninth century. Rome was an exception in receiving a new but reduced fortification. The Aurelian Wall was 18 km long, with sixteen massive gates at the end of the major streets. The walls were raised twice, reaching an enormous height of over 15 metres in 402–3. Over 380 square towers projected from the wall at intervals of 47 metres, and the towers and gates were linked by an arcaded gallery. The wall left some inhabited areas outside, even cutting some villas in two.[24]

The Romans had distinguished between the inner city and its suburb even in the republican period, but the trunctated walls of the late Empire necessitated a further distinction, which is enshrined in legislation of the emperor Constantine, between the *civitas*, which included the walled area and a suburb of some 1,000 paces around it, and the 'territory', which was the rural portion beyond the suburb.[25] The emergency utilisation of a small fortress by residents of extended suburbs is a decisive stage in the developing appearance of the early medieval city. Most late Roman fortifications in Gaul, although not in Britain, enclosed a much smaller area than had been inhabited previously. The third- or early fourth-century wall was the only fortification that many smaller centres received from the Romans, and they were never intended to be more than citadels,

22 Pérouas, *Histoire de Limoges*, 6–37.
23 Rivet, *Town and Country*, 92, 96–7.
24 Krautheimer, *Rome*, 4, 6–7, 17; Krautheimer, *Three Christian Capitals*, 7, 12; Février, 'Permanence et héritages', 83–5, 90–1; Bullough, 'Urban change', 83–9.
25 Mengozzi, *Città italiana*, 12–15, 21–2.

sheltering civilian populations during emergencies. The wall of Tours enclosed only 9 ha, in the northeastern corner of an inhabited area of 40 ha. Paris had originally been on the left bank of the Seine, but it was moved to a fortress enclosing 13 ha on the island in the river around 280. The Île de la Cité became the nucleus of medieval Paris. Although settlement continued on the left bank after the island was walled, medieval and modern Paris originated with the linkage of the island and a right bank settlement. The left bank remained a semi-rural and university quarter through the Middle Ages.[26]

The impact of the new walls on the Roman street plan was mixed. At Amiens and Senlis the Roman quadrilateral plan was kept intact by the reduced wall. At Amiens, however, the wall of 10 ha was based on the amphitheatre and a few islands near it. Most of the still inhabited islands were not included in the walled area. Only one street – the Boulogne–Beauvais road – that was left outside the late third-century Roman wall at Amiens survived into the Middle Ages.[27]

Autun shows that while the population of most Gallo-Roman centres declined, it did not drop to the degree suggested by the contracting lines of the fortifications. The city's first wall, enclosing 180 ha, was destroyed in 269–70. Its fourth-century successor contained only 10 ha on the southern edge of the city. Yet during the fourth century the inhabited area was almost as great as in the third, for the unfortified suburbs of Autun became centres of manufacturing. As late as 861 the fourth-century fortress, the *castrum*, was still distinguished from the rest of the settlement, called the *civitas*.[28]

Of course, some fortifications were larger than these. The wall of Sens enclosed 43 ha, while Reims, which the Romans made the chief city of the province of Gallia Belgica and was eventually the seat of an archbishopric, contained 60 ha. The wall of Reims is unusual in leaving no inhabited area outside.[29] Trier is also an extreme case. It began as the *civitas* capital of the Treveri but became a colony in the first century. The Romans gave it a regular street plan and made it an important centre for wine, textiles and metalworking. Trier's famous baths, amphitheatre and many temples were all built during the second century. While most Roman centres in Gaul suffered during the disasters of the third century, Trier actually became more important after the prefecture

26 Galinié, 'Reflections on early medieval Tours', 58; Kolb, *Stadt im Altertum*, 236; Roblin, 'Cités ou citadelles . . . Paris', 301; Roblin, 'Cités ou citadelles . . . Senlis', 368–91; Nicholas, 'Urban origins', 60–1; Konvitz, *Urban Millennium*, 3.
27 Février, 'Permanence et héritages', 99.
28 Kolb, *Stadt im Altertum*, 236–7.
29 Kolb, *Stadt im Altertum*, 236; Desportes, *Reims*, 47.

of Gaul was moved there in 293. The city was a frequent imperial residence in the fourth century. When Christianity was legalised, several major abbeys and churches were established in Trier and its suburbs. The fourth-century wall of 285 ha included farmland and Celtic shrines southeast of the city centre as well as the urban core. Trier probably had a population of about 50,000 in the mid-third century, growing to 60,000 in the mid-fourth.[30]

The Romans' decision to build large fortresses caused other cities to become more prosperous in the fourth century than the third. Toulouse is rarely mentioned until the third century, but then the Romans gave it an enormous fortification of 90 ha, the largest in Gaul. Evidently because of its defences, it became the capital of the Visigoths in the fifth century. The Roman wall was never even partially abandoned, and most of the population remained Roman.[31] The Roman city at Poitiers initially occupied most of a hilltop between two small rivers, but the wall of the late third century took in only the lowland eastern half and did not extend all the way to the river. Yet even with a much reduced area of 42 ha Poitiers was the third largest city of Gaul, behind Toulouse and Reims, more important in the fourth and fifth centuries than previously.[32]

But these are exceptions. The extent of the problem is shown by places, most of them in southern Gaul, that received a first fortification during the early Empire and a second in the third century. Although the second fortification of Metz abandoned a quarter of the area formerly enclosed, it still contained 67 ha, and the city benefited from the great prosperity of Trier nearby. Lyon's site should have made it one of the greatest Roman cities. The Romans built a fort near the summit of a hill on the right bank of the Saône, near its junction with the Rhône but west of both rivers. The place was at the edge of the Massif Central and was linked to the Loire commercial area by four river valleys. During the fourth century settlement was moved downhill to the island between the rivers, which was now fortified. Lyon is the only major case in France of a Roman city that moved toward the plain away from a promontory, and it was not successful, for this area was too marshy for the settlement to prosper. The contrast with Paris, also on an island but drier, is stark.[33]

---

30 Vercauteren, 'Spätantike *civitas*', 127; Wightman, *Gallia Belgica*, 234–9; Barley, *European Towns*, 193, 195.
31 Wolff, *Histoire de Toulouse*, 7–52.
32 Dez, *Histoire de Poitiers*, plans 1 and 3; Claude, *Bourges und Poitiers*, 27–35.
33 Nicholas, 'Urban origins', 73–4; Dollinger-Léonard, 'Cité romaine', 195–7; Butler, 'Late Roman town walls in Gaul', 40–1; Latreille, *Histoire de Lyon*, 10–14; Février, 'Vetera et nova', 416 and plan, 345; Février, 'Permanence et heritages', 61–2.

The Romans also fortified some smaller centres, evidently attempting to have garrisons at intervals of roughly thirty kilometres on all major rivers and roads. Some of them developed into cities in the Middle Ages, while more exposed larger places nearby dwindled into insignificance. The growth of Namur reinforces the lesson drawn from the decline of Besançon. A small civilian settlement on the Sambre near its confluence with the Meuse, extending downhill from the Celtic hill fort on the Meuse, was at almost exactly the site of the medieval town. After it was burned in the third century, the Romans extended the walls of the Celtic fort downhill. Combining an almost impregnable defensive site with a port on the Meuse, which became the major commercial artery of northern Europe in the seventh century, medieval Namur was far more significant than its Roman ancestor had been.[34]

THE FOURTH CENTURY

The Mediterranean basin

During the fourth century the central government assumed increasing control of political and economic life in the Mediterranean cities, where most of the wealth of the Empire was concentrated. The government had strategic goods produced in state workshops, beginning with arms and extending to other manufactures. The central government and local authorities regulated quality and prices and collected taxes through occupational associations (*collegia*). These had originated as charitable fraternities but became state agencies after membership in them was made hereditary in the fourth century. Many craftsmen, particularly in the smaller cities, simply left and became clients of powerful patrons.[35] The imperial government also controlled municipal politics, generally appointing outsiders as judicial 'defenders' to protect the lower orders from extortion and the unlawful actions of powerful persons. Diocletian added the 'exactor' to collect taxes, but imperial control weakened in the late fourth century. A law of 387 gave the city councils the right to appoint the defender and exactor.[36]

34 Février, 'Vetera et nova', 411; Nicholas, 'Urban origins', 73, 77, after Rousseau, *Namur*, 12–34; Barley, *European Towns*, 161, 175.

35 Jones, *Later Roman Empire* 1: 689–700; 2: 858–64, 834–9; Jones, *Decline of the Ancient World*, 250.

36 Ward-Perkins, *Urban Public Building*, 17; Jones, *Decline of the Ancient World*, 65, 239–42; Jones, *Later Roman Empire* 1: 726–7; Claude, *Byzantinische Stadt*, 117–18; Vittinghoff, 'Verfassung', 34.

Even as their resources diminished with the loss of population and wealth, the cities had to assume new expenses. Their buildings fell into ruins. Grand though the public buildings of antiquity had been, virtually all of them before 300 had been erected and maintained not by the city government, but with private funds, through a combination of private munificence, personal pride and status-seeking. Where generosity and social ethics did not suffice, compulsion was applied. Decurions normally had to post a substantial bond on entering office or use their own resources to finance an important public project, such as an aqueduct or an arcade.   ·

During the fourth century private building of monuments virtually ceased. The city governments were so poor that the central government assumed control of whatever building was done. The emperors confiscated civic lands and incomes, then set high tax rates and collected them directly. When they made the decurions personally responsible for paying taxes that they were unable to collect, persons eligible for membership on the municipal councils tried to avoid service, and this in turn caused the emperors to make curial rank hereditary. Thus municipal aristocrats tried to leave the cities for their rural estates. Others escaped by entering the imperial civil service or the Senate, taking holy orders or joining the army, although imperial statutes formally barred these avenues of exit to decurions.[37]

Relief was given and new obligations imposed with bewildering inconsistency. By Constantine's time most cities had the right to choose their own officials and to legislate. But although the towns still had corporate legal personalities, gradual restrictions on urban autonomy had made that a dead letter by the sixth century. Although Diocletian had withdrawn the cities' rights to confiscate vacant land, Constantine allowed them to take the property of decurions who died intestate or left. From 374 the emperors ordered one-third of the income of the rents of former civic lands to be returned to the cities, but imperial officials administered the transfer of funds. Although the emperors in 396 required the cities to pay for their own fortifications, in 400 the central government leased buildings and other property formerly belonging to the cities to those same cities in perpetuity.[38]

---

37 Ward-Perkins, *Urban Public Building*, 3–16; Jones, *Decline of the Ancient World*, 250–1; Jones, *Later Roman Empire* 1: 738–53; Vittinghoff, 'Verfassung', 27; Jones, *Greek City*, 240–50.
38 Claude, *Byzantinische Stadt*, 151–2; Jones, *Greek City*, 251–3; Jones, *Decline of the Ancient World*, 248; Jones, *Later Roman Empire* 1: 732–4.

Gaul and Britain

Less is known of municipal institutions in the north than in Italy. Although most of the fourth century was relatively peaceful, the nature of urban life was modifying radically if gradually. Changes in nomenclature give subtle indications. The Romans had renamed most tribal *civitates*; but even in the fourth century, long before the garrisons withdrew, many Roman names were replaced by Celtic words. Bourges, which the Romans initially called *Avaricum*, became *Bituricas*, after the Bituriges. Poitiers, initially *Lemonum*, became *Pictava* (Pict City). Tours (*Caesarodunum*) became *civitas Turonorum*, the city of the Turones.[39] Changes of name were less frequent along the Rhine and in Switzerland, although the degree of Romanisation was much less strong than in Gaul, for the Romans had initially bestowed fewer new non-tribal names there. Some alterations are found in Britain. Leicester was first called *Ratae Coritanorum* for the Coritani, but this yielded to *Legorensis civitas*, City of the Legora, a Celtic name for the river Soar. The eventual place name combined Legora with *cester*, from the Latin *castrum* (fortification). Evidently by the late Roman period the name of the tribe had receded from consciousness, but that of the natural feature had not.[40]

The problems of the third century affected Britain less severely than the continent, and numerous English cities show stability at a low level of urbanisation in the fourth century. London revived as a political capital when the emperor Septimius Severus (193–211) divided Britain into two provinces with capitals at London and York. As elsewhere the craft and merchant element, never strong in Roman towns, was being replaced by bureaucrats and soldiers. During the fourth century the two provinces were subdivided into four, but London was the headquarters of the praetorian prefect, to whom the governors reported. New civic construction virtually ceased in the third century but revived in the fourth. To new political troubles after the 360s, however, was added a rise in sea level, which caused flooding that obliterated some settlements. Nearly all of Southwark was abandoned, and the rest of London had a sharp population decline. As civilian buildings and streets were being abandoned when population declined, fortifications and, perhaps paradoxically, churches were erected.[41]

39   Claude, *Bourges und Poitiers*, 36, 43–4; Galinié, 'Tours', 58. Chartres and Limoges, the *civitas Lemovicum*, also illustrate reversion to Celtic place names; Pérouas, *Histoire de Limoges*, 28; Chédeville, *Histoire de Chartres*, 26–45; Chédeville, *Chartres*, 398–400.
40   Brown, *Leicester*, 11–18; Simmons, *Leicester*, 1, 12.
41   Reynolds, *English Medieval Towns*, 4; Merrifield, *London*, 90–114, 140–71, 173–83; Rivet, *Town and Country*, 93–4; Jones and Wacher, 'Roman period', 35–7.

CHRISTIANITY AND THE URBAN FABRIC
OF LATE ANTIQUITY

The most important changes in Roman urbanisation during the fourth century came from the impact of Christian churches on the governance and spatial relations of the cities. As an outlaw religion Christianity left little imprint on the urban landscape of the Empire until after Constantine's edict of toleration of 312. Thereafter numerous churches were erected and quickly became major foci of continuity between antiquity and the Middle Ages. Some historians have seen the 'episcopal city' as a specifically medieval urban type.

The bishop's territory was normally the *civitas*, and this included both the urban core and its rural environs. By the sixth century the term *civitas* was normally being used only for once-Roman settlements that were bishoprics. The bishops moved into the power vacuum left by the declining municipal senates and provincial governors. In 409 the emperor Honorius ordered that the bishop, the clergy and local landowners not of curial rank should join the decurions in choosing the defender of the city. Power struggles were already beginning in some *civitates* in the fourth century between the bishop and the secular rulers. By the fifth century bishops were virtually unchallenged rulers of most cities in both Italy and Gaul; only from the late sixth century would their power be curbed in some places by the rise of counts.[42]

The central parts of most cities in Gaul had little vacant space left for churches by the time Christianity was legalised. This was less invariably true in Italy, where the cathedrals sometimes occupied the territory of one or more decayed islands without disturbing the grid street plan. This happened at Milan, Turin and Parma. At Pavia, by contrast, the churches were all outside the Roman wall until the Ostrogothic period. Where possible the Christians built churches adjacent to or even on the site of the ruined but centrally located imperial palaces, thus suggesting that they were continuing Roman rule. The Christians normally did not reuse pagan temples. Although the temples had been closed in 356 and ordered to be converted to new uses in 408, the first one in Rome itself to be reconsecrated directly to Christian purposes was the Pantheon, which was Christianised in 609 as Santa Maria Rotunda.[43]

With the city centres thus difficult to penetrate, most Christian

---

42 Jones, *Decline of the Ancient World*, 247; Goudineau, Février and Fixot, 'Réseau urbain', 114–15.

43 Barley, *European Towns*, 483; Krautheimer, *Rome*, 35, 72; Hodges and Hobley, *Rebirth of Towns*, 43–5; Février, 'Permanence et héritages', 103–4; Bullough, 'Urban change', 90–1.

churches were built near the walls and in the unprotected suburbs. Even at Rome the only churches inside the Aurelian wall were those erected on the outskirts by the imperial family. Faced with a largely pagan population, Constantine did not put Christian churches inside the *pomerium*, which was sacred to the traditional gods. The Romans had forbidden burial within the limits of cities, although they did not require the removal of established cemeteries when town walls contracted. Thus the older churches were joined in the fifth and sixth centuries by numerous shrines around martyrs' tombs.[44]

In Gaul, where most city defences were more truncated than in Italy, many Christian sanctuaries were built near the cities and became rivals to the pagan temples within the walls. Settlement continued around suburban churches and cemeteries at Périgueux and Paris after their fortresses had been reduced. At Clermont-Ferrand the cathedral was enclosed in a tiny wall, but there were seven sanctuaries within 10 ha of it. The geography of early Christianity, urban but often extramural, contributed both to a continuation of some urban habitation and to a displacement of its focus toward the peripheries. The spread of Christianity, combined with the distaste of the Germans for living in walled areas, thus cushioned the shrinking of the fortified areas of the Roman cities.[45]

THE FIFTH CENTURY: THE CATASTROPHE OF ROMAN URBANISATION

The Mediterranean

After the Rhine frontier fell in 406 and the Visigoths sacked Rome in 410, the cities of Italy and Gaul received shocks that were far worse than the disasters of the third century. Italy was once thought to have been an exception to the pattern of breakdown of classical urban life, at least until the Lombard period, but recent scholarship has suggested considerable decline, even in comparison to some episcopal centres of the north.[46] The physiognomy of Italian urbanisation was revolutionised between the fifth and early seventh centuries. Chris Wickham has argued that three-quarters of the roughly 100 Roman municipalities in northern Italy still functioned as cities in 1000; yet fewer than one-quarter of them kept their Roman street plans, and all suffered massive depopu-

---

44 Krautheimer, *Rome*, 18–24; Krautheimer, *Three Christian Capitals*, 16–18, 31; Kolb, *Stadt im Altertum*, 168–9.
45 Guillerme, *Age of Water*, 3–15; Février, 'Vetera et nova', 411–14 and plan, 344.
46 For the older view, see Ward-Perkins, *Urban Public Building*, v.

lation. At most, they preserved the central site of the *forum*, which was the main market, together with decayed shells of imperial buildings, churches and particularly cathedrals. The Roman *decumanus* and *cardo*, which were linked to the gates, persisted at Piacenza, Aosta, Turin and Verona. Como lost virtually all trace of its *cardo*, for the building of San Fedele and its baptistery in the centre disturbed the main street, but the secondary roads that joined it are better preserved. Bologna declined from an occupied surface of 50 ha to under twenty, and the reduced area was walled at some point, probably between the fifth and seventh centuries. In contrast to the situation in the north, no Italian city developed mainly around a church or monastery, although the bishoprics did have a great impact on some individual cities.[47]

Milan is an excellent case study. Although it was at the junction of the major land routes across Italy, it remained a simple provincial town until Diocletian's co-emperor Maximian (293–305) made it his residence and built a new wall, circus and palace. Milan enjoyed a virtually constant imperial presence between 340 and 402. Its prosperity as a political capital was complemented by the prestige and church building of its bishop, St Ambrose (374–97). The population probably exceeded 100,000 and became partly suburban. The older section of Milan had a grid plan, with the *forum* somewhat south of the geographical centre of the city, but the street network in the peripheral areas within the wall circuit on the north was fixed by the course of several waterways. The cathedral was built in the mid-fourth century on the outskirts of the old city near the government buildings. The Germans settled in the suburban quarters that developed around villas and sanctuaries east of Maximian's wall. Yet despite its prominence, and although a chronicler reports that 30,000 male civilians were executed when the Goths seized Milan from a Byzantine garrison in the 530s, so little of Milan's Roman street plan survived as to suggest a virtual break in habitation. Milan owes less to its Roman antecedents than any other major medieval city in Italy. It seems to have grown relatively late from independent roots.[48]

Rome itself (Plan 1) was no exception to the decay of the Italian cities in the late fourth and fifth centuries, but it began from such a base of grandeur that it always functioned as a city. Although the emperors were rarely present after 312, Rome kept a municipal organisation as late as the Byzantine occupation in the sixth century. Statutes suggest that by 419 the city was recovering from the sack of 410 and had a

47 Wickham, *Early Medieval Italy*, 80–3; Février, 'Permanence et héritages', 101–2; Bocchi, 'Développement urbanistique oriental de Bologne', 136.
48 Krautheimer, *Three Christian Capitals*, 68–75; Barley, *Medieval Towns*, 475–9; Ward-Perkins, *Urban Public Building*, 29. See also Chapter 2.

population of some 400,000 in 452, but this figure must be balanced against the fact that only 120,000 persons were still receiving the grain dole that Rome guaranteed to its citizens. Rome was becoming increasingly isolated and a drain on its depopulated hinterland. Regular grain imports continued into the seventh century, but by then Rome had declined to fewer than 50,000 inhabitants.[49] Settlement gravitated toward the lowlands as peripheries near the Aurelian wall and the ancient temple precincts on the centrally located hills were abandoned until the seventh and eighth centuries.

Although numerous churches were built at Rome in the early fifth century, much of the construction material came from the ruins of other buildings, including but not limited to the pagan temples. Suburbs developed around martyrs' tombs, as in Gaul. After 432 the popes concentrated on developing their own suburb, the Lateran, which was isolated on the eastern edge of the city near the walls and distant from the habitations of most Romans. The pilgrimage trade to Rome gave birth to another suburb, around the shrine of St Peter, which would eventually surpass the Lateran.[50]

Gaul and Britain

The decline of urban life also quickened in Gaul. Trier atrophied after the prefecture of Gaul was moved to Arles around 400. The Franks took the city four times between 411 and 428, for its enormous wall was impossible for the reduced population to defend. Trier disintegrated into independent nuclei around parish churches. But while settlements around suburban churches determined the medieval townscape elsewhere, Trier's fortification was so enormous that the cathedral inside the Roman wall became the major focus of settlement. The decline was not total. Trier still had a mint in the early fifth century, and the baths along the Mosel were still being used. Its merchants traded with Metz and with Frisia and in the Mediterranean, and Trier had a Jewish colony, suggesting long-distance commerce.[51]

Other capitals were moved and new cities founded as the Romans suffered military reverses. Most marked was the decline of some early Roman centres in favour of late foundations on Celtic sites nearby. Thus

49 Ward-Perkins, *Urban Public Building*, 40–1; Hodges and Whitehouse, *Mohammed*, 24–6; Jones, *Later Roman Empire* 1: 687; Hodges and Hobley, *Rebirth of Towns*, 30; Février, 'Permanence et héritages', 66–7.
50 Krautheimer, *Three Christian Capitals*, 93–102; Krautheimer, *Rome*, 46–56.
51 Kolb, *Stadt in Altertum*, 229–32; Owens, *City*, 129–30; Nicholas, 'Urban origins', 74; Dollinger-Léonard, 'De la cité romaine', 215–19.

Augst yielded to Basel, Lillebrune to Rouen, Carentan to Coutances and Alba to Viviers. Capitals of bishoprics of *civitates* had a better chance of survival than did others, but this rule is not invariable. By the early fifth century the canton capital of the Triboci had been transferred from Brumath to Strasbourg. *Civitates* that were not on rivers frequently did not survive. Tournai and Cambrai, both on the Scheldt, surpassed and eventually assumed the *civitas* status of Cassel and Bavai, which were less accessible.[52]

Germanic rulers used some Roman centres as capitals. Tournai's fortunes rose when the Scheldt became a frontier under the Salian Franks. Although the city was destroyed in 406, it was repopulated even before the Franks occupied it and converted the centre of imperial government to a royal residence. There was little if any break in settlement. Tournai is the best example in the far north of continuity of settlement and to some extent continuity of Roman street plan. Yet even though settlement continued across the invasions, the centre of habitation gradually shifted away from the Roman site toward suburban churches.[53]

Conditions on the Rhine were worse. A provincial capital and military base near the northeastern extremity of Roman expansion in Gaul, Cologne (Plan 2) was the first Roman city in the area to be fortified. But the catastrophe of 406 was so complete that little of the Roman street plan remained into the Middle Ages; only three thoroughfares that were aligned with the gates and the streets that followed the interior trace of the wall stayed roughly the same. Internal politics could also determine the short-term fate of cities. Cologne declined in part because it was the capital of the Ripuarian Franks, who yielded to the Tournai-based Salian branch of the tribe.[54]

The changes were even more drastic on the Danube. Even at Salzburg, the centre of heavy Gallo-Roman settlement, habitation continued in the hilltop fortification for a time, but the civilian town was abandoned and covered by forest by the seventh century. In the extreme east, the trace of the small Roman fortress at Vienna survived, but nothing of the street plan. The Roman element died out at Regensburg. As at Trier, churches within the wall rather than in the suburbs became nuclei of Germanic settlement.[55]

When the Rhine frontier collapsed in 406, the Roman legions were

---

52   Goudineau, Février and Fixot, 'Réseau urbain', 110; Barley, *European Towns*, 203–4, 307.
53   Barley, *European Towns*, 159, 162–5; Petri, 'Anfänge', 233–5.
54   Kolb, *Stadt im Altertum*, 232–5; Janssen, 'The rebirth of towns in the west', 50; Meynen, 'Grundriss Köln', *Stoob FS*, 281–94.
55   Klein, *'Juravum*-Salzburg', 77–85; Klebel, 'Regensburg', 87–93; Barley, *European Towns*, 343.

withdrawn from Britain and never returned. Some towns, notably Winchester, reinforced their fortifications after the mid-fourth century, while Cirencester maintained its *forum* into the fifth. Verulamium was still inhabited in 429, and in the sixth century Gildas, admittedly not the best of sources, mentions occupied towns.[56] Yet loss of settlement was severe after 420. Saxon burials within city areas are rare. To suggest on the basis of a few huts that 'urban' life continued is absurd. Nineteen eventual Anglo-Saxon cities were on Roman sites, but in most cases there was repopulation at a later date rather than continuity. Even London probably experienced a complete break in settlement between 450 and 600.[57]

With a few exceptions British cities do not follow the continental pattern of settlement around suburban sanctuaries; what continuity there was came inside the walls. At many places, including Leicester and London, the surviving Roman wall fixed the limits of settlement in the medieval successor city. Although the ruined Roman government buildings probably evoked memories of public administration as in Gaul, there is no evidence from Britain that they attracted settlement. Repopulation on Roman sites was fostered by two considerations. First, even ruined towns presented physical barriers that probably tended to promote settlement. Secondly, the Roman road system, which linked the cities as garrisons, survived more nearly intact in Britain than on the continent.[58]

Although some medieval streets paralleled their Roman predecessors, they rarely if ever followed the same track precisely. At Winchester the High Street linking the two gates in the Roman wall virtually replicated the Roman *decumanus*, but there is no evidence of the rest of the Roman street plan. Roman gates continued in use at Gloucester, York, Colchester, Chester and Canterbury, and the need to use the shortest route between them caused elements of the Roman street plan to persist, although so much territory was abandoned inside the walls that survival was minimal. The distortions included removing buildings and entire islands to make way for farm settlements around the cathedrals.[59]

---

56 Biddle, 'Towns', 104; Rivet, *Town and Country*, 97; Reynolds, *English Medieval Towns*, 8–10; Barley, *European Towns*, 294.
57 Merrifield, *London*, 236–68; Reynolds, *English Medieval Towns*, 12; Jones and Wacher, 'Roman period', 36–7. Aston and Bond, *Landscape of Towns*, 50–2 argue continuity between 450 and 600 on the basis of pre-450 evidence.
58 Reynolds, *English Medieval Towns*, 14; on Leicester, see Simmons, *Leicester*, 3–11, 21; Brown, *Leicester*, 13, 17–18, 30. Brown claims continuation of the Roman street plan at Leicester that is not evident to me on the plans of the Roman and medieval cities.
59 Reynolds, *English Medieval Towns*, 11; Barley, *European Towns*, 9–10; Biddle, 'Towns', 106–10.

The boundaries of the late medieval Bail of Lincoln, including the castle, were the same as those of the Roman upper city, and its medieval street plan shows superficial similarities to the Roman; but the plan of the medieval town, on the site of the Roman lower city, does not.[60]

Although Roman urbanisation became very weak on the Rhine frontier and virtually ended in Britain and on the Danube, a stronger case for continuity can be made for some cities of interior Gaul, particularly those that housed bishoprics. The transformation of the Roman mononuclear, political/governing, consumer city into its generally polynuclear successor that was a producer of goods and above all services began in the early Middle Ages. We shall explore this metamorphosis in Chapter 2.

60 Hill, *Medieval Lincoln*, 3–15 and Figures 1 and 5.

CHAPTER TWO

Suburbanisation and Deurbanisation in Merovingian and Carolingian Gaul, 500–830

The Merovingian age (481–751) brought important changes to the urban configuration of Europe. Most Roman fortifications had been quadrilateral, enclosing regular street plans. In many cities the Roman wall fixed the alignment of the main streets, but the rest of the street plan was different. As population declined, churches and fortresses became foci of discrete villages, oval or circular settlements with their own street plans inside the quadrilateral Roman fortresses. Only a few cities, notably Basel and Constance, were eventually repopulated in the same approximate pattern as under the Romans. Thus the medieval city with Roman antecedents in a sense is a third type, corresponding exactly neither to planned nor nuclear towns.[1] All cases about which there is a serious question of functional continuity between Roman and early medieval city are on the continent west of the Rhine, and most are south of the Scheldt. There is more continuity further south, where the *civitates* of Boulogne, Thérouanne, Arras and Cambrai were inhabited across the invasions and continued to be centres of government through their churches.[2] In Italy there was generally continuity of settlement and often of governmental functions, but there, too, the norm was the 'fragmented city', with separate nuclei of population just inside the walls and generally along the major roads. Florence, for example, became several farm villages, with small ceramics the only known industry. Such new building as there was was coarse, often from the ruins of Roman

---

1   Planitz, *Deutsche Stadt*, 26, 33; Lavedan and Hugueney, *Urbanisme*, 1, 6–8.
2   Clarke and Simms, 'Comparative history', 671; Nicholas, 'Urban origins', 76; Ennen, 'Städtewesen Nordwestdeutschlands', 149; Verhulst and Doehaerd, 'Nijverheid en handel', 201.

buildings. But – and this point must be emphasised – the wall guaranteed the survival of the 'urban fabric': barring complete abandonment or ruin, the places occupied by the Romans would continue to exist in some form.[3]

The city enjoyed a distinct status. In late Merovingian Gaul houses in the cities, but not in the rural areas, were alienable apart from the land on which they were built. King Rothair of the Lombards in the early seventh century destroyed several Byzantine *civitates* and ordered that they be called villages in the future.[4] Furthermore, the *civitas* generally was a bishopric on a Roman site by the fifth century. The bishoprics founded in Germany in the ninth century and later were also *civitates*. The word initially referred to the bishop's diocese, which included territory outside the walls; but as the many bishops' secular authority became confined to the walled area, *civitas* was increasingly used for only the urban part of the diocese. As cities assimilated suburbs, *civitas* often meant only the area inside the late Roman wall, while other terms were used for the entire agglomeration. In 797 Bishop Theodulf of Orléans ordered 'priests who are in the circuit of the city or in the city itself [to] convene [the people] into a single group for celebrating public mass'. This distinction between the city and its circuit is Roman; and although all other references to it from this period are for Italian cities, Orléans could hardly have been unique in Gaul. The churches were a unifying force of city and suburb, since the two could act jointly for public religious ceremonies.[5] Thus the 'city' in many French places of Roman origin is only the old walled *civitas*. When 'City' is capitalised in the rest of this book, it refers to the fortified Roman city; lower case 'city' means the entire urban complex.

Received opinion has held that the Germans were not city dwellers and that such habitation as continued inside Roman walls was largely Gallo-Roman except for a German warrior aristocracy. The examples of Flanders, the least Romanised part of Gaul, and England certainly suggest this. This notion has been criticised, but unconvincingly, on grounds that some prehistoric Germanic and Celtic forts, Roman towns, and eventually medieval cities occupied the same sites. No medieval city sprang from purely Germanic roots during the period of the great migrations. In Strasbourg the Frankish settlement developed outside the Roman wall and more than doubled the area of the total agglomeration. Some purely Germanic sites developed urban characteristics during or after the Carolingian period; but with all others the question is over

3   Ciampoltrini, 'Città "frammentate" e città-fortezza', 629.
4   Claude, *Byzantinische Stadt*, 236, 238; Claude, *Bourges und Poitiers*, 91–2.
5   Mengozzi, *Città italiana*, 98.

whether once-Roman sites experienced continuity of settlement or were simply repopulated. The medieval city was always so different from its Roman ancestor in economic function, social structure and street plan that it seems misplaced to speak of continuity.[6]

The economic base of city life was reoriented fundamentally in the Merovingian age. Some cities had Jewish and Syrian merchants in the sixth century, but they were usually not permanent residents of the cities. As Mediterranean trade declined in the seventh century, the North Sea became a major trading area. Yet even in the neo-Roman forts in the Meuse valley, which conducted substantial long-distance trade in the early Middle Ages, local trade was more important in establishing the resident population base. No settlement of early medieval Europe that based its economy exclusively or even primarily on long-distance trade developed into a city. Although long-distance trade was important in establishing the capital base of the most important cities, it rarely if ever overshadowed local trade and merchant activity.

Capitals

Virtually all cities where continued occupation can be proven were favoured residences of bishops, kings or counts. The 'town lord' originated in the Middle Ages. Examples abound on the continent of kings occupying government buildings in the residual Roman cities, especially the *praetorium*, the residence of the military commander, which was generally close to the wall. The later Merovingian kings sometimes resided in the *praetorium* at Cologne. Clovis occupied Paris, and Paris, Orléans, Soissons and Rheims were the favoured residences of his sons. Worms was the capital first of the Visigoths and eventually of the Burgundians, and Metz later became the capital of Austrasia. Although in most places the Franks simply used Roman buildings, they built their own in others. Merovingian palaces were erected in Cologne on the later cathedral hill, in Mainz around the abbey of St Alban and in Worms and Basel.[7]

The Lombards were using Pavia as a capital by the seventh century. Ravenna, the capital of late Roman and Byzantine Italy, preserved most of its Roman street layout, but enough was lost to suggest considerable

6   Nicholas, *Medieval Flanders*, 3–13; Nicholas, 'Urban origins', 88. Planitz, *Deutsche Stadt*, 26–34. The map (p. 32) does not substantiate Planitz' claim that the legionary fort at Strasbourg became the nucleus of the medieval city.
7   Brühl, 'Town as a political centre', 423–5; Ennen, *Frühgeschichte*, 150; Ennen, 'Städtewesen Nordwestdeutschlands', 160; James, *Origins of France*, 48; Thompson, *Romans and Barbarians*, 23; Planitz, *Deutsche Stadt*, 36.

displacement. But as secular authority waned in the other cities of Lombard Italy, the government palace near the old Roman city centre lost importance. Habitation gravitated toward the cathedral, which in most places was on the periphery of the Roman town. In Milan the open area in front of the cathedral, in the northeastern part of the city, was used for assemblies, while the old *forum* was still the marketplace. In cities such as Brescia that lacked Milan's commercial importance, the area around the *forum* declined, as the line of the Roman wall bisected the medieval city.[8]

Princes lived in the cities longer in Italy than in the north, where the Frankish kings had stopped using Roman cities as residences by the early seventh century. By Charlemagne's period (768–814) the only royal palace in a city was at Worms, and he abandoned it. As royal power declined, cities became capitals of local counts. Carolingian palaces were built in Maastricht, Utrecht, Speyer, Regensburg, Nijmegen, Aachen, Frankfurt and Vienna, but counts rather than kings lived in most of them. Even in places that had never been *civitates*, such as Ghent and perhaps Bruges and Antwerp, the memory of the Roman occupation may have caused the Franks to continue to use the site as the capital of a local district (*pagus*). Destruction was so total at Rouen, the capital of medieval Normandy, that we know scarcely anything of the Roman city; but Merovingian Rouen was the chief place of a province whose borders corresponded to the later limits of Normandy.[9]

The bourgs

An important new word reflects the changed urban landscape of the early Middle Ages. Late Roman authors had used *burgus* (Fr. *bourg*, Germ. *Burg*, Ital. *borgo*), which was of Germanic origin, to refer to a fort. But the word originally had meant an unfortified place outside a *civitas* or other fort, and during the invasions *burgus* reverted to this meaning. Most bourgs mentioned between the seventh and ninth centuries were unwalled suburban settlements near *civitates* and around an abbey or church. When juxtaposed to another part of the town, *burgus* indicated a more recent section, while *civitas* or *cité* (City) was used for the original fortification. The bourgs of Merovingian Gaul are indistinguishable functionally from the later *Wike* of Germany. Until the ninth century *burgus* in northern

8 Ewig, 'Residence and capital', 163–73; Ward-Perkins, 'The towns of northern Italy', 16–18 and especially map p. 17; Vaccari, 'Pavia', 160; Wickham, *Early Medieval Italy*, 83.
9 Fixot, 'Image idéale', 499; Verhulst, 'Aspect', 175–206; Mollat, *Histoire de Rouen*, 13–26; Planitz, *Deutsche Stadt*, 36.

Europe was used only in central France and the Loire and Saône areas. *Suburbium* and *portus* were used in the Oise and Marne basins for this settlement type, while *portus* was favoured in the Low Countries. *Burgus* was unusual in Germany until the twelfth century, and then it meant the entire walled city; in France it continued to mean a suburb. Suburban churches were also nuclei of settlement in early medieval Italy. Several new churches founded by the Ostrogoths and Byzantines became nuclei of settlement outside the original Roman colony of Bologna.[10]

The growth of extramural suburbs was accelerated in the Merovingian age, as shrines and cemeteries became centres of population. The polynuclear character of most medieval cities on the continent is of cardinal significance. Neighbourhood consciousness was very strong throughout the Middle Ages. Few people this early thought of themselves as living in the 'city of . . .' unless they actually resided in a fortified enclave formed by a castle, bishopric or Roman ruin. Instead their identity was centred on the bourg where they lived. Before the twelfth century the area of Cologne had thirteen separate communities, each with its own bourg master (*burmeister*), which collected the land tax and maintained shares of the common city wall. Probably no medieval city had a continuously occupied urban space. Instead, 'towns within cities' developed with site-specific street plans that sometimes did not merge well when they grew together into a city.[11]

Episcopal cities and merchant suburbs

Cities require permanent buildings and a resident population. They must also exist at the intersection of supply and demand. The early medieval cities developed as a service sector of the economy, for until the central Middle Ages few cities produced many manufactured goods. They were centres for the redistribution and reconsignment of goods grown or produced elsewhere, and they provided temporary shelter or homes for merchants who moved about for much of the year selling their goods. Demand for the cities' marketing services came from the rural economy generally, but the internal demand within the pre-urban nuclei came from the fortification around which merchants congregated. Since the

---

10   Büttner, 'Frühmittelalterliches Städtewesen', 164–5; Nicholas, 'Urban origins', 100–1, summarising recent literature, particularly Schlesinger, 'Burg und Stadt' and Schlesinger, 'Stadt und Burg'; Mitterauer, *Markt und Stadt*, 187; Schumann, 'Decadenza e ascesa di Bologna', 178, 188.
11   Hall, *Mittelalterliche Stadtgrundrisse*, 53–61; Barel, *Ville médiévale*, 59, 61; Strait, *Cologne*, 6–7; Braunfels, *Urban Design*, 19.

churches were permanent structures, while most secular rulers were itinerant, the demand for goods generated by the ecclesiastical nuclei was
constant, while that from princes' fortresses was intermittent. Especially
in the early Middle Ages, before internal demand in the merchant suburbs themselves was high, the *civitates* were thus critically important as
points of demand for merchants' goods and services. Far fewer charters
for markets were issued in the west than east of the Rhine, because
market activity had persisted all along in the French *civitates* and did not
need the stimulus of charters.[12]

The episcopal city thus became an important urban type of the early
Middle Ages. Most Roman *civitates* that would evolve into cities had
been occupied or reoccupied by bishops by the early sixth century. But
in addition to the bishopric within the walls, numerous other churches,
some within the walls but most suburban, became foci of settlement. Including both churches and monasteries, Metz had some twenty-eight religious foundations in the eighth century, Trier eight, Paris sixteen, Reims
twenty-two, Lyon eighteen and Arles between fourteen and twenty-
three. Churches were more important than secular traditions in continuing some degree of urbanisation across the Merovingian period.[13]

Thus most neo-Roman cities in Gaul became polynuclear, with a
fortress surrounded by bourgs that developed during and after the Merovingian age. The geographical relation to the parent fortification varied.
When the stronghold was on a hill, the bourg was almost invariably
downhill and sometimes at some distance. Narbonne and Arras had contiguous but distinct city and bourg, but at Limoges the *civitas* was 500
metres from the larger abbey of St Martial, which was being called the
'fort' (*castrum*) in the tenth century.[14] Many bourgs developed around
shrines, but others grew in locations propitious for trade. Some were
settled mainly by merchants, especially those immediately adjacent to
the fortification. At Rouen, Orléans and Bordeaux the merchant bourg
was at the gate on the riverbank, and the plans of bourg and city thus
evolved compatibly. At Verdun and Lyon the bourg was across the
river from the city at the bridge. For Roman cities in the plains, such
as Troyes, bourgs developed along the main street leading into the
settlement. Dijon had several suburbs: in addition to the bourg Saint-
Benigne north of the fortress, the church of Notre-Dame and several

---

12 Reynolds, *English Medieval Towns*, 28; Clarke and Simms, 'Comparative history', 671.
13 Ennen, 'Städtewesen Nordwestdeutschlands', 159; Claude, *Byzantinische Stadt*, 231.
     See in general Prinz, 'Bischöfliche Stadtherrschaft', 1–26; Büttner, 'Frühmittelalter-
     liches Städtewesen', 153. France had 129 bishoprics by 800, compared to 17 in Eng-
     land; Hilton, *English and French Towns*, 27.
14 Büttner, 'Frühmittelalterliches Städtewesen', 181–2.

nearly parallel streets named after occupations were included in the eventual city wall.[15]

Urban society in the Merovingian age

It is difficult to determine the extent to which merchants were part of the city elites of Merovingian Gaul. Many landholders from the surrounding countryside lived in the cities, which offered defence and a place to market the surplus produced by their farms. Bishop Bertram of Le Mans owned one house there and others at Paris and Bordeaux.[16] Noble families used Mainz as a stronghold in the civil wars against the late Merovingian kings. The first traces of a parish organisation come in the eighth and ninth centuries, when the nobles required their dependants to attend their proprietary churches. This important aspect of urban social relations was doubtless present in other cities but cannot be documented this early.[17]

Little else is known of the social composition of the Merovingian cities apart from the large number of clergy and princes. Gregory of Tours shows extensive relief of pilgrims and the poor by urban churches. Lists of the poor were kept in all major cities of Gaul in the sixth century, but by the seventh such registers are associated more with rural monasteries. Conditions were so deplorable for all but the richest that 'poverty' is a dubious problem. By the Carolingian period the term 'poor' (*pauperes*), which had meant modest landowners in the Merovingian age, referred to those who were weak enough to be damaged by the 'powerful' (*potentes*). Indigents were thus a subgroup of the poor, but other politically impotent persons were also 'impoverished'.[18]

Episcopal cities and public lordship in Merovingian Gaul

Most bishops established themselves as town lords during the sixth century, particularly in areas on the periphery of royal control. Counts disputed power in the *civitates* with the bishops, whose palaces were characteristically near the city walls but on the opposite side from the prince's palace. The powers of most bishops declined in the seventh century as the counts' powers grew and trade declined in the bishoprics, but there are exceptions. Around 630 Bishop Desiderius restored the

15 Lavedan and Hugueney, *Urbanisme*, 18–20.
16 Claude, *Bourges und Poitiers*, 79.
17 Falck, *Geschichte der Stadt Mainz*, 18–21.
18 Mollat, *Poor*, chs 3 and 2; Claude, *Bourges und Poitiers*, 82; Bullough, 'Social and economic structure and topography', 370.

aqueduct at Cahors and had a wall constructed. The Rhenish archbishops generally maintained their powers better than those of Gaul. In the dioceses of Cologne and Trier the count generally spent most of his time in the rural areas while the bishop ruled the city and oversaw its defences.[19]

Information about civic government is tantalising but too fragmentary to permit solid conclusions. 'Courts' continued to meet in the Roman *fora* at Tours and Angers. City militias were active at Bourges and Orléans. The citizens of Limoges burned the tax registers, and only the bishop's intervention saved the collector's life. At Reims in 686 the bishop made a land grant with the consent of his 'brothers and fellow citizens'. By the mid-sixth century the defender of Bordeaux, heir to a Roman title and perhaps functions, was chosen by the bishop and clergy rather than the citizenry and confirmed by the king. The same situation is found in the seventh century in Burgundy and at Orléans, Tours, Sens, Le Mans and Paris.[20]

Poitiers has the clearest evidence that Roman civic life persisted. Citizens negotiated and made political decisions. They were landowners, but many of them lived within the city wall. Decurions and 'great men' (*viri magnifici*) constituted an advisory council to the bishop. The still undamaged wall was so enormous that the *civitas* housed a diverse population, including some Germans by the seventh century. Although the site of the later castle was probably vacant, Roman bridges were still used, and the areas around the churches were densely settled. Merovingian Poitiers probably had between 4,000 and 8,000 inhabitants inside the walls and 1,000 in extramural settlements.[21]

Monastic cities

The monastery became a new element in the townscape in the early Middle Ages, particularly in France and Germany. While the bishops' complexes created demand but generated little supply of goods or services, the monasteries supplied food in addition to consuming luxuries. Most of them collected more food rents from their estates than could ever have been eaten by the monks, and markets developed on their estates to dispose of this surplus. The development of regular markets

19 Prinz, 'Bischöfliche Stadtherrschaft', 19–20; Strait, *Cologne*, 7; James, *Origins of France*, 44; Nicholas, 'Urban origins', 83.
20 Claude, *Bourges und Poitiers*, 59–60; James, *Origins of France*, 56–7; Vercauteren, 'Meuse et Loire', 465; Février, 'Vetera et nova', 454.
21 Claude, *Bourges und Poitiers*, 51–4, 64.

around monasteries preceded the significant revival of long-distance trade by several centuries.[22]

A monastery alone in the absence of other stimuli would not give rise to a major city, although some secondary centres, such as Tiel, Montreuil-sur-Mer and Bury St Edmunds were monastic. Monasteries that were close to bishoprics, as at Arras, or to princes' fortresses, as at Ghent, were especially likely to affect city development. Some kings who did not inhabit the *civitates* had residences in the suburbs near monasteries that they patronised. In this way the abbeys of Saints Rémi at Reims, Medard at Soissons, Martin at Tours, Arnulf at Metz, Alban at Mainz, Emmeram at Regensburg, Ambrose at Milan and Zeno at Verona helped to preserve continuity of habitation in the area while displacing the city centre.[23]

Most monasteries whose bourgs were important for city development were suburban and were named after local saints whose burial shrine had generated a small settlement before the abbey was founded. Arras and Tours were the greatest abbatial cities. Arras had been a Roman *civitas*, and a bishopric remained inside the fortification, but most commercial life centred on the nearby bourg of the abbey of St Vaast, which was founded in the seventh century. The fame of the miracles performed at the tomb of St Martin near Tours had made the bourg around his shrine more populous than the Roman City by the sixth century. The *civitas* was economically active, although less so than the abbey village, and its prosperity was enhanced when counts lived there. Tours thus developed as two distinct cities. The area between them was pocketed with small settlements. Yet despite its prosperity in the early Merovingian period, Tours had declined into a district capital by the Carolingian age. Its medieval street plan owes nothing to its Roman ancestor.[24]

Later examples confirm the importance of monasteries for city development. The shrine of the martyr Benigne west of the Gallo-Roman town at Dijon was converted into a Benedictine abbey in 871. The Bourg-Saint-Benigne was walled and had a weekly market and annual fair by 925. St Remigius was buried in the 'Christian street' (*vicus christianus*) south of Reims. An abbey was established that had been walled by 924–25. The oratory of St Frontinus near Périgueux gave rise to an abbey in the tenth century that was soon the centre of a bourg that had its own mayor, consuls and eventually a wall of about 17 ha, triple

---

22 Mumford, *Culture of Cities*, 17; Doherty, 'The monastic town in early medieval Ireland', 55.
23 Nicholas, 'Urban origins', 106; Hodges and Hobley, *Rebirth of Towns*, 43–5.
24 Van Dam, *Leadership and Community*, ch. 11; Büttner, 'Studien zum frühmittel-alterlichen Städtewesen', 183; Galinié, 'Tours', 59–60; Nicholas, 'Urban origins', 106.

the size of the fortified city. The two towns of medieval Périgueux never had a common wall. The shrine of St Martial on a hill west of the *civitas* at Limoges was converted to a monastery in 868 and gave rise to a bourg that was walled in the tenth century. When the *civitas* was finally walled at the end of the twelfth, its area was one-third that of the bourg Saint-Martial, and the two settlements remained legally distinct municipalities.[25]

The fate of Roman urbanisation in southern and western Gaul

In contrast to the scattered evidence of continuity in the north, many cities of southeastern Gaul persisted into the early Middle Ages with plans essentially unaltered. The hiatus there seems to have come with Muslim raids that damaged but did not destroy their commerce in the eighth and ninth centuries. Jewish colonies persisted in the major centres, and the sources speak of trade with Muslim Spain.[26] The main street of medieval Marseilles, the Great Street [*Grande Rue*], followed the track of the Roman *decumanus*. Marseilles still had some commerce with the east during the Merovingian period, but it was mainly in the hands of Syrians and Jews. Church politics divided the citizenry, and after the severe plague of 588 the bishop moved to the abbey of Saint-Victor across the river, which in turn altered settlement patterns in the city. Although only one bishop is known by name between 614 and 780, the mint at Marseilles remained active until the end of the seventh century and was the last one in Gaul to strike gold coins.[27]

Southwestern Gaul more closely approximates to the situation in the north. At least eleven *civitates* lost their bishoprics in the early Middle Ages and only regained them after several centuries. Our only knowledge of sixth-century Toulouse is an episode of 585, when the bishop and some citizens tried to keep a pretender to the throne out of the city. Bordeaux still had a substantial Gallo-Roman population in the sixth century, with a royal mint and Jewish and Syrian merchants, but the inhabited area contracted in the seventh. The episcopal complex was at the southwestern corner of the fortress, while the swampy suburbs contained scattered nuclei of settlement. There is little more information about Bordeaux until the tenth century.[28]

25   Lavedan and Hugueney, *Urbanisme*, 16–18.
26   Nicholas, 'Urban origins', 66; Duby, 'Villes du sud-est', 233–40.
27   Baratier, *Histoire de Marseille*, 42, 52–5; Février, 'Vetera et nova', 463–6, 477.
28   Goudineau, Février and Fixot, 'Réseau urbain', 123; Wolff, *Histoire de Toulouse*, 52–4; Higounet, *Bordeaux*, 201–7, 230–3, 251.

Episcopacy and urbanisation in the Rhineland

Although in some west German cities the Roman *civitas* remained the centre of habitation during the Frankish occupation, there was less continuity than in Gaul. Farm villages inside the Roman walls radically altered the character of the medieval city at Mainz and Trier. Taxes were collected at Trier as late as 548, and the city has numerous Merovingian inscriptions. Although the population was much reduced, trade continued on the Mosel with Metz. Jews were still active at Trier, and the city's merchants still traded in the Mediterranean in the sixth century. The bishops were town lords by 630. Roman Trier was only obliterated in the Scandinavian attacks of the 880s, for the wall was too large for the population to defend. The survivors fortified the cathedral complex, completely obliterating the Roman street plan. This cathedral city of about 8 ha, not the enormous Roman city, was the nucleus of medieval Trier.[29] Speyer, although much smaller, developed similarly. The surviving Gallo-Roman population withdrew into a corner of the wall. Merchants settled around the residence of the Merovingian duke in the northern part of the city. By 614 the Roman city had been largely resettled and had a bishop. There was no significant suburban development at Speyer, but the bishop did not perpetuate the Roman tradition.[30]

Roman funerary inscriptions show that settlement continued at Mainz. A fourth-century wall around the civilian settlement along the Rhine outside the army camp was still used in the Frankish period, but the Roman fort further from the river was deserted. Several late Roman churches near the Rhine, including the eventual cathedral of St Martin, and Roman suburban cemeteries continued in use. Mainz became a residence of the Frankish kings. Several churches of landowners whose manors were inside the civilian wall became nuclei of settlement and transformed the town plan. Bishop Sidonius built new defences along the Rhine in the mid-sixth century, but a century would pass before the next bishop is known by name; the same gap in the episcopal list occurs at Cologne. Yet new churches were still being founded, and Mainz was also a commercial centre in the early seventh century. Shippers with 'friends in the city' furnished St Columban's monks with provisions around 610. Mainz has more coin finds than the other episcopal

---

29 Nicholas, 'Urban origins', 82–3; Ennen, 'Städtewesen Nordwestdeutschlands', 159; Dollinger-Léonard, 'De la cité romaine', 220–2.

30 Nicholas, 'Urban origins', 84, after Doll, 'Zur Frühgeschichte der Stadt Speyer', 133–200.

centres of the mid-Rhine. Most are from the Mediterranean, but coins with the Mainz mint imprint are also found in Frisia.[31]

Bonn illustrates especially clearly the displacement of settlement on former Roman urban sites in Germany. The Roman fortress was in the northern part of the modern city, but settlement after the invasions was concentrated in its southwestern corner around the church of St Cassian, at some distance from the Rhine at the intersection of several small roads leading into the interior. Other suburban settlements developed around parish churches in the eighth and ninth centuries. Bonn was a farm market, not a centre of long-distance trade; the Roman port on the Rhine silted over. The fortress was eventually destroyed by the Vikings and never rebuilt. Medieval Bonn developed with no reference whatsoever to its Roman ancestor.[32]

Urban life in pre-Carolingian Italy

Despite the advantage of a Mediterranean location, urban life in Italy declined sharply in the wake of attacks by Huns, Goths, Greeks and Lombards in the late fifth and sixth centuries. The Ostrogothic rulers (493–555) did not neglect the cities. There was actually some recovery at Brescia, where the wealthy area east of the *forum* declined in the fifth century but revived in the Ostrogothic period. Yet both Roman buildings and their Gothic successors were falling into disrepair in the southern part of the city, and the Lombards eventually walled an area only one-third the size of the late Roman enclosure.[33] 'Possessors, defenders and decurions' continued to oversee walls and sewers in some centres. Naples had a general assembly led by two 'advocates', and local notables handled the defence of the city in the 530s. The Ostrogoths in the citadel had their own assembly that was distinct from that of the rest of the town. As late as 670 Bishop Agnellus of Naples built a deanery and monastery that were to see to the distribution of grain and soap twice a year, suggesting both a substantial population and continuation of the public baths.[34]

Numerous references from the Ostrogothic and Byzantine periods show collective action or at least some sort of civic militia or government in the north Italian cities. King Theodoric (493–511) made the

---

31 Barley, *European Towns*, 190–3 and Figure 5, p. 192; Falck, *Geschichte der Stadt Mainz*, 3–6, 9–12.
32 Nicholas, 'Urban origins', 72; Ennen, *Frühgeschichte*, 85 ff.; Ennen and Höroldt, *Kleine Geschichte*, 15–17, 23–9.
33 Brogiolo, 'Città longobarda', 557–60.
34 Claude, *Byzantinische Stadt*, 123–4; Février, 'Permanence et héritages', 111.

collegium of a man who raped a virgin collectively responsible for paying the fine. Ostrogothic Pavia preserved its Roman grid plan in nearly perfect state. Its decline was slow enough to prevent the bishopric from moving inside the walls until the turn of the eighth century, since there was no vacant land until then. Although the Ostrogoths destroyed many buildings within the walls, Theodoric built his palace and repaired the Roman baths and amphitheatre. He communicated in writing just before his death with the 'counts, defenders and decurions' of Pavia, which shows that both the militia and the civic aristocracy were still functioning. State granaries were maintained at Pavia in 535.[35]

Colleges of notaries governed Ravenna and Naples, with functions similar to those of the Roman *curiales*. Ravenna had an assembly of nobles, but its duties are uncertain. Municipal administration continued in Rome. The title 'Senator' was still used for distinguished persons, but there were no Senate meetings. The city declined to a population of 30,000 in the early sixth century but was back to 90,000 by 590. From the time of Gregory the Great (590–604) the popes were generally its lords, handling finances and public works, but they faced competition from noble families and particularly from the Byzantines, who tried to turn Rome into an administrative district under a duke in the early eighth century. Gregory appointed a prefect and a supervisor of the aqueducts, and a curator of the palaces is mentioned in 686. But no inscriptions record actual repairs undertaken by the prefect or his deputies, and there are only two references to secular building works in the late sixth and early seventh century.[36]

Aqueducts, baths, palaces, theatres and walls were restored at the royal residences of Ravenna, Verona and Pavia, but the Ostrogoths did not pay such attention to the smaller cities. We hear little in the Gothic period of *fora*, basilicas, porticoes, markets and street paving, and scarcely anything about repairing ruined structures. Virtually all late Roman churches in Italy were built from material scavenged from ruined public buildings, not from new material; the Ostrogothic kings encouraged this to prevent vacant structures from collapsing. Until the eighth century urban buildings continued to be gutted for other constructions, converted to a use other than the original purpose, granted to retainers as rewards, or simply allowed to decay. Decurions continued to function into the early seventh century, but thereafter there is little written evidence of habitation even in the larger cities except bishoprics.

---

35 Mengozzi, *Città italiana*, 70–1; Bullough, 'Urban change . . . Pavia', 92–3, 101–2.
36 Ward-Perkins, *Urban Public Building*, 48; Krautheimer, *Rome*, 59–68, 74–8, 90; Fasoli *et al.*, 'Struttura sociale', 293; Previté-Orton, 'Italian Cities Till c. 1200', 209.

The pattern of pockets of settlement around shrines and abbeys, both inside and outside the walls, is found in the Italian cities as well as the north.[37]

In frontier areas bishoprics were sometimes instrumental in continuing or reviving settlement on Roman sites, although this was less usual than in the north. The Lombards destroyed Padua in 602 and for strategic reasons made Monselice the chief place of the region. The bishop fled but quickly returned to Pavia and settled in the ruins. The medieval city grew up around the bishopric, but only from the tenth century did Padua become the political centre of its region. Roman Modena had been an important city, but it was ruined in the seventh century because it was on the frontier with the Lombards. When the drainage system of the ancient city ruptured, the buildings were inundated. A 'New City' was founded five miles west of Modena around 740, and the Lombard *gastaldus* made it his headquarters. But the church remained in Modena, with the relics of St Gimignano, the patron saint of the diocese. Around 879 the bishop fortified the cathedral precinct, and this became the nucleus of the medieval city.[38]

Urbanisation in early Britain

There was no functional survival of Roman urbanisation in Britain. Excavations at London, Canterbury, Gloucester and Winchester show a break in soil type that makes it most unlikely that any substantial population existed there between 450 and 600. Contrary to their practice in Gaul, the Germans did not reuse Roman fortifications in Britain before the seventh century. Canterbury may have the best claim to continuity of the English cities. It was probably a residence of Bertha, the Frankish queen of Ethelbert of Kent, for St Augustine found a settled community when he arrived in 597. The cathedral complex around which settlement congregated is in a corner of the Roman wall. Christ Church cathedral and St Martin were reused Roman churches, while the four churches outside the walls and the abbey of St Augustine were on the sites of Roman cemeteries. Yet even at Canterbury the medieval street plan has scarcely any relation to its Roman predecessor.[39]

37 Ward-Perkins, *Urban Public Building*, 30–2, 56–61, 131–3, 203–29; Jones, *Later Roman Empire* 1: 760–1.
38 Rippe, 'Commune urbaine', 660; Hyde, *Society and Politics*, 22–3.
39 Clarke and Ambrosiani, *Towns in the Viking Age*, 9; Barley, *European Towns*, 296; Brooks, 'Early medieval Canterbury', 487, 494.

THE ECONOMY OF THE EARLY CITIES: THE PROBLEM OF THE SEVENTH CENTURY

There is no consensus concerning the extent to which the Mediterranean-based commercial economy of late antiquity persisted into the Merovingian period. There was little urban industry except in coastal emporia that lacked Roman antecedents. There is clearer evidence for trade in the *civitates* of the sixth century than in the seventh, but much of this is because seventh-century chroniclers have less economic information than is provided in the *History of the Franks* of Bishop Gregory of Tours (d. 594), our best source for the sixth-century urban economy.

The tantalising fragments, however, suggest a highly developed market economy in the sixth-century cities. Narbonne had such a polyglot population of Goths, Romans, Syrians and Jews that the church imposed a common calendar on them in 589. Oriental merchants are mentioned in several communities of southern France and in a few as far north as the Loire valley. Auch, Narbonne and Arles had Jewish communities in the seventh century. The Jews of Orléans asked royal aid in rebuilding their synagogue, which the Christians had destroyed. The bishop of Arles complained of regular Sunday markets in the forum that attracted more people, specifically goldsmiths, shipbuilders and other craftsmen, than the church.[40] Gregory of Tours describes merchants' houses on the Île de la Cité at Paris. Clogged drains beside the bridges that linked the island to both riverbanks were being cleaned in the 580s. The Roman bridges across the Loire were still used at Tours.[41]

The bishops took an active interest in economic matters. Several councils condemned prelates who loaned money at interest to their citizens. Returning to Verdun from exile to find the inhabitants of the city 'destitute', the bishop in 540 negotiated a loan from the king, which he agreed to repay with interest 'as soon as the men who are in charge of the commercial affairs of my city have reorganised their business, as has been done in other cities'. Gregory of Tours added that 'as a result the businesspeople of Verdun became rich and they still remain so today'.[42]

For most cities except the coastal emporia we have little economic information between roughly 650 and 800. Virtually all indices of trade are down. Population was devastated by a series of plagues that began

---

40 Février, 'Vetera et nova', 466–7; James, *Origins of France*, 58.
41 Büttner, 'Frühmittelalterliches Städtewesen', 154; Gregory of Tours, *History*, ch. 33, pp. 466–7; 5, ch. 17, pp. 48–9.
42 Gregory of Tours, *History*, chs 34–5, pp. 190–1.

in 543 and continued into the mid-seventh century. Even at Tours excavations have shown continued occupation of administrative buildings and churches but little else.[43] Mediterranean trade declined in the sixth century and more sharply in the seventh, although it was reviving by then along the North Sea coast. Imports from the Mediterranean to northern Europe were rare after the mid-sixth century, as special arrangements between trading partners and a 'gift culture' replaced market relations as the determinant of trade.[44]

The Romans had not used rivers much for trade. Although some of their cities were along streams, the purpose was more defensive than economic. The roads of Gaul decayed in the Merovingian period, for the rivers, which were safer and could accommodate larger cargoes, became the major arteries of long-distance trade. Roman *civitates* that were not on navigable streams declined, while small forts on streams that had not carried much trade in antiquity now grew. Examples are Dinant, Namur and Huy on the Meuse and Ghent on the Scheldt. The shift to river traffic may explain the mysterious eclipse of Roman *Venta Icenorum* near Norwich and of Silchester near Reading. Norwich and London and most continental ports of the early Middle Ages that survived to become cities, such as Bordeaux, Hamburg and Bruges, were not coastal and hence exposed to attack from the sea, but rather were within easy reach of the shore, at crossing points on inland rivers.[45]

Yet this point must not be overdrawn; for local trade, most of it along land routes, was more important than long-distance commerce in establishing the economic base of permanent settlements. Although the Meuse was the leading long-distance artery in northern Europe in the seventh century, its prosperity had little impact on urbanisation along its banks. Huy is at the junction of the Meuse with the Hoyoux, which was too shallow for large boats and passed through a narrow valley that gave little room for the town to expand. Yet Huy in fact developed there rather than on the Meuse, as the market between regions producing different raw materials. Huy is an exception to the rule that the early cities had little industry. Even in the fifth and sixth centuries it had two clearly defined industrial quarters, one each on the Meuse and the Hoyoux. Although Huy had a *portus* on the Meuse for long-distance trade by 862, while a street (*vicus*) on the Hoyoux handled local trade, settlement on the Meuse remained suburban until the central

---

43   Février, 'Vetera et nova', 463, 477; Clarke and Ambrosiani, *Towns in the Viking Age*, 7.
44   For this argument, see Hodges and Whitehouse, *Mohammed*, ch. 3 and pp. 90–1.
45   Wightman, *Gallia Belgica*, 234–9; Claude, *Bourges und Poitiers*, 63; Clarke and Ambrosiani, *Towns in the Viking Age*, 7.

Middle Ages. The city expanded into the interior along the Hoyoux and a land route that crossed it.[46]

Quentovic and Dorestad

Since the *civitates* had permanent populations of clerics and landowners who generated demand for the goods and services provided by non-aristocratic residents of both the fortification and the suburbs, they had an intrinsic advantage over more recently occupied settlements. This can be explained by a model that is critically important for the rest of our study. Urban populations may be divided into rough categories of 'basic' and 'non-basic' economic factors. A basic factor's income is derived from sources outside the community, while non-basic factors are the support personnel needed to provide goods and services to the basic factors. In the Merovingian city, priests who lived from the yield of rural estates were basic factors. Bakers, transport workers and brewers were non-basic. The classifications cannot be applied rigidly, for the same person might fit into two categories, for example a weaver who produces fine woollens for export and coarser cloth for the local market. Particularly as the cities became industrialised, most households below the apex of the social pyramid had more than one wage-earner. In social units that are as differentiated as cities, with numerous interdependent specialists, the presence of one basic factor normally requires one non-basic factor to care for the needs of the worker and his or her family. Thus in theory when a basic factor moves to a city, a non-basic factor should also come. When their two families are taken into account, the basic worker's appearance should raise the population by between seven and ten persons. Earlier established cities with firm roots in the economy and social structure of their environs thus had a tremendous advantage over later foundations. We have seen that basic factors continued to reside in the shrinking Merovingian *civitates*.[47]

The 'Frisians', a term evidently referring generally to North Sea merchants, were the principal long-distance traders in the north between the seventh and ninth centuries. They had resident colonies in several major commercial centres. As the *civitates* declined due to troubles in the Mediterranean, the shift to riverine commerce and declining local markets, commerce quickened in coastal emporia that could handle the growing trade between princely courts.

None of these new markets survived to become a true city, but they

46   Nicholas, 'Urban origins', 108; Joris, *Ville de Huy*, 69–91 and maps.
47   See discussion in Russell, *Medieval Regions*, 34–8.

show 'urban thinking' and city planning better than the *civitates*. Quentovic on the Canche and Dorestad on the Lek and Kromme Rijn, the
ports of the Frankish subkingdoms of Neustria and Austrasia respectively, are the best examples from Merovingian Gaul. The exact site of
Quentovic has never been discovered, but excavations at Dorestad show
an unfortified commercial settlement of 250 ha and a population of perhaps 2,000 by 800. The houses were adjacent on small, rectangular plots
in a planned layout in two rows along a single street. Each house had
frontage along the river and a back yard for outbuildings. Settlement was
more dispersed in an agricultural sector away from the river. The farmers
had cottage industries in shipbuilding, carpentry, basket-making, leather,
iron, bone, amber and textiles. As at Quentovic and Hamwih in England,
royal administration supervised the port and controlled the coinage.
Although long-distance trade was controlled by aliens, local traders and
craftsmen also lived at Dorestad.[48]

Urban life in Britain in the seventh century

Apart from Quentovic and Dorestad, the best examples of seventh-
century coastal emporia are in Britain. Hamwih was probably founded
in the late seventh century as the outpost of Winchester, 18 km up the
Itchen. The two were complementary in function: Winchester was
the residence of the king, bishops and aristocrats, while Hamwih was
the port and market. With an area of 46 ha at its height, it had a grid
street layout along the river. Iron, bronze, lead, silver, pottery, wood,
bone and antler and especially textiles were worked there. The notion
that 'foreign enclaves' may have existed at Hamwih is now discredited;
but it was apparently 'not a family-oriented settlement', for a graveyard
has been excavated with a male-female ratio of 2:1. Wares were imported from France and northern Germany. Yet despite its promising
beginnings and continued growth into the early Carolingian age,
Hamwih, like Dorestad, did not evolve into a city.[49]

Although urban life collapsed more completely in Britain than on
the continent in the fifth and sixth centuries, the cities revived there in

48 Verhulst and Doehaerd, 'Handel en nijverheid', 204–7; Steuer, 'Urban archae-
    ology', 82–3; Fixot, 'Image idéale', 535; Hodges and Whitehouse, *Mohammed*, 93–
    5; Verwers, 'Dorestad', 52–6. Recent summaries of Quentovic and Dorestad are
    given in Clarke and Ambrosiani, *Towns in the Viking Age*, 16–19, 25–9 and Hinton,
    Alfred's Kingdom, 3–9.
49 Biddle, 'Towns', 112–14; Clarke and Ambrosiani, *Towns in the Viking Age*, 22, 35–
    6; Aston and Bond, *Landscape of Towns*, 62–3. The pairing of a political capital with
    an outport is reminiscent of Cairo and Fustat in Egypt.

the seventh, just when most centres in Gaul were declining or stabil-
ising. 'Prefects' are mentioned at York and Carlisle. York had a church
by 627, and King Edwin of Deira probably had a palace there. By the
mid-seventh century the Roman defences were being rebuilt and
strengthened by an entirely new stone tower; York is the only English
city that is known to have rebuilt its Roman defences this early. Gold
coins were minted at York by this time. London, after being deserted
for more than a century, grew rapidly in the seventh century, acquiring
a bishopric, a mint, a port and by 674 a royal trading hall and reeve.
St Paul's cathedral was founded in 604. There were actually two Londons
in the late Saxon age. Lundenwic, whose 'wic' name suggests trading,
was an unwalled settlement west of the Roman city extending along the
Strand toward Whitehall and the eventual Westminster. The Roman
city was Lundenburh, whose 'burh' name reflects the fortification, but
the lack of archaeological finds there until after 850 suggest that it was
deserted for Lundenwic, whose area was comparable to that of Dorestad.
The rise of urban life in seventh-century England led to reciprocal trading relations in the North Sea area and contributed to the changes that
become clearer in the Carolingian age.[50]

URBAN LIFE IN LOMBARD AND EARLY CAROLINGIAN ITALY

The Lombard invasions had a more severe impact on urbanisation in
northern Italy than those of the Ostrogoths. They destroyed some cities,
but once they began to settle permanently, their constructive function
was in making the cities governmental and particularly military centres.
The 'count of the *civitas*', a descendant of the Roman *curator* of the
civitas, is found throughout northern Italy. Some cities also had 'tribunes', who were military commanders attached to *castra*, but they were
under the command of the count. Some duchies were formed of *civitates*
and *castra* that were subordinated to a duke, as at Ravenna. This created
some lines of dependence that later urban growth rendered anachronistic, such as the subordination of the count at Como to the duke at
Milan and of the counts of Pistoia and Pisa to the duke at Lucca. The
Lombard monarchs started living in the cities just about the time the
Frankish kings were ceasing to do so, bringing with them a German
and rural aristocracy. The Lombards evidently had their own enclaves

50   Biddle, 'Towns', 118–19; Hill, *Medieval Lincoln*, 20; Tillott, *City of York*, 3–9; Mer-
     rifield, *London*, 267; Reynolds, *English Medieval Towns*, 12; Hobley, 'Lundenwic and
     Lundenburh', 59–73; Biddle, 'Development of the Anglo-Saxon town', 207–8.

in some towns. At Pavia, which became their capital, they lived in the east and northeast around the public buildings, while the native Romans lived in the western parts of the city.[51]

Internally, the Roman distinction of city–suburb–territory within a *civitas* organisation persisted through the Lombard period in most of Italy, even in places where castles replaced the city as the chief royal centre, and it was taken over by the Franks. A capitulary of 806 distinguished Italian *civitates* and their suburbs from their counties and subordinated suburb and territory to the *civitas*. A text of 815 mentions a 'suburb of the *civitas* of Verona', while 'circuit' is used in 873 for the territory within the *civitas* at Lucca.[52]

The Lombards subordinated their cities to much firmer territorial organisation than was possible for any northern princes at this early stage. In some cities the 'citizens' (*cives*), who lived in the *civitas*, were required in the Frankish period to do labour on public works, but whether this obligation extended to the 'people' (*populus*) of the suburb is unclear.[53] The Byzantines and after them the Lombards kept the Roman practice of dividing the area of the *civitates* into neighbourhood associations that were attached to a gate of the *civitas*. These units became centres of the militia and later of administration. Each of them had assemblies. This led eventually to the division of the cities into quarters or sixths, which were defensive in character, in charge of maintaining and defending a sector of the wall. There is no evidence of such organisations in northern Europe until the late ninth and tenth centuries. The entire urban territory had a military organisation whose chief commander was the count, even if some counts were technically subordinate to a duke. These officials seem to have had a role in preserving urban life that was comparable to that of the northern urban bishops.[54]

For all the destructiveness of the Lombard invasions in their early phase, the Italian cities revived rapidly in the early eighth century. Most of them had more and larger public buildings by 750 than the northern towns. Some aristocrats had stone houses. The Roman drainage system at Pavia was still functioning. Milan and Verona were thriving by 800 as residences of the aristocracy and seats of administration and government. An anonymous author wrote of Milan in 739 that 'There are towers with high tops around the circuit [of the Roman wall], finished with great care on the outside, decorated with buildings on the inside.

51 Bullough, 'Social and economic structure and topography', 373–6.
52 Mengozzi, *Città italiana*, 91–3.
53 Mengozzi, *Città italiana*, 150–1, 252.
54 Santini, *Europa medioevale*, 201–9; Haverkamp, 'Städte im Herrschafts- und Sozialgefüge Reichsitaliens', 166; Previté-Orton, 'Italian cities till c. 1200', 211.

The walls are twelve feet wide; the immense base is made with squared blocks, elegantly completed on top with bricks. In the walls are nine marvellous gates, carefully secured with iron bars and keys, before which stand the towers of the drawbridges'.[55] Pavia had forty-five churches, Lucca fifty-seven by 925. Most of them were family churches, established by powerful notables who dominated both the truncated cities and their environs. As in the north, the bishops were town lords in these places, holding lands in the city and the suburbs in immunity, which in practice gave them sole exercise of public authority.[56]

The Lombard period brought a radical change in domestic architecture in Italy, as the single-family dwelling spread in the wake of the destruction of the islands with multistoreyed buildings. The Lombards rebuilt much of what their ancestors had destroyed, but their structures were cruder than those of the Romans. Most buildings were still in stone or brick, as they had been in antiquity, but they now faced the Roman streets, and the interior of the 'islands' had gardens or outbuildings. Most houses had only a ground floor or at most one storey above ground. This form dominated until the aristocratic towers of the eleventh century and after. The kitchen, bathhouse, shop, occasionally an exterior portico and often the family habitation were on the ground floor or occasionally the storey above ground. A masonry or stone solarium might be found if the house had a second level. There is no evidence of interior latrines. Roofs were straw, wood or tile, occasionally with lead. The novelty was in having the living area, including the reception chamber, at the ground level. Smaller houses did not have all these amenities. Though it required space and land, this type of house was found both within the walls and in the suburbs of the cities. Examples have been excavated or described in written sources for Ravenna, Rimini, Lucca, Verona and Rome.[57]

With the exception of Milan most larger centres in early medieval Italy were non-Roman, like Venice, or kept more of the Roman street plan than was usual in the north. Tradition holds that Pavia was abandoned and then rebuilt by the Lombards, who made it their capital, but the fact that Pavia kept its Roman grid in nearly perfect state makes this unlikely. The street plan of Verona, too, survived virtually unaltered, those of Turin and Vicenza with slight modifications. There are some

---

55 Quoted by Wickham, *Early Medieval Italy*, 82.
56 Ward-Perkins, 'The towns of northern Italy', in Hodges and Hobley, *Rebirth of Towns*, 19–25; Bocchi, *Città italiane*, 9–10; Wickham, *Early Medieval Italy*, 84–6.
57 Cogiano de Azevedo, 'Aspetti urbanistici', 652–7; Wickham, *Land and Power*, 111; Brogiolo, 'Città longobarda', 562.

survivals at Genoa and even Ravenna, the capital of Byzantine Italy, but enough was lost to suggest considerable displacement. The colossea, games and temples declined. Churches were the only significant new public buildings, and they were considerably smaller than those of the Romans.[58] The Roman central city at Lucca survived intact, and the *forum*, colosseum, royal palace and mint were still used. It was the seat of powerful counts. Although the cathedral complex was on the periphery inside the wall, the other churches were already becoming neighbourhood centres throughout the city. Lucca also had extramural buildings, the palace of the duke of Tuscany, churches and dwellings. The city was divided before 739 into quarters based on the gates. It had the wide range of occupations not found in northern cities until much later. We can only speculate about how typical Lucca was of the north Italian cities.[59]

On balance, Roman street plans were virtually obliterated in northern Europe, but they survived to some degree in most large Italian cities except Milan. This would have been impossible if public control had not survived or been reinstituted quickly to prevent encroachments on the streets. Similarly, although virtually all early medieval *fora* were smaller than in the Roman cities, their space continued to dominate the city centres. They became the market squares. The Lombards placed public thoroughfares under a separate legal status, as the Romans had done. Work also continued on town walls, although whether only during emergencies or as a programme of continuous maintenance is uncertain.[60]

Although the bishops and the landed aristocracy dominated the Italian cities through the Carolingian period, the cities also display traces of corporate organisation. Public meetings are found in most cities of late eighth- and early ninth-century Italy. Consultative assemblies that are variously called 'council of the *civitas*' or 'assembly' usually met on the square in front of the cathedral church or some other important public building, usually an abbey. An act of 808 calls the ancient amphitheatre at Lucca the 'place where discussions are held' (*parlascium*). Ancient amphitheatres continued to be used in this way in the tenth and eleventh centuries at Arezzo, Pisa, Florence, Cremona and Bergamo. As late as 1059 public assemblies at Milan were meeting in the amphitheatre for secular issues, in the cathedral of St Ambrose for church matters. A document of 790 shows the 'men' of Piacenza without the intervention

---

58 Claude, *Byzantinische Stadt*, 124–5; Février, 'Towns in the western Mediterranean', 330–1; Ward-Perkins, 'The towns of northern Italy', 16–18 and esp. map p. 17; Ward-Perkins, *Urban Public Building*, 22, 179–80.
59 Wickham, *Early Medieval Italy*, 84–5.
60 Ward-Perkins, *Urban Public Building*, 180–99.

of bishop or count receiving new citizens according to 'their precept', which implies organisation and law. While under the early Lombards the ancient courts and the *exceptor* of the *civitas* had lost their function of transcribing municipal documents, both had revived by this time.[61]

Although the aristocracy of the Italian cities at this stage was Lombard or Lombard–Frankish and largely rural, the Italian cities also display a stronger local market network than their northern counterparts. A Lombard statute of 750 divided the 'merchants' of the kingdom into three groups of 'greater', 'followers' and 'lesser' in requiring military service from each. Commercial transactions were already being centred in the *civitas*. Merchants of Milan who are mentioned in ninth-century documents were always residents of the city, although they also bought and sold in the surrounding countryside and witnessed transactions there. The greater Italian merchants even this early were displaying a characteristic that would mark medieval urban elites: one Donato of Milan was identified in 803 as 'merchant of Sertole street' in which, coincidentally, he owned 120 *denariae* worth of land.[62] We shall see that in northern Europe as well as Italy the oldest elite families of the medieval city were landowners as well as merchants, in many cases before they were merchants.

Signalling a situation that the authorities would see as a problem for the rest of the medieval period, church officials and Charlemagne himself forbade holding markets on Sunday and other religious festival days, but this shows that it was being done on a large scale. In most Italian cities the market was in the urban centre, at the intersection of the *cardo* with the *decumanus*. That of Milan was inside the cathedral precinct, in front of the church. The problem about Sunday sales may have been that after the ancient temples were destroyed, the Christian bishops located their seats on the sites of the old temples, which happened to be on the site of the ancient forum. This happened in Vercelli, Cremona, Brescia, Lucca, Piacenza, Bergamo, Parma, Pavia, Pisa, Ferrara, Verona, Florence, Arezzo and other cities. The siting of the bishopric thus postdated that of the market, the reverse of what generally happened in northern Europe.[63]

Most of the markets seem to have dealt with grain, other necessities such as salt and petty artisan work. The monasteries of the Po valley used their cells in the cities for warehousing grain, which they naturally sold on the urban market. The Venetians bought food from churches at

---

61 Fasoli *et al.*, 'Struttura sociale', 295–6; Mengozzi, *Città italiana*, 262–3, 267–70, 279–80; Keller, 'Soziale und politische Verfassung Mailands', 52–3.
62 Violante, *Società milanese*, 54–5.
63 Mengozzi, *Città italiana*, 255, 232–3, 235–8.

the market of Pavia, both for their own consumption and for export to Byzantium. Although some luxuries from the east entered Italian trade in the eighth and early ninth centuries, the basis of eventual economic growth in the cities was provisioning the local market with necessities. The large number of urban churches that collected rents in kind from tenants on their rural estates provided a surplus for sale in the city markets.[64]

The Italian cities also had artisans, although even less can be said about them than of the merchants. Some of them already had occupational organisations – the soapmakers of Piacenza were making an annual payment of thirty pounds of soap to the king before 744 – although continuity in such cases with Roman antecedents is unlikely except perhaps at Rome and Ravenna, which came under Byzantine influence in the sixth century.[65]

The situation of Venice requires special consideration. While coastal locations fostered trade, they were also hard to defend. Venice was the only coastal city that is known to have had extensive trade before the tenth century. From the fifth century onward the lagoons had been a refuge for Po valley inhabitants who were fleeing invaders. Thus Venice remained in the portion of Italy claimed nominally by the emperor at Constantinople, since the Lombards were never able to take it. 'Tribunes' built castles on the islands, which became nuclei of discrete settlements. They in turn were linked under the *doge* (duke) at the end of the seventh century. The *doge* was appointed by the Byzantine emperor at first, then by the Venetians themselves after the religious struggles of the Carolingian period caused Italy to break away from Constantinople. In 840 the western emperor Lothair gave Venice control over traffic on the Po and its tributaries, probably in a confirmation of the *status quo*. This permitted the city to develop a lucrative two-way trade with Byzantium, despite the political break, conveying the raw materials of the Po valley to Constantinople in exchange for luxuries.[66]

URBAN LIFE IN NORTHERN EUROPE IN THE EARLY CAROLINGIAN AGE

The consolidation of royal power in the eighth century in Gaul, Britain and northern Italy had a great impact on urbanisation. Establishing an

64 Luzzatto, *Economic History of Italy*, 27–8; Violante, *Società milanese*, 12–13.
65 Previté-Orton, 'Italian cities till c. 1200', 210; Luzzatto, *Economic History of Italy*, 29–30.
66 Van Werveke, 'Rise of the towns', 9; Luzzatto, *Economic History of Italy*, 32–5, 51–2.

episcopal organisation in Germany east of the Rhine created the basis of urban growth there. The kings gave power in the cities to the bishops, while the counts were more clearly rural figures. Hamburg, with a bishopric by 831, had a fortress that included both the cathedral and the merchant settlement, but the other Carolingian bishoprics in Germany were polynuclear. The centrifugal tendency that was so apparent in Gaul was even stronger across the Rhine, where no Roman wall made a nucleus. The cathedral complex was more often walled in Germany than in the west, and it was then characteristically joined by other churches within a radius of 300–1,500 metres.[67]

The neo-Roman *civitates* of southern France continued to decline in the Carolingian age. In the Rhône valley the Muslims were a constant threat until the mid-tenth century. Commercial development was stunted, while the bishops and rural lineages jockeyed for military advantage. Some commerce continued at Marseilles into the early ninth century, but then it was ruined by the Muslim raids. Poitiers was a royal residence and fortification with a truncated civilian settlement. Its walls were reinforced by King Pippin but were damaged in fighting during the ninth century.[68]

Further north, however, most *civitates* were reviving in the late eighth and ninth centuries, and some new bishoprics were established in response to changing settlement patterns. Laon, which had not been a Roman *civitas*, was a bishopric by the early sixth century and became the seat of a powerful family of Frankish counts.[69] From the early ninth century the clergy who were attached to the bishoprics were being required to live near the cathedral, thus fostering concentration rather than dispersal of settlement. In the larger *civitates* of the west many bishops were still competing with counts for control inside the city walls. When the count became the town lord, as at Poitiers and Bourges, he generally limited the bishop to an immunity district around the cathedral. The count also replaced the bishop as town lord at Bordeaux, Saintes, Angoulême, Bourges and Poitiers in the Carolingian period. All of them were in the forefront of the Norman attacks and thus relied on a secular defender. The bishop also lost lordship to the count at Le Mans and in the areas of the south that were threatened by the Muslims. At Limoges, Périgueux and Clermont, which were further from the Normans, the bishop continued to rule. The bishops also were more successful in keeping

67 Schlesinger, 'Frühformen', 300; Hall, *Mittelalterliche Stadtgrundrisse*, 69–72.
68 Dez, *Poitiers*, ch. 2; Claude, *Bourges und Poitiers*, 94–5, 98–9; Baratier, *Histoire de Marseille*, 58; Fixot, 'Image idéale', 521–5.
69 Bur, *Laon*, 11–37.

control in the smaller *civitates*, which had too little space within the walls to provide bases for competing powers.[70]

Trade in Carolingian city and suburb

The early Carolingian period saw a general growth of the local markets that were so important for the population base of the early cities. Trade is not of itself necessarily an urban activity, but the regulation of trade usually is. By establishing markets the Carolingian rulers were trying to centralise trade into specific places where it could be controlled. Mints and toll stations show that a bureaucracy was trying to tap the resources of the economy. Just as the English kings would later try to confine commercial transactions to *burhs*, Pippin the Short limited minting to *civitates*, a few *vici* and some great suburban abbeys. In 820 Louis the Pious made the count in each city responsible for its mint. The kings were trying to foster the cities as centres where trade could be controlled.[71]

The famines of the Carolingian age, however deplorable in human terms, also promoted the growth of an exchange economy, for scarcity creates demand, and lords who collected grain rents sold food to the hungry. This contributed to the development of commercial centres. A synod in 744 ordered bishops to provide food at legal measures 'through all *civitates*', a directive that shows that a regular market mechanism existed for grain. Commerce with the Islamic east and in the North Sea area was active until around 820. Dorestad, Hamwih and Quentovic expanded in the second quarter of the eighth century, declined between 750 and around 790, then experienced a new boom, perhaps connected with the revival of cross-channel ties under Charlemagne and King Offa of Mercia. While long-distance trade was largely patronised by the princely and episcopal courts through the eighth century, local trade was more broadly based, and long-distance trade became less dominated by luxuries in the ninth century.[72]

More of the numerous suburbs outside the *civitates* were being described in the Carolingian period in terms suggesting trading and merchants. Extramural settlements called *portus*, where tolls and taxes were collected, developed outside virtually all cities in Gaul on navigable waterways, both *civitates* and other forts. At Tournai the *portus* was used for interregional trade, while a separate market existed for local exchange.

70 Hall, *Mittelalterliche Stadtgrundrisse*, 66; Claude, *Bourges und Poitiers*, 101, 104, 112.
71 Fixot, 'Image idéale', 525–8.
72 Büttner, 'Frühmittelalterliches Städtewesen', 158–9; Hodges and Whitehouse, *Mohammed*, 98, 101, 115–18.

Mints were often in the *portus* rather than in the city proper, particularly in the Scheldt network, which was beginning to supplant the Meuse in commercial importance in the Carolingian period. Some of the greatest cities of northern Europe would be in this area. They began demonstrating urban characteristics in the eighth and early ninth centuries. Valenciennes was the earliest Scheldt town to develop from non-Roman roots. It was three miles from the nearest Roman fortress and six miles from the Roman road, but the growing Scheldt trade caused a *portus* to develop outside a royal fortress that had been on the site by 693. Like Ghent, Norwich and later Lille, Valenciennes also grew at a geological/economic frontier, the intersection of the marshy Scheldt valley and the chalk plateaux. By the early eighth century it had a parish organisation. Charlemagne's biographer Einhard mentions shipping and merchandise there in the ninth century.[73]

The topographical distinction between fortified nucleus and commercial suburb was becoming clearer in the Carolingian age in the older centres as well. Examples abound: Amiens, Troyes, Provins, Le Mans, Cambrai and especially Beauvais, where the separation was still felt in the seventeenth century. At Lyon the Saône ran between the *civitas* and bourg. The merchant colony in Paris was on the right bank of the Seine, while the *civitas* was the Île de la Cité. Nucleus and suburb were also separated by a river at Verdun, Mechelen, Utrecht and Maastricht. Where the fortress was on a hill, as at Basel, Erfurt, Namur, Dinant and Huy, the merchant settlement was at its foot. Much also depended on the size of the fortification. Merchants lived inside the large *civitates* at Regensburg, Passau and Cologne, but all of them also had merchant suburbs. Cologne is one of the earliest examples of the market developing at the gate leading into the old city from the suburb. But when a small fort rather than a *civitas* was the nucleus, lack of space within the walls often forced the merchant settlement outside, particularly in the Low Countries, where it was often immediately under the count's castle. In Flanders, where there were no major Roman fortresses, castles were the nuclei of virtually all cities. Thus while many Flemish cities were binuclear, they were not polynuclear, as was common in France.[74]

The coastal emporia

The fate of the coastal emporia in the Carolingian period shows the inherent limitations of such agglomerations. All would yield to more

73 Nicholas, 'Urban origins', 97; Deisser-Nagels, 'Valenciennes, ville carolingienne', 51–90, esp. 53–64; Platelle, *Valenciennes*, 11, 15–16, 19.
74 Ennen, *Frühgeschichte*, 135–8; Chédeville, 'De la cité à la ville', 81.

protected sites inland in the ninth century. But Quentovic and Dorestad were declining even before the Scandinavian attacks, for their prosperity was too tied to demand generated by royal courts whose power was waning. This is particularly true of Dorestad, which declined drastically after 830 and was abandoned after 863, when its mint was closed. The Danes founded Haithabu after 810 to force the Carolingians to redirect their trade away from Dorestad. Hamwih traded with more scattered markets in northern France and the Low Countries and thus survived into the tenth century. Hedeby, which in contrast to the earlier coastal emporia was fortified, was established in the mid-eighth century, flourished in the ninth and tenth, then declined in favour of Schleswig in the eleventh.[75]

The Islamic cities

In conclusion, the primitive level of development of European urban life may be illustrated graphically by comparing the much larger and socially differentiated cities of the Islamic east with those of the contemporary Carolingian west. Islamic cities typically had a citadel surrounded by a royal city, then by a central urban complex that included homes of the great burgesses and religious leaders, the great mosques and religious schools and the main markets, where craftsmen and traders had spaces assigned by occupational group. The larger streets were lined with shops. The diffusion of commercial and industrial activity throughout the city, and the use of the home as a workshop, that are characteristic of the cities of Europe, especially the north, is not true of the Islamic cities. Residential quarters outside the central area were strongly differentiated by religion, family and profession. Immigrants tended to settle in compact groups in the Islamic cities. The suburbs of Baghdad had separate quarters occupied by the descendants of the Companions of the Prophet, the people of Kufa, Greeks, and others, with each group having its own military and civilian leader. The quarters became the basis of taxation and the militia, and the leaders of the quarters thus had important governmental functions. Suburbs were populated by recent migrants and some occupations were concentrated there. While the central area generally displayed some planning, the suburbs did not. When superimposed on cities that had been occupied by the Romans, Islamic street plans were more crooked, with shops and houses encroaching on the streets.

75 Hodges and Whitehouse, *Mohammed*, 108–14, 162. The excavations at Hedeby are described in Clarke and Ambrosiani, *Towns in the Viking Age*, 56–63.

Community solidarity in the Islamic cities tended to be felt within the quarters, especially when they were divided along religious lines. This element was not present in the west except for the Jews, who were much less important there than the Christian and Jewish communities were in the cities of the Near East. Although most early medieval western cities were communities separated from each other by considerable space within the walls or between walled and suburban areas, as they 'grew together there were rarely confessional or other hindrances to their eventual union under a single urban government, in contrast to the Muslim cities. Thus, although there were revolts between the eighth and tenth centuries in the cities of Mesopotamia and Syria, these incidents were not a prologue to the development of civic institutions, as happened in western Europe. 'Committees', usually dominated by the *kadi*, did lead the cities of Muslim Spain after the collapse of the Umayyad caliphate of Cordova. But while government by council lasted in the north, the Spanish cities soon reverted to the rule of military emirates.

The Muslim cities were loosely structured, with few institutions in the European sense. The city did not become independent of the central government. Islamic law recognised no corporations; thus, although the early Islamic cities had professional associations, they were not guilds in the later western sense, with officials and rights of self-government. The state police regulated artisans and set standards for their work, and the leaders in each craft reported back to the police.

The caliphs were strong enough to be able to plan enormous new cities successfully. Baghdad was a more startling example than anything in the west of a planned city that succeeded. It did not begin as an economic centre but rather as a political capital that attracted economic development. Founded in 762 as a centrally located capital on a flat area between the rivers Tigris and Euphrates, it had a network of avenues, major streets that were one-third the width of the avenues and side streets, and alleys that could be locked at night. In contrast to the more rectangular shape of the later western planned cities, Baghdad had the form of concentric circles. An inner area, the 'Round City', of public buildings was surrounded by symmetrical arcaded rings of city blocks. Although initially inhabited mainly by members of the imperial family, army and officials, Baghdad developed more ethnic diversity than the other Islamic cities and had more public buildings and amenities.[76]

76 Discussion based on Stern, 'Constitution of the Islamic city', 25–6, 33–4, 42–4; Sourdel, 'L'organisation de l'espace dans les villes du monde islamique, 2–4; Hourani, 'Islamic city', 15–17, 21–4; Cahen, 'Corporations', 51–63; El-Adi, 'Foundation of Baghdad', 93–100; Lassner, 'City Plan of Baghdad', 103–10.

The infant pre-urban settlements of post-Carolingian Europe underwent a series of crises in the ninth and tenth centuries from which a recognisable urban network would emerge. Although no European city would approach the sophisticated planning or socioeconomic differentiation of the Islamic cities of the early caliphs before 1200, the basis for the great expansion after 1000 was being created in this time of trial.

CHAPTER THREE

Challenge and Response: the Scandinavian and Muslim Attacks and the Revival of Urban Life in the West, 830–1000

The Scandinavian attacks and urbanisation

The Scandinavian attacks of the ninth and early tenth centuries were a major shock throughout northern Europe. The raids first became serious in England, then in France and the Low Countries, where nearly every major population centre was seriously damaged or destroyed. The worst onslaughts came between 855 and 892 in areas drained by the Seine, Loire, Meuse, Scheldt and their tributaries. Archaeological evidence shows that many existing settlements were destroyed. New fortifications were built, some on the same site, but many were in previously uninhabited places. Yet any break in continuity of settlement was brief, and all embryonic cities recovered.[1]

The cities were unprepared for the crisis. Although the *civitates* had been fortified for centuries, some of their defences had been torn down and the stone reused for civilian buildings during the peaceful early Carolingian period. The bourgs were still unwalled in the early ninth century, and in many places they housed more inhabitants than the *civitas*. Paris (Plan 3) had several populous bourgs when the Normans came, particularly Saint-Germain-des-Prés on the southwest and Saint-Germain-l'Auxerrois on the west, which suggests substantial growth in the early ninth century. Unfortunately, since the Gallo-Roman wall had been

---

1 Nicholas, *Medieval Flanders*, 15–18; Chédeville, 'Cité', 37.

destroyed, the Normans took Paris easily, leaving only the Île de la Cité inhabited. At Chartres the survivors of the sack of 858 took refuge in a corner of the Roman stockade. A second wall may have been built around the cathedral. The Northmen pillaged Poitiers in 857, then returned to destroy the three convents outside the walls in 863. The *civitas*, however, ransomed itself, a deed that implies a municipal organisation, able to raise money. The city was burned again in 865, but in 868 citizens defeated the Scandinavians.[2]

Thus most of the larger suburban shrine-settlements in areas struck by the Vikings were walled between 875 and 925, including those of St Vaast at Arras (884–87), Saint-Martial at Limoges (ca. 900), Saint-Rémi at Reims (923–25) and Saint-Géry of Cambrai. Saint-Arnoul of Reims and Saints-Hilaire and Radegonde at Poitiers were enclosed slightly later. The half-century time lag between destruction and fortification seems common for both the bourgs and new centres that lacked Roman or episcopal antecedents. In addition, particularly in western France, the inhabitants of the area within five leagues (11 km) of the wall, called the *defensaria* or *quinta* of the city, were obliged to help maintain the fortress. Forts that might be used by an enemy were forbidden in the *quinta*. The area within the *quinta* of Poitiers was identical to that of its vicariate and may go back to the Romans. The development of *quintae* is also attested at Saintes, Tours, Angoulême, Périgueux and Limoges. This is very similar to the arrangement imposed on Wessex by Alfred the Great's Burghal Hidage, although its impact on urbanisation in France was less profound than in England.[3]

Yet the Scandinavians traded as well as raided. This fact explains the paradox that although they were more destructive along the Scheldt and in northern France than along the Meuse, the climax of their attacks in the late ninth century coincided with a definite shift of commercial activity from the Meuse to the western rivers. The repopulation that began in the early tenth century marked the beginning of the continuous habitation of most cities in the north. Most *civitas* walls in France that were rebuilt followed the trace of those the Scandinavians had destroyed. The only significant exceptions were cases where the bishop ordered an old wall to be extended to incorporate a suburban sanctuary, as happened

2 Boussard, *Paris*, 11–16; Dez, *Poitiers*, ch. 2; Chédeville, 'Cité', 37.
3 At Bourges it was called the *septema* and at Besançon the *sexta*, probably because the radius was seven and six leagues respectively. The *quinta* disappears in the eleventh century. Chédeville, 'Cité', 40–4; Claude, *Bourges und Poitiers*, 122. Peasants were required to labour on Russian city walls, but evidently only after the plagues had seriously depleted the labour supply in the cities in the second half of the fourteenth century. Langer, 'Medieval Russian town', 26.

at Vienne and Cambrai around 900 and at Châlons and at Metz after the Magyar raids.[4]

The Low Countries

Although the agricultural and commercial elements were stronger and industry weaker in the Flemish pre-urban nuclei than was once thought, the Flemish cities were almost unique in owing so little of their early development to the seigneurial power of a lay prince or church. They were as exclusively economic entities as anything the Middle Ages produced.

The rise of the southern Low Countries as an urban region after the Scandinavian attacks is an anomaly. Although the Vikings destroyed the *portus* of every town on the Meuse or Scheldt in the 870s and 880s, the Scheldt cities became the largest of northern Europe as trade shifted westward from the Meuse. They were far enough inland to avoid the fate of Dorestad and Quentovic but close enough to the coast to take advantage of overseas contacts. Perhaps most importantly, despite the poverty of the area, they had enough inhabitants to link the sea to a strong overland trade.

Flanders and Brabant have more examples than other regions of cities that developed on opposite sides of a river or on two rivers without one settlement really dominating. At Ghent (Plan 4) a Merovingian settlement and harbour around the abbey of St Bavo on the Scheldt was called a *municipium* in the eighth century; in the ninth a merchant *portus* with a semicircular moat developed across the river. The merchant *portus* of Bruges, which was evidently a response to Scandinavian contacts, was simultaneously taking shape around rural churches. Bruges (Plan 12) had a mint by 875. But the catalysts of urbanisation at both cities were fortresses erected by the counts of Flanders, at Bruges by 851 and at Ghent before 939, that protected the infant cities and also determined much of their topographical development. Bruges developed along the land route leading to the castle, which was at the port. The castle at Ghent, which was later called the 'Old Burg', was along the Leie, the smaller of the two streams that merged at the city. As happened at Huy, London, Utrecht, Passau and other centres, settlement backed down the smaller stream, away from the castle toward the source of food; for grain coming downstream on the Scheldt was provisioning communities farther south, and Ghent thus obtained its food via the smaller river. The count's settlement on the Leie was linked during the tenth century

---

4   Nicholas, *Medieval Flanders*, 29; Verhulst, 'Vie urbaine', 189–94; Chédeville, 'Cité', 37, 40; Fixot, 'Image idéale', 520; Nicholas, 'Urban origins', 94.

to the now repopulated agglomeration along the Scheldt by two arteries: a street, the High Port (Hoogpoort), and further south a canal that effectively completed the moating of the central city.[5]

Ghent thus began as a grain market attracted by the demand generated in the count's castle. It is at the intersection of the prosperous grain-producing loam area of southern Flanders with the sandy, pastoral north, and much of the city's later trade would be in re-exporting grain brought from France to grain-poor northern Flanders. The first craftsmen mentioned at Ghent were leatherworkers in the 'Old Burg'; the clothmaking that would later make Ghent's fame is not attested until the late tenth century, and the textile quarters developed in the suburbs, particularly on the Scheldt and the canal linking it to the Leie. Ghent is thus unusual in having two *portus*. The one on the Leie, the later 'port of Ghent', originated in local trade, particularly grain and provisioning the residents of the count's complex (the 'Old Burg'), while the *portus* on the Scheldt handled long-distance trade. Although it originated in local trade, the Leie settlement contained the three food markets of Ghent and the grain staple, and it eventually became the centre of banking and most manufacturing except textiles.[6]

Since both in this area and further south merchant settlements developed before castles (in the case of Ghent by half a century) the importance of the fortresses for the embryonic cities was less because they provided defence than because their residents' demand for food, manufactures and luxuries stimulated trade and economic development. The Scheldt castles were as large as some smaller *civitates* elsewhere and incorporated settlements of merchants and craftsmen. The diffusion of centres of political power as the Carolingian state declined meant that consolidation of the authority of local conspicuous consumers would bring economic growth.[7]

---

5 Valenciennes shows a strikingly parallel development later. The wall begun by Count Baldwin IV (988–1035) was a semi-circle beginning and ending at the Scheldt, which was the eastern border of the city; but the inhabited area of Valenciennes was bisected by the tiny Ruonelle. The primitive fort and the merchant *portus* had been on the left bank of the Scheldt, but later settlement backed away from the fort down both sides of the Ruonelle. Platelle, *Histoire de Valenciennes*, 39–41 and Figure 3.

6 Discussion of the origins of Ghent and Bruges based on Chédeville, 'Cité', 55, Nicholas, 'Urban origins', 95–6 and Nicholas, *Medieval Flanders*, 32–5, and literature cited, particularly the magisterial studies of Adriaan Verhulst. English readers should note particularly Verhulst, 'Aspect of continuity' and Verhulst, 'Origin of towns', 3–35; Ryckaert, 'Origines et l'histoire ancienne de Bruges', 122–6; for Passau, where the salt trade on the Inn river far surpassed the incomes from Danube traffic, see Brandl-Ziegert, 'Sozialstruktur', 45–6.

7 Verhulst and Doehaerd, 'Nijverheid en handel', 212.

The *Wik*

The development of permanent city life is tied to a word that enters the urban vocabulary in the Scandinavian period: *Wik* (bay) and its compounds. At least eight hundred *Wik* names survive in North Germany, Scandinavia, the Baltic coastal cities and England. France has about seventy-five, of which fifty are south of the Loire and evidently transliterations of the Latin *vicus* (street), whose original meaning was closer to *burgus*. Dorestad was described as a *vicus*, but Quentovic, which was older, had *Wik* in its name.

The earliest *Wike* were not permanent market settlements – that was a later extension of meaning – but rather were places where travelling merchants traded and thus where commodities were stored and often where locally based industry was practised. Traders stopped for rest and business in the *Wike*, where they found resident populations that could provide for their needs. Although most *Wike* were suburban, the name thus implies a population of non-basic producers and suggests the early growth of a permanent market network. In London (*Lundenwic*) and other English towns the *Wike* were under a royal '*Wik* reeve', who was being called 'port reeve' by the tenth century. Later the *Wiek* or *Weichbild* might refer to an entire urban quarter (for example the Alte Wiek, the market settlement at Brunswick) or even a whole city.[8]

Urbanisation in England in the Viking age

The Scandinavian influence on urbanisation is most evident in England. While in France most older centres were declining or at best had stable populations in the eighth and early ninth centuries, English cities were growing. Not only were Roman cities reoccupied, but towns also developed on non-Roman sites. Hereford, in Mercia near the abandoned Roman fort of Kenchester, may have become a bishopric in 676. It developed administrative, ecclesiastical and commercial functions and had a planned grid street layout that may precede the more famous example of Hamwih. Its mid-ninth century wall may be the earliest urban wall on a non-Roman site in England. Although the first written record of Ipswich is from 991, it was occupied by the late sixth century. Its modern street plan is mid-Saxon. Cottage industries have been found throughout the town, particularly pottery, which shows Rhenish influence. Grave finds show that some of the inhabitants were wealthy. Ipswich traded mainly with Flanders, the Rhineland and to a lesser extent

8   Discussion based on Vogel, 'Wik-Orte und Wikinger', 205–25.

northern France. Its economic orientation seems comparable to Quentovic and Dorestad. Between the late seventh and early ninth centuries at least one commercial emporium was founded in each kingdom in Britain: Hamwih, the outport of Winchester, for Wessex; York for Northumbria; *Lundenwic* for Essex; Ipswich for East Anglia; and Fordwich in Kent as the port for Canterbury.[9]

But the Scandinavian raids ruined the coastal emporia. The trade of Hamwih was already diminishing before it was sacked in 842, then abandoned in the tenth century. Its population gradually moved to the site of its successor, Southampton, on the other bank of the Itchen.[10] The fortified centres offered more chance of survival, for suburban commercial settlements could move inside the walls. York grew rapidly during the eighth century. New streets obliterated the Roman grid plan inside the walls, suggesting that there was little habitation there. The heart of Saxon York was between the Roman fortress and Marygate, on the right bank of the Ouse, extending back along the river outside the fortification toward the confluence of the Ouse and the Foss near Fishergate. A trading centre across the Ouse that had housed a Frisian merchant community by the 780s moved inside the walls after the Viking attacks and occupation after 866. Although York had been a Roman colony, its modern name is a *Wik* compound (Anglian *Eoforwic*, Anglo-Scandinavian *Jorvik*). The Roman name *Eboracum* was entirely abandoned.[11]

The permanent location of London (Plan 5) was fixed during the Scandinavian period, as civilian populations sought the protection of walls. The Roman fortification was nearly deserted until the early ninth century, when settlement began in Eastcheap and continued westward downhill to the harbour. Cheapside thus became the major east–west artery of early medieval London, inside the Roman fortification but not precisely on the track of the main Roman road. The Scandinavians evidently destroyed the suburban commercial settlement of *Lundenwic*, which is never mentioned after King Alfred occupied the fortress of London in 886. The revived London was a consumer city. It imported fine goods, mainly from elsewhere in England through the late tenth century and thereafter from overseas, but it had scarcely any manufacturing.

9   Clarke and Ambrosiani, *Towns in the Viking Age*, 19–21, 37, 45; Maddicott, 'Trade Alfred', 6–10; Biddle, 'Evolution', 23–5; Biddle, 'Towns', 115–16, 121; Barley, *European Towns*, 10; Martin, 'New beginnings', 410–11; Wade, 'Ipswich', 93–100.
10 Maddicott, 'Trade Alfred', 9–10; Hodges and Whitehouse, *Mohammed*, 163; Hodges and Hobley, *Rebirth*, 101–8; Aston and Bond, *Landscape of Towns*, 63.
11 Reynolds, *English Medieval Towns*, 26; Hall, 'York 700–1050', 125–30; Clarke and Ambrosiani, *Towns in the Viking Age*, 33; Tillott, *City of York*, 101.

The Roman wall was rebuilt, and London received a grid street plan in the east and south with an interior street along the line of the walls, as was generally true of Alfred's *burhs*.[12]

The Burghal Hidage and English urban organisation

Virtually all major English cities originated as fortifications that later developed commercial functions. Roman forts and bishoprics were the major stimulus on the continent, to which commerce along the great rivers was added in the eighth and ninth centuries. But no English bishopric evolved directly from a Roman antecedent; and since England had so many small navigable streams, some of the forces promoting urbanisation along the great rivers on the continent do not apply in Britain.

English urban development received its greatest impetus from the *burhs* (fortifications) erected by King Alfred the Great of Wessex and his heirs in the late ninth and tenth centuries. There is no continental parallel for town foundation on such a large scale as the *burhs*. Alfred first built *burhs* on the frontiers of Wessex with Mercia and the Danelaw and at intervals of 28 km in the interior of Wessex. The Burghal Hidage, a document probably written before 890 and certainly before 920, lists thirty *burhs* in Wessex. Some were completely new, while others reused Roman or even prehistoric Celtic forts.

Most *burhs* had rectangular tenements with boundaries between the them and streets generally at right angles, but they were less absolutely rectangular than Roman layouts had been. In places that had been Roman the new design was superimposed on any traces of the Roman plan. Alfred was familiar with the plan of Hamwih and undoubtedly knew of the Mercian plan and fortification at Hereford. The fact that the Roman towns in Britain had been completely depopulated, in contrast to many on the continent, meant that little habitation or occupied building had to be removed to create a street network. Other princes were fortifying their domains at this time, but the level of systematic planning in Alfred's creation is exceptional. The continental emporia were very small, with fewer urban characteristics, and the fortresses of such princes as Alfred's son-in-law Count Baldwin II of Flanders were much smaller than the *burhs* and did not give rise to cities; furthermore, they were rounded, while most *burhs* were quadrilateral. The forts of Henry the Fowler in Germany a generation later likewise gave rise to no cities.

12 Hobley, 'Lundenwic and Lundenburh', 73–80; see also Clarke and Ambrosiani, *Towns in the Viking Age*, 32; Rosser, *Medieval Westminster*, 10–13; Maddicott, 'Trade Alfred', 15; Schofield, *Building of London*, 24.

The *burhs* were principally refuges for peasants and accordingly cannot in each case be considered urban. The Burghal Hidage required each hide of land (about six hundred acres or 243 ha) to provide one man to defend the *burh* fortress. Each 5.5 yards (5 metres) of the wall required four men. The similarity to the west French *quinta* is obvious. Comparing length of wall with number of hides at Winchester, Bath and Oxford shows a close correlation. Thus the Burghal Hidage is not a comprehensive urban list for Wessex. It lists fortifications that never developed urban characteristics, and some large walled places (London, Canterbury and Rochester) were not in it. Thus it is often hard to determine the extent to which the fortifications stimulated places to evolve into genuine cities. The impact is clear at Oxford, which had a stone wall and was the capital of its shire by 912. It had a grid street plan inside the wall, suggesting that it was a planned foundation, but the streets remained irregular on the outskirts.[13]

The great period of urban foundations in England was between 870 and 920. All *burhs* built after 920 remained small. Before the reign of Athelstan (924–39) organic cities such as York, London and Canterbury developed in response to local economic circumstances, but virtually all places founded in the century before the Norman Conquest had defence as their primary function. They adapted less rapidly than the organic cities and the first founded *burhs* to the economic changes that were calling an urban network into being.[14]

The Saxon *burhs*: the example of Winchester

Winchester (Plan 8), at 144 acres the largest of Alfred's *burhs*, has been the most thoroughly investigated of them and is of special interest because it had also been a Roman centre. As at London, Colchester, Lincoln, Canterbury, Chichester and Exeter, the medieval wall at Winchester followed the Roman trace exactly. The Burghal Hidage assigns 2,400 hides to Winchester for the maintenance of its wall, which converts to a circuit of 3,017 metres; the Roman wall was 3,034 metres.

13 Salter, *Medieval Oxford*, 7–8, 12–13, 22; Biddle, *Winchester*, 273. Discussion of the *burhs* and their continental analogues is based on Biddle, 'Towns', 125–8; Hinton, *Alfred's Kingdom*, ch. 2; Biddle, 'Towns', 126–8; Barley, *European Towns*, 10; Reynolds, *English Medieval Towns*, 31; Clarke and Ambrosiani, *Towns in the Viking Age*, 45, 91; Hodges and Hobley, *Rebirth*, 5; Brooke and Keir, *London*, 61–2; Nicholas, *Medieval Flanders*, 20.
14 Aston and Bond, *Landscape of Towns*, 69; Biddle, 'Towns', 137; Hill, *Atlas*, 133 and 143, map, 235.

Although the Alfredian street plan filled out the entire area of Roman Winchester, the Roman street plan disappeared except for High Street. The fact that the entire area within the walls was laid out suggests that most of Winchester was unoccupied at the time, so that little had to be removed or built around. Even the High, although generally following the trace of the main Roman east–west street, ignored Roman property boundaries and frontages and thus was diverted in places.[15] The eastern end of the High was called *ceap straet* by 900, and the name was soon extended to the entire street, which also became known as *forum* or *mercatum* (market), the Latin words for *ceap*. This became the nucleus for the street plan of Winchester. Dispersal of the market along the entire length of the main street is also found in the other larger *burhs*. Where a separate market square developed, it was often just outside the wall. At Winchester too, although the High was the main market, there were smaller markets around the gates. The market thus became centrally located as the suburbs were enclosed, but it was not planned that way in the *burhs*, although the later town plantations from the eleventh century often display this feature.

The Saxon plan was characteristically rectangular. The burgages were nearly the same size but not absolutely standardised, and all were large enough to permit subdivision into tenements. While the Romans generally had two main streets, the *burhs* had only one. A street also ran around the interior circuit of the wall, and a moat surrounded it. Defences and the street plan were thus integrated, for defenders would have access to any point of the circuit along the cross streets. Waterways had been aligned to the new street layout by the late ninth century to power mills and provide drinking water.

Most *burhs* were large enough to accommodate a substantial increase in population; English urban development thus lacked the suburbs that were so characteristic of the continental cities. But Winchester grew so rapidly in the tenth and eleventh centuries, more as a governmental than a trading centre, that suburbs developed on the west and south. The three minsters had enclosed complexes, and streets named after merchandising or crafts – Ceap, Tanner, Fleshmonger and Shieldwright – are found before 1000.[16]

---

15 Canterbury displays diversion within the walls so that the gate of exit is not opposite the gate of entry. London is ambiguous: Westcheap and Eastcheap both follow Roman roads roughly. Biddle, 'Evolution', 22.

16 Discussion based on Biddle, *Winchester*, 259, 272–9, 286, 450–3, 461–2; Dyer, 'Recent developments', 74; Biddle, 'Evolution', 20–1, 27–8; 'Towns', 128–34; Hill, *Atlas*, 133; Barley, *European Towns*, 11.

The Scandinavians and urban development: the examples of York and Dublin

As Alfred's successors conquered first English Mercia and later the Dane-law, they restored Roman fortresses and built new *burhs*. King Edward 'the Elder' (899–918) seized Derby, Leicester, Stamford, Lincoln and Nottingham, which together were called the 'five boroughs'. The Danish conquest seems to have stimulated the growth of these places, although Stamford, at least, had been settled in the mid-ninth century and had a recognisable street plan and a substantial pottery industry. Five Danelaw forts – Hereford, Buckingham, Bedford, Stamford and Nottingham – were 'double *burhs*', with a nucleus on each side of a river.[17] The *burhs* in the Midlands and north had a closer tie with urban development than those in Wessex. There were fewer of them, and virtually all became county towns, market centres for their environs and seats of local government. The shire organisation is thus extremely important for city development in the Midlands.[18]

York, which became a capital of the Danelaw in the sense that Winchester was for Wessex in the tenth century, displays some features in common with the southern cities but also distinctive characteristics. The Vikings restored the Roman wall on three sides but extended it on the southeast. They completely changed the street layout of York; and since the fortress had been inhabited when they arrived, this meant displacing population. Many of York's street names still have the Scandinavian suffix 'gate', and personal names known from the tenth century include a high percentage of Scandinavian names. The commercial centre of York shifted from Fishergate on the Foss to the Ousegate-Coppergate-Pavement area.[19]

Like the southern *burhs*, York had rectangular plots of land at right angles to the streets, but in Ireland the Scandinavians introduced a new element into the European townscape; for although they planned their cities, they did not use grids. The streets of Dublin (*Dubb Linn*, the black pool), which the Vikings established in 841 and refounded in 917, are curved, following the contours of the land and creating trapezoidal tenements.

Excavations in Coppergate at York show that each plot was fronted with a rectangular building made of panels of wattle, serving both as a

---

17 Biddle, 'Towns', 135–6; Lobel, *Atlas* 2 . . . Cambridge: 1–3.
18 Clarke and Ambrosiani, *Towns in the Viking Age*, 42–5; Simmons, *Leicester*, 14–16; Hill, *Atlas*, 85, Map 17.
19 Clarke and Ambrosiani, *Towns in the Viking Age*, 91–3, including plan of Viking York; Biddle, 'Towns', 123.

home and a workshop. Posts in the walls supported the roof. The floors were covered by boards or rushes, and the Coppergate buildings had centrally situated hearths. The back yards were used for wood- and leatherworking and other crafts. Wattle fences served as property boundaries. Evidently neighbourhoods did not specialise in particular industries, for the same crafts were practised throughout York except that the mint was in Coppergate. Excavations in Fishamble Street at Dublin have revealed many similarities to Coppergate in York. Regular plots, each with an individual path that gave access to the waterfront and probably to a main street, were bounded by wattle fences. The walls of buildings were wattle and daub, as at York; but while in York the gable side fronted the street, in Dublin the short side faced the street and steep gables faced the river. Thatch roofs were supported on two pairs of posts in the windowless exterior wall. The posts divided the interior into three aisles, with the side passages slightly higher than the central aisle, which contained the hearth and the living area. The houses had underground drains, which almost certainly indicate the coordination provided by government authority. Houses of this type were typically about 8.5 metres long, 4.75 wide. Others were smaller and lacked some of the amenities, notably the side aisles and hearth.[20]

THE TENTH-CENTURY REVIVAL

Although the tenth century has traditionally been portrayed as a period of economic deterioration, recent scholarship has shown substantial urban growth everywhere. The bases of the urban network of the eleventh and twelfth centuries were established in the tenth. Political decentralisation fostered the interdependence of regional economies that is so essential to the exchange of goods and services that are the reason for the cities' existence. The Muslims, although their raids devastated the centres of southeastern France, traded with Italian merchants, particularly those of Genoa and Pisa, which was then on the Mediterranean coast. Venice had developed a prosperous eastern trade before 1000.

In the north most tenth-century information suggests only topographical rather than economic growth. Although commerce was reviving, rarely is a merchant identified with a particular city. More certain indices of their linkage only appear in the eleventh century.

20 Discussion of Scandinavian York and Dublin based on Wallace, 'The archaeology of Viking Dublin', 107–9, 112–14, 117–18, 122–6; Clarke and Ambrosiani, *Towns in the Viking Age*, 94–6, 102–6; Tweddle, 'Craft and industry', 17–41.

France

The cities of southern France were still being hurt by Muslim attacks and the displacement of major trade routes away from the Mediterranean and toward the North Sea. The Muslims were the source of considerable bullion for the court economies of northern Europe, but in Mediterranean France and the Rhône delta they were plundering more often than trading. Although trade in slaves and oriental luxury crafts did not end completely, it was too weak to be a basis for the commercial development of a city. Mint activity slowed and in some areas ended in the tenth century; and the Jews, whose presence usually meant trade, were buying and even farming land. Only the salt trade generated much commercial activity in southern France. Urbanisation in southern France was also retarded by the fact that the area, which had been so important politically and economically under the Romans, now had more *civitates* than were needed to handle commerce at the reduced levels of the tenth century. Thus the cities in this region remained fortresses. Noble families turned episcopal elections into power struggles.

There was some revival of population at the end of the tenth century. The new quarter of Sauveterre at Marseilles was formed around 980; Narbonne, whose walls had been in ruins at the beginning of the tenth century, had three densely populated *bourgs* by 990, one of them called Villeneuve. But most Roman walls in this area were so large that suburban settlement was unusual even as population expanded. Thus the signs of topographical expansion that illustrate urban revival in the north are rarer for southeastern France until the early eleventh century.[21]

Elsewhere in France recovery was perceptible in the tenth century, particularly in episcopal centres that were on major arteries for interregional trade. The occupied area initially contracted, as sanctuaries moved nearer the walls of the episcopal complex, vacating space on the peripheries and suburbs. In France, but not in Germany, where the episcopal complexes were more recent, the distinction became clearer between the increasingly clerical 'City' (the old fortification) and the rest of the settlement.[22]

Although few new bourgs were established in the tenth century, the older ones became less clerical, and toward the end of the century some were walled. Metz (Plan 6), like London, Ghent, Huy and other cities, was at the junction of a major artery for long-distance trade (the Mosel) and a small stream suitable for local trade (the Seille). In the early tenth

21   Chédeville, 'Cité', 46; Duby, 'Villes du sud-est', 235, 239–46, 249–50.
22   Chédeville, 'Cité', 50–1.

century the bishop restored the Roman wall and gave a separate fortification to part of the *portus* on the Mosel and to the 'suburb of [the canons of] St Stephen'. The new quarters of Metz developed primarily between the wall and the Seille, not along the Mosel. Metz was renowned for its wealth in the tenth century, with three fairs and a Jewish colony, and the settlement plan suggests that local trade dominated the city's thriving economy.[23]

The number of bourgs on a site is thus not a key to whether a city would develop; Bayeux, which did not become a major city, had five bourgs, but Rouen only one. Similarly, the size of the old fortification is no key to the number of bourgs. Toulouse, whose wall was one of the largest in France, also had six bourgs. Whenever a suburban nucleus existed before the commercial revival, it generally attracted more settlement than either the City or newer bourgs. This happened at Tours, Limoges, Périgueux and Reims (Plan 7), where a new quarter developed around the fortress-abbey of Saint-Rémi. Of thirteen parish churches in Reims in the fourteenth century, eleven existed by the end of the tenth century. At Toulouse the older bourg Saint-Sernin outstripped newer ones founded in the eleventh and twelfth centuries. Here and at Arras the bourg became more important than the City, which was too small and crowded for a market to develop inside the walls. The larger the fortified area, the less likely the market was to be situated in the suburbs.[24]

The eventual major cities of northern France began to outstrip their rivals in the tenth century. Rouen, the chief city of Normandy, grew more rapidly than Paris. Although Normandy's rulers were Scandinavian, the population of the city remained generally Frankish. Rouen's prosperity was based on handling the Seine trade with England and transferring river-borne goods by the land route into the Vexin. 'Merchants of the water' were active at Rouen and Paris. The Billingsgate tolls (ca. 1002) record merchants of Rouen passing the port of London with wine, which they must have acquired from southern French suppliers. Several authors note many foreigners at Rouen, including political refugees and pilgrims as well as merchants.[25]

Paris also revived in the tenth century, although not yet as a political capital; Laon was the favoured residence of the later Carolingians. The fair at the suburban abbey of Saint-Denis, established in the seventh century, revived as a trading link between the Mediterranean and northern France. Paris had a Jewish colony and benefited from the close interdependence between the Île de la Cité and the rich suburban abbeys,

23 Dollinger-Léonard, 'Cité', 199.
24 Chédeville, 'Cité', 84; James, *Origins of France*, 68.
25 Mollat, *Histoire de Rouen*, 40–3.

of which the area had an unusually dense concentration. A bourg formed in the tenth century around the abbey of Saint-Germain-des-Prés along the road to the Petit-Pont.[26]

Elsewhere in France, Dijon remained bipolar in the tenth century, but an important step towards uniting the two communities was taken in 913, when the market, which had been in the eastern part of the fortress, was moved just outside the wall. The bourg of the abbey of Saint-Benigne still had its own market.[27] A new wall around the *civitas* at Tours was constructed between 903 and 918. Decrepit Roman buildings were demolished and new construction undertaken. Extramural settlements around the tomb and monastery of Saint-Martin prospered. The abbey's bourg was walled after 919. A third settlement developed in the 940s around the church of Saint-Julian between fort and City, although the most economically important settlement was the bourg-Saint-Martin. The four settlements only received a common wall in 1356.[28]

England

The Burghal Hidage and the conquest of the kingdom of Mercia in the midlands in the early tenth century had given a marked impulse to urbanisation in England, which had more large towns in the tenth century than the areas directly across the channel. Many *burhs* and a separate category, the 'ports', overlapping with the larger *burhs*, display urban characteristics. Contemporary sources distinguish the *ceaster* (a Roman site) from the *port* (a purely commercial settlement with a market, often unfortified), and each from the *burh*, which was simply a fortification.[29] King Edward the Elder (899–924) required that all commercial transactions be conducted in ports in the presence of witnesses and the king's port reeve. This apparently strained his administration, for his successor Athelstan (924–39) limited this to transactions involving more than 20 pence. Athelstan also linked this statute to one concerning repair of the borough walls and restricted minting to ports. Borough courts are mentioned in a statute of 962 that distinguishes large boroughs, where thirty-six standing witnesses had to be appointed, from small boroughs and hundreds, where twelve sufficed. An early eleventh-century tract distinguishes 'land-right' from 'borough-right'.[30]

---

26 Boussard, *Paris*, 49–51, 61, 73–4, 82–4, 92.
27 Desportes, *Reims*, 48–9; Büttner, 'Frühmittelalterliches Städtewesen', 186, 188.
28 Chédeville, 'Cité', 46; James, *Origins of France*, 66–7.
29 Aston and Bond, *Landscape of Towns*, 63.
30 Reynolds, *English Medieval Towns*, 32–3; Hilton, *English and French Towns*, 30; Maddicott, 'Trade Alfred', 11–12; Loyn, 'Towns', 122–3; Tait, *Medieval English Borough*, 27.

Several centres began to outstrip the others after 950. Perhaps because most English cities had had such tiny populations as late as Alfred's time, there is little growth of suburbs until after 1066 except at Winchester and London. The Alfredian walls sufficed for the larger towns, the term that we may now employ for the urbanised *burhs*. By 1000 most Anglo-Saxon towns on Roman sites were larger than their ancestors had been.[31]

Little is known of tenth-century London, but it was the political centre and the largest city of England. The number of moneyers at London suggests that the city was pulling ahead of others in the late tenth century, but Lincoln, York, Chester, Oxford, Exeter, Stamford and Norwich also had large coin outputs. The *Anglo-Saxon Chronicle* reports that London paid about 12 per cent of England's Danegeld in 1018. The Billingsgate toll shows the port of London with extensive trade with the Low Countries and western France and what seems to have been most favoured trading status for subjects of the German emperor.[32]

Norwich is the outstanding case of urban growth in tenth-century England. The city was formed by the merger of five settlements, two of them with *wic* names, along the river Wensum near the track of a Roman road. Norwich did not grow much before the Danish occupation. Edward the Elder made it a *burh*, but the numerous 'gate' street suffixes suggest continued Scandinavian influence. The 'Nordwic', the area around the eventual cathedral that became the pre-urban nucleus and gave its name to the entire settlement, had a mint by 930. Several suburbs developed later in the century, including a trading settlement around the church of Saints Vaast and Amand, whose patrons suggest Flemish influence. Norwich had a substantial pottery manufacture. Most importantly, it became the site of the county courts of Norfolk and Suffolk. Paired counties elsewhere were small or thinly populated, but these two had some of the highest rural population densities in England. With few competing towns in a thriving agrarian hinterland, in contrast to the many small boroughs of southwestern England, Norwich developed primarily as a political and local trading centre in the tenth century, adding overseas trade and some industry in the eleventh. Parish boundaries suggest rapid growth in the first half of the eleventh century, as happened at London; by 1086 Norwich had an area of about 200 ha, twenty-four churches and a population of at least 5,000.[33]

31 Reynolds, *English Medieval Towns*, ch. 2; Biddle, 'Towns', 140.
32 Brooke and Keir, *London*, 22–3; Hodges, *Dark Age Economics*, 166–8; Reynolds, *English Medieval Towns*, 39.
33 Lobel, *Atlas 2* . . . Norwich: 3–6; Clarke and Ambrosiani, *Towns in the Viking Age*, 101–2; Biddle, 'Towns', 137–8.

Germany

Urban growth was slower in the tenth century in Germany than in the west, perhaps because trade centred on the powerful but still itinerant royal court as opposed to the more dispersed but increasingly permanent foci of power in France. Thus most demonstrable expansion came in the episcopal cities of the Rhineland and in the new bishoprics further east. Between 969 and 982 the monarchs gave the bishops of the upper Rhenish cities full rights of secular government, and the grant to Worms included both city and suburb.[34]

The German cities were repairing and extending their walls in the tenth century. Mainz's fortification made commerce difficult, for the Roman wall around its civilian settlement had allowed access only on the land side. As long-distance trade on the river grew in the Carolingian period, a gate was cut on the Rhine side of the wall; but it was resealed after the Vikings destroyed Mainz, and the city lacked direct access to the river thereafter until the thirteenth century.[35] Some Rhenish cities, beginning with Worms between 891 and 914, made quarters of the city responsible for maintaining parts of the wall, similar to the English situation of the Burghal Hidage and the French *quinta*. At Mainz certain sectors of the city paid no market toll to the bishop because they brought their produce to the Mainz market for sale. In return, each was responsible for maintaining a number of *Zinnen* (about 3 metres) of wall. The *Zinnen* were marked with stones in the wall that were still visible in the fifteenth century. At Novgorod the quarters were also responsible for segments of the common wall, but they were such ferocious rivals that they did not coordinate their efforts; the wall's varying construction styles betray the diverse origins of each sector.[36]

Much of the evidence of urban growth in tenth-century Germany is the presence of foreign colonies in the cities. The Frisian settlement was outside the Roman wall at Worms, and probably in the later 'Rhine suburb' at Cologne. An annalist called their quarter along the Rhine at Mainz the 'best part' of the city in 886. At Regensburg a merchant settlement developed in the early tenth century along the Danube west of the Roman city, then gradually expanded toward the abbey of St Emmeram. Some cities in the Empire had Jewish communities, suggesting distant trade rather earlier than in France. They are first noted at Metz in 888, Worms in 960, Regensburg in 981, then at Cologne, Trier and

---

34 Dollinger, 'Aufschwung', 137.
35 Barley, *European Towns*, 190–3 and Figure 5, p. 192.
36 Falck, *Geschichte der Stadt Mainz*, 74–5; Dejevsky, 'Novgorod', 396.

Speyer in the eleventh century. There were over 550 Jews in Mainz by 1096, which would have meant a sizeable percentage of the population of the city. Mainz had a rabbinical school by the late tenth century. Its Jewish community handled trade with Hungary. Although the Tortosa Jew Ibrahim Ibn Jakub mentions arable fields and fruit trees within the walls of Ottonian Mainz, the city also had a mint, and spices from India were found there.[37]

Much urban activity east of the Rhine in the tenth century was connected with German missions to the Slavs. The most rapidly growing city in tenth-century Germany was Magdeburg, on the border of Germanic and Slavic settlement, at the intersection of land routes from the west and where the Elbe develops several tributaries while the main river continues on toward Krakóu. The Carolingians had fortified the site of the eventual cathedral square, and the Ottonians rebuilt it and added a palace. A second nucleus would be the New Town founded by Henry the Lion in the twelfth century. Inhabitants of the surrounding area owed labour service on the city wall. Some merchants lived in the fortification, but more were in the suburb just outside it, around the Old Market and the 'merchant church' of St John. In 965 Otto I gave the abbey of St Moritz jurisdiction over the 'Jews and other merchants living there permanently'. By the early eleventh century the merchants were storing their goods at St John under the supervision of the 'best men of the city'.[38]

While few cities in France had market charters, since commercial activity in and around the *civitates* was assumed, the German kings authorised numerous markets in the tenth and eleventh centuries. While most French cities and some in Germany had several markets, with the main square developing just outside the wall of the nuclear fortification, the more usual form in Germany and England was for the market to develop as an irregular quadrilateral or triangle from a broadening of the main street going through the city. The church of the merchants was normally built on this market. The merchant settlement around St John at Magdeburg created a triangular street market. When the town hall was built in the thirteenth century this was divided into the Old Market, on the side away from the river, and the separate square around St John. At Augsburg, Speyer and Würzburg the original street market was widened into a marketplace in the late eleventh or twelfth century.

37 Planitz, *Deutsche Stadt*, 43; Falck, *Geschichte der Stadt Mainz*, 105, 112–18, 125; Agus, *Urban Civilization* 1: 88–9; Bullough, 'Social and economic structure and topography', 397.
38 Schwineköper, 'Magdeburg', 392–410, 446; Janssen, 'Non-Roman town', 232–3; Lavedan and Hugueney, *Urbanisme*, 51.

Markets in the form of streets broadened into elongated triangular shapes are also found at Strasbourg, Speyer, Tiel and Liège.[39] Although suburbs were less important in the initial phase of German urbanisation than in France, some German cities had exterior markets on the French pattern. The fortification of suburban *Wike* represents an important stage in medieval urbanisation that is distinct in form and function from the walling of multiple ecclesiastical nuclei, such as the City and a suburb. The *Wik* characteristically developed along one side of the main road, which was then joined by a cross street, then a third street paralleling the first, and thus a simple and often irregular market complex developed. Trier, Halle and Quedlinburg have examples.[40] Cologne was the earliest city in Germany to have a walled suburb. Since the Roman wall had not been directly on the Rhine, a merchant *Wik*, the quarter of St Martin, developed between it and the river in the ninth century. Deutz, the 'Rhine suburb', was planned by Archbishop Bruno of Cologne with a rectangular street pattern, market and an overall shape of a long triangle that was eventually bisected by the mint into two distinct markets. The Rhine suburb was brought inside the larger walled city around 950 and became the commercial nucleus of medieval Cologne.[41]

The walled settlement at Regensburg was divided into sectors held by the king, the clerks and the merchants who were dependents of the abbey of St Emmeram. Around 920 the duke of Bavaria walled the precinct of St Emmeram with the cooperation of the local leaders, but soon afterward the townspeople and 'Senate' tore down the west end of the Roman wall and brought the abbey into the larger fortification. Thus the 'New City' of Regensburg was created around the abbey of St Emmeram west of the Roman wall. This gave Regensburg the only walled *Wik* in the Danube region until the twelfth century.[42] Only two other cities in the area controlled nominally by the emperor, Namur and Verdun on the Meuse, had fortified *Wike* in the tenth century. The chronicler Richer mentions an 'enclosure of the merchants' across the Meuse from the citadel of Verdun around 985. The merchants are unlikely to have been wanderers, for such people would hardly have built

39 Stoob, *Forschungen*, 43–9; Planitz, *Deutsche Stadt*, 67; Schwineköper, 'Magdeburg', 434, 448–9; Herrmann, 'German Democratic Republic', 250; Janssen, 'Non-Roman town', 220–2.

40 Stoob, *Forschungen*, 49; Hall, *Mittelalterliche Stadtgrundrisse*, 83–9, 95–8.

41 Meynen, 'Grundriss Köln', 281–94; Ennen, *Frühgeschichte*, 156–8; Planitz, *Deutsche Stadt*, 67; Lewald, 'Köln und Deutz', 378–82.

42 Strobel, 'Regensburg', 69–70; Klebel, 'Regensburg', 96–100; Ennen, *Frühgeschichte*, 157.

a permanent wall. It appears more likely that the City was too small and the bishop's authority too stifling for the growing merchant community of Verdun, so the tradesmen moved across the river. In Germany, particularly in cities lacking Roman antecedents, *Wik* and *civitas* were generally enclosed within a single wall, while in former Roman centres and in France they were more often walled separately.[43]

Apart from the domination of the bishop and count, little is known of the governance or social composition of the tenth-century German cities. The bishops had rights of temporal rule in the cities of the Rhineland that the king usually gave to the count elsewhere. Although the archbishop was the lord of Mainz, other nobles had land and dependants within the walls. The 'citizens' barred the archbishop from the city in 939. The prelate generally governed through a 'prefect of the city', 'urban judge' or 'advocate'. The burgrave (count of the borough) and town lord's advocate were the same person at Mainz, Worms, Speyer, Trier, Würzburg and Magdeburg. They were distinct at Cologne, Regensburg, Strasbourg and Augsburg. In some cities the burgrave was the higher official, in others the advocate. Nothing in the tenth century suggests either a large merchant element or more than occasional opposition to the landlords who controlled the cities.[44]

Eastern Europe

The Scandinavian ventures also stimulated urban growth in eastern Europe. The Swedish leader Rurik had a base at Novgorod (New City) in the north by 862; his followers, called Varangians and Rus by the Slavs and Byzantines, gave their name to Russia. Farther south the Varangians established the great trading route between the Baltic and Constantinople along the Dnieper via Kiev, where they dominated a pre-existing Slavic settlement by 882. Kiev evolved as a political capital, perhaps the first genuine one in Europe apart from Muslim Cordoba in Spain.

Before the great growth of Moscow in the late Middle Ages, Kiev and Novgorod were the only sizeable Russian cities in the lands that would become Russia and its neighbouring states. Both were on the Varangian route, on major rivers and at the intersection of land routes leading into the interior. Both were polynuclear. The Russian cities developed large resident foreign colonies earlier than those of the west, and the Varangians found Slavic habitation on three sites on the area

---

43 Ennen, *Frühgeschichte*, 152–3; Hall, *Mittelalterliche Stadtgrundrisse*, 100–1; Planitz, *Deutsche Stadt*, 68; Hubert, 'Evolution de la topographie et de l'aspect', 553–4.
44 Falck, *Geschichte der Stadt Mainz*, 75–8, 82–3.

of Novgorod when they arrived. The place became urban in the tenth century as these three grew together and a common market was laid out as the 'new town' in the formerly swampy area between the hill and the river. Novgorod had a permanent settlement of Swedes by 980 that was large enough to sustain a riot and massacre in 1015. The city developed on both banks of the river Volkhov, with a centrally located hilltop fortress containing the prince's complex, the residences of government officials and nobles, and the cathedral of St Sophia on the left bank, and a lowland commercial and craft settlement with the main market across the river. The western half of Novgorod is still known as the 'Sophia side', the east as the 'trade side'. The individual quarters of the city retained their separate administrations throughout the Middle Ages, a reflection of their origin as farm villages. Novgorod was in a marshy area that gave access to the interior by small streams, but the swampy environs meant that Novgorod always had to import food over a considerable distance. Although both Novgorod and Kiev were politically important, Novgorod was more developed economically as the terminus for Russian trade with Scandinavia and Germany.

Kiev developed as three separate towns without a central citadel: the first established by the Varangians, then in the late tenth century by Grand Prince Vladimir, and a third town just south of it was added by his son Yaroslav. Yaroslav's town had a planned but contour-driven street layout. Only the last of Kiev's boroughs, established in the thirteenth century, shows a grid plan. Monasteries were more important in urban development in old Russia than in the west, serving as population nuclei both within the cities and in the suburbs. They were especially important on the peripheries of Novgorod, providing a fortified line of defence a few miles from the city.[45]

Poland's urban development lacked the external stimulus provided by the Scandinavians in Russia and generally followed the pattern illustrated by the west, but more slowly. By the eighth century, Gniezno, Poznan, Warsaw and Kraków existed as Slavic fortresses along the major rivers. The suburbs that developed around these strongholds were walled even in the tenth century and housed merchants, craftspeople and lesser knights. The main market was a third nucleus. The duke as lord of the fortification controlled the entire area strictly. As in the west, the great churches were in the citadel, while the later foundations were in the market suburb. The first settlement on the area of Kraków was a

---

45   Birnbaum, 'Kiev, Novgorod, Moscow', 1–26, 43; Dejevsky, 'Novgorod', 392–3; Birnbaum, *Essays in Early Slavic Civilization*, 137, 147–54; Langer, 'Medieval Russian town', 19.

prehistoric fort on the Wawel hill. By the tenth century it was a for-tified residence of the local prince and had a church. A second church built there after 1025 became the site of the bishopric, and the establish-ments of government officials and other aristocrats controlled the rest of the hill. The suburb of Okól was settled as early as the ninth century at the foot of the Wawel, and a market developed there at the junction of two major land routes. The suburb, however, only became densely settled at the end of the eleventh century.[46]

Merchants and craftsmen in post-Carolingian Italy

Most Italian cities did not experience significant topographical expansion until the eleventh century or even later. The coastal centres suffered from Muslim raiding, and northern Italy was affected by the Magyar forays. Civil discords, particularly in Rome and the Romagna, prevented the sort of rural economic growth that occurred in northern Italy and was a precondition to the expansion of the market cities there. We must keep a proper perspective, however, for even the shrunken Italian cities of the early Middle Ages were considerably larger than most of those north of the Alps. The Italian centres whose late Roman or early me-dieval wall had seriously disrupted settlement do show signs of growth. . Bologna expanded substantially in the tenth century, particularly east of the ancient nucleus, which became known as the 'old rump *civitas*'. Several suburban monasteries founded during the Lombard period be-came nuclei of growth, including the eventual main market of the medi-eval city at the junction of the Ravegnana gate in the Roman wall and the suburb that was growing around the monastery of Santo Stefano.[47] Signs of growth become much clearer in the late tenth century, particu-larly in Lombardy. Following a century of stable prices and money, late tenth- and early eleventh-century evidence from 'Cologne Street' (the name was used by 875) shows a progressive subdivision of plots in the wake of population growth and a rise in the prices of land and houses in Milan and its suburbs.[48]

The Italian cities show a definite increase in merchant activity during the tenth century. Pavia reached its height in the early tenth century as the capital of Carolingian Lombardy, yielding to Milan in the eleventh. A description of Pavia written around 1025 but clearly bearing on the tenth century shows an international clientele in the market of Pavia,

46   Knoll, 'Urban development of medieval Poland', 65–73, 79–81.
47   Bocchi, 'Développement urbanistique oriental de Bologne', 137, 147–9.
48   Violante, *Società milanese*, 59, 123–38, 143–9.

including merchants of Salerno, Gaeta, Amalfi, Venice and even England. The chamberlain of the royal palace regulated the economy. The foreign merchants were 'licensed' and paid for the right to do business in Pavia. The Venetians paid a huge premium in return for the right to buy food in any market in the Lombard kingdom. Pavia's own merchants were 'men of great worth and wealth'. In contrast to the artisans mentioned in the description, they did not pay tribute, but they depended on the king for charters of protection to give them free access to markets in the kingdom outside Pavia. They had the right to pre-emptive purchasing in those markets and in Pavia itself: no merchants could trade in the market 'before the merchants of Pavia do, unless he is one of the merchants of Pavia'. This in effect gave them the essential privilege later enjoyed by merchant guilds. The document mentions customs posts at the exits of Alpine valleys. The trade of all north Italian cities, Asti, Vercelli, Milan, Verona, Cremona, Piacenza and Lucca as well as Pavia thus was enhanced by controlling the routes to the passes.[49]

The Italian cities continued to have an artisan component in the tenth century, but the sources say less of them than of the knights (*milites*), nobles (*nobiles*) and merchants (*negotiatores*). Especially around the markets many streets were named after the crafts practised in them. At Milan references to free persons as artisans are much more numerous and show them with higher standing in the tenth century than in the ninth. The most frequent appearances are by minters, who sometimes passed the trade on to their sons, but smiths were also numerous, and some of them had land outside the city. The craftsmen were usually identified by their streets of residence. According to the chronicler Landulf the elder, in 961 Milan had five 'master bakers' with whom the bishop contracted to feed the local population with breads of a set weight and price.[50]

Some Italian cities had a level of occupational differentiation that we can only document later in the northern cities. By the 830s, craftsmen at Pavia were producing for the royal palace, which sold their goods, and references to the city's merchants become numerous after 887. The description of 1025 shows Pavia with organisations (misteries–*ministeria*) of minters, tanners, mercers, fishmongers and shippers. The minters of Pavia had nine masters, those of Milan four. The other misteries had two masters to handle their dealings with the royal chamberlain. These

49 Of numerous convenient commentaries on this document, see Bullough, 'Urban change . . . Pavia', 95; Vaccari, 'Pavia nell'alto medioevo'; Luzzatto, *Economic History*, 57–60; and Hyde, *Society and Politics*, 21–2. Substantial translated portions of the text are printed by Lopez and Raymond, *Medieval Trade*, 56–60; the quotation is from p. 60.
50 Violante, *Società milanese*, 86–7.

organisations owed tribute to the royal court and payments on their boats. The tribute was paid in return for the sole privilege of exercising the trade: 'No man is to perform these activities unless he is one of the masters'.

The references to urban militia, communities and artisan organisations are difficult to interpret, but they show at the very least that the Italian cities were much larger, more socially and economically differentiated, coherent, corporative, and powerful than any in northern Europe.[51] Yet the fact that occupations were being practised does not mean that their practitioners were organised. The late Roman *collegia* appear to have died out by 800; for after the seventh century the only unambiguous evidence of organised craft guilds in Italy before the twelfth century is for the misteries of Pavia mentioned in the text of 1025, the Milanese crafts and an organisation of fishermen with at least eleven members in Ravenna in 943. The misteries do not seem to be heirs of the ancient *collegia*, for the trades mentioned in the Pavia text were those that had business at the royal court.[52]

Pavia illustrates an important and often neglected point about the Italian cities, particularly in this early phase. Most major cities of early medieval northern Europe originated on rivers, although at the points where they joined important land routes. Only later was the land route network strong enough in the north to give rise to major cities. But the Italian rivers except the Po were too small to give rise to much trade. In neither northern Europe nor Italy were port cities generally as large or prosperous as the centres of the interior. Pisa and Genoa did not become major trading cities until the eleventh century and only grew rapidly when the Crusades gave them better penetration of the eastern markets. Amalfi, the chief port of the Tyrrhenian Sea, had a thriving commerce between the tenth and early twelfth centuries. The Amalfitans controlled the trade of the Byzantines and Muslims together with the interior of southern Italy, and even cut into Venice's sphere of influence in the Adriatic. They had their own quarters in the cities of the east and owned shops at Pisa and Genoa. But Amalfi declined when the Normans ended the political infuence of the duchy of Amalfi, for the other ports had better natural locations, particularly bigger harbours. Thus overland routes were much more important than the rivers or coastal shipping for the commercial revival in the tenth and eleventh

51 Bullough, 'Urban change . . . Pavia', 110; Luzzatto, *Economic History*, 60; Violante, *Società milanese*, 58–9, 67–9, 74–5, 86; Fasoli *et al.*, 'Struttura sociale', 303; Lopez and Raymond, *Mediterranean Trade*, 60 for quotation.
52 Bullough, 'Social and economic structure and topography', 368.

centuries of the cities of Italy, which were doing a lively pilgrim and merchant trade with northern Europe. The lesson is clear: the large Italian cities grew as centres of agricultural exchange and as political capitals. The courts and the large urban populations attracted foreign capital. Although Italian merchants would later dominate the capital markets and much of the commodity exchange of northern Europe, there is no mention of them at the north European fairs until the early twelfth century.[53]

The markets of the major cities were also expanding physically in the tenth century. As the landholding aristocracy consolidated its position, the merchants were concentrated increasingly around the palace and the bishopric, where lucrative markets and opportunities for office could be found. In 952 the emperor gave the cathedral church of Milan five plots of land in the city where the public market is. On two of the five, which do not seem to have been contiguous, there were already sale booths, and one bordered the still usable city sewer on one side. The prince included with the donation a hall on the market, with stands inside it. This grant was thus the expansion of an existing facility. By 901 the 'enclosed market' of Pavia had 'stations', presumably booths. As in northern Europe, the larger Italian cities, including Pavia, also had subsidiary markets by the tenth century in addition to the main market.[54]

City and *contado* in early medieval Italy

The close connection of the greater Italian merchants to minting, toll collection and the demand market of the urban courts (which after the Carolingian period were stronger in Italy than in northern Europe) and the fact that the trade of the larger Italian cities except Venice was in basic goods tied to the immediate hinterland rather than luxury imports, explain the continued symbiotic relationship of merchant activity and landownership in Italy. Bishop Rather of Verona distinguished merchants whose main interest was acquiring money and movable property from nobles whose nobility was 'not in family, but in possession', which in the context clearly meant land. Numerous tenth-century texts show merchants as landowners, but usually in the city rather than the environs. The connection becomes clearer in the eleventh century, but the quasi-rural nature of the urban nobility, and the fact that nobles who

53 Luzzatto, *Economic History*, 49–51.
54 Lopez and Raymond, *Medieval Trade*, 55–6; Violante, *Società milanese*, 14–15, 61–2; Bullough, 'Social and economic structure and topography', 385–6; Bullough, 'Urban change . . . Pavia', 110.

held castles had powers of command over rural populations, helped city and citizens to control market relations in the countryside to a greater extent than was possible in northern Europe.[55]

The Italian cities were thus intimately involved with princely territorial governance in a way that prefigured the eventual political and economic subordination of the countryside (*contado*) to the city. In the early tenth century the count normally ruled the *contado*, the bishop only within the city. But some bishops had received immunity privileges that made them independent of the counts even in the ninth century, and the weakened kings tended increasingly to foster the bishop's power as a counterweight to the count and to make the count's officials in the city into royal servants.

It was unusual for a bishop to supplant a count completely, but virtually all cases where this did happen involved important cities that would later achieve considerable autonomy. Mantua's bishops, by contrast, were unable to gain comital rights (the rights normally exercised on behalf of the prince by a count) in the countryside and thus enjoyed powers similar to those of north European urban bishops. The town of Mantua fell under the lords of Canossa. Its location was less propitious for overland traffic than that of nearby Piacenza, and Mantua never became more than a local farm market. Although the citizenry would eventually turn against the bishop and establish governments independent of him, the bishop's authority in city and *contado* seems to have fostered a sense of cohesion and community at this early stage. Even before the city governments began to sponsor town formation, fortification and infrastructure improvement in the *contadi*, the bishops had been doing so. The archbishop of Milan tried to control the roads leading to the Alps and over the tributary streams of the Po. He had built a canal by 1037 that linked Melegnano and the Lambro to Milan.[56]

The bishops' authority certainly strengthened the power of the larger cities. Although most bishops in Lombardy came from rural aristocratic families, the centre of their power was in the city proper. They ruled the environs of the city through viscounts or advocates or, increasingly, in the tenth century, by enfeoffing 'captains' with church land and castles, thereby making them their vassals. The captains were petty rural lords who came to the city because the bishop's court was there and became powerful landowners in the city as well. Although they tried to break away from the bishop's control after 1000, they were his agents

55 Violante, *Società milanese*, 55–7; Haverkamp, 'Städte im Herrschafts- und Sozialgefüge Reichsitaliens', 174.
56 Racine, 'Città e contado in Emilia e Lombardia', 106–8.

against the count in the tenth century. The counts were generally pushed to the periphery of the *contado* in cases where the bishop was strong.[57] This process can be seen most clearly at Milan, whose bishop was the most powerful in Italy.

Thus many Italian bishops, particularly in the north, made city lordships even more formidable than did their northern counterparts. At Padua, for example, the king gave the bishop the task of fortifying the town in 911, after the Magyar invasions. His powers were confirmed in 964 by Otto I. When a count returned to Padua at the beginning of the eleventh century, it was too late for him to contest the bishop's lordship. The bishop also exercised comital authority in the *contado*, basing his power on defined but expanding nuclei where he held land and strongholds. At Padua and elsewhere the court of the bishop's vassals was the council of the city. A text of 945 notes that the bishops of Mantua, Verona and Brescia held mints, which had to be held from the king. In some places no competition with a count was necessary. The bishop's court took the place of the count's court in many cities. Bishops thus had temporal power in most cities at the beginning of the eleventh century, due to Carolingian grants of immunity and Ottonian grants of comital powers, often forced. The tenth century thus saw the dissolution of the counties and separation of city from county.[58]

Immunity and comital grants are worthless without a means of putting them into effect. During the tenth century the counts' gradual loss of power led to the building of numerous castles in the *contadi* of the cities. The owners of the castles were often clients or vassals of city nobles or of the bishop. Just as secular princes did, the bishops enfeoffed their relatives with castles as a means of solidifying their control of the rural areas. This process was accompanied by the expansion of the bishop's court, consisting of captains, viscounts, advocates, 'emissaries', and functionaries. As the bishop's immunity district grew in size, so did the importance of these officials, who ruled it for him. Thus the famed castle building of the tenth century solidified the bishops' power in the *contado*. The bishops were lords of the cities and of considerable rural land around them, but their power was still weaker outside than inside the urban areas. The growing power of the bishoprics made them attractive to competing lineages in the cities and their *contadi*. The four great 'kinship groups' of the diocese of Florence at the end of the tenth century – Aldobrandeschi, Gherardeschi, Guidi, Cadolingi – used control

---

57 Hyde, *Society and Politics*, 44; Racine, 'Città e contado in Emilia e Lombardia', 116.
58 Rippe, 'Commune urbaine', 660–2; Haverkamp, 'Städte im Herrschafts- und Sozialgefüge Reichsitaliens', 167–70; Racine, 'Evêque et cité', 130–2.

of the bishopric as part of larger strategies to gain power.[59] What is perhaps most important for our purposes is that the rights that bishops, counts and other lords gained in the Italian countryside in the tenth century would eventually pass to the city governments that eroded their power.

But the bishop's lordship is not the whole story. The citizens of some places were beginning to participate in policy decisions with the bishop. Even as early as 851 the 'inhabitants of the city of Cremona' claimed at the royal court in Pavia that a tax demanded on their boats demanded by their bishop was illegal. By 924 the merchants of Cremona were so powerful that they tried to move the city harbour to a place not controlled by the bishop.[60] King Berengar I in 904 gave the bishop of Bergamo 'power and defence' over the towers, walls and gates; but the walls were to be rebuilt 'wherever the bishop and his fellow citizens think necessary'. Thus the bishop was placed on the same legal footing as the other citizens and had to consult with them, in effect becoming their leader. Peaceful citizen involvement with the bishop is also attested at Mantua. In 958 Kings Berengar and Adalbert gave the inhabitants of Genoa minor immunity, recognition of their customary law, and the right of public officials to enter citizens' homes to collect tax. The citizens thus received executive and legislative power, but judicial power remained in the hands of the marquis as town lord until 1056, when he gave the city the right to a court. This is the first surviving charter given to a group of citizens acting apart from their bishop.[61]

There were more urban uprisings in tenth-century Italy than in the north, where the only serious rebellions were the Mainz affair of 939 and the famous but brief 'commune' formed at Cambrai against the bishop in 967. As early as 886 a 'sedition' occurred at Pavia between the king's entourage and the 'citizens'. Milan rebelled between 948 and 953 in favour of a canonically elected bishop against the emperor's nominee. The count of Verona on behalf of the emperor deposed Bishop Rather in 968 in response to the advice of the residents of the city in an assembly. The Milanese rose against their bishop in 983, but Cremona is the most conspicuous early example of hostility between bishop and citizenry. The emperor gave a charter in 996 to 'all free citizens of Cremona, rich and poor' that granted them 'everything appertaining to the state' between the mouth of the Adda and the port of Vulpariolo,

59 Volpe, *Medio Evo Italiano*, 17–72, 110–12; Dameron, *Episcopal Power and Florentine Society*, 25–60; Keller, 'Soziale und politische Verfassung Mailands', 38–9; Racine, 'Evêque et cité', 132.
60 Haverkamp, 'Städte im Herrschafts- und Sozialgefüge Reichsitaliens', 175–6.
61 Vaccari, 'Pavia', 178–80; Wickham, *Early Medieval Italy*, 190; Tabacco, *Medieval Italy*, 172–3, 190, 331–2; Pavoni, 'Evoluzione cittadina in Liguria', 244–5, 250.

which in practical terms meant control of an outport and the territory between it and the city. But the charter was revoked later that year as a violation of the bishop's right to control the riverbanks. Hence a 'conspiracy' and 'sworn association' began that would persist into the mid-eleventh century.[62]

The Low Countries

The cities of the Low Countries grew modestly in the tenth century, but nothing suggested the spectacular development that would commence in the eleventh. While in Germany and France the episcopal complex was most often the nucleus of the eventual city, in Flanders the castle of the count generally served that function. During the tenth century the two ports of Ghent were linked by a canal and street, and the entire settlement was surrounded by a moat. The Scheldt was diverted westward to facilitate contact with the main settlement around the castle. By 1000 *portus* was used for the entire settlement, not just the ports. Saint-Omer originated on a flat-topped hill surrounded by swamps around the abbey of Saint-Bertin. Although nothing except the monastic complex existed until the late ninth century, Saint-Omer developed quickly thereafter by exporting grain from Artois. It received a wall in the early eleventh century, the earliest in Flanders apart from the castle complexes.[63]

The Flemish cities began as grain markets. Ghent and Saint-Omer grew in the tenth century because they were situated where rich farmland met thinner soils useful mainly for pasture. At Ghent overpopulation and subdivision of tenements in the abbey suburb of St Peter were so severe that the abbot permitted the residents to do industrial labour in lieu of farm work. As commerce expanded and the cities developed some industry in the eleventh century, the grain networks were joined by other regional linkages that had not been present earlier. Their social structures consisted mainly of serf-farmers, abbey personnel and lesser nobles. These elements, including aristocratic 'serf-knights', become clearer in the eleventh century.

Retrospect: a millennium of urban development

We have covered one thousand years of urban evolution in Part One of this book. Except for the oldest Italian cities, notably Rome itself, all cities of the Roman Empire had a planned grid layout. No strictly

62   Wickham, *Early Medieval Italy*, 190; Tabacco, *Medieval Italy*, 324; Previté-Orton, 'Italian cities till c. 1200', 213–14; Haverkamp, 'Städte im Herrschafts- und Sozialgefüge Reichsitaliens', 176.

63   Nicholas, *Medieval Flanders*, 26, 32–7, summarising substantial recent literature.

organic Roman city existed north of the Alps, and even in Italy some with irregular central sectors received regular plans as they expanded.

The capital itself was a consumer city, using the products of the Empire that were channelled to Italy as tribute. Rome had a commercial aristocracy of generally recent ancestry, as did the other Italian cities, but they had a larger craft element. In no city, even in Italy, did long-distance trade, let alone artisanry, become the major occupation or generator of capital. In the north most of the originally unfortified cities began as military and governmental outposts, to which civilian elements were added to provide food and other necessities to the officials. As bureaucrats and former soldiers intermarried with the local populations, and as the native Celts traded with the Romans, a mixed 'Gallo-Roman' population inhabited the cities.

The Roman cities were fortified in Britain from the late second century, on the continent after the political and military collapse of the third century. But only a small part of the inhabited area was enclosed. The city became a citadel. These fortresses, most of which were very small, in their turn became the geographical nucleus of many medieval cities. But as insecurity became chronic, the now suburban settlements were deserted. When more settled conditions returned, the areas outside the truncated fortification were resettled, but often in a direction away from where the bulk of the Roman population had been.

As the cities became citadels, the Christian church, legalised in 313, became an important element of urban topography; for most of the citadels were inhabited by bishops and their entourages, sometimes with smaller parish churches as well. Some lay counts or dukes also centred their authority in the urban citadels and disputed temporal power with the bishops. These town lords, both ecclesiastical and lay, generally controlled substantial lands outside the walls. Monasteries, usually but not always in the suburbs, became focal points of settlement as the urban area was gradually repopulated in the early Middle Ages.

The aristocratic clergy and princes who inhabited the citadel constituted a demand market. Most of them received food as rent from their rural estates, but they required manufactures and luxury goods, most of them from the Greek or Muslim east at this time. Thus the early medieval cities had a small floating population of Jews and Syrians, and by the eighth century some Muslims in the south. Much of the substantial resident population, which consisted principally of natives of the area, also engaged in long-distance trade. The shift of long-distance trade from the Mediterranean and overland roads towards the rivers did not bring about the quick decline of most Roman centres that had not been on navigable streams; but as the cities became less demand-driven and produced more goods, and the inhabitants of the suburbs gained capital by trading in regional markets, Roman centres that were not on sites favourable to long-distance trade began to atrophy, and eventually some were extinguished.

Although the capital base of most early cities was in long-distance trade, almost entirely importing, their resident population was concentrated in local trade. The need to provision the inhabitants of the growing suburban nuclei outside the residual Roman cities, and the growing use of rivers to handle large-scale shipments of grain between fertile and infertile agricultural regions, meant that the early cities also had substantial trade in grain and other foods.

The eighth and ninth centuries brought perceptible alterations to the urban map of Europe. The expansion of a Christian church organisation to Germany east of the Rhine meant that bishoprics there served the same functions as stimuli to urbanisation as in the originally Roman centres of the west. But suburban settlements developed less often in Germany than in France. More often expansion was planned, as new sectors of an expanding town were laid out. In the west, in the wake of the Scandinavian attacks, cities began to develop in the Low Countries, which would eventually have the highest urban density in northern Europe, and in England. The English cities are associated with the *burhs* of King Alfred of Wessex and his successors, for there had been little continuity of habitation in the older Roman centres. In the Low Countries the new cities were mainly along or near the Scheldt river, which began to displace the Meuse as the chief commercial artery of northwestern Europe during the late ninth century. All developed outside fortifications, but these were the castles of local lay princes rather than the neo-Roman cities of the bishops.

As their populations grew and became more socially and occupationally diverse, the cities developed some utilitarian manufacture. Artisanry, although it was doubtless more important than can be proven directly except by archaeological finds, was at a generally low level and was usually for local exchange rather than export. Industry was less specifically an urban activity at this stage than commerce was. As contacts with distant regions, including the east, quickened in the ninth and tenth centuries, much of it under the stimulus of Scandinavian traders, there is increased evidence, for the first time since the sixth century in significant quantity, of resident colonies of foreign merchants in some cities, most conspicuously in Russia along the Varangian route established by the Swedes. But these colonies remained small. The cities remained principally governmental, cult, and military centres. Commerce remained incidental and artisanry insubstantial.

To speak of any settlement in the Latin West except Rome as a 'city' before 1000 is probably misplaced. Thereafter commerce quickened, population grew, and Europe developed industries that, in contrast to earlier manufacturing, were labour-intensive, centred in the cities, and produced goods of high enough quality to be exported between regions. By 1200 the city had become a primarily commercial organism, in some exceptional cases joining substantial industry to trade, weakening the mainly governmental–ecclesiastical–landowner elements that had dominated urban society since classical antiquity. Most major cities of medieval Europe existed before 1000, although not all of them were displaying signs of their eventual greatness this early. Some places were founded in the eleventh century that developed into major cities. Although they were exceptional, the list of latecomers includes some of the largest and most turbulent of the medieval cities. We must examine next the development of urban life in the eleventh century on the solid foundations laid before 1000.

PART TWO

The Eleventh and Twelfth Centuries

From Seigniorial to Economic Urbanisation: Landowning, Commerce and Industry in the Cities of the Eleventh and Twelfth Centuries

Residence and city

The earliest cities of medieval Europe had been primarily residences of nobles, temporal princes or wealthy churchmen, with enough craftspeople and particularly merchants to supply them with the goods and services that they needed or desired. The urban economy was dominated by the demand markets that those sources generated. Particularly in Italy, with its large number of bishoprics, the collection of rents and tithes became centred on the urban churches.[1]

During the Merovingian and Carolingian periods the cities were regional grain markets and stopping-off points for itinerant merchants. All cities transferred raw materials from producers to consumers, and the most successful of them were located on economic frontiers, at the intersection of supply and demand, between regions needing and those lacking essential goods, services or personnel. In addition to their political and defensive functions, they were central places for their rural environs, transmitting their products to more distant markets. But the rise of a city is also conditioned by the distance that people are willing to travel to obtain its goods or services. A rarely purchased commodity has a greater range than something more common. Thus cities that developed a high degree of specialisation, producing or cornering the

---

1 Wickham, *Mountains and City*, 91.

market in rare luxuries or strategic necessities, became larger than those that did not.[2]

Even the earlier English borough charters gave the central places monopolies within their shires, although more to facilitate the task of the king's tax collectors than to stimulate the city. Henry I forbade the transfer of ship and wagon cargoes in Cambridgeshire except at the borough of Cambridge, where a toll would be levied. By 1086 the city's geld payment was ten times the average for the villages of its shire, suggesting that much of its rise was due to its being the only substantial place in its county at the time. The burgesses of Cambridge were also given the right to hold a fair at Reach, ten miles upriver. The city elite made its fortune by exporting the raw materials of Cambridgeshire and importing luxuries, especially wine. Henry II ordered foreign merchants in Lincolnshire to trade only in Lincoln. Such provisions centralised commerce in the early cities and gave them jobs and patronage, although these monopolies did not last permanently; Boston quickly surpassed Lincoln within Lincolnshire.[3]

Lords and fortresses

Most cities were still dominated in the eleventh century by the fortified complex of the town lord and often the strongholds of persons high in his entourage. Large stone buildings were conspicuous both in Italy, where rural nobles spent much of their time in the cities, and in the north. In the early twelfth century the bishop's officials had fortified houses at Laon, while the Flemish count's chamberlain had a moated complex at Bruges. Until city halls became common in the thirteenth century, churches were the main public buildings. They were used for assemblies, inquests, audits, oath-taking and contracts. Although the suburbs were growing, they were still secondary to the settlement inside the original fortification in economic and political importance.[4]

The older conflicts between rival lords in the city, bishop and count or bishop and abbot, continued to be divisive, particularly when each controlled a clearly defined area. The bishop of Marseilles was lord of the new quarters, while the viscount held the hilltop. Conflicts at Narbonne only ended in 1112, when the viscount did homage to the archbishop.

---

2   Vance, *Continuing City*, 96–8, 102, criticises this notion in favour of a purely commercial model. I consider the functions complementary.
3   Ballard, *British Borough Charters*, lxvi; Lobel, *Atlas* 2: 4, 6.
4   Barel, *Ville médiévale*, 37; Platt, 'Evolution', 53; Mollat, *Rouen*, 56; Chédeville, 'Cité à ville', 98.

Similar divisions occurred at Nimes, Arles, Aix-en-Provence, Avignon, Cahors and Agen. Each lord within these places fortified his quarters, which accentuated their military character and evidently stunted their commercial development. Cathedral chapters also had their own domains and were often a third territorial element in addition to bishop and count.[5]

As governments became more sophisticated, princes spent more time in their chief cities. Favoured residences continued to grow through demand from personnel at the court, particularly in Germany, which had a lucrative eastern trade. While the kings before Henry II (1002–24) usually moved between rural castles and royal domains, thereafter they preferred bishopric-cities. From the period of Henry IV (1056–1106) the fact that the episcopal cities were fortified meant that the kings paid increasing attention to them. Local as well as royal courts contributed to the prosperity of some cities, notably Toulouse, Arles, Angers, Orléans, Mainz and particularly Vienna in the twelfth century. The fact that Troyes and Provins were residences of the counts of Champagne contributed more to their steady growth as urban centres than did the transients who visited their famous fairs.[6]

Withdrawal of the court meant certain decline for the city. Aachen, Charlemagne's capital, atrophied in the eleventh century. Speyer, a favourite residence of the Salian emperors, received three new walls between the tenth century and 1180; but the city did not grow much after the dynasty ended in 1125, for it had no economic potential beyond its local market.[7] Winchester, the virtual capital of Norman England, is the most spectacular illustration of the impact of withdrawing royal patronage, for the Angevin kings after 1154 favoured Westminster. Winchester's population of over 8,000 in 1148 was its medieval apogee.[8]

Jewish capital and urban growth

In addition to generating demand for goods and services, princely courts attracted investment. Most eleventh-century cities that would become centres of long-distance trade had settlements of Jews, who loaned money to the town lords and may have provided capital for industries that were developing in the suburbs. The traveler Benjamin of Tudela

5   Chédeville, 'Cité à ville', 151; Büttner, 'Frühmittelalterliches Städtewesen', 185.
6   Chédeville, 'Cité à ville', 144; Duby, *Early Growth*, 235; Chapin, *Villes de foires*, 15–20, 141; Diestelkamp, 'König und Städte', 256–7, 264.
7   Opll, *Stadt und Reich*, 26–32; Jansen, 'Handel en nijverheid', 162; Nicholas, *Medieval Flanders*, 117–23; Dollinger, 'Oberrheinische Bischofsstädte', 135.
8   Biddle, *Winchester*, 290–6, 387–92, 493–4; Rosser, *Medieval Westminster*, 13.

noted the size of Jewish communities in Italy and southern France in the early twelfth century: most had several hundred inhabitants, although Genoa, Pisa and Lucca are conspicuous exceptions. Although in most cities they were associated with moneylending, each of the ten Jews of Brindisi was a dyer. Critics complained as early as the sixth century of the bishops' dealings with Jewish moneylenders, and Benjamin of Tudela noted that the Jews of Rome in his time 'occupy an honourable position and pay no tribute, and amongst them are officials of the Pope Alexander, the spiritual head of all Christendom'.[9]

The Jewish quarters were usually in the old fortified City but near its edge, and some 'Jew Streets' were near the new industrial quarters. The Jewish *call* in Barcelona was in the City across from the palaces of the bishop and the count. Marseilles had a 'corporation of the Jews' under the leadership of three syndics, but they were assimilated into the Christian community as citizens and landowners and had the same rights in guilds as Christians. Both the upper and lower city of Marseille had a synagogue with a Jewish market and baths. Excavations at Rouen have revealed a synagogue of about 1100 under the courtyard of the modern Palace of Justice.[10]

The Jews were very important in Paris until Philip Augustus began persecuting them in 1182 and demolished their quarter. Jewry Street [*rue de la Juiverie*], joining Small Bridge Street [*rue du Petit-Pont*] on the south, was the economic centre of the Île de la Cité, containing the grain hall and the residences of many Christians. The English cities also had Jewish communities. The largest were in London and Lincoln, followed by Canterbury. That of Norwich had about two hundred persons at its height, settled near the castle and the market in the Saddlegate/Haymarket area.[11]

THE PHYSICAL EXPANSION OF THE CITIES

The terminology of urbanisation

As the cities' populations grew, substantially in the eleventh century and extremely rapidly in the twelfth, settlements merged that had previously been discrete entities. Terminology used in the sources for the cities thus became less precise. *Villa*, which had meant a rural estate in the early Middle Ages, was sometimes used for a city. *Burgus* or *Burg* had

9   Benjamin of Tudela, *Itinerary*, 2–8, with quotation p. 6.
10   Bisson, *Aragon*, 77–8; Lesage, *Marseille Angevine*, 38–9; Mollat, *Rouen*, 65–6.
11   Boussard, *Paris*, 147–51; Urry, *Canterbury*, 109–11; Lobel, *Atlas* 2: 10. On the Jews in Italy, see Chapter 7.

originally meant a suburb, but by the eleventh century it could also mean everything in the environs outside the original city wall; but the *Annolied* (1076–1126) used it to mean the entire city of Cologne. Curiously, in Germany burgess [*burgensis*] came to designate the inhabitants of the city at precisely the time when *Burg*, with its suburban connotation, was yielding to *Stadt* as the preferred vernacular usage. *Burgenses* later meant only residents with full rights of citizenship, as groups within the city became differentiated.[12] In France *burgenses* was being applied without discrimination to the inhabitants of suburbs and *civitates* alike by the twelfth century. Burgess of the city [*Burgensis ville*] is first used at Bourges in 1100, synonymously with citizen [*civis*]. The contrast between *burgensis* and *civis* is found after 1100 only in such places as Toulouse, Limoges and Tours, where the topographical division of sections of the town continued to be sharp. In the Low Countries *burgus* compounds generally designated only the area just in front of and inside the castle complex, although *burgenses* could mean the inhabitants of the entire city.[13]

The urban parishes

Except in England the inhabited area of virtually all cities expanded in the central Middle Ages. The multiplication of parishes is an indicator of expanding population. Most cities in France and the Low Countries had several small parishes within the walls, dominated by that of the central cathedral, while the suburban parishes were larger in area but less densely populated. At Metz nine of the eventual twenty-six parishes were inside the Roman wall, eleven in the suburbs, and the others in abbey villages. Curiously, most churches mentioned there in the eighth century did not become centres of parishes, which were demarcated in the eleventh and twelfth centuries as the city expanded.[14]

Many inner-city parishes became too populous for the church staffs to handle and thus were subdivided. Toulouse had only three parishes in 1000 but seven by 1200. The central city of Ghent initially had one parish apart from the count's palace church, but this grew to four when three densely populated areas near the markets and quais were withdrawn from the cathedral parish of St John. The densely populated suburbs contained four other parishes. The expansion of Strasbourg's

12   Ennen, 'Forschungsproblematik', 16, 19–20, 23; Ammann, 'Städtewesen Spaniens und Westfrankreichs', 133.
13   Chédeville, 'Cité à ville', 103–5; Joris, 'Burgus', 195–6. Ghent, Bruges and Namur illustrate this terminology.
14   Schneider, *Metz*, 28–9.

size from 19 ha to 54 ha brought with it two new parishes making a total of six. Like the Flemish example, the Italian cities had a single major parish church until the twelfth century, but with numerous small subsidiary parishes (*pievi*).[15]

Comparisons are difficult, for the older English cities had numerous small parishes, the heirs of the estate churches of the lords on whose lands the cities were built. This is the converse of the norm in France. Many of them were so tiny that they went out of existence in the late Middle Ages for lack of support. Parishes multiplied particularly rapidly between 1000 and the Norman Conquest, then declined sharply, suggesting as do other indices that the Normans stunted English urbanisation. By the second half of the twelfth century, however, Lincoln and Norwich had forty-five parish churches, York forty, Exeter thirty, Canterbury twenty-two, and London 107 within the walls. Winchester probably had fifty-seven parish churches, many of them private foundations. The post-Conquest English cities resembled the continent in having fewer parishes; even Great Yarmouth and Boston had only a single parish each.[16]

Extension of the walls

By 1100 many cities had walled the first suburbs around the nucleus, and by 1200 all large places on the continent had defences. Most cities grew enormously in the eleventh and twelfth centuries. Florence added two walls within a century, in 1078 and between 1173 and 1175, the latter creating a sort of quadrant with the Arno. It enclosed several *borghi* that had been left outside the earlier wall. As with most city walls, these enclosed vacant space to leave room for further expansion, but the even stronger population growth of the thirteenth century rendered obsolete many of the new enclosures, including that of Florence.[17]

Indeed, the fact that suburban quarters were developing and were walled is often a secondary stage of population growth, for space for more inhabitants was also being created by subdivision of tenements and expansion into previously vacant territory inside the principal agglomeration, especially in the older centres. In Rome, for example, the normal form of private house into the twelfth century was the street floor and

15 Wolff, *Histoire de Toulouse*, 68–70; Gysseling, *Gent's Vroegste Geschiedenis*, 33–4; Dollinger, 'Oberrheinische Bischofsstädte', 136; Bocchi, *Città italiane*, 10.

16 Platt, 'Evolution', 55; Urry, *Canterbury*, 208–9; Schofield, *Building of London*, 32; Brooke and Keir, *London*, 126; Brooke, 'Ecclesiastical centre', 468; Biddle, *Winchester*, 498–9; Aston and Bond, *Landscape of Towns*, 106–7.

17 Sznura, *Espansione urbana di Firenze*, 43–7.

one storey above ground. There were many independent, stand-alone houses, with gardens behind and courtyards in front. But multistorey houses became more common as population grew in the twelfth and thirteenth centuries. The subdivision of the ground floor into clearly discernible rooms becomes more usual in the late twelfth century. As in the rural areas, lords who were trying to gain income by promoting settlement of suburban *borghi* normally gave tenements at perpetual rent (emphyteusis) as an inducement to immigration, but real property values and rents rose sharply in the central cities at Milan and Piacenza in the eleventh century, although they remained low in Rome until the 1140s.[18]

The wall was an important aspect of the corporate personality of the city. In England it was owned in principle by the king, but walls on the continent were municipally owned. In addition to the obvious military importance of the wall, taxes were collected on imports at the gates. Seville's gates were opened early in the morning, but guards were to detain anyone whose identity they could not verify.[19] Public ceremonies often started at the walls or involved them. Posterns in the wall were used to collect fresh water. Some walls already had habitations. Describing the capture of Waterford by the Normans in 1170, Giraldus Cambrensis reported a house jutting out over the wall, held up by a beam, which the Normans cut to breach the wall.[20]

Although the wall demarcated city from suburbs, the notion of burgesses huddling inside the walls for defence is anachronistic, for the city without suburbs is rare until the wars of the fourteenth century. Canterbury had extramural suburbs even before 1066, and single-street suburbs developed on the north and west in the twelfth century. There was enough space inside the walls to accommodate the inhabitants of these suburbs had they desired to live there. Winchester had major suburbs outside each of the gates along the Roman roads. The Domesday Book also shows houses outside the walls in 1086 at Colchester, Hereford, Leicester, Oxford and Lincoln, all of which had suffered massive depopulation inside the walls after 1066.[21]

Perhaps because conditions were relatively peaceful, perhaps because most cities there were not growing significantly, few new city walls were built in England in the Norman period. Some used their Roman walls

18 Miller and Hatcher, *Towns, Commerce and Crafts*, 267; Bocchi, 'Développement urbanistique oriental de Bologne', 139–40; Hubert, *Espace urbain*, 166, 174, 201, 350–1.
19 Lévi-Provençale, *Séville musulmane*, 71–2.
20 Ladero Quesnada, 'Fortifications urbaines', 145–6; Barry, *Archaeology Ireland*, 129.
21 Urry, *Canterbury*, 187–90; Biddle, *Winchester*, 259; Darby, *Domesday England*, 293.

unchanged or, as happened at London and Leicester, expanded them only slightly. Chester, Rochester and Gloucester expanded their circuits, using only part of the Roman wall. Most other evidence of city wall construction in England only comes in the thirteenth century, when the kings began making 'murage' grants to help some cities finance new fortifications.[22]

Most city walls of the eleventh century in the Empire were in the episcopal cities of Burgundy and the upper Rhine (Besançon, Speyer, Basel and Worms) and in the German northwest and the Low Countries. In Flanders and adjacent northwestern France the earliest of the more comprehensive walls – apart from the primitive nuclei forts – is that of Saint-Omer, which had been built by 1071, enclosing 30–35 ha. At Bruges and Ghent walls of about 1090 enclosed 70–80 ha. Douai and Arras were also fortified by 1100. Other cities were walled in the early twelfth century on the Rhine and in Flanders, but not on the Meuse, which was losing its commercial importance; even Maastricht remained unfortified until 1229. Elsewhere walls were built in the early eleventh century to link the episcopal complex with the suburban merchant settlement in the non-Roman episcopal cities of Liège and Magdeburg. These elements remained distinct in most older cities until a second wall was built. At Cambrai the bishop linked the City and the quarter of Saint-Sépulchre with a stone wall. Chartres, Toulouse and Senlis had built more rudimentary defences for their suburbs by 1100.[23]

Except in the northwest most French cities only built walls beyond the primitive City in the twelfth century and particularly the thirteenth. Troyes and perhaps Strasbourg had walls before 1125. The bourg Saint-Sernin was linked to the City at Toulouse before 1150 by a fortification. Amiens walled two suburban quarters between 1117 and 1135, and the wall of the Neufbourg at Metz dates from the same period. Dijon and the bourg-Saint-Benigne were walled together in 1137. The Norman dukes fortified Rouen, Poitiers and Angers in the mid-twelfth century. Bordeaux continued to have separate walls for the City and the bourg-Saint-Eloi until the early fourteenth century.[24]

Fortification usually followed substantial settlement by at least a generation, and accordingly some walls linking City and suburb were quite late. Paris (Plan 3) was not a frequent royal residence until the time of Louis VI (1108–37). The palace and the episcopal complex were on the small and densely populated Île de la Cité. Its central location led to a

22   Aston and Bond, *Landscape of Towns*, 103.
23   Ennen, *Frühgeschichte*, 160–3; Chédeville, 'Cité à ville', 101; Wolff, *Histoire de Toulouse*, 71.
24   Chédeville, 'Cité à ville', 101; Lavedan and Hugueney, *Urbanisme*, 22–4.

roughly concentric settlement on both sides of the Seine. (This was in contrast to London, where the location of government in the royally patronised abbey suburb of Westminster entailed a more linear development, with most habitation on the north bank of the Thames.) Three bridges linked the Island to the banks: the Small Bridge [*Petit-Pont*] in the centre, the Great Bridge [*Grand-Pont*] on the north and a wooden footbridge on the site of the later Notre-Dame Bridge. Growth began on the right bank, which became the commercial centre of Paris half a century before the left bank was economically active. Most food coming to Paris on the Seine was unloaded at the Grève, a large market square on the right bank upstream from the Grand-Pont. On the northeast, the Champeaux began growing rapidly after 1117, particularly after Louis VII founded a 'new market' there in 1139. The most significant suburban population centre on the north was the bourg-Saint-Denis, where Louis VI situated a new fair in 1124. The left bank also grew as the area between the three abbey bourgs of Saints Germain, Genevieve and Marcel was settled. The vacant area between the Small Bridge and Saint-Marcel was already becoming the student quarter. The right and left banks were bisected by two parallel north–south streets leading to the Petit-Chatelet and Small Bridge and to the Great Bridge and royal palace.

Paris began a growth in 1180 that would transform it into a national capital. King Philip Augustus (1180–1223) spent much more time there than his predecessors. Parisians were on the royal council and were entrusted with the royal treasury during his crusade. He transformed the schools into the university, paved streets and built the Louvre palace. Paris received its first comprehensive wall in his reign. The left bank wall, which survived into the seventeenth century, was 2 metres thick and over 8 metres high, with six gates along the major roads. Since this was still largely vacant area, the king was clearly planning expansion. He thus financed the left bank wall, while the city paid to fortify the more populous right bank.[25]

Although the first city walls had evidently been undertaken at the initiative of the lords, some city governments were taking responsibility for their own defences by the twelfth century. In 1106 the burgesses of Cologne built a fortification that was strong enough to withstand a three-week siege by the emperor. In 1180 they built a new and final wall that enclosed suburbs that were still mainly agricultural.[26]

---

25 Discussion based on Boussard, *Paris*, 99, 130, 151–2, 159, 169–73, 194, 283–5, 319–22, 326–7, 380.
26 Strait, *Cologne*, 30–3; Ennen, 'Erzbischof und Stadtgemeinde', 40–1.

The planned towns of the central Middle Ages

In addition to the spectacular growth of the older cities, lords were founding new places on their domains and endowing others with charters of liberties. Virtually all 'founded' cities were preceded by some settlement on the site or were simply grants of town law to previously existing communities. Alexandria, for example, was 'founded' by Frederick Barbarossa in 1167–8, but it had a prehistory as eight separate communities.[27]

Although the charters made the plantations 'towns' in a juridical sense, few in the former Roman west became genuine cities. Most boroughs in Wales were plantations, as were Zutphen in the Netherlands and sHertogenbosch in Brabant.[28] Neither Italy nor Flanders, on the peripheries of Europe and its most densely urbanised areas in the twelfth century, experienced the proliferation of 'new towns' that France and Germany did, perhaps because the older cities sufficed for the need. The subordination of the *contado* to the older cities in Italy stifled the development of new places until the large cities themselves began founding them for strategic reasons in the thirteenth century.[29] The counts of Flanders planted several towns, but only the North Sea outposts and particularly Lille and Ypres became substantial. Ypres developed around a castle whose moat created an island. At the point where the river Ieperleet ceased to be navigable, Ypres was crossed by land routes leading to Bruges and Lille.[30]

Germany had the largest number of plantations that became major cities. Except for Bamberg, founded as a bishopric by King Henry II (1002–24), the great founded towns of Germany came in the twelfth and thirteenth centuries. Most benefited from the great revival of Baltic trade. The most famous founder of cities in Germany was Henry the Lion, Duke of Bavaria and Saxony. He established Munich in 1158 by moving the bridge over the river Isar there, which entailed diverting the main salt route from upper Bavaria. Few medieval cities survived without having a monopoly on the exchange of a strategic commodity; the salt toll would be Munich's most important income until the mid-fifteenth century. In Saxony Henry established Göttingen and Hannover and refounded Brunswick. Frederick Barbarossa, Henry's great rival,

27 Opll, *Stadt und Reich*, 183; Braunfels, *Urban Design*, 19, 23.
28 Delaney, 'Welsh Urban archaeology', in Barley, *European Towns*, 37; Petri, 'Städtewesen', 274–5; Sarfatij, 'Town in the Netherlands', 206–7.
29 Chittolini, 'Italian city-state', 591.
30 Van Uytven, 'Stadsgeschiedenis', 196; van Houtte, *Economic History*, 47; Derville, 'Gravelines et Calais', 1051–4; Nicholas, *Medieval Flanders*, 110, 119. Curiously, although urban foundations typically have a discernible street plan, Ypres is the only Flemish example.

granted charters to several eventual cities: Ulm and Kaiserslautern, which were favoured royal residences; Chemnitz, Zwickau and Frankfurt-an-der-Oder in the east, and Rothenburg and Schwäbisch Gmund.[31]

A distinction should be made between bastides, which were founded on completely virgin territory and were often used as much for defence as for civilian settlement, and the 'planned town', where habitation had evolved organically on a previously inhabited site that was now being given a charter in recognition of its commercial possibilities.[32] Lübeck (Plan 14), the greatest German founded city, shows how 'planned' towns actually developed on previously inhabited sites. The Slavic settlement of Old Lübeck goes back at least to 817. By 1100 it had a fortification on the left bank of the Trave near its intersection with the Wakenitz, with artisan suburbs and a merchant settlement on opposite sides of the river. This settlement was destroyed in 1138, refounded in 1143 and burned again in 1157. It finally fell in 1159 to Henry the Lion, who hoped to divert the Gotland trade there and thereby control the route to Russia and Sweden. Henry established a new marketplace by using a model previously found at Brunswick: straight streets intersected to create an absolutely rectangular market, which was then surrounded by a parallel street. Side streets led to the two rivers. Henry relocated the settlement away from the tip of the peninsula created by the river junction and made the market and church square its midpoint. As in most German towns that were superimposed on Slavic centres, Lübeck had a grid plan and was more uniform in architectural type than the older cities of the Rhineland. It became the greatest port of the Baltic. Lübeck fell to the emperor with Henry's disgrace in 1180, then in 1226 became the first fully free imperial city.[33]

Freiburg-im-Breisgau, whose law was given to many other foundations, was not new either. A castle and monastery became dual foci of settlement when in 1120 the duke of Swabia offered a charter. A grid plan was laid out with a triangular market, and standard-sized tenements were to be held in return for a ground rent that was fixed in perpetuity. There was already a municipal elite, called 'members of the sworn association of the market', 'merchants' or *burgenses* – the first time that this word was used in a charter east of the Rhine. The document was

---

31 Braunfels, *Urban Design*, 33–5; Gleba, *Gemeinde*, 119; Ammann, 'Städtewesen Spaniens und Westfrankreichs', 148; Fuhrmann, *Germany*, 166; Maschke, *Städte und Menschen*, 44–5.

32 Morris, *Urban Form*, 82–95.

33 Fehring, 'Early Lübeck', 269–77, 279–82; Fehring and Hammel, 'Topographie', 169–70; Ebel, 'Lübisches Recht', 261; Steuer, 'Urban archaeology', 91; Planitz, *Deutsche Stadt*, 96–7; Hall, *Mittelalterliche Stadtgrundrisse*, 110–21 discusses the founded towns of the twelfth century.

witnessed by them and by twelve officials of the duke. The merchants chose a 'rector' and received the right to settle disputes according to their own law or 'that of the merchants, especially those of Cologne'. The sworn association of 1120 was eventually represented by twenty-four persons, all from old families with lands in the city and rural areas. Their descendants were the twenty-four members of the city council in the thirteenth century. By that time each of the twenty-four had an establishment in one of the three arcades on the market that had been erected when the city was founded.[34]

All town foundations in England required royal confirmation. Most plantations that evolved into cities were founded before 1170. The most successful was Newcastle-upon-Tyne, in an area devoid of large cities and well positioned to benefit from the growth of the coal trade in the thirteenth century. Rye and Ludlow became major secondary centres. Boston and King's Lynn were important coastal markets for the Baltic trade in grain, but neither became a large city. The riverbank dictated their street patterns and limited their expansion. Salisbury was the largest plantation of the thirteenth century. Its success was due to a strong campaign by its bishop to move settlement after 1220 from the prior site, Old Sarum. English plantations were less likely than those of the continent to have grid plans. Even Salisbury was not completely rectangular, especially the east–west streets.[35]

Urban expansion in the Middle Ages came much more from the growth of established places than from the foundation of new cities. Except for Salisbury, La Rochelle and in the Baltic east, no major medieval city resulted from a plantation after 1200, although many were founded, then stagnated. As cities became more economic than religious and governmental entities, the number of places that could develop was necessarily restricted by the need for merchants' services and the demand for craftsmen's products. The urban map of medieval Europe was essentially fixed by 1200.

City plan and city wall

The new walls and their relationship to the primitive fortress had differing effects on city plans. Some walls bisected parishes, particularly in Italy, disrupting neighbourhood solidarity, although probably not in towns

---

34 Steuer, 'Urban archaeology', 84; Müller, *Freiburg*, 48–9; Fuhrmann, *Germany*, 80; Keller, 'Charakter Freiburgs', 254–7, 262–70, 280–1; Maschke, *Städte und Menschen*, 46.
35 Hilton, *English and French Towns*, 40; Butler, 'Planted towns after 1066', 38–46. See in general Beresford, *New Towns*, esp. 241–2, 272, 319–38.

where the division into parishes did not long predate the walls.[36] But as second and third walls were built around the cities, the interior walls, which like the outer circuit had gates that could be locked at night, separated quarters from one another and permitted the authorities to isolate trouble spots during disturbances. By 1181 Philip Augustus was allowing houses to be built on the old Roman wall at Bourges, since it was no longer the defensive perimeter.[37]

Although founded towns generally had more regular street plans than did 'organic' or 'nuclei' towns, this distinction is not always valid. The most irregular street plans in Europe were those of Muslim Spain. Some organic cities, such as Leipzig, had regular grid plans. Many Dutch towns developed organically but parallel to a canal, which enforced a regular street pattern.[38] Planning is also found in the newer areas of many older cities. The linkage of unplanned nuclei with planned suburbs is most common when the nucleus was a hilltop settlement. Kraków, established about 1000, had a nucleus containing the cathedral and a fortress linked by a corridor to a planned city down the hill beyond the marketplace. But the reverse could also occur. At Metz the part of the *civitas* around the bishopric had a more regular street plan than did the areas nearest the wall and the suburbs.[39]

Whenever the prince took the initiative, the city plan was regularised. At Augsburg the episcopal town in the southern corner of the Roman wall had a chaotic mixture of streets and squares. The Salian kings tried to plan a southward expansion linking the cathedral to several monasteries, although most of Augsburg's trade went north. The great merchants lived in the western part of the planned settlement around the markets and major streets; the craftsmen were in the east, closer to the river. This part of town had street markets. A planned section centred on a huge street market also developed outside the cathedral complex at Speyer.[40]

Erfurt (Plan 9), where the *Erpf* land route from Eisenach crosses the Gera, was one of the most important German medieval cities. It was walled by 1066 and had twenty parish churches and a dozen abbeys in the twelfth century. A subsequent wall of 1168 enclosed 133 ha. Erfurt's topographical growth illustrates changing land use in the growing cities. It was binuclear, having an organic settlement on the left bank around the church of St Severi and a planned settlement, initially under royal

---

36   Bocchi, *Città italiane*, 10; Schneider, *Metz*, 41.
37   Claude, *Bourges und Poitiers*, 158–63.
38   Hohenberg and Lees, *Making of Urban Europe*, 30–1.
39   Brooke, 'Ecclesiastical centre', 461–2; Schneider, *Metz*, 35.
40   Bosl, *Augsburger Bürgertum*, 11–12.

lordship, on the right bank, with a merchant church and a more regular street plan. The earliest and ultimately the largest market of Erfurt was in front of St Severi. It became the centre of the trade in daily necessities, eventually containing sixty cobblers' shops, a leatherworkers' hall with thirty-six stalls and a bakery. The merchant church on the left bank was at the midpoint of what was effectively an interior 'ring street' and was linked by an alley to the Little Market [*Wenigenmarkt*], the centre of cloth wholesaling on the Gera. In the virtual city centre the Mercers' Bridge [*Krämerbrücke*] contained the shops of dealers in luxuries such as silks and spices. The third and most recent market of Erfurt, the Fish Market, was on the left bank near the Jewish quarter and was eventually called 'New Market'. The public buildings of the early thirteenth century, including a hospital, the City Hall and probably a Merchant Hall were there. The merchant suburb on the right bank continued to develop but less rapidly than did the earlier organic settlement on the left bank, attracted by the demand generated by the bishop, his officers and the local market.[41]

Expansion and form of the urban markets

The shape of the market squares influenced the topography of the entire city, for they required open space that either had to be cleared or was initially suburban. We have seen that 'street markets' in which a main thoroughfare was widened for shops were the most common form during the early period. St Catherine Street, the renamed Roman *cardo*, became a street market at Bordeaux. Even in London there was no large market square, for the wide main streets of the old city were the markets. The Old Market of Bristol began as a widened space with special privileges for booths and stalls on the London road east of the castle gate. In Worms the Roman road through the city centre was broadened into a marketplace that bisected the town. Some markets were even unwidened streets, including those of Goslar, Naumburg, Bamberg, and in the twelfth century Hamburg. A separate market square was laid out in most plantations. Even in some older towns the relocation of the market could determine the direction of later growth; while the line of the walls gave the tone to most pre-Conquest towns in England, the market did so after 1100. In 1067 the earl of Hereford revolutionised the town plan by moving the market to a funnel-shaped crossroads north of the minster.[42]

41 Schlesinger, 'Frühformen', 313–31.
42 Lobel, *Atlas* 2: 5; Chédeville, 'Cité à ville', 97; Planitz, *Deutsche Stadt*, 89–97; Platt, 'Evolution', 51.

Several characteristic forms of market thus develop. When the market developed inside the fortification, as in Alfred's *burhs* and in London, or was planned to link the stronghold with another settlement outside, as at Augsburg, it tended to be of the widened street type. English Street (the modern High) at Southampton still has 'swells' where the medieval markets were. The High or Cheap in Saxon Winchester was a long area with specialised segments for the sale of meat and perhaps fish, and for minting.[43] Many mature medieval markets at the gate between City and unplanned suburb were triangular, especially in southern Germany and Austria. Frankfurt-am-Main, Soest, Halle, Aachen and Bonn had triangular markets that were either broadenings or reconstructions of old streets and thus are variants of the street market type.[44] The only large triangular market in England was at Nottingham, evidently accompanying the establishment of the French colony there.[45]

Founded cities usually had the market centrally located, with artisan groups congregated in alleys specific to their occupations nearby, but in some the market square was detached from the rest of the plan. This is also found in older cities such as Magdeburg, Worms, Dortmund, Cambrai, Arras and Douai that built new markets in the suburbs to replace older ones. At Namur and Maastricht the new market of the eleventh century was across the Meuse from the merchant *portus*. The shape varied: the markets of Utrecht, Cambrai and Douai were quadrilateral, Namur nearly square, Maastricht triangular, while the twelfth-century market at Halberstadt was an irregular hexagon.[46]

Most early medieval cities began with a single market, often the corrupted residue of the Roman *forum*. Exceptions are most common in cities without a Roman past, those with unusually extended walls and in England. Multiple markets became common when the suburbs, which often had their own markets, were incorporated into the main fortification. In the larger cities markets often developed along quais or were linked to the docks by small alleys. This was especially important for the grain trade, which was generally riverine until at least the twelfth century, by which time the essential urban map of medieval Europe had been established.[47] Central Ghent (Plan 4) illustrates this, with four major market squares in addition to street markets that developed near

43 Schofield and Vince, *Medieval Towns*, 49; Platt, 'Evolution', 53; Platt, *Medieval Southampton*, Figure 3, p. 44; Biddle, *Winchester*, 460.
44 Sydow, *Tübingen*, 60–6; Planitz, *Deutsche Stadt*, 94.
45 Lobel, *Atlas* 1: 3.
46 Reinecke, 'Kölner Recht', 149; Planitz, *Deutsche Stadt*, 94–7; Hall, *Mittelalterliche Stadtgrundrisse*, 79–109.
47 Britnell, *Commercialisation of English Society*, 86.

the main churches. The enormous Grain Market paralleled the harbour and was adjacent to the Fish Market. The Long Mint led to the Friday Market, where most small-scale local exchange was handled, while the Animal Market was nearby outside the church of St Jacob.[48] Except in England and the larger continental cities the eventual main market was often the first market to be established outside the primitive nucleus during the first phase of expansion. It was often at the gate or outer extremity of the City wall where it joined the suburb. The market of Cologne in the 'Rhine suburb' was one of the largest. Buildings had surrounded the square before 989. The square was bisected initially by the archbishop's mint; then in the second half of the eleventh century there was a further division by rows of shops. The harbour and foreign merchants were south of this, and their quarter included the market church of St Martin.[49] The market of Barcelona was just outside the northeastern gate of the wall at the 'Old Castle'. A commercial bourg developed outside the New Gate [*Puerta Nueva*] at Zamora in the late eleventh century, at the intersection of three roads. When the two settlements joined in the thirteenth century, the *Puerta Nueva* became the square where the town council met. Salamanca, Oviedo, Zamora and Segovia developed similarly.[50]

Neighbourhoods, occupational segregation and public amenities in the twelfth-century city

Urban social geography first becomes clearly discernible in the twelfth century. Although most medieval urban neighbourhoods would eventually have both rich and poor residents, in the twelfth-century cities the richest inhabitants lived either in the government quarters of the old City or in 'fashionable' suburbs, such as the bourg-Saint-Sernin at Toulouse. London, whose government centre was suburban, and Bristol were the major exceptions.[51]

The growing industrialisation of the cities led to the development of occupational quarters. Many streets took the name of the crafts that dominated them at some point. Late tenth-century Winchester had streets named after the tanners, shield-makers and butchers, joined in the eleventh

48 Nicholas, *Metamorphosis*, 68–9.
49 Ennen, 'Europäische Züge', 13.
50 Bisson, *Aragon*, 77–8; Glick, *Spain*, 117; Ladero Quesnada, 'Fortifications urbaines', 152; Chédeville, 'Cité à ville', 91.
51 Keene, 'Suburban growth', 81; Platt, 'Evolution', 53; Aston and Bond, *Landscape of Towns*, 107.

century by shoemakers' and goldsmiths' streets and a haymarket.[52] In northern Europe the fact that a street was named after a craft did not mean that practitioners of other trades did not live there. The same building was used successively in German cities by people practising very different crafts, and different occupations were practised in adjacent houses.[53] Tradesmen requiring water or posing environmental problems, notably dyers, butchers, fullers, potters and smiths were especially likely to be segregated. Tanners were usually relegated to the moats on the outskirts, but some lived away from the main nucleus of their trade. Moats that brought goods to the city could be channelled and dammed to satisfy the needs of the crafts. Millers and fullers were thus generally near canals.[54]

But while in the north such occupational specialisation of neighbourhoods was a matter of convenience, in some Mediterranean cities it was enforced by the authorities. Some craft organisations promoted occupational segregation, for the guilds could fix rents and control quality more easily when most members lived in the same quarter or street. The practice was most rigid at Montpellier. Streets and squares were named after linen bleachers, ring makers, moneychangers, carpenters, drapers and leatherworkers during the mid-twelfth century and after the vegetable dealers by 1205. A law of 1204 forbade artisans thus compartmentalised to leave their residential quarters, and newcomers were admonished to settle in neighbouring streets. The fishmongers, who were about to move to a new location, were the only exception.[55]

Metz (Plan 6) illustrates how occupational differentiation accompanied the physical expansion of a large city in the twelfth century. By the twelfth century three distinct quarters had developed between the Seille and the Gallo-Roman wall: first Vesigneul and Port-Sailly, then Champ-à-Seille, which was only occupied densely from the mid-twelfth century. The wall of the late twelfth and early thirteenth centuries doubled the area of the Roman wall and enclosed a New Bourg [*Neufbourg*] along the Seille adjacent to the old wall. The Seille area was more fragmented territorially than the City. The parish of Saint-Martin, which was in both the City and New Bourg, was vital for local provisioning, containing Old Butchery [*Vielle Boucherie*], the chief street of the City.

---

52 Biddle, *Winchester*, 427–8.
53 Steuer, 'Urban archaeology', 88.
54 Guillerme, *Age of Water*, 52–6, 61–2; Keene, 'Suburban growth', 81.
55 Mickwitz, *Kartellfunktionen*, 23; Gouron, *Réglementation des métiers*, 69–70. Faber and Lochard, *Montpellier*, 94–5, argue against Gouron that the efforts of the authorities at Montpellier to centralise trades were not completely successful. Even leather and cloth trades, which by their nature tended to congregate, had some artisans living away from the main concentration.

The church was reached by a large main street containing patrician houses. Port-Sailly was even more active, with its own meat hall and poulterers. Italian moneylenders were here, and trades included the cordwainers. Baker Street [*Fournirue*] led from the cathedral to Port-Sailly, where the bakers yielded to smiths and goldsmiths and especially armourers. Most patrician families stayed out of the densely populated areas. On the steep hill overlooking the Seille the streets characteristically converged to form a quiet quarter of clergy and patricians. Champ-à-Seille had the largest market in the city. It was originally the seat of the government of the count of Metz but became an animal market after the countship was suppressed.

Outre-Moselle was a quiet quarter, unlike the Seille. On the east, Port-Sailly had some foodmongers' stalls, but it was too cramped to contain a major market. The bourg of Vesigneul, the site of the Monday market, was south of it along the Roman wall. Moneychangers and bankers, who were originally at Port-Sailly, were moving into this area by the thirteenth century. The mercers' shops were along the Roman wall on the other side of Vesigneul. Guildhalls were built in the first half of the thirteenth century on the extreme south of the square, but the old lineages avoided Vesigneul. The entire area on this side of the river took the name 'Quarter' [*Quarteau*] in the twelfth century. Port-Sailly, Vesigneul, and Champ-sur-Seille were to be the economic centre of the city in the thirteenth and fourteenth centuries. Outre-Seille had irregular streets and was settled late. Characteristically, the earliest artisans here were those needing the waters of the Seille: tanners in the twelfth century, dyers in the thirteenth. Outre-Seille was thus artisanal and would be the centre of revolutionary movements in 1283 and 1326.[56]

THE BEGINNINGS OF ECONOMIC URBANISATION

Cities could not develop until the rural economy could feed a large number of people who, instead of growing their own food, compensated the farmer by reconsigning his products and later by manufacturing items that the more prosperous peasants desired. The 'takeoff' of the European economy in the central Middle Ages is closely linked to changes in the rural economy that created an agricultural surplus that could feed large cities. Although it has been argued that the growth of the Italian cities in the eleventh century was stunted because the rural aristocracy controlled them more strongly than in the north, the size of the Italian centres in

56 Discussion based on Schneider, *Metz*, 28–50.

comparison to those of France and Germany, together with the large numbers of toll exemptions and navigational privileges granted by princes after 1050 show that localised, overland trade was the basis for the changes, in Italy as in the north. The cities had large enough populations even by 1100 to make famine a real threat, and controlling the large cities' food supplies became a major element of the wealth of their elites. Even in the twelfth century the archbishop's toll at Mainz was used to guarantee that the city itself had enough food before re-export was permitted, but the cities also had storage facilities and could import and keep grain for resale when conditions were propitious.[57]

Even in enormous London the food markets had a fundamental importance in the evolution of the city plan. Densest settlement was not in the south and east toward the continent, nor south and west toward the government suburb of Westminster, but rather north and west, toward the food source. The city was centred on the two Cheaps, East and West. The Saxon bridge of London, which served the city until 1209, crossed the Thames at the site of the meat market on a line separating two wards.[58]

The cities were thus still principally centres of consumption, with trade and manufacturing decidedly secondary until well into the twelfth century and in many cases thereafter. The trade that centred in the growing towns of the eleventh century was chiefly in food and basic industrial products of the surrounding area. Overseas trade was concentrated mainly in the larger cities. Until the twelfth century most long-distance trade in the cities was importing, both for the demand market of the citizens and the urban court and to provide a transit service for goods passing through the tolls. This is particularly true in the case of the Italian cities, which, except for the coastal ports, grew as political and market centres of their environs and were less affected by international trade than were most great cities of the north. Coin was used mainly for long-distance, luxury trade and wholesale local trade; the purchasing power of the penny, the smallest coin minted, was so substantial that it was unfeasible for smaller retail transactions, which were still handled by barter.[59] This rudimentary exchange apparatus meant that the main sources of wealth continued to be provisioning the city

---

57 Diestelkamp, *Beiträge* 1; Britnell, *Commercialisation of English Society*, 86; Falck, *Mainz*, 161; Bordone, *Evoluzione delle città*, 20.

58 Schofield, *Building of London*, 33; Brooke and Keir, *London*, 171–7, 159; Honeybourne, 'Bridge of London', 31–4.

59 Britnell, *Commercialisation of English Society*, 30; Miller and Hatcher, *Towns, Commerce and Crafts*, 10–16; Diestelkamp, 'König und Städte', 253; Hyde, *Society and Politics*, 74.

with necessities and renting property to new residents. Moneylending, often with real property as security, was also important for the aristocracy. Merchants rarely exercised political power until the twelfth century, when artisans who made exportable goods streamed into the cities and sometimes made common cause with the merchants against the older landowning elite. But although merchants and knights had guilds in the eleventh century, artisan organisations as such are rare before 1100 outside Italy.

The growth of urban industry in the twelfth century is connected with a shift in fashion and industrial technology. Early medieval industry had been largely rural, producing utilitarian goods for local use but exporting little. Linen, made on simple stretch frames, was the preferred textile. But in the mid-eleventh century the treadle horizontal loom appeared at Troyes, followed by the heavy horizontal broadloom, which required two and later three people to use it. These machines produced a much heavier woollen textile that became the favoured cloth of the rich during the twelfth century. The manufacture of luxury woollen fabrics required the services of many specialists, who could only be found in large numbers in the cities. The textile trades that required high technical competence, such as weaving and dyeing, became almost exclusively male-dominated and urban, while other cloth trades, notably spinning, remained centred in the villages. The development of an exportable industrial commodity and its concentration in the cities had been accomplished in the west by the end of the eleventh century, in Germany by the end of the twelfth.[60]

Transport and urbanisation

A revolution in transport also contributed to the changes after 1100. Most early medieval cities that became important commercial centres in the twelfth century were on navigable rivers, which were better suited to moving cargoes than the rough overland roads. Boats became larger in the late twelfth century, necessitating a shift to deeper harbours. Thus Haithabu was abandoned for Schleswig, which could handle bigger boats. The development of Saintes was halted by the foundation of La Rochelle, an unusual case of a plantation overcoming the early advantage of an organic city. Flooding along the North Sea coast in the early twelfth century made Saint-Omer the natural port of western Flanders. As the waters receded, the city dug a canal to the sea at Gravelines, became

---

60 Desportes, *Reims*, 103; Diestelkamp, *Beiträge* 1: xii. See summary of literature on cloth technology in Nicholas, 'Poverty and primacy', 35–7.

that town's proprietor, and acquired a staple on the river Aa, forbidding discharge of cargoes between Saint-Omer and Gravelines. Bruges, which the flooding had turned into a natural port, dug the Reie canal and founded Damme as its port in 1180. The Flemish counts established Nieuwpoort in 1163 as the outport of Ypres and Biervliet in 1183 for Ghent, in each case giving the parent city firm control over the new foundation. Thus the greatest Flemish cities were dependent on overseas trade, but by 1200 none was a seaport. Some English cities on estuaries also had extraterritorial rights on coastal wharves or docks, as Exeter did at Topsham and Colchester at Hythe. By 1200 the urban coastal landscape had essentially been established.[61]

The transport revolution also affected overland trade. During the twelfth century the increased use of horse teams with collars, and of four-wheeled carts that could carry as much as 600 kg of grain 40 km per day, meant that grain could be marketed more easily. As land routes became more competitive with rivers, they contributed to the success of the Champagne and other fairs and to the prosperity of some cities that were not on rivers. The professional grain merchant who provisioned a city market by buying from farmers who lacked other distributive facilities made his appearance and became an object of distaste for peasants and nobles alike. Even in such a small place as Laon in 1112 most merchant wealth came from the grain trade. The city merchants were accused of swindling the peasants, and the bishop used armed farmers from his domains against the townspeople.[62]

In addition to making possible the urban growth of previously small places, the wheeled cart caused important changes in urban morphology, particularly in Spain. Large cities developed earlier in Muslim areas than in Christian Spain, and canals and pack mules made more sense there than wheeled carts, since the roads were so poor. These conveyances are suited to narrow streets and dead-end alleys, which can provide security and family cohesion. As the Christians conquered Muslim cities, they gradually widened streets and opened alleys to accommodate carts, which require flat, paved streets that are at least as wide as an axle. But the fact that Muslim cities were already so developed made it hard to adapt to the change to the wheeled transport that was so important

---

61 Jansen, 'Early urbanization in Denmark', 183–216; Ammann, 'Städte-wesen Spaniens und Westfrankreichs', 126–31; van Uytven, 'Stadsgeschiedenis', 196; van Houtte, *Economic History*, 47; Derville, 'Gravelines et Calais', 1051–4; Derville, *Histoire de Saint-Omer*, 36–7; Nicholas, *Medieval Flanders*, 110; Britnell, *Commercialisation of English Society*, 86.

62 Derville, *Histoire de Saint-Omer*, 35; Chapin, *Villes de foires*, 12; Chédeville, 'Cité à ville', 140–1.

in the continuing development of urban life in the north, where suburban quarters were often planned with wide streets.[63]

Nuremberg is the best example of a great European city that prospered by building a network of overland routes, but its great expansion
came later. Land routes were critical for the development of the cities
of Brabant. In the twelfth century the Flemings started going directly
overland to the Rhineland markets by using a new route from Cologne
to Bruges over Tongeren, Sint-Truiden, Louvain, Brussels, Aalst and
Ghent. Except for Antwerp, which was on the periphery of Brabant
and really a part of the Flemish economic region, urban life in Brabant
was negligible until stimulated by this route.[64] Coventry was not on a
navigable stream, but it was at the centre of a road network and of many
small streams that could be used for fulling mills. By the late twelfth
century the southern sector of Coventry, fostered by its lord, the earl
of Chester, was an important cloth centre.[65]

The site of Milan, the largest city of northern Italy, was also super-
ficially unfavourable. In a plain between two rivers, Milan was linked
by canals to the Ticino and Adda but never to the Po. The city was
at the junction of a rich alluvial area and an arid sector and thus at the
intersection of supply of and demand for food. The rural district that
was initially controlled by the powerful archbishop and later became the
contado of the commune of Milan was mainly north of the city, toward
the Alpine passes. This brought Milan into a fateful competition with
Como for the traffic coming from the north, which became extremely
lucrative, particularly after the rise of the fairs of Champagne in the
mid-twelfth century. The roads from Milan through the Alpine passes
led onward to the Champagne fairs. Milan, in turn, controlled the flow
of north European goods to the cities of southern Lombardy. The southern roads were important, too, for Milan's trade with Genoa, which
furnished wool and other industrial raw materials from overseas in exchange for grain from Lombardy, which Milan controlled.[66]

Politics and urbanisation

Political considerations and the establishment of frontiers of principalities had a strong impact on the establishment of some cities. Lille had been
a small regional market, at the junction of two agrarian systems, alluvial

63 Glick, *Spain*, 118–19, 24–5 after Richard W. Bulliet, *The Canal and the Wheel*
    (Cambridge, Mass.: Harvard University Press, 1975), 10.
64 Pfeiffer, *Nürnberg*, 4; Jansen, 'Handel en Nijverheid', 161–75; Charles, *Ville de
    Saint-Trond*, 120–6.
65 Lobel, *Atlas* 2: 1–3.
66 Mazzi, 'Milano', 374–6, 381, 401–3; Volpe, *Medio Evo Italiano*, 109, 221–3.

and prosperous on the south and sandy and infertile on the north, before it became a favoured residence of Count Baldwin V of Flanders after 1054. It was also between river systems, linked to the Leie and Ghent by the Deûle. The city commenced at the point just north of the castle where the lower Deûle became navigable, then expanded entirely southward, so that the castle was eventually on its northern extremity. This is a common feature of urban origins in this part of Europe: the city developed where a river became navigable and thus intersected traffic that had been overland to that point.[67] Bristol was at the border of ancient Wessex with Mercia and at the junction of the Severn estuary and the Avon. At the lowest point where the Avon could be bridged, it was a point of transshipment where agricultural, mining and industrial areas met. The growing Irish trade in the twelfth century, cemented by Bristol's links with Dublin, contributed to its growth as well as to that of Exeter, which owed its rise primarily to the revival of the Cornish tin trade with Ireland.[68]

Political influence on urban development in the eleventh and twelfth centuries is clearest in England. The tenth-century *burhs* and ports in which the kings tried to centralise coinage and large-scale marketing transactions had created a dense network of places with urban characteristics before the Norman Conquest. The Norman conquest depressed what had been a buoyant urban civilisation and created the basis for the dependence of the English economy on exporting raw materials to the continent. English merchants had an active trade in the Mediterranean before the Conquest, but after 1066 there is no record of English ships in the Mediterranean for more than a century, while Italian merchants appear in England in the 1120s.[69] Rather than serving as nuclei around which settlement congregated, English castles were agents of destruction. The Normans built huge forts in virtually all cities, depopulating burgages to make room for them. The number of burgesses paying rent to the king at Canterbury dropped from fifty-one in 1066 to nineteen in 1086. At Norwich ninety-eight messuages were demolished to make room for the castle and 199 for all other reasons. Ipswich had about 540 messuages in 1066, of which 328 were waste by 1086.[70]

The Normans demolished twenty-seven burgages for their castle at Cambridge. Lincoln was comparable in size to Norwich in 1066; but

67 Trenard, *Histoire de Lille*, 45–50, 57–9, 22–30; Sivery, 'Histoire économique et sociale', 146–51, 161–3.
68 Lobel, *Atlas* 2: 2–3; Maddicott, 'Towns Alfred', 17–22.
69 Miller and Hatcher, *Towns, Commerce and Crafts*, 20–6; Nightingale, *Medieval Mercantile Community*, 13.
70 Platt, 'Evolution', 51; Urry, *Canterbury*, 40–3; Darby, *Domesday England*, 296–8.

of its 1,150 inhabited messuages, 240 were waste by 1086, of which 166 were torn down to make room for the castle and 74 were deserted due to poverty and fire. In the fourteenth century Lincoln had fewer inhabitants than before 1066, despite the stimulus of removal of a bishopric to Lincoln in 1072. Oxford had been the largest city in the Midlands in 1066 but was down to half its former size by 1086. It did recover more rapidly than did Lincoln and Cambridge in the twelfth century. Adding insult to injury, the Normans raised taxes on the depressed cities. William the Conqueror raised the tax farm at York from 53 pounds to 100 pounds, despite a population decline of 50 per cent in twenty years. Lincoln's taxes were more than trebled, Colchester's quintupled.[71]

Accompanying their new castles the Normans settled colonies of Frenchmen in many cities. London was a conspicuous exception, although some individual foreign merchants came there. The French boroughs cushioned the population decline to some extent, and some became more prosperous than the Saxon settlement. They were all in eastern England, a fact that, with the rise of the newly founded ports of Boston and Lynn, suggests that the Normans were shifting trade away from London and were furthering the increasing Flemish involvement in a lucrative wool trade. The Norman borough at Nottingham was between the hilltop castle and the Anglo-Saxon *burh* further east. It had its own defences and became the commercial centre, while the English borough declined. The two had separate inheritance customs, bailiffs and sheriffs into the fifteenth century. At Norwich a 'new burg' west of the castle where 124 French and a scattering of English and others lived made up for some of the decline, but it is still likely that total population had declined by one-quarter by 1086. Norwich did recover spectacularly in the twelfth century, but the French sector was considerably richer than the English. Winchester also had numerous French settlers after the Conquest, although they did not have a separate borough. Although 85 per cent of the citizens had English names in 1086, only 35 per cent did by 1110, and most of the newcomers were Norman, concentrating in the aristocratic High.[72]

The early development of urban/economic regions

Political conditions were tied to international trade and finance and to the interdependent urban regions. The temporary separation of Normandy

71 Lobel, *Atlas* 2: 1–6; Hill, *Medieval Lincoln*, 35, 45, 53–5; Salter, *Medieval Oxford*, 20–2, 29–31; Tillott, *City of York*, 22.
72 Lobel, *Atlas* 1: 2; 2: 8–9; Darby, *Domesday England*, 298–9, 305–6; Hill, *Lincoln*, 63; Biddle, *Winchester*, 475–6; Nightingale, *Medieval Mercantile Community*, 20.

from England prompted a rebellion at Rouen in 1090. The restoration of a common prince after 1106 rekindled ties. Gilbert Becket, father of the famous archbishop Thomas, was born at Rouen, married a woman of Caen, then moved to London before 1119, eventually becoming sheriff. Guillaume Trentegerous farmed the viscounty of Rouen in 1150 and loaned money to the future King Henry II. In 1156 he farmed the tax of Southampton, then was succeeded by his wife until 1163. She returned to Rouen before 1180 and leased the viscounty. She invested in land and houses in Rouen and environs, but she also entered trade, selling salt and herring cargoes at Paris and forming a partnership with the Englishman Gervaise of Hampton. Members of Guillaume Trentegerous' family stayed at Rouen, and one was mayor in 1218. The common features in these stories of twelfth-century urban fortune are easy movement between England and Normandy, usury, collaboration with the royal treasury, and, in a second stage, long-distance commerce. At the end of the twelfth century officeholding was declining and trade rising as the chief source of wealth of the Rouen aristocracy.[73]

The Crusades also fostered interregional trade, although not to the extent once thought. From 1080 Venice had a colony at Constantinople that virtually monopolised the city's western trade. Other Italian and southern French cities followed suit after the Latin Kingdom of Jerusalem was established. Then-coastal Pisa and Genoa became the leading ports of the western Mediterranean and each other's bitter rivals. Marseilles maintained merchant offices in foreign ports, governed by a consul chosen by the city government. Northern cities also had resident colonies of foreign merchants. William Cade of Saint-Omer loaned money to English prelates and princes in the early period of Henry II. He may have been responsible for the privilege given to Saint-Omer merchants of buying and selling through England and having hostels in London, which in turn extended the market for Flemish textiles in England at the expense of the native product.[74]

The cities of Slavic Europe had conspicuous foreign colonies before 1200. We have noted the example of Novgorod, where Swedes became extremely prominent. Before 1200 all major Polish towns had large colonies of foreign merchants, especially Germans, who were living under their own law. Kiev had a Jewish quarter in the eleventh century, although Novgorod never did. As the cities of Russia expanded beyond their early nuclei, *slobody*, amounting to bastides, were established as

73   Mollat, *Rouen*, 58–61.
74   Lesage, *Marseille angevine*, 52; Derville, *Histoire de Saint-Omer*, 38.

foreign colonies, particularly for Greeks but also for some west European traders.[75]

During the twelfth century western Europe developed clearly defined urban economic regions that flourished through trade with one another. Although the English link seems to have fostered urban growth in Normandy, most English cities continued to decline. Those of Flanders and northwestern France grew, and the cities of northern Italy expanded tremendously. This created a bipolar urban network whose supply and demand mechanisms stimulated population growth and industry in their trading partners. The urban density of Flanders was higher than in Italy; within a radius of 25 km of Lille were Tournai, Douai, Ypres and Courtrai. Flanders was also bordered by principalities that had large cities. By contrast, 'every great Italian city controlled a territory as large as Flanders', creating *contadi* whose administration we shall discuss separately.[76]

The cities of east-central France also grew, particularly with the stimulus provided by the Champagne fairs; but most other French cities except Paris and those on the Mediterranean coast did not continue in the twelfth century to display their earlier potential. In west-central France urban growth slowed in the twelfth century as the northwest lured trade away from them, and long-distance exchange became centred at the Champagne fairs. The cities of southwestern France initially developed in a similar pattern to those of the north, but they stagnated in the twelfth century because they did not develop export industries.[77]

Muslim Spain had a precocious urban culture, containing one-third of the cities of Europe with a population of more than 10,000 in the tenth century. Córdoba probably had a population of 90,000 at its height, declining to 50,000 in the twelfth century with the collapse of the Caliphate. Seville, the second largest city of Islamic Spain, had a population of 52,000 in the tenth century, 83,000 in the eleventh. Toledo grew from 28,000 in the tenth century to 37,000 in the eleventh, Granada from 20,000 to 26,000. Zaragoza, Valencia and Malaga were larger than all but a few north European cities.[78]

As in the north the larger and older Spanish cities developed suburbs, but some Spanish *civitates* were so thoroughly altered in the eleventh and twelfth centuries that they amounted to new towns. French settlement was stimulated by the pilgrimage trade and trading concessions

75 Knoll, 'Urban development of medieval Poland', 74–5; Birnbaum, 'Kiev, Novgorod, Moscow', 30–3, 39, 45.
76 Sivery, *Histoire de Lille*, 164–5.
77 Ammann, 'Städtewesen Spaniens und Westfrankreichs', 146, 126–31.
78 Bairoch, *Cities*, 117 ff.; Glick, *Spain*, 110–16.

given by the Christian kings of Spain. At Pamplona, which had been a deserted Roman ruin until the eleventh century, 'Franks' occupied an entire bourg, San Cernin, with a regular street plan. A large market square was between the original settlement and the Frankish suburb. Oviedo, which was revived by the pilgrim traffic to Compostela in the eleventh century, also developed a French merchant colony outside the episcopal city. Barcelona, which would become the largest city of medieval Spain, first became a major port in the twelfth century, with suburbs dominated by merchants and sailors.[79]

Spain is especially notable for frontier settlements that were founded as outposts against the Muslims. Many of them, as in northern Europe, were settled before receiving formal charters. Jaca, the leading city of Old Aragon, had a royal castle, a monastery, and a commercial and agricultural centre west of the castle. Each nucleus had a discernible street plan and developed separately before a single charter was given to Jaca in 1076.[80] The frontier towns between Tagus and Duero and along the Ebro – Salamanca, Avila, Segovia, Cuenca and Guadalajara – were more military than those of northern Spain, many of whose charters limited the military service that the prince could exact. These towns were typically polynuclear, reflecting the ethnic or regional origin of their citizens. They actively repopulated lands under their control, established new settlements, and controlled routes and mountain passes. Avila had a granite wall with 88 towers. Its cathedral was built into the wall and was as important as the castle in defending the town.[81]

Fairs and urbanisation

Fairs are attested by the sixth century, and much of the commercial activity of the twelfth century was handled at them. The fair of Saint-Denis outside Paris is especially renowned. Jewish merchants living at Worms and Mainz obtained goods on credit through the fair of Cologne, which contributed to a large extent to the city's prosperity. The Stourbridge fair at Cambridge, together with the university, was the basis of much of the city's prosperity.[82]

However, the long-term impact of most fairs on urbanisation is

79 Glick, *Spain*, 113; Ammann, 'Städtewesen Spaniens und Westfrankreichs', 112–13, 117; Bisson, *Aragon*, 42–5.
80 Powers, 'Creative interaction', 53–80; Nelson, 'Foundation of Jaca', esp. 696, 700, 705–6.
81 MacKay, *Spain*, 53–4; Ladero Quesnada, 'Fortifications urbaines', 149–55.
82 Mitterauer, *Markt und Stadt*, 159; Agus, *Urban Civilization* 1, 108–9; Rubin, *Cambridge*, 34.

problematical, for they attracted a transient population but very little permanent support personnel in the host sites. The great Flemish cities had fairs early, but that of Ghent is not mentioned after 1200, and those of Saint-Omer and Douai did less business than the 'five fairs' of Flanders, only two of which – Bruges and Lille – were in major cities. Most of the great international and regional fairs were in small towns, such as St Ives, rather than the larger or older places. The great fair of St Giles was held outside Winchester but was not enough to halt the decline of the city after 1148.[83]

The greatest fairs were the six held in four places in the county of Champagne. Roughly equidistant from the Low Countries and northern Italy and accessible only overland, the fairs eventually stimulated the bipolar urban axis centred on these two regions and also the growth of regional networks of fairs. These were scheduled so that merchants could establish an inventory locally, then visit the Champagne emporia. Of the four fair sites, Lagny and Bar-sur-Aube were never cities, but Provins and Troyes were important long before they received charters in 1230. The fairs of Troyes (Plan 10) were held in a commercial/industrial suburb with an unplanned street layout west of the old City that had been walled by 1125. A later suburb on the north, Bourgneuf, has a grid plan. Even the swampy eastern and southern suburbs were walled by 1171. A final wall was built in the 1230s, and the Seine and its tributary the Vienne were diverted and the marshes drained into moats around the walls, coincidentally making the east more habitable. Troyes thus grew during the period of the fairs, but whether because of them is unclear; for the place had considerable native industry and was the chief residence of the counts of Champagne.

The impact of the fair on the urban economy is clearer at Provins, which originated as a Carolingian hill fort and district capital and was a major textile centre and market for the cloth production of the Durtain valley. A lower city had a common wall with the fortress by the early twelfth century. In 1137 the count granted a charter for the fair of St Martin, providing space for lodgings for traders from Arras and Flanders. The second or May fair is mentioned in 1141. By 1203 the fairs occupied virtually the entire upper city near the castle. The industrial lower town grew toward the fair site. The fairs clearly stimulated the textile production of Provins and its region to a greater extent than at Troyes.[84]

83   van Houtte, *Economic History*, 47; Biddle, *Winchester*, 286–7.
84   Chapin, *Villes de foires*, 11–22, 30–9, 53–6, 141.

URBAN SOCIETY IN THE ELEVENTH AND TWELFTH CENTURIES: FROM LANDOWNING ELITE TOWARD MERCHANT PATRICIATE

The elite of the eleventh-century cities was a small but never stable group of persons who exercised political power and controlled the assets that constituted the basis of their communities' wealth. Long-distance merchants contributed substantially to the capital assets of some early cities but were never the population base, since they were gone for most of the year. A permanent resident population is necessary for the city, which is founded in local governance, trade, cult relations and to some extent in providing shelter for wanderers, including merchants.[85]

Accordingly, although commerce was expanding in the eleventh century, the elite of the cities still consisted of their lords, their officials and others who owned and rented land inside the City or the adjacent suburbs. This interpretation is a truism of scholarship on the Italian cities,[86] but studies of Arras, Metz, Reims and Ghent have shown it to be essentially accurate for northern urbanisation. Loaning and exchanging money were also important, for they developed through the lord's mint. Moneyers were an important part of the early officeholding aristocracies in Germany, Italy and England. Since their business required some knowledge of merchant activity and overseas contacts, some also traded as merchants. They were among the earliest members of city councils at Milan and Pavia, and in England at Winchester and Lincoln. Of the aldermen of London who are known by name from the twelfth century, at least four were moneyers. Several of them were knights.[87] Most persons of substance in the early municipal elites thus were not newly rich wanderers; rather, their roots go back far into the community.[88]

As town populations grew, landowners could take considerable profits from immigrants. Much of the population base of the cities was composed of serfs or other tenants of the elite. The inhabitants of Poitiers were 'free villeins' or 'customary serfs' of the abbey of Montierneuf into

---

85 Petri, 'Städtewesen', 268–9; Ennen, *Frühgeschichte*, 217–22; Schneider, *Metz*, esp. 88; Lestocquoy, *Villes*, 13–24; Blockmans, *Gentsche Stadspatriciaat*; Nicholas, 'Urban origins', 109–10.

86 Of perhaps 10,000 inhabitants of the Lombard city of Bergamo who are known by name before 1100, only one was exclusively a merchant; as late as 1277 landless citizens were forbidden to participate in elections to the town council. Kolb, *Stadt im Altertum*, 262.

87 Nightingale, *Medieval Mercantile Community*, 23–4.

88 See formulation of Chédeville, 'Cité à ville', 134–9; Hilton, *English and French Towns*, 88–9.

the twelfth century. The abbey of St Vaast at Arras had a problem in the early twelfth century with free merchants living in the city trying to prove that they were serfs so that they could claim the abbey's toll exemption. Arras, virtually alone of the places in northwestern Europe that eventually became major cities, did not have a *portus* in the ninth century. Although its trade included gold and slaves, there is no trace of the wandering merchant at Arras. It is the best example of the origins of a merchant urban aristocracy on a monastery's domain.[89]

This thesis is confirmed by several German cities. At Augsburg the 'noble unfree' (the bishop's officials, called ministerials) in the old city were distinguished from persons living mainly in the suburbs, who could be freed from servile obligations by paying a ground rent (*cens*) in wax to one of the churches. The patron saint of that church thus became their fictive lord as they became 'free unfree'. In the late tenth century the 'property owners of the city' of Passau were serfs who had been freed on condition of paying ground rent in perpetuity. As at Arras, dependence on the powerful conferred advantages; many 'freemen' also made themselves dependants of the altar of the church of St Stephen, a status so desirable that some noblewomen wanted to marry them. The 'free unfreedom' of the *censuales* (persons paying *cens*) thus permitted serfs to rise from 'city dwellers' to 'citizens' and finally in the twelfth century to 'burgesses'. Later sources show that 'citizen of Passau' and '*censualis* of St Stephen' were the same. The *censuales* included ministerials (serfs who performed honourable services much as castle guard for their lord, or had responsibilities in his household or bureaucracy) of the cathedral; but from the late eleventh century some ministerials began distinguishing themselves from other *censuales* by adding 'lord' to their names. Nearby Regensburg developed similarly, but the ministerials in its elite, who were also *censuales*, were differentiated more sharply from the merchants who were 'upright men', although both groups were citizens. The serfs of Novgorod could likewise be freed through dependency on a church and thereby become 'black people' (free craftsmen).[90]

The earliest urban elites in England were also landowners, particularly in *burhs*. At Lincoln the 'lawmen' of the late eleventh century were moneylenders and landowners in town and countryside. The elites of Durham, Colchester, York and especially Cambridge were heavily involved in the land market in the city and its environs.[91] Even in the

89   Claude, *Bourges und Poitiers*, 145; Nicholas, *Medieval Flanders*, 105; Petri, 'Städtewesen', 273.
90   Brandl–Ziegert, 'Sozialstruktur', 19–31, 64–71; Bosl, 'Regensburg', 121–34; Bosl, *Augsburger Bürgertum*, 13–14; Goehrke, 'Novgorod', 369.
91   Hilton, *English and French Towns*, 91–2; Rubin, *Cambridge*, 36–8.

Flemish cities, which are often portrayed as prototypes of medieval commercial and industrial urbanisation, landownership was so important that it became the basis of a social rank. The charter of Saint-Omer of 1127 mentions that two 'landed men' could attest the validity of a transaction. This terminology had spread to Ghent by 1168. The 'landed men' were the first patricians, descendants of landowners in the original *portus*. The aristocrats who ruled Ghent in the thirteenth century were thus defined by their landowning and had probably originated as a group by the tenth century.[92]

The example of Metz also should caution us against over-emphasising the role of long-distance trade in the composition of the early elites. Although Metz was one of the largest cities north of the Alps, it had an almost purely local commerce, as the only significant urban regional market within a 60 km radius. The patricians were members of five 'paraiges' (peerages or lineages) that originated in the bishop's household. Most of their property consisted of land and vineyards in nearby villages. There was scarcely any investment in long-distance trade.[93]

City and *contado* in the Mediterranean basin

Landowners and knights were strongest in the Italian and Iberian cities. Even in the eighth century the wealthiest residents of the Lombard cities had been required to fight on horseback, and this obligation was the constituent mark of a knight by the twelfth. Many of the military towns of central Spain were collective lords of their regions and had reserved offices for knights and squires. The population of the suburb of Zamora was divided in the eleventh century into 'greater persons', who had a horse, and 'lesser persons'.[94]

The domination of the lesser landowners of the embryonic cities is clearest in Italy. The nobles of the *contado* (surrounding countryside) had had property or family branches in the major cities from the onset of urbanisation. The first aristocrats of Venice were landowners who had property on the mainland. From the eleventh century the 'old houses' [*case vecchie*], consisting of landowners who had turned to commerce, were already distinguishing themselves from the purely commercial 'new houses' [*case nuove*]. Studies have shown that there was no significant distinction between rural and urban nobilies during the tenth and eleventh centuries in Tuscany and Lombardy, although one developed later.

92 Blockmans, *Gentsche Stadspatriciaat*, 64–97.
93 Dollinger-Léonard, 'Cité', 200; Schneider, *Metz*, vi, 24–5, 60–5, 89–93, 123.
94 Glick, *Spain*, 158; MacKay, *Spain*, 56; Lansing, *Florentine Magnates*, 148.

The cathedral clergy and the bishops themselves came mainly from families that included captains, who held castles in fief of the bishop and were in his court. The captains had land in both *contado* and city. Some families included both judges in the city and captains, although the judges of Milan came from the middle social groups as well as from captain families; several sons of merchants were judges. They were the major source of penetration of the captain group from below.[95]

In Tuscany and Lombardy we have seen that many bishops exercised temporal power, and some even had the title of 'count.' Many municipal aristocrats were vassals both of their bishops and of the German emperor. Events in the eleventh century at Milan, whose archbishop Aribert was *de facto* imperial regent for Lombardy, seem to have marked a turning point in the relations of the embryonic cities with the nobility and the bishops. By the early eleventh century contemporary writers were dividing the population of Milan into 'captains' (greater knights), their vassals ('valvassors') and the 'people'. A fine scale of 1067 distinguished four 'orders': captains, vassals, merchants and 'others'. Clearly such distinctions were not rigid, for the terminology used in the narrative sources for social groups does not correspond exactly to that in legal sources.[96]

By the early eleventh century the captains upon whom the bishops had relied to limit the powers of the counts were becoming more independent of them. The captains had seized control of rural parishes and threatened the bishop's control in the city. Some captains held rights of jurisdiction as early as the Carolingian period, and some came from families that had served the royal house, while the valvassors were lesser landowners and from newer families, less often with lordship. Their ancestors were not noble in the ninth century, but they were trying to gain this status in the eleventh.[97]

Captains and valvassors, the two levels of urban/rural nobility, thus fought in several Italian cities in the early eleventh century, but the valvassors also had problems with the archbishop. The valvassors were vassals of both the bishops and the captains. Most were from families that lacked the means to create lordships. Thus they were comparable in status to the ministerial vassals of Germany, a considerably less distinguished group than the vassals of eleventh-century France and England. Thus the revolt of the valvassors in 1035 was also directed against

95   Barel, *Ville médiévale*, 26; Fasoli, 'Città italiane', 312; Dilcher, 'Comuni italiani', 75; Keller, 'Soziale und politische Verfassung Mailands', 35–8; Racine, 'Città e contado', 118–22.
96   Dilcher, 'Comuni italiani', 76–7.
97   Keller, *Adelsherrschaft und städtische Gesellschaft*, 194–5, 240–50, 302.

the archbishop, who was no more willing than the captains to grant them heredity over their fiefs. The emperors saw the valvassors as a counterweight to the increasingly unruly captains and gave them hereditary tenure of their fiefs in 1037.

At Milan the non-noble citizens had fought with archbishop Aribert against the valvassors, but they feared the emperor Conrad II's invasion in 1037, which had been directed chiefly at the archbishop and the captains. Thus the alliances shifted, and in 1042 the captains supported the valvassors against the commoners. The archbishop and nobles were expelled, and knights and commoners made a pact. Fighting continued until 1045, when Lanzo, a jurist of captain rank who was leading the 'people', mediated a settlement. But internal divisions over episcopal elections had broken the fragile unity by 1055. In 1059 the valvassors, now called Patarenes (ragpickers) by their opponents, allied with the pope against the archbishop of Milan. Yet the Patarenes, far from being poor citizens, as has been maintained, were led by the captains Erlembald and Landulf, both of them born into families of Milan that had served kings. The rising was only ended by the emperor in 1073.[98]

The union of 1045 was called a 'federation of peace'. The Patarenes swore a 'communal oath' (*juramentum commune*) at Milan in 1067, the first collective oath-taking of an urban population recorded in Italy, and a new vocabulary of terms involving some form of *commune* developed from that point. The oath of 1067 concerned church matters, but it involved all participants in the peace association. Penalties were prescribed for violating the truce of God. Although it is probably premature to speak of a 'communal movement' in Italy at this time, this peace agreement between knights and commoners at Milan, which is documented more clearly in developments between 1067 and 1074, has similarities to the sworn peace associations that were at the base of the northern communes (see Chapter 5), although the language is less explicit than in the north.[99]

The Patarene movement was connected to the papal programme of church reform and was directed against imperially-designated bishops who were accused of simony. It was not limited to Milan. The agitation was also serious at Padua, whose bishop had a large territory but

98 Tabacco, *Medieval Italy*, 184–5; Barel, *Ville médiévale*, 35–6; Keller, 'Italienische Stadtverfassung', 56–7; Mazzi, 'Milano', 398; Violante, *Società milanese*, 179–89, 201–2, 243–7; Jakobs, *Stadtgemeinde*, 24–5; Keller, 'Soziale und politische Verfassung Mailands', 37; Previté-Orton, 'Italian cities till c. 1200', 218–19; Racine, 'Città e contado', 123–6.
99 Dilcher, 'Comuni italiani', 79–80; Keller, 'Soziale und politische Verfassung Mailands', 49–52; Racine, 'Evêque et cité', 137.

few great vassals to help him control it. There and in the other Lombard cities where disturbances occurred they weakened the secular powers of the bishop. Particularly from the 1070s the movement was directed more explicitly at the bishops and became linked to the development of papal parties in the cities. This struggle would result in the institution of the commune at the end of the century, which we shall discuss in Chapter 5.[100]

The nobility at the turn of the twelfth century included the valvassors of the eleventh century and their descendants. While most twelfth-century chroniclers distinguish captains from valvassors, even by 1100 the two were being lumped together as the 'order of nobles'. But nobility and knighthood, although related, were not the same at the beginning of the twelfth century. Knighthood was a lower status than valvassor, and some 'people' or 'commoners' became knights. Just after 1100 two Milanese 'citizens and equestrians', a baker and a functionary in the archbishop's household, were elevated to knighthood. The imperial chronicler Otto of Freising and others called the city folk 'knights' and 'equestrians' and saw them as a revival of the Roman equestrian order. The noble group was thus being replenished from below as townspeople bought land and were dubbed. Much of the cause of this was the break-up of great rural estates, creating a mobile market in land for townspeople to buy.

Thus the terms 'captain', 'valvassor', 'equestrian burgess' and 'lesser citizens' gradually yielded to the simpler categories of 'nobility' (*nobilitas*) and 'people' (*populus*), which continued in use through the thirteenth century. They do not correspond to modern meanings of these words. By 1200, with the rise of the commune and its subordination of the *contado*, most Milanese writers distinguished between two 'societies': those of the captains and valvassors, which, however, included some merchants, and those of the 'people' (*popolo*) to which most knights seem to have belonged. The hardening of corporate distinctions that do not correspond to modern notions of 'class' becomes a problem that will engage our attention in Chapter 8.[101]

The question naturally arises of the relationship between merchant activity and landholding. While the most socially prominent urbanites were landowners, this does not necessarily mean that they were merchants. In both the north and in Italy landowners were beginning to trade as merchants as the economic changes made that activity more

---

100 Racine, 'Evêque et cité', 135–7; Rippe, 'Dans le Padouan', 143.
101 Keller, 'Soziale und politische Verfassung Mailands', 45–8; Keller, *Adelsherrschaft und städtische Gesellschaft*, 20–59.

lucrative. Whether the land buyers of the late eleventh and twelfth centuries were generally new men or sons of previously prominent merchant families is more difficult to answer. Family and professional continuity can be shown among merchant lineages between the tenth and eleventh centuries, but in most cases it is hard to document that the eleventh-century land buyers were descendants of tenth-century merchants. There was not a merchant patriciate this early, but the increasing availability of land gave the new merchants a chance to solidify a dynasty and provided a new opportunity for landed families to engage in merchant activity. Whatever may be said of their ancestors, the newly rich Milanese merchants of the eleventh century were buying land and even becoming vassals, despite the archbishop's objection.[102]

Nobles owned or held in fief strategically important urban properties, such as gates and bridges. They also extended their rural feuds into the cities and became a public menace. Although cities are often faulted for weakening family cohesion, this was not true of the Italian nobles. Florence contained 150 noble towers by the early thirteenth century, some as high as 250 feet. Benjamin of Tudela noted that 'each householder [at Genoa] has a tower to his house, and at times of strife they fight from the tops of the towers with each other'. Although Pisa still lacked a wall, it had 'about 10,000 turreted houses for battle in time of strife', a figure that betrays the habit of exaggerating numbers so often found in medieval chroniclers. Even the purely merchant aristocracy of Amalfi lived on hilltops.[103]

To counter the towers, 'popular' military companies called 'tower societies' developed, based on the city gates. They were not kin groups, although they overlapped with families, but rather were peace associations whose members paid a fee to keep the tower in repair. When the rectors of the society heard that one member was in danger, they gave him the keys to the tower until the threat had passed. The tower societies and parish-based military associations were the most effective means for Italian merchants to fight the aristocracy and gain a measure of political participation commensurate with their numbers and economic importance.[104] The power of the nobles was strongest in Rome, which was ruled by popes who were often seen locally as family chiefs rather than spiritual figures. Noble families dominated entire quarters. Most of their palaces had two elements: one or more single-storey houses and a tower, generally on an ancient ruin, to which the family

102 Violante, *Società milanese*, 158–65.
103 Fasoli, 'Città e feudalità', 365–6; *Itinerary of Benjamin of Tudela*, 5, 9.
104 Tabacco, *Medieval Italy*, 222–3; Lansing, *Florentine Magnates*, xii, 3, 89–92; Fasoli, 'Città italiane', 307.

fled during emergencies. Most noble lineages acquired large blocks of land around the central complex, which was reserved for the family, for lease and rental to clients.[105] To combat the violence, some city governments began forcing nobles of the environs to become clients of the municipality. This was a key aspect of a more comprehensive conquest of a *contado*, generally starting with the city's own diocese and the commune's gradual assumption of the bishop's rights. It was a natural outgrowth of the close involvement with the rural environs that had distinguished urban life in Italy since classical antiquity. But the conquests had another dimension. For the cities, desperately needing control over the roads and security of trade, had to secure and pacify the surrounding countryside, and this included preventing strategic localities in their sphere of influence from passing into the power of rival cities. The fact that the Italian cities were growing as centres of overland exchange and that their size made it imperative for them to ensure a regular supply of food also contributed to the perceived need to subordinate the *contado*. Thus most pacts were with nobles whose powers were on the peripheries of the *contado* and controlled border strongholds or castles that could hinder trade. The arrangements required the nobles to submit their lands to the commune, make war or peace at their own expense at its behest, give hospitality twice a year to the city's officials, live in the city for part of the year, and pay a fine or post bond.[106]

The process actually began in the late eleventh century. The emperor Henry IV gave charters in the 1080s to cities that were aiding him against the pope. We shall discuss their significance for urban government in Chapter 5, but they also involved rights outside the cities. The prince guaranteed Pisa's lordship over communities and fortifications on key roads around the city. As a reward for keeping pro-papal Parma from seizing control of the Alpine passes, in 1119 Henry V gave the 'people' of Piacenza in fief the toll at Fiorenzuola, twenty-five kilometres from Piacenza. The emperors' opponents 'fought fire with fire'. In 1098 Countess Matilda invested certain named 'men' of Cremona with 'Fulcher's Island', including the castle of Crema, which had long been disputed between Cremona and solidly imperial Milan. These were to be held for the use of the episcopal church and the commune. She extended the powers of the Florentine commune in the *contado*, where individual Florentines had previously shown little interest, as a

---

105 Krautheimer, *Rome*, 157; Hubert, *Espace urbain*, 189–94, 281–6.
106 Waley, *Orvieto*, 4–5; Ennen, *Frühgeschichte*, 254–5; Haverkamp, 'Städte im Herrschafts- und Sozialgefüge Reichsitaliens', 197.

counterweight to lords who opposed her. By 1090 the countess had delegated the right to collect taxes in the *contado* to the city. After Matilda's death in 1115 most of her powers in rural Tuscany were taken by the cities.[107]

During the half-century of the 'Investiture Contest' the German episcopal cities, whose elite consisted of merchants and ministerials, gained economic privileges, freedom from servile obligations and in some cases the right to participate in regulating markets, mints and tolls (see Chapter 5). But in no case did city regimes get corporate rights of lordship in the rest of the bishop's diocese or the county outside their walls. The Italian cities, by contrast, obtained enough rights of lordship in the *contado* to make it easier for them to encroach on the remaining powers of the bishops and counts.

Thus by the 1120s, by which time the cities had their own governments, their expansion into the *contado* became more direct. The process often took many years. Perugia was gaining the submission of rural villages by 1139, and by 1208 its *contado* included thirty-three communes. Bologna began subjugating its environs in 1116, culminating in the conquest of Imola in 1151. Cremona and Lucca both made substantial gains during the cities' war with Frederick Barbarossa after 1159. The commune of Florence was seizing noble castles by the 1130s.

Pisa illustrates the process well. The emperor Lothair in 1132 gave Pisa all political and juridical rights in specified localities in its *contado*. Frederick Barbarossa rewarded Pisa in 1162 for helping in the siege of Milan by defining its *contado* as an area of between forty-five and ninety kilometres around the city. He gave Pisa complete dominion over the coast between Civitavecchia and Portovenere, together with full civil and criminal jurisdiction over the territories and cities. Pisa divided its *contado* into administrative quarters in the late twelfth century. The villages were generally administered by 'syndics', who were often in fact consuls of Pisa under a different title, and a variety of other officials, judges and arbitrators. There were few noble seigniories (estates with rights of jurisdiction) near the city, for many townspeople had properties there. Incorporation into Pisa's lordship was largely 'organic' and uncontested. Further away, conquest and negotiation were needed.[108]

Florence has been seen as the prototype of a conquest by the city of a backward 'feudal' aristocracy, but it was untypical in the extent to which its elite was little involved in rural landholding before 1100. The

---

107 Haverkamp, 'Städte im Herrschafts- und Sozialgefüge Reichsitaliens', 184–9, 193; Racine, 'Evêque et cité', 138; Dameron, *Episcopal Power and Florentine Society*, 66–7.
108 Volpe, *Studi sulle istituzioni comunale a Pisa*, 1–7, 113–15.

only major rural landowner at Florence was the bishop. Given Florence's pro-papal political stance against the emperor, until the late twelfth century the bishops usually helped the city regime, collecting municipal taxes in some rural locales, providing grain and military service to the city and using castles to help the commune to control roads. The bishop was never the lord of Florence, and perhaps for that reason the movement of the commune into the rural areas was delayed. But during the twelfth century the city gradually made itself the defender of the interests of the bishop in rural Tuscany and, in the course of doing so, required nobles to come to the city. This did not occur at Milan, where the nobles were already urban landowners.[109]

A lengthy debate has raged about the extent to which the *contado* was being exploited by and for the benefit of the city. We shall explore this theme further in later chapters. Before 1200, however, relations between the two seem to have been more symbiotic than even potentially antagonistic. The internal cohesion of the Garfagnana and Casentino area was fostered by extensive landholding of the elites of Arezzo and particularly Lucca even as early as the ninth century. Elsewhere, particularly at Florence and even Milan, most landholding by citizens who were not nobles was near the city. The consolidation of the city regime in the *contado* was thus accomplished in the immediate vicinity by using these properties as juridical footholds, elsewhere in the bishop's diocese by taking over his jurisdictional rights, and on the peripheries by conquering the castles of nobles.[110]

The military expansion of the city governments into the rural areas was followed by the influx of urban capital. Individual landowners and the city councils sponsored public works, notably water mills and canals, and continued investment in land and reclamation. By the late twelfth century, when the emperors were no longer a threat, Milan was building navigable canals and drainage conduits in lower Lombardy, making it more profitable for agriculture. Prompted by a grain shortage, Verona in 1199 reclaimed a marsh in which the commune and several rural villages had a share. The city kept a small portion as pasture for its warhorses and leased the rest to four hundred men, each of whom paid the commune one-tenth of the yield and a cash rent. The government of Pisa gave charters of liberties to villages similar to those granted by princes in northern Europe.

However, the results of urban penetration of rural Tuscany were not

---

109 Dameron, *Episcopal Power and Florentine Society*, 65–7, 72, 76.
110 Wickham, *Mountains and City*, 131–4. Dameron, *Episcopal Power and Florentine Society*, 8.

entirely beneficial. Wealth and jurisdictional rights were moving to the city. Some urban landowners were reimposing servile obligations on their peasant tenants by the late twelfth century. Free immigration to the city was not permitted to *contadini*. At the end of the twelfth century Pisa provoked a revolt by imposing a salt quota on its *contado*, to be purchased through the city. Indirect taxes on village and castle populations had become property taxes before the mid-twelfth century. There were disturbances in the Pisan *contado* in 1164 and 1169 against the consuls.[111]

Even as urban penetration of the *contado* became more intense in the twelfth century, a social separation was also in process. Rural populations were clearly understood as being under a different legal regime from those who lived in the city proper. A text of 1117 has captains, valvassors and people (*populus*) understood as citizens, but particularly after 1150 such terms as 'inhabitant' and 'citizen' were being used to distinguish persons who lived in the city as those who enjoyed the special status of citizen, either by swearing an oath to the commune or by inheriting it from parents. In texts describing the subjection of the *contado* by the new communes in the twelfth century, 'citizen' is often used in distinction to 'knight', while within the city 'nobles' and 'commoners' were separated. When 'people' and 'citizens' were distinguished within the city, the 'citizens' were the more influential politically.[112]

MINISTERIAL ELITE OR COMMERCIAL PATRICIATE?

The urban elites of the eleventh century were thus nobles, joined in Italy by knights and valvassors and in Germany and the Low Countries by ministerials, who were technically unfree persons who held offices and often fiefs from the town lords. Although many eventually entered the nobility, most early urban ministerials were from the lower echelons of the group: tollkeepers, dependants of ecclesiastical foundations and minor officials. Merchants and craftsmen were rarely in city elites before the twelfth century. But after 1100 commercial wealth became increasingly powerful, gradually weakening the older ministerial families even though many merchants invested in land.

Urban populations were juridically diverse. The archbishop of Mainz gave a privilege to the city before 1135 on the advice of clergy, 'counts'

111 Volpe, *Studi sulle istituzioni comunale a Pisa*, 113–21, 128–9; Luzzatto, *Economic History*, 95; Hyde, *Society and Politics*, 76; Haverkamp, 'Städte im Herrschafts- und Sozialgefüge Reichsitaliens', 200, 232.

112 Dilcher, 'Comuni italiani', 77–8; Keller, 'Soziale und politische Verfassung Mailands', 39–40, 41–3.

(probably the family of the burgrave, conceivably ministerials), citizens (probably both merchants and ministerials), freemen and *familia* (dependants of the archbishop), both free and unfree.[113] Ministerials were distinguished from the rest of the citizenry in some cities. While the tenth-century treaties of Genoa with nobles of its *contado* had obliged the nobles to make Genoese marriages for their children as long as this could be done without derogation of status, Lübeck forbade daughters of burgesses to marry nobles. More often the ministerials had special privileges but were nonetheless citizens. Most of them preferred to be judged at the court of the town lord, not the court that he had been obliged to permit the burgesses for themselves. As early as 1101 the ministerials of Speyer were given the right to be judged at the episcopal court, not in the *forum* or according to 'public law'. Citizenship might also deprive ministerials of the financial benefits of service to the town lord. In 1182 the emperor ruled that the church of Worms and its 'ministers' did not have to contribute to the tax that the city owed him.[114]

The landowning aristocrats of medieval Novgorod, called boyars, display functional similarities to the ministerials of the German cities, but they kept their power much longer and lacked the ministerials' servile ancestry. Most of the population of Novgorod lived on one of the approximately four hundred 'urban estates' owned by boyars. Their domination was facilitated by the fact that they had estates throughout Novgorod, not simply in or near a central citadel as tended to occur in the west European cities. Some boyars were in the entourage of the prince of Novgorod, who was forced to live outside the city in 1136 and exercised a purely nominal overlordship thereafter. Some boyars became long-distance merchants, although most operated indirectly, selling the raw materials from their estates to professional merchants. The boyars also loaned money, suggestive of the later control of minting by ministerial families in the Rhineland cities. The boyars controlled the general assembly of Novgorod, the *veche*, and monopolised offices in the individual quarters of the city.[115]

The notion that the first medieval urban elites were ministerial or other noble landholders is based on newer works that have modified the emphasis that Pirenne, Planitz and their disciples gave to long-distance traders. Yet the example of Novgorod shows that the two views are not

113 Opll, *Stadt und Reich*, 152–3.
114 Opll, *Stadt und Reich*, 115; Keutgen, *Urkunden*, nos. 11, 13, pp. 6–7; Ennen, *Frühgeschichte*, 260.
115 Langer, 'Medieval Russian town', 29; Goehrke, 'Novgorod', 359–62; Birnbaum, *Studies*, 177.

mutually exclusive. Municipal elites were never closed in the twelfth century and only rarely in the thirteenth; and landowners sold the products of their estates, while merchants bought real estate as an investment and for the social status that landownership conveyed.

Cologne, which would become one of the greatest commercial and industrial cities of Europe, illustrates the problem of a rigid 'class' analysis. Although it had some industry, the wealth of medieval Cologne was in trade. A merchant guild probably existed by 959, but many merchants did not belong to it. The rebellion of Cologne against its archbishop in 1074 is alleged by a chronicler to have been led by 'six hundred of the richest merchants', implying that there were more. He seems to equate townsmen with merchants and artisans and does not mention ministerials or landowners as a separate group. Yet other sources show that landowning was a major indicator of social distinction and economic prosperity through the twelfth century.

The agendas of extended families are the key to understanding medieval urban elites. Merchants of Cologne intermarried with noble and ministerial families to improve their social position, but they also married into other merchant lines. Although most twelfth-century patricians of Cologne founded no lasting dynasty, at least eight prominent families of the thirteenth and fourteenth centuries had origins in the twelfth. Many of the Cologne elite of the twelfth century were ministerials. Gerhard Ungemaz [Immoderate] made his fortune in property, particularly rents and foreclosures in the central parishes of the city, and by serving as the archbishop's tollkeeper, which provided an easy transition into moneylending. He was called 'master of the senates' in 1171 and was an official of the *Richerzeche* (Rich Club) that ruled the city after 1180. 'Werner', the ancestor of the Jude family, was a tollkeeper and ministerial, and his sons were *scabini* (members of the lord's court). He owned residences near the city centre, market stalls, granaries, bakehouses, gardens and rural land. Most land speculation was in the outlying parishes of the city, which were still partly agricultural in the twelfth century, but this land became more profitable as it was brought into the urban complex. Of four elite families that did not hold public office until the early thirteenth century, only two came from a mainly merchant background, and even they owned some land, including rural property.[116]

Arras shows an even more striking persistence of patrician lineages than does Cologne. Landowning was the constituent element of the

---

116 Discussion based on Strait, *Cologne*, 14–21, 27–8, 81–5, 90–1, 100–3, 112–13, 118–19, 121–7. On the Rich Club and the *scabini*, see Chapter 5.

patriciate, but more of Arras's elite expanded early into moneylending. Some member of the Lanstier family was in the magistracy of Arras from 1111 until 1450. The elite maintained kin ties among themselves and in neighbouring villages. Mathieu Lanstier found stealing from the city treasury more profitable than rents. He seized inheritances and forced rich orphans to marry into his family. The Huquedieu, initially officers of the abbey of St Vaast, became moneylenders and rentiers. The moneylenders of Arras, notably the richest of them, the Crespins, were without exception also landowners in the city.[117]

The link among landowning, ministerial and servile status, and expansion into long-distance trade is usually veiled, but several texts elucidate it. A charter of 1069 for Toul, near Metz, exempted 'citizens' from the toll on salt taken from foreigners. The beneficiaries were dependants of the cathedral chapter who used it to further their own trading interests. Some years later the emperor ruled that 'public merchants' of Liège, even if they were dependants of the cathedral chapter, were subject to 'market justice'. In 1182 the imperial court freed the servants of the cathedral chapter of Worms from some taxes on condition that they did not engage in commerce nor enter the chapter's service merely to avoid taxes. 'Definite and public merchants' were excluded from this exemption. The bishop of Toul in the same year confirmed the judicial and fiscal immunity of the dependants of the local chapter, except that 'the men of the chapter who are merchants will be bound at fairs and market days to answer those to whom other merchants answer in matters concerning commerce, but only in that. Neither the citizens of Toul nor other persons may hinder the men of the chapter from becoming merchants'. A charter forged around 1160 at Liège placed the ministerials of the church of St Servatius under the 'civil law' or the 'judges of the city' only if they were 'public merchants'.[118]

Thus servants of cathedral chapters in the Empire, even if they were merchants, gained tax exemption through the churches' immunity privileges for most of the twelfth century. This was being limited at the end of the twelfth century, precisely when the newer, non-ministerial 'merchant patricians' were gaining political influence at the expense of the landowning patriciate by forming the city council in opposition to the town lord's court, the *scabini* (see Chapter 5). But the escape clause of the earlier charters show that ministerials, who were exempt from toll, gained an early advantage over other merchants who lacked links to the cathedral chapters and accordingly had to pay.

117 Lestocquoy, *Dynasties bourgeoises d'Arras*, 14–80.
118 Schneider, 'Toul', 185–6; Van de Kieft, 'Städte im niederländischen Raum', 160–1.

GUILDS AND SOCIAL ORGANISATION

The early guilds: landowners and merchants

A guild is a group of persons, generally bound by oath, who enjoy the right to regulate an aspect of their corporate behaviour that poses special problems or concerns. Guilds thus assumed many forms. We have seen that the ancient occupational *collegia* may have continued in some Italian centres into the seventh century. Thereafter the only evidence of occupational organisations, as distinct from occupations merely being practised, in the Italian cities before the twelfth century is from a single document concerning Pavia and Milan, and the fishermen's *schola* of Ravenna in 943. All other early references to urban guilds are northern. Canterbury had a guild of *cnihtas*, aristocratic landowners, by the 860s, London in the tenth century, and Cambridge and London had guilds of thegns before 1066. Since thegns and *cnihtas* were landowners, these organisations have caused some to argue that the English cities were retrograde. Yet royal statutes of the eleventh century provided that when three generations of merchants were able to travel abroad three times at their own expense, they and their descendants became thegns. The urban guilds of thegns could easily have been such merchants, particularly in view of other evidence of merchant guilds in England in the late eleventh century.[119]

Comparison with Scandinavia is instructive. There *kundsgilden* included merchants, farmers and warriors in the late twelfth century but gradually evolved toward purely merchant associations.[120] Another suggestion of the link between thegnhood and trade is found at Oxford. Of 946 houses in the city in 1086, 225 were 'mural mansions', which were attached to shire manors (215 of them held by royal tenants-in-chief) and were responsible for maintaining sections of the city wall. Although this arrangement is a survival of the military obligations of the Alfredian *burhs*, the mural mansions at Oxford were probably town houses of thegns whose motive for being in the city would have been to market the produce of their rural estates.[121]

The *cnihtengild* of London had corporate possession of the court jurisdiction outside Aldgate, which had passed by 1137 to Holy Trinity Priory, and exercised jurisdiction over its members wherever they were. The guildhall of London, which is first mentioned in 1127, was adjacent to a royal property, like that at Winchester. The king still owned

---

119 Urry, *Canterbury*, 124; Bullough, 'Social and economic structure and topography', 368.
120 Nyberg, 'Gilden', 29–40.
121 Salter, *Medieval Oxford*, 22–3, 43–5.

it as late as 1228, but the municipal Husting court was meeting there by the late twelfth century. Dover had a 'guildhall of the burgesses' in 1086, while the *cnihtas* of Winchester had a hall where they 'drank their guild'. Post-Conquest Winchester had at least four guilds with halls. They were apparently religious, social or convivial organisations, since no connection with an occupational group can be proven. The Easter guild in the western suburb may have evolved into the merchant guild, first mentioned in 1155. The merchants' guildhall was on the site where the city court of Winchester eventually met.[122] The merchant guild of Canterbury contained *cnihtas*, suggesting that the ninth-century guild had become the merchant organisation of the eleventh, and was presided over by the royal portreeve. It owned real estate by 1100. A borough guild existed by Henry II's time, but whether it was new or a renaming of the old guild is unclear.[123]

The ties of the guilds of *cnihtas* to guilds of merchants and to the city governments explain why merchant guilds gained political influence in some larger English cities in the late eleventh or twelfth century, earlier than on the continent. In contrast to the merchant guilds that came to dominate the cities of northern France and Flanders, however, the English guilds were organisations of local monopolists whose interest in long-distance trade was only in importing goods to sell on the local market.[124]

The volume of evidence is compelling. By 1200 merchant guilds are found in six seigniorial and twenty-three royal boroughs. The list includes virtually all true cities and some smaller towns. Many of them evidently go back to the early Norman period. Lewes had a merchant guild by 1088. King Stephen confirmed one to Chichester 'as in the days of [his] grandfather', William I (1066–87). The merchant guild of Burford in 1107 was the first in England to receive a charter that has survived, but it then received the liberties of the 'guild of merchants' of Oxford, whose statutes were granted by Henry I (1100–35). Henry's charter may thus have been recognition after the fact.[125]

Initially all citizens were in the merchant guild, though some guilds included outsiders. In excluding some groups of inhabitants from membership the guilds were in effect barring them from citizenship. This was the case with artisans in many places in the twelfth century. The merchant guild of Oxford contained fewer than half the city's residents,

---

122 Brooke and Keir, *London*, 35–6; Loyn, 'Towns', 123; Urry, *Canterbury*, 125–6; Biddle, *Winchester*, 498, 427, 463.
123 Hilton, *English and French Towns*, 94–5; Urry, *Canterbury*, 105, 126–9; Nightingale, *Medieval Mercantile Community*, 46.
124 Hilton, *English and French Towns*, 91–2; Rubin, *Cambridge*, 36–8.
125 Miller and Hatcher, *Towns, Commerce and Crafts*, 290–2.

and some of its members were non-residents. In 1200 the corporate seal of Gloucester read 'seal of the burgesses of the guild of merchants'. Gloucester also received the liberties given to Winchester in 1190, in which guild membership was the prerequisite of citizenship. Leicester's first guild charter, a confirmation of the terms of William I, is somewhat different. Membership gave exemption from some tolls and a monopoly of trading inside the borough. Not all burgesses were members of the guild, and some guild brothers were not residents of Leicester. Yet the merchant guild was not aristocratic. About two hundred persons were admitted between 1196 and 1223, including a villein, cooks, bakers, merchants and dyers. Thus in England, in contrast to France, the merchant guild did not consist only of wholesalers, but also retailers who sold the goods that they made.[126]

The merchant guild of Southampton, which existed by the time of Henry I, required members to attend biannual guild meetings, which lasted for several days. The guild was a peace association, handling quarrels among members, and provided charity and burials for indigent members. The franchise of the city was not restricted to guildsmen; however, persons who enjoyed it but were not in the guild were imprisoned and lost the franchise for injuring a guild brother. Membership usually descended to the eldest son; but although it might be purchased, it could not be obtained by marriage. Guildsmen were to share goods available for purchase with other members and had a right of first refusal of items offered for sale in the town. They had a monopoly on tavern-keeping, retail cloth sales, and the purchase of honey, fat, herring, oil, millstones, hides and skins. They controlled the grain trade, for only guildsmen could store more than five quarters of grain for retail sales. They shared exemption from local tolls and customs with all who enjoyed the franchise. The guild had officers and a treasury. Although Southampton did not have a communal movement in the twelfth century, the guild had the organisational apparatus needed to form a town government.[127]

The economic and governmental aspects of the merchant guilds are shown in a case of 1304 from Bury St Edmunds. The abbot as town lord complained that a syndicate had been extracting payments from other townsfolk. They did not deny his allegation but said that they had a legally recognised merchant guild, which would have a customary right to these payments. Although their claim was disallowed, these

---

126 Lobel, *Historic Towns* 1: 4–5; Simmons, *Leicester*, 26–7; Miller and Hatcher, *Towns, Commerce and Crafts*, 292–5.
127 Platt, *Medieval Southampton*, 17–19.

are good indications of what merchant guilds could ordinarily do. The defendants took 'hansing silver' from all persons in the town, with the amount depending on the value of the payer's chattels. Thus they were trying to force all inhabitants of the town to join their organisation. They were in effect acting as a town government, for they had 'decreed among themselves that no man should stay in the aforesaid town beyond a year and a day without being distrained to take oath to maintain their aforesaid assemblies and ordinances', evidently without regard to whether they had joined the guild. Twelve burgesses of the town had been accustomed to elect 'four men of the same town yearly to keep their gild merchant, each of whom shall have chattels to the value of 10 marks'. The guild had an alderman and a guildhall. The aldermen of the guild and burgesses of the town had 'been accustomed to distrain every man in the same town having chattels to the value of 10 marks, wishing to trade among them and to enjoy their market customs. And thus each of the aforesaid four men so elected should enjoy burgess-ship among them'; thus only members of the merchant guild enjoyed citizenship in the town.[128]

The guildsmen's monopoly of trading in the borough was meaningless outside their home towns, where others enjoyed the same monopolies. The authorities were concerned not only with the monopoly of the guildsmen, but also with ensuring adequate provisions for the city. Suburban residents engaged in forestalling, buying from merchants en route to the city market, saving them the problem of city tolls and a more extended trip, then selling in the city and hurting the trade of urban merchants. Cities as diverse as London and Arles prohibited forestalling but seemed powerless to stop it.[129]

Some charters, generally those incorporating towns rather than establishing or confirming existing merchant guilds (Dublin and Bristol are exceptions), confer the local merchandising monopoly on the burgesses at large. Thus the charter of Newcastle-upon-Tyne, which had no merchant guild until 1216, gave the burgesses a monopoly of buying wool, leather or cloth within the borough. This privilege was called 'freedom of the borough' in places lacking a merchant guild. The majority of inhabitants of most English towns were thus not 'free', for freedom of the borough had to be bought or gained through membership in the guild.[130]

128 Summarised and quoted from Bland, Brown and Tawney, *English Economic History. Select Documents*, 128–30.

129 Britnell, *Commercialisation of English Society*, 27, 73–4; Agus, *Urban Civilization* 1: 215.

130 Ballard, *British Borough Charters*, lxx; Salter, *Medieval Oxford*, 33–5; Hilton, *English and French Towns*, 92.

Merchant guilds in Germany and the Low Countries

On the continent, Cologne had a merchant guild by 1070, Arras and Ghent in the late eleventh century, Bruges in 1113. They were protective groups, binding merchants from the same town to mutual assistance in necessary travel outside the home city. They were not established to regulate market or employment conditions.[131]

The earliest surviving statutes of a medieval merchant guild are those of the 'Charity' of Valenciennes, originally given just after 1066, with new provisions added around 1120. It was principally a charitable and peace association of merchants, although it could exercise coercive justice in some actions between guildsmen. The guild held festivals and drinking rituals, especially honouring St Nicholas, the patron saint of merchants, and guaranteed decent interment for its members. Guild brothers swore to leave the city armed (probably travelling in caravan to the fairs), to stay together for at least three days in case of need, and to contribute as much as possible to fines levied on a brother in foreign territory. A provost was the chief officer of the Charity, which also had mayors and a minister and chancellor.[132]

Slightly later statutes survive from the guild of Saint-Omer, but the terms suggest that they had been in force for some time. Called a merchant guild in the eleventh century, it fostered 'common utility' by maintaining the streets, gates and town wall. The guild provided relief for the poor and lepers and restricted the right to bear arms in the city. A foreigner had to leave his weapons at the gate and only retrieve them when he left or found someone, presumably a kinsman or business partner, who would vouch for his peaceful intentions. The guild helped members on their travels and gave them the right to pre-empt sales on the market of Saint-Omer. Yet knights and clerks could also be admitted, and most clauses concern devotion and charity. The fact that the city *échevins* met in the merchants' hall and that the guild had peace-keeping and administrative functions creates a strong presumption that the city government of Saint-Omer evolved directly from the guild, but most scholars reject this view on the technical grounds that the hall was the property of the count of Flanders until 1157.[133]

The charter given to the residents of Saint-Omer in 1127 guaranteed the merchants 'their guild', evidently referring to toll exemptions outside the city. In court proceedings members of the Flemish guilds were

---

131 Duby, *Early Growth*, 241; Ennen, 'Städtewesen Nordwestdeutschlands', 189–90.
132 Platelle, *Histoire de Valenciennes*, 26–7; Blockmans, 'Société urbanisée', 66.
133 Derville, *Histoire de Saint-Omer*, 45; Chédeville, 'Cité à ville', 131; Monier, *Institutions judiciaires*, 82–4.

believed on their own word; others had to have two witnesses. Guildsmen could also certify documents. The major difference from England is that the French and Flemish charters never give a monopoly of trade in the city either to the burgesses as a whole or to the merchant guild, and usually give less comprehensive immunity from toll than do the English charters.[134]

The numerous places in Germany whose merchants received trading privileges probably had merchant guilds, for their rights presuppose an organisation; for example, the merchants of Duisburg had 'elders' in 1155. In 1105 the bishop of Halberstadt gave judicial power to the town merchants for 'themselves or those whom they wanted to represent them'. Merchant guilds can also be confirmed before 1200 in Soest, Schleswig, Bremen, Magdeburg, Dortmund, Goslar, Naumburg and Minden.[135]

It has been argued that the merchant guild at Cologne, like that of Saint-Omer, was the germ cell of the sworn association of the commune, with its chief officer, the 'provost of the merchants', as the leader of the townspeople against the archbishop. The officers of the guild of the parish of St Martin were simultaneously the government of the *Wik*. But membership lists show that although members were generally admitted simultaneously to the parish guild and the merchant guild, and the same prominent people often held offices simultaneously in each, they were not a single organisation. The fact that merchant law was originally personal rather than territorial strengthens the argument that some city governments originated in parish associations rather than sworn occupational fraternities.[136]

Merchant guilds in France and Italy

Evidence is much scarcer for France. Rouen had a merchant guild in the early twelfth century, but it is not mentioned in John's charter of 1199. A text refers to the customs that the 'Merchants of the Water' of Paris enjoyed under Louis VI (1108–37). This guild had a monopoly of Seine commerce except around Rouen, whose guild had a similar local privilege. In 1141 Louis VII gave the merchants control of the 'Old Market' at the Place de Grève. As it became the major market of Paris, their local powers were extended.[137]

134 van Uytven, 'Stadsgeschiedenis', 217; Wyffels, 'Hanse', 4; Blockmans, 'Société urbanisée', 67; Ballard, *British Borough Charters*, cxv.

135 Planitz, *Deutsche Stadt*, 76–7; Frölich, 'Kaufmannsgilden', 18–19; Berthold, 'Köln', 236.

136 Planitz, *Deutsche Stadt*, 70, 78; Ennen, *Frühgeschichte*, 166–73; Strait, *Cologne*, 60; on the merchant law, see Chapter 5.

137 Mollat, *Rouen*, 68; Boussard, *Paris*, 162.

Some Italian cities in the twelfth century were developing merchant organisations with their own officials to judge infractions of commercial regulations. Milan, whose artisan organisations are relatively late, had 'consuls of the merchants' by 1159, and they were involved in town government by 1177. The 'association of the merchants' had its tribunal by the early thirteenth century. Artisan guilds precede merchant guilds in Italy, perhaps because the urban economies were so locally based until the twelfth century, when the opening of trade routes to the Champagne fairs gave them a market for the luxuries that were coming from the east.[138]

Craft guilds

England References to craft organisations are rare in the northern cities before the twelfth century. Fewer statutes have survived than for merchant guilds, but most were at least as concerned with charity and devotions as with quality control or market monopolies. While the merchant guild officers did not usually become the city council on the continent, they often did in England, with royal cooperation. But the English kings were more hostile to craft organisations than were most continental princes. They considered them subversive, particularly weavers' guilds. Although craft guilds seem to have been widespread before 1200, they declined and in the thirteenth century gained political power officially only in London.

The Domesday Book mentions 'cobblers and drapers' of Canterbury jointly paying a fee to the king, while a twelfth-century rent-roll records 'land of the smiths' guild'. England was developing a significant textile industry in the twelfth century, and most substantial towns had one or more clothmaking guilds. By 1130 the king was collecting fees from guilds of weavers and bakers at London, weavers and millers at Winchester, weavers at York, Nottingham, Huntingdon and Lincoln, and weavers and cordwainers (makers of cordovan leather) at Oxford. Monopoly is implicit, for the payment to the king gave these artisans exclusive rights to practise their trade in the town and, in some cases, its rural hinterland. The charter of the weavers of Oxford permitted them to compel all weavers within a five-mile radius of the city to join their guild. Henry I gave the weavers' guild of Nottingham a monopoly of working dyed cloth within ten leagues of the city. But the authorities were wary. From John's time the king rather than local authorities authorised craft guilds. Before 1200 weavers and fullers were generally

138 Mazzi, 'Milano', 399–400, 408–9.

denied the freedom of the borough. At Marlborough they were required to sell to the merchants of the town rather than directly to foreign buyers.[139]

Nineteen illegal guilds in London were fined in 1179. All had their own aldermen, and seven were identified only by the alderman's name. The goldsmiths, pepperers (later called grocers, the only purely merchant organisation of the nineteen), clothmakers and butchers were named, as was a guild of foreigners, probably merchants living in London. Cordwainers had a guild in Oxford and glovers, hosiers, saddlers and curriers in York. Guilds were declared illegal in several other towns at this time, but the nature of their organisation is not stated.[140]

Italy   While merchant organisations might develop to control either a local or long-distance market, craft guilds usually did not evolve before a place had either an enormous local market, as for construction- and leatherworkers, or was developing an export industry. Except for coastal places, notably Genoa, long-distance trade continued into the twelfth century to be less important for the Italian urban economies than local town–countryside ties. Lucca was the only Italian city with a major export industry in the twelfth century (silk), and it did not employ many people. These considerations may explain the relatively late development of craft guilds in Italy.[141]

Religious brotherhoods provided a model for some of the earliest occupational guilds, to which professional statutes were appended later, as in southern France; further north most fraternities postdated the appearance of the crafts with which they were associated. The statutes of the cobblers of Ferrara in 1112 expressly used those of religious brotherhoods as models. They punished interfering with the business of a brother, and specifically enticing away journeymen or apprentices. They also pledged mutual help before the courts. Rome had organisations of metalworkers, vegetable sellers, farmers, Tiber shippers, cobblers, sandal sellers and gardeners. An eight-person branch of the gardeners had its own statutes. They owned land, chose a prior, had a guild court and common treasury and made rules for their trade.[142]

139 Urry, *Canterbury*, 132; Salter, *Medieval Oxford*, 31–2; Ballard, *British Borough Charters*, lxx; Lobel, *Atlas* 1: 3; Hilton, *English and French Towns*, 69–70; Urry, *Canterbury*, 132; Miller and Hatcher, *Towns, Commerce and Crafts*, 104–6.
140 Bland, Brown and Tawney, *English Economic History. Select Documents*, 115–16; Hilton, *English and French Towns*, 70; Nightingale, *Medieval Mercantile Community*, 43.
141 Haverkamp, 'Städte im Herrschafts- und Sozialgefüge Reichsitaliens', 204.
142 Tirelli, 'Lucca', 183; Mickwitz, *Kartellfunktionen*, 36–8; Hilton, *English and French Towns*, 74; Ennen, *Frühgeschichte*, 235–7.

By 1200 virtually all cities of northern Italy had several artisan guilds that were clearly organisations of masters without a necessary link to a devotional fraternity. Verona, Cremona and Bologna had such associations of masters before 1150 in a form resembling the ancient *collegia*. Ravenna had *scholae* of fishermen, merchants and butchers. The emperors and municipal authorities alike were sometimes suspicious of such organisations. The imperial charter of 1162 to Pisa obliged the city magistrates to extirpate the 'companies of citizens and villeins' that they knew had been formed 'against the commune's honour', a designation that a text of 1164 gives to organisations of stone workers and tilers. Guilds of furriers, leatherworkers and builders appeared at Pisa in the 1190s. Some early Tuscan craft guilds appear to have originated, as we have seen in Lombardy, in trades that produced mainly for the court of the local prince. The viscount of Pisa, as heir of the Lombard *gastaldus*, had control of the weight, ovens, wine trade, and all crafts; this control passed to the city consuls in the twelfth century.[143] These seigniorial rights of some town lords were assumed by the municipal governments. Members of the construction guilds of Venice were obligated to work on public buildings. At Piacenza the bishop required labour of the millers and bakers and rented stalls to the butchers. Verona had a 'greater guild' with officers and organisations of butchers and fishmongers. The emperor named his own officials as guild leaders.[144]

The tremendous surge of population in the second half of the twelfth century, resulting in a greater division of labour, led to the formation of more craft associations, many of them with a neighbourhood base. The moneychangers of Lucca already had an organisation by 1111, the millers by the end of the century. Four separate wood trades of that city had their own guilds by 1200 (the stonemasons, wallers, carpenters and cartwrights).

France The magisterial works of André Gouron have elucidated the history of craft organisations in southern France. He distinguishes between regulated occupational guilds and the charitable fraternities that gave birth to some of them. Provence shows few artisan organisations before 1200, probably because nobles dominated city governments, but thereafter they grew rapidly. Marseilles had seventy crafts by 1243, one hundred by 1255. Thirty-five guilds were in the government of Arles in 1247.[145]

---

143 Volpe, *Studi sulle istituzioni comunale a Pisa*, 3–4, 236, 263, 302; Fasoli *et al.*, 'Struttura sociale', 306.

144 Mickwitz, *Kartellfunktionen*, 18–22, 28–9.

145 Gouron, *Réglementation des métiers*, 37–9; Lesage, *Marseille angevine*, 39–40.

Craft organisations emerged earlier in Languedoc, where they developed with the cooperation of the fledgling city governments and their princes, who used the guilds to collect taxes and enforce standards of production. The statutes of Toulouse show a minute attention to regulating trades, especially the foodmongers. The earliest guilds mentioned were the cordwainers of Toulouse (1158); the moneychangers of Saint-Gilles (statutes from 1176); the dyers of Montpellier; the masons, carpenters, fishmongers, butchers and wood dealers of Toulouse (1181); and the masons of Nîmes (1187), who received privileges in return for work on the city walls. By the early thirteenth century seventy-two craft guilds, some burgesses and the advocates and notaries took it in turns to be responsible for each day's defence of the gates of Montpellier. But the craftsmen were rarely on city councils this early except at Montpellier, where the moneychangers and drapers each chose two of the twelve consuls after 1204. Nine other guilds, one of them the 'labourers', also had political rights.[146]

Paris was unusual in having both a merchant guild and strong craft organisations, fostered by the royal government as a way to control quality and collect taxes. The victualling trades were the earliest organised crafts, beginning with the butchers in 1146 and the fishmongers in 1154; evidence of other crafts at Paris is after 1200. Philip Augustus in 1182 confirmed the butchers' customs, notably a monopoly over the sale of meat and a central abbatoir at the Chatelet where sales could be controlled.[147]

Evidence from other French cities suggests that occupational groups were becoming large and sophisticated enough to have group consciousness. Except in Flanders leatherworkers developed occupational differentiation earlier than did woollen clothmakers. At Rouen the cobblers had a guild in the early twelfth century, while the tanners were given a charter prohibiting anyone not in the guild from working in or within a league of the city. Chartres had a Tanners' Street along the Eure, and texts distinguish tanners, cordwainers, shoemakers, skinners, saddlers and harnessmakers. Streets named after the cordwainers, feltmakers, saddlers and cobblers appeared in the twelfth century in the lower town, the artisan quarter.[148]

Although some of these are simply occupations that may or may not have had organisations, the tavernkeepers of Chartres had a guild by 1147 with 'masters' who were probably appointed by the count. The

146 Gouron, *Réglementation des métiers*, 39, 47, 52–8.
147 Boussard, *Paris*, 162–4, 168, 301.
148 Chédeville, *Histoire de Chartres*, 80, 124; Chédeville, 'Cité à ville', 116.

furriers also had a guild before 1200. The king also appointed a master of the bakers of Pontoise when he gave the guild a sale monopoly in 1162. At Bourges, Beauvais, Châlons and Toul, all of them in the Paris basin, one or more trades had masters in the twelfth century. The earliest craft statutes in northern France are for the smiths of Caen before 1180, but only the last two clauses address professional concerns; the rest are charitable.[149]

The Low Countries and Germany Despite the early industrialisation of the Low Country cities, they lacked legally recognised occupational craft associations until the late thirteenth century, although Arras had craft-based religious brotherhoods of tailors, minters and cloth shearers.[150] Evidence is stronger in Germany. The fishmongers of Worms were the first attested craft guild in an episcopal city of the upper Rhine. In 1106 the bishop gave twenty-three named fishermen the hereditary right to practise their profession and included a monopoly on the resale of fish within the town area. Those who died without heirs would be replaced by the city community. At Strasbourg the burgrave had jurisdiction over eleven trades and chose their masters. Nothing is known of their organisation or monopolies. Craft guilds are only attested later at Speyer and Basel.[151]

Further north, the cushion weavers of Cologne received statutes in 1149 and the turners in 1180. The weavers were to share shops on the market with the linen weavers, so both groups were probably organised. The wool weavers in 1230 and the cloth wholesalers were called fraternities in 1247, so they probably had organisations before that date. Mainz had a religious fraternity of weavers by 1175, by which time craftsmen occupied some lower city offices. The minters were already an important guild, often ministerials of the archbishop. The minters of Worms were given their own court for civil cases in 1165 and were freed from the obligation to serve in other municipal offices.[152]

Craft statutes, quality control and regulation of the market

Scarcely any craft organisation outside Italy drafted its own statutes before the thirteenth century, for most lacked the right to compel all practitioners of their trades to join the guild. Without such a privilege, which does

149 Mickwitz, *Kartellfunktionen*, 77, 80, 91; Chédeville, 'Cité à ville', 119.
150 van Uytven, 'Stadsgeschiedenis', 210; Mickwitz, *Kartellfunktionen*, 96.
151 Dollinger, 'Oberrheinische Bischofsstädte', 142; the Worms text is translated in Herlihy, *Medieval Culture and Society*, 185.
152 Strait, *Cologne*, 62, 70–1; Berthold, 'Köln', 240–1; Falck, *Mainz*, 161; Opll, *Stadt und Reich*, 175.

not preclude competition between brothers within the guild, regulation of quality and price could only hurt those who were subjected to them. Although merchant guilds customarily had such privileges, Louis VII of France was the first prince who gave many of them to craftsmen. Thus the earliest craft organisations were regulated by the city governments and town lords, not by themselves. Basic to this were public control of weights and measures and protection of the consumer by regulating prices, profits and quality.[153]

Weight-and-measure legislation at the turn of the thirteenth century in France affected mainly sellers of food and beverages, not makers of goods for export. Public measures were placed at convenient spots on the market and in the main streets. In return for the craft organisations' cooperation in quality control, the authorities gave them monopolies over sales of their specialities or provision of their services. The consuls of Toulouse held an inquest in 1184 about the quality of meat and allegations of collusive profiteering by various associations of butchers. They prohibited societies of more than two persons in the trade except among family members. Innkeepers, who dispensed food retail to their guests, could not bake their own small bread, but had to use the public weights furnished them by the bakers and keep duplicates of the public measures for wine in their establishments.[154] Muslim Seville controlled weights and measures of food and of bricks and other construction materials. Sanitation measures for food were precisely specified. Each guild was assigned a specific place on the market in front of the mosque, but street markets were used for legumes and fruits.[155]

Merchants thus became increasingly powerful economically in the twelfth-century cities, particularly as ministerials and nobles used their commercial exemptions to gain advantages in the growing local and interregional trades. Craftsmen entered the urban areas in increasing numbers. Most produced for the increased local demand, but Europe was now producing some industrial goods that could compete in a wider market.

The twelfth century also witnessed the emergence of governments in most large cities that were semi-independent of their lords. Although merchants played some role in these regimes, the ministerial element remained strong and the craftsmen were largely absent. Our next chapter thus examines the political side of the movement toward urban autonomy whose economic aspect has been discussed in this chapter.

153 Mickwitz, *Kartellfunktionen*, 8–9.
154 Gouron, *Réglementation des métiers*, 58–64.
155 Lévi-Provençale, *Séville musulmane*, xxiii, 74–85, 95, 118, 120.

CHAPTER FIVE

Urban Law and Government in the Eleventh and Twelfth Centuries

Lords and corporations: the beginnings of urban government in northern Europe

Virtually all cities had governments before a charter formalised their rights, but they functioned alongside the city lord's officials. The first municipal governments were courts, but they quickly either acquired administrative functions or were joined by other bodies that did. Although by 1200 most cities had the right to judge cases involving their citizens, and at least some financial independence, few outside Italy had broadened the right to judge into a right to legislate.

Some English cities had governments before the Norman Conquest. Exeter had a *witan* or council in 1018. Hereditary 'lawmen' functioned as borough courts in the Danelaw, with jurisdiction over persons and land and enjoying 'custom' as income. Cambridge, Lincoln and Stamford still had 'lawmen' in 1086, while Chester and York had 'judges'. York, which had a large Scandinavian population, had 'portmen' and 'burhmen' in 1069, but this may have ended during the rebellions against William I.[1]

Even in the tenth century London had a thrice-yearly 'borough court' or folkmoot (*burhgemot*) consisting of all citizens. This conclave continued to function into the twelfth century, but policy was in the hands of smaller groups of 'judges' who met indoors and were presided over by the king's reeve. This assembly was being called 'husting' by the period of Danish rule in the early eleventh century, when it had become an assembly of ward representatives called 'aldermen'. The husting was probably the municipal council that assisted in drafting the customs of London that were incorporated into royal statutes of the early eleventh century.

---

1 Tait, *Medieval English Borough*, 42, 124; Tillott, *City of York*, 12, 18, 21; Darby, *Domesday England*, 294; Hill, *Lincoln*, 38–40.

William I then agreed to respect the laws and customs that the city had enjoyed in the Confessor's time.[2]

Canterbury's charter of 1155 is more detailed. It gave the same procedural guarantees as the London charter and added that the borough court would meet bi-weekly. Property conveyances were published in both borough and ward courts. Security of tenure, protection against unpaid debt and freedom from manorial duties were guaranteed, and actions concerning lands, tenures and pledges would be handled according to the custom of the city. Canterbury thus had extensive self-government and a custom that goes back at least to the time of Henry I.[3]

Although most cities on the continent had magistrates by the eleventh century and virtually all gained them in the twelfth, most north of the Loire initially had courts staffed by dependants of the town lord called *scabini* (Fr. *échevins*, Germ. *Schöffen*, Fl. *scepenen*). These officials were judges and assessors, but not yet a city council with legislative power. The earliest *échevins* were also witnesses to oral contracts, which had legitimacy by virtue of being made in the *échevins'* presence.[4] Most cities of the southern Low Countries had *scabini* before 1133, but in the northern Netherlands the only cases before 1200 are Utrecht, Tiel and Zutphen. South of the Seine and in Italy 'good men' or 'upright men', or in the extreme south 'noble men' or 'noble laymen', formed the town court instead of *scabini*.

In Flanders and some cities of northern France the *scabini* became the city council. Elsewhere in France a separate group of *jurés* ('sworn men') who represented the sworn association of the community assumed control in the late twelfth century, usually functioning alongside the earlier *scabini* and drawn from the same social circle. In Germany this group was designated the *Rat* (council). In many cities the *jurés* became a court, but usually they shared functions with the town lord's existing court, the *scabini*, rather than absorbing it. The *scabini* usually held life appointments. Arras and Tournai in the 1190s were the only large cities of the Flanders-Artois region to receive annually appointed *scabini* before 1200, but the practice became general in the early thirteenth century.[5]

Particularly in the Empire, lords initially governed the cities through deputies, usually called advocates or bailiffs. The advocate convened the court, controlled the mint and handled criminal actions. His powers

2 Brooke and Keir, *London*, xix–xx, 29, 36–41; Nightingale, 'Origin of the court of Husting', 562–3.
3 Urry, *Canterbury*, 80–2.
4 Bedos-Rezac, 'Civic liturgies and urban records', 34–7.
5 Strait, *Cologne*, 12; Chédeville, 'Cité à ville', 155–6; Ballard, *British Borough Charters*, lxxxviii; van Uytven, 'Stadsgeschiedenis', 214, 224–7; Monier, *Institutions judiciaires*, 26.

remained significant until the thirteenth century. At Cologne the advocate in turn was represented by 'judges', but they had lost most of their functions to the *scabini* by 1160. In some cities a *Schultheiss* was the urban judge. The bishop of Metz kept a separate administration for his City and governed the rest of the diocese, including the town, through the twenty *échevins* of his palace, who by 987 had a 'first *échevin*'. To keep any lineage from becoming too powerful, in 1180 the bishop made the first *échevin* an annual office, open to knights and burgesses but not to serfs. By 1162 the *échevins* were no longer merely a court but were regulating economic matters to the extent of ordering local merchants to stop overcharging pilgrims.[6]

Before 1100 many bishops were using the burgrave to restrict the scope of their own advocates. The burgrave handled the defences of the city while exercising criminal justice and in some places collecting tolls. While the advocates were usually titled nobles, most burgraves came from ministerial families over whom the town lord originally had more control, although many were becoming knights during the twelfth century.[7]

The German kings had initially tried to control the cities by extending the privileges of the bishops who were their lords. By the twelfth century, however, church and monarchy were political opponents, and the kings encouraged revolutionary movements in the episcopal cities. The bishop of Speyer had to appoint an 'urban tribune' in 1084 to handle actions between 'citizens'. A 'common council' and a 'law of the citizens' in apposition to those of the cathedral immunity are mentioned in 1101. Henry V gave charters to the citizens of Speyer in 1111 and Worms in 1114 that were the first of a new type, in which the citizens were given more than a trade privilege: all citizens of these communities were freed from servile obligations. Citizens of Speyer were exempt from the court of the royal bailiff outside the walls, and no one could be forced to go outside the city to finish a lawsuit begun inside. At Worms the charter of 1106 for the fishmongers' guild mentions 'the common council of the townspeople'.[8] A movement against the bishop began at Metz in 1097 led by butchers and supported by the cathedral canons. By the 1120s the cathedral and the burgesses were allied against the bishop and the suburban abbeys. The townspeople were represented by deans, and

---

6   Falck, *Mainz*, 131–4; Strait, *Cologne*, 44, 11–16, 66; Schneider, *Metz*, 67–9, 83–5, 94–5, 100.
7   Opll, *Stadt und Reich*, 42–5, 160–3; Dollinger, 'Oberrheinische Bischofsstädte', 138–40.
8   Strait, *Cologne*, 37; Köbler, 'Exemter Rechtsbezirke', 12; Diestelkamp, 'König und Städte', 270–1.

by 1130 by 'ministers' who became the three mayors of the city. The symbolic head of the city government was the mayor of the quarter of Porte-Moselle.[9]

The archbishop of Mainz gave freedom from trial outside the city to 'citizens' of Mainz shortly after the emperor gave it to Speyer. By 1143 municipal officials functioned alongside the archbishop's, administered a 'native law' and controlled the town seal. The bailiff was excluded from justice and administration within the walls. In 1129 the king gave this right to Strasbourg but with the exception of lands held outside the city by citizens. In 1119 Henry V had given all 'citizens' of Strasbourg civil law and abolished the bishop's wine tap. Even before the civil law a 'public law of the city' at Strasbourg had been enforced by 'rectors', officers more often found in the Italian communes. Cologne also had rectors, later called 'councillors', who levied taxes. A 'law of the city of Cologne' is mentioned in 1159.[10]

Most cities in Saxony also had their own magistrates before 1200. The bishop of Halberstadt in 1105 confirmed the citizens' customary 'rights and civil statutes', specifically control over weights and measures and over food. This suggests strong local government. By 1168 the community of Soest chose *Schöffen* who judged misdemeanours, controlled weights and measures and the food supply, summoned the population with a bell, and had a seal. The archbishop of Magdeburg appointed *Schöffen* from the 'better persons' of the city, but not until the 1190s did they take oaths to the city corporation. Bremen already had sixteen 'sworn men of the city' before an imperial privilege recognised a 'community of the city' in 1181.[11]

Receipt of a charter did not necessarily make a city independent. Most lords were still owed heavy payments and kept control of the cities' foreign policy. They owned public buildings and frequently walls, gates and bridges. Payments to use mills persisted, as did monopolies on strategic goods. The advocate of the bishop of Erfurt collected ground rent in the city, held criminal cases and until 1235 controlled the gate through which the main street entered the city.[12] Augsburg's charter of 1156 confirmed the bishop's right to appoint the advocate, burgrave and mintmaster, but he was to consider the 'petition' of ministerials, residents of the city and the entire people. The advocate had criminal affairs, while

9 Schneider, *Metz*, 73–82.
10 Planitz, 'Stadtgemeinde', 80–1, 84–5; Dollinger, 'Oberrheinische Bischofsstädte', 141; Falck, *Mainz*, 143–5, 148; Opll, *Stadt und Reich*, 116–17; Köbler, 'Exemter Rechtsbezirke', 13; Fink, 'Rhein und Maas', 173–4.
11 Planitz, 'Stadtgemeinde', 85–9.
12 Chédeville, 'Cité à ville', 163; van Uytven, 'Stadsgeschiedenis', 206; Opll, *Stadt und Reich*, 141, 173; Schlesinger, 'Frühformen', 332–3.

the burgrave handled civil actions and economic regulation.[13] Most German cities took decades to buy out such rights.

Cologne is unusual in the extent of its independence. The *scabini*, the archbishop's court for the city, controlled a separate city seal by 1149. They pursued an independent diplomacy with other towns and controlled tolls. Any of them individually could give judgement in a legal action, subject to confirmation by his colleagues. A brotherhood of *scabini* who were out of office chose the new board. By 1179 Cologne had a two burgomasters as chief executive officers. They had to be citizens, a characteristic that distinguishes them from the rectors and *podestàs* of the north Italian cities. By 1179 the king could only rule even on blood offences with the advice of 'the masters of the citizens and our *scabini* of Cologne and officials of the Rich Club [*Richerzeche*] . . . since they are familiar with the laws of Cologne and have had its privileges put into writing'. The elite from this time consisted of the *scabini* and the 'Rich Club', a private organisation that gradually took over public functions from the *scabini*. Although no separate guild of merchants is mentioned at Cologne after 1179, the Rich Club consisted primarily of landholders and rentiers. One burgomaster was chosen from its members, the other from the *scabini*.[14]

Novgorod limited the pretensions of its lords even more significantly than did Cologne. An uprising led by boyars in 1136 forced the prince of Novgorod to live at some distance from the city. Thereafter the *veche* (the general assembly of the free males living in the five villages that by now made up the city) appointed and removed the princes of Novgorod. The city was ruled thereafter by the *veche*, with a Council of the Notables that it chose, presided over by the bishop, and the *posadnik* or mayor and other administrative officials. All free male citizens, including the 'black people' (mainly free craftsmen, but they held no offices) and the boyars controlled the *veche* through their powers as landlords of virtually the entire city. The *veche* was not a democratically organised mass meeting, as some have maintained. Novgorod, however, was exceptional in its degree of independence. In other Russian cities, notably Kiev, the prince always controlled administration, justice, finance, defence and foreign policy, all of which city governments in the west came to handle in varying degrees. Only at Novgorod and Pskov did the *veche* function as a court.[15]

13   Opll, *Stadt und Reich*, 33–8.
14   Keutgen, *Urkunden*, 10–11; Strait, *Cologne*, 39, 61–6, 71, 77–80, 141–3; Ennen, 'Erzbischof und Stadtgemeinde', 38; Berthold, 'Köln', 232–3; Opll, *Stadt und Reich*, 97–9.
15   Birnbaum, 'Lord Novgorod', 171; Goehrke, 'Novgorod', 357; Langer, 'Medieval Russian town', 24, 28; Dejevsky, 'Novgorod', 396.

Municipal liberties in France, England and the Low Countries

By the late tenth century Saint-Omer had an 'urban judge', *échevins* appointed by the abbot of Saint-Bertin and perhaps 'burgage' tenure, which gave owners the right to alienate their land without constraint by the lord. The charter given to Saint-Omer and other Flemish communities in 1127 shows the *échevins* as a territorial court handling most cases arising in the town area. Landowners in the city witnessed and authenticated contracts.[16] The guild of Saint-Omer lost power in government and confined itself to economic and charitable activity. The burgesses were freed from arbitrary taxation, specifically the head tax. The count recognised the citizens' 'commune' and made collective vengeance obligatory to redress injuries to citizens by outsiders. By 1164 Saint-Omer had two mayors and *jurés* who functioned as a second court with high justice in addition to the *échevins*.[17]

An important step in gaining independence in France was for a city to purchase the office of the king's provost, who collected his incomes in the town. By 1204 Compiègne, Poissy, Pontoise, Montdidier and Sens had already farmed their own revenues and those of their provosts, and most other French cities did so soon afterward.[18] Removing the provost corresponds to the provision in English urban charters giving the 'farm of the borough' to the inhabitants. This gave the cities, rather than the sheriff, the right to collect what they owed the king. It implied the existence of a financial administration and perhaps also the right to elect officials. Eight boroughs were being farmed separately from their counties in 1130, including London. Nevertheless, although Henry II gave short-term grants of the borough farm to several municipalities and often leased it to citizens as individuals, the grant in perpetuity was rare until John's time. Most of his numerous charters to boroughs included it.[19]

The communal movements

Particularly in northern France the movement to establish communes has often been seen as the genesis of the quasi-independent medieval city.

16 Although this is not common in French cities, at Amiens and Rouen two or more *jurés* could validate transactions on their oaths; Ballard, *British Borough Charters*, cxix.
17 Derville, *Histoire de Saint-Omer*, 45; Nicholas, *Medieval Flanders*, 117–20. English urban charters do not have the obligation to take collective vengeance. Ballard, *British Borough Charters*, cviii–ix.
18 Mollat, *Rouen*, 61–3; Baldwin, *Government of Philip Augustus*, 64.
19 Platt, *Medieval Southampton*, 14–15; Tait, *Medieval English Borough*, 156–7, 162–83; Brooke and Keir, *London*, 33; Ballard, *British Borough Charters*, cxvii; Young, *English Borough*, 17–21. There is no German equivalent of the farm of the borough.

Although sworn associations of inhabitants were important, the self-governing city cannot be equated with the commune. Urban government preceded the communal movement, which touched only a score of towns between Rhine and Loire before the mid-twelfth century. Most were suppressed or ended in a compromise between the town lord and the citizens. Some of France's largest cities were not communes. Although the enormous cities of Flanders gained a large measure of independence from their counts, none received a communal charter, although Saint-Omer, Aire and Courtrai were called 'commune' in narrative sources.[20]

Communes have been associated with uprisings against town lords. Disturbances occurred at Liège between 957 and 971. Riots against the new Norman lords of Le Mans from 1063 culminated in a commune in 1070. Most participants were artisans in the victualling trades or were domestics of the churches; but there were also cloth merchants, tailors, many tanners, furriers, shoemakers, saddlers, construction workers and a few goldsmiths and moneyers. Conflict continued until the bishop authorised a commune in 1108–9.[21]

Cambrai's struggles lasted for more than two centuries. In 968 the bishop's ministerials demanded that he recognise their sworn association. Another rising in 1077 was involved more with diocesan questions than with an effort to gain urban autonomy. In 1107 the emperor quashed another commune at Cambrai, which had evidently legislated for itself. An aristocracy of 'better people' is mentioned in 1107 and 1121. Another commune in 1138 had its own militia, bell, belfry, archives and arsenal. The bishop complained that the commune was arrogating the right to tax. The townspeople claimed unsuccessfully in 1167 that the emperor had enfeoffed them with the right to control buildings and fortifications. Agitation continued until the commune was ended by the emperor in 1182. Two years later he restored a city government in a diploma that exempted the clerics, knights and ministerials from the town's jurisdiction. He studiously avoided calling Cambrai a commune.[22]

Perhaps the most famous French commune is that of Laon in 1112, described colourfully in the *Memoirs* of Abbot Guibert of Nogent. The town was dominated by clergy and knights, who were often each other's kinsmen and who oppressed the traders (most of those mentioned were

---

20 Petit-Dutaillis, *French Communes*, 9–62; Chédeville, 'Cité à ville', 166–7; Claude, *Bourges und Poitiers*, 146–9.
21 Latouche, 'The commune of Mans (1070 AD)', *The Vézelay Chronicle*, 347–51; Chédeville, 'Cité à ville', 166; Vermeesch, *Essai Commune*, 84.
22 Van Uytven, 'Stadsgeschiedenis', 214–15; Vermeesch, *Essai Commune*, 88–98; Opll, *Stadt und Reich*, 55–62.

foodmongers) and craftsmen, many of them serfs. The bishop and the king were joint lords of Laon. While the bishop was in England in 1111, the archdeacons and the magnates decided to raise money by selling the inhabitants a commune. On his return the bishop tried to abolish the commune – an action requiring royal authorisation – and he and the inhabitants offered bribes of ascending amounts to the king's councillors. When Louis VI abolished the commune, an uprising began that cost the bishop his life. The rebels were led by a serf who had begun his career as a noble's tollkeeper, then joined the commune. Intermittent fighting continued until 1128, when a charter was issued, the 'Institution of Peace'.[23]

The princes thus considered the communes revolutionary. In 1139 Louis VII quashed a commune at Reims; in 1182 the city received a new charter that restored old liberties, including the townsmen's right to choose their own *échevins*, but the king did not call Reims a 'commune'. Philip II (1180–1223), the first king who favoured communes – and then only to weaken rival lords – distinguished between 'his burgesses' and the inhabitants 'of his communes'. He issued twenty-eight urban charters between 1180 and 1190 and another forty-six before 1223. Many were simple confirmations, which the towns had to seek from each new king.[24] The few English communes – Gloucester and York in 1170 and 1176 and London in 1141 and 1191 – were accepted by the authorities as a means of perpetuating the existing oligarchy. The London commune granted by Prince John in 1191 gave a reduced borough farm, which was paid by sheriffs evidently chosen by the citizens. The commune was directed more against the magnates who were controlling London in Richard I's absence than against him. When he returned, he confirmed the liberties in the charter but avoided calling the place a commune.[25]

In Germany most communes arose as townspeople played on the rivalry between emperor and bishops during the Investiture Contest. Traces of citizen organisations begin in the Rhenish episcopal cities around 1070, notably a 'conspiracy' at Worms in 1077. The Cologners rose against their bishop in 1074, but no city magistracy is mentioned in either until the early twelfth century. The only hint of a commune at Cologne is a dubious reference to a 'conspiracy' in 1112.[26] Although

---

23 Petit-Dutaillis, *French Communes*, 53–6; Vermeesch, *Essai Commune*, 109, 112; Guibert of Nogent, *Memoirs*, 157–82, esp. 166–7; Bur, *Laon*, 66–71.
24 Desportes, *Reims*, 78–88; Petit-Dutaillis, *French Communes*, 7, 9, 33–4; Baldwin, *Government of Philip Augustus*, 60–3.
25 Hilton, *English and French Towns*, 129–30; Lobel, *Atlas* 1: 4–5; Brooke and Keir, *London*, 45–7; Nightingale, *Medieval Mercantile Community*, 50.
26 Dollinger, *Oberrheinische Bischofsstädte*, 140–1; Planitz, *Deutsche Stadt*, 103–5.

the emperor Frederick Barbarossa never recognised communes, by the 1170s he was giving communities that would make him their overlord the right to choose magistrates and build walls. This is not unlike the town policy of the Capetian kings of France: unfavourable to the autonomy of large and/or older centres except those whose lords were the king's political opponents. Thus Barbarossa gave extensive privileges to Goslar, Dortmund and particularly Lübeck, which were cities of Henry the Lion.[27]

Yet most communes were peaceful. In 1066 the bishop of Liège gave the first surviving commune in the Empire to Huy. The charter contains the first use of *burgensis* for 'citizen' in the Empire and uses 'liberty' in the sense of 'immunity' or 'franchise'. It made Huy privileged territory where someone who had committed a crime or serious injury could go without fear of private vengeance, on condition that he accept justice by offering compensation to the victim or his family and having the matter decided in court. The charter did not change the status of inhabitants who were serfs. Burgesses were exempt from the ordeal and the judicial duel, modes of proof that favoured the nobles; proof in debt cases was by the sworn testimony of three oath helpers. Military service due to the prince was limited to periods of general mobilisation. The burgesses had an organisation, although we cannot say whether it was a sworn association, for they were to occupy the fortress of Huy and collect the payments due to the bishop while the bishopric was vacant.[28]

Much of the confusion is terminological. 'Commune' is normally used in English to mean a group that is virtually independent of the town lord. The Latin *coniuratio*, which is often translated 'commune', can mean either 'sworn association' or 'conspiracy'; hence scholars have taken some peaceful movements as revolutionary organisations against the town lord. Matters are complicated by the famous castigation by Guibert of Nogent: ' "Commune" is a new and evil name for an arrangement for them all to pay the customary head tax, which they owe their lords as a servile due, in a lump sum once a year, and if anyone commits a crime, he shall pay a fine set by law, and all other financial exactions which are customarily imposed on serfs are completely abolished'.[29]

The only characteristic that seems generally valid is that the commune was a sworn association of inhabitants. The communal oath excluded other corporate oaths, for most charters prohibited commune members

27   Stoob, *Städtewesen*, 51–72.
28   Joris, *Huy*, 38–50; Monier, *Institutions judiciaires*, 94–5; Baldwin, *Government of Philip Augustus*, 64.
29   Guibert of Nogent, *Memoirs*, 167.

taking one another to court outside the town. Most communes called themselves 'peace associations' or 'friendships', suggesting solidarity of the members against outsiders. They exacted severe penalties for injuring fellow-members of the commune and required mutual help for members as 'brothers', enforced by penalties against recusants. The Charter of Peace that Count Baldwin of Hainault sold to Valenciennes in 1114 was a sworn association of most inhabitants over age 15, excluding foreigners, those such as serfs and clerks who did not have control over their own persons, and residents of several private jurisdictions inside the city. His *échevins* were limited to civil cases, while *jurés* representing the community were instituted for criminal cases, thus dealing with those who would disturb the peace association. The *jurés* were also given broad authority to handle problems not mentioned in the charter. The city hall itself was called the 'house of peace'.[30]

Although the charters came to have a territorial element, they were not given to all residents, but only to members of the sworn association. The major social difference in the twelfth-century cities was between 'sworn burgesses', to whom the rights granted in the borough charter applied, and mere 'inhabitants', who were the majority in some English cities, where the freedom of many cities was restricted to members of the guild.[31]

Communal institutions and the growth of municipal government

The Institution of Peace of Laon, versions of which were given to other French communities, presupposed that the inhabitants would choose a mayor and *jurés*. The commune had begun as a sworn association of persons, but it now had a territorial boundary. Newcomers had to build or purchase property or bring their movables into the town area within a year. Lords were forbidden to seize freemen or serfs without due process. The magistrates were to seize the property of persons convicted of misdeeds against a member of the commune or who refused to appear for judgement. Fighting was not permitted inside the town area. Servile exactions except the head tax and tallage were ended. Far from being a haven for serfs, the commune promised that 'no alien from among those subject to a poll-tax owed to any church or knight

---

30   Monier, *Institutions judiciaires*, 76–9; van Uytven, 'Stadsgeschiedenis', 215; Platelle, *Histoire de Valenciennes*, 28–32, 41–3; Vermeesch, *Essai Commune*, 135–48; Chédeville, 'Cité à ville', 167, 176.
31   Ennen, *Frühgeschichte*, 280; Britnell, *Commercialisation of English Society*, 149.

of the state shall be received into this institution of the peace unless his lord agrees'.[32]

Saint-Quentin illustrates less colourfully the connection of urban emancipation to the grant of a commune. By 1151, when the first formal charter (the 'Establishments' of Saint-Quentin) was given by the countess of Vermandois, a municipal government already existed, consisting of a mayor, *jurés* and the lord's *échevins* who designated a 'first *échevin*' as *de facto* mayor.[33] Local nobles could not have fortified houses within three leagues of the town. But the communal movement was peaking in the late twelfth century, with increased royal intervention. A new charter in 1182 shows the organs of municipal administration more developed than in 1151, though the town had actually lost some freedom of action. The commune had become a sworn association that one joined; membership was not automatic with residence. It did not include knights or serfs of the town lord, even if they lived in the town area, but the king's freemen and those owning allegiance to other lords could join.

The countess' viscount, who does not figure prominently in the text of 1151, played a greater role by 1182. He helped keep order and had the sole right to impose capital sentences, although the *échevins* decided guilt or innocence. The mayor and *jurés* handled civil actions, had cognisance (the right to deal judicially) of 'heinous crimes against the commune' and could order the demolition of the house of anyone who offended a member of the association without offering peace. They were responsible for the militia and maintaining the city walls and had the authority, if the 'community of the burgesses' agreed, to tax lands, capital and income and to fine recusants. Members of the commune were guaranteed freedom from criminal trial outside the town and from debt prosecution outside except inside a fortified place. Security of debt was guaranteed, including the right to arrest outsiders at Saint-Quentin for debts there. Residence at Saint-Quentin unchallenged for a year and a day guaranteed possession of one's land. The charter of 1182 was thus for a fully developed commune, and it still provided a large role for the town lord.[34]

Some communal charters, particularly those from the late twelfth century and those given to cities that were already large, gave the lord or

---

32 Hugh of Poitiers, *Vézelay Chronicle*, 351–7. Hugh describes the communal uprising at Vézelay in terms reminiscent of Guibert's account of events at Laon, focusing on the shifting alliances of the commune and the abbot who was town lord. *Vézelay Chronicle*, 318–27.

33 The Beauvais charter of 1182, which provided for the election of mayors, is the first of its type. Ballard, *British Borough Charters*, cxix.

34 Petit-Dutaillis, *French Communes*, 36–47.

a municipal aristocracy more rights than they had had previously. The 'Establishments' of Rouen became the model for other communal charters in Normandy and areas south of the Loire where the Angevins ruled. The first twenty-nine clauses were probably given in the 1160s, the rest after 1204. They provided a tightly controlled regime, with minute regulations on everything from choosing magistrates to gossiping. All city officials were drawn from one hundred 'peers', a hereditary aristocracy of persons who were probably in the king's favour and not really representatives of the commune. The peers chose twelve *échevins* and twelve *jurés* from their number to handle middle and low justice and civil cases, while the king's officers kept high justice. The peers met every two weeks, the *jurés* weekly, the *échevins* twice a week. The prince named the mayor annually from three persons nominated by the peers. He chaired all meetings, received incomes, kept keys to the gates and controlled the militia.[35]

Jurisdictional heterogeneity in the cities

Our analysis of government in the early cities is complicated by the fact that few if any cities outside Italy were single jurisdictional units in the twelfth century. Many in France were unions of several bourgs with separate jurisdictions. Various lords, primarily but not exclusively the king, had jurisdiction in the English boroughs. Although most larger English towns were royal, they had sokes (private jurisdictions) corresponding to the immunities of the continental cities. Wards and parishes had their own governing boards. The Danelaw cities before 1066 commonly had ten wards, while those further south had varying numbers. By 1166 Canterbury had six wards called 'hundreds', named after the chief gates. The ward court was presided over by an alderman; it published land transactions and owned real estate, but little else is known of its functions before the fifteenth century.[36]

Although the king was also the major landlord in most English cities, the exceptions illustrate the still close ties of the cities with their rural environs. The earl of Chester controlled a district peopled with craftsmen who were not considered townspeople. All residents of the town had to grind their grain at his mills. Two-thirds of the houses at Leicester

35 Mollat, *Rouen*, 61–3; Petit-Dutaillis, *French Communes*, 63–6.
36 Lobel, *Atlas* 2: 4; Martin, 'Domesday Book and the boroughs', 160; Tillott, *City of York*, 20; Biddle, *Winchester*, 463; Urry, *Canterbury*, 92–8; Ballard, *British Borough Charters*, lvi; Keller, 'Italienische Stadtverfassung', 60; Hilton, *English and French Towns*, 46–7; Bonney, *Durham*, 7–30; Miller and Hatcher, *Towns, Commerce and Crafts*, 27.

were owned by Hugh de Grandmesnil, the largest landowner in Leicestershire. His holding had passed by 1107 to the Beaumont counts of Meulan, who become earls of Leicester. Much of Bristol's expansion came on two manors of the Harding family, who seem comparable to the German ministerials; they began as royal reeves and had a stone house in the early twelfth century. At Cambridge the Dunning family had a stone house by 1066. The first Dunning known by name died around 1150, leaving two sons. One was a county landowner; the other occupied his father's house, Dunningstede, the modern Merton Hall, and left a fortune to his own son, Harvey, who was a knight, alderman of the merchant guild and the first known elected mayor of Cambridge. Winchester is an especially good example of the multiplicity of jurisdictions in the Anglo-Norman boroughs. The main landowners were the bishop, the prior of the cathedral church, the abbess of St Mary's and the abbot of New Minster (Hyde Abbey). In the thirteenth century the bishop's soke, based on the manor of Chilcomb, which virtually surrounded Winchester, was still separated from the walled city and some of the northern and western suburbs.[37]

Some parishes on the continent had well-developed governments that may have preceded the central city administration. Parish guilds at Cologne elected masters who issued statutes. Persons who owned land and paid taxes in the parish were members of its guild. *Scabini* and parish courts recorded property transactions on request and adjudicated misdemeanours. The precise relationship of the parishes to the city government is unclear, but parish magistrates, rather then *scabini* or 'better persons', acted on behalf of the entire city in 1174 in loaning money to the archbishop.[38]

Our tendency to refer to 'city' in the singular is thus based on later developments rather than on conditions before 1200. The bishop and cathedral chapter of Paris kept jurisdictional and economic rights in their bourgs. Several lords had jurisdiction in Poitiers, and the bourg of Saint-Hilaire was independent until the late sixteenth century. Languedoc had many 'double towns'. The City of Narbonne, around the viscount's castle and the cathedral, was separated by the Aude from the bourg around the abbey of Saint-Paul. The two settlements had separate seals, town halls and administrations until 1338. Carcassonne is the most striking example. Several suburbs around the City were destroyed in 1240

---

37   Hilton, *English and French Towns*, 47–8; Urry, *Canterbury*, 40–1; Simmons, *Leicester*,
      18–19, 22; Brown, *Growth of Leicester*, 29; Lobel, *Atlas* 2: 5–7; Biddle, *Winchester*,
      5, 255.
38   Braunfels, *Urban Design*, 86; Strait, *Cologne*, 35, 45–56, 143–6.

and population moved to the plain across the Aude, where a bourg developed that became a major textile centre. The two Carcassonnes had separate consulates until 1789.[39]

Merchant law and urban law

Urban law is sometimes equated with the law merchant, but imprecisely. A commune was initially a group of persons without territorial competence, and merchant privileges were personal. Local custom applied to all inhabitants. Yet the two notions do overlap. Princes had extended safe-conducts to merchants for centuries, and some of them were site-specific by the late tenth century. In 965 and 975, for example, the merchants of Bremen and Magdeburg were placed under royal protection. The law of the merchants of Dortmund was given in 990 to the merchants and inhabitants of Gandersheim. The bishop of Naumburg in 1033 wrote of the 'law of all merchants in our region'. In 1134 the emperor confirmed the privileges of the merchants of Quedlinburg: 'just as the merchants of Goslar and Magdeburg had'.[40] Cologne had a personal 'law of the merchants' by 994 and a territorial 'peace and ban of the market' in 1000. The origin of territorial jurisdiction in the cities must thus be sought in the institutions of the town lords, since the earliest territorial magistrates were their officials, even though they would eventually yield many of their functions to representatives of citizen associations.[41]

Although urban law had considerable local variety, it developed in broad families as the customs of older cities were given to newer ones, particularly founded towns. The newer city generally appealed doubtful cases to the older one, which was its 'head'. Some daughter cities grew to a size and prosperity equal to or exceeding that of the parent, and in such cases no real subordination existed. Dublin, where a colony of merchants from Bristol lived before 1169, received the liberties of Bristol in 1172 and became its equal trading partner.[42]

The most widespread French town law families were those of Lorris and Beaumont-en-Argonne for the small centres, while the liberties of Soissons were the most common for genuine cities; they were eventually

---

39 Boussard, *Paris*, 285–6; Dez, *Poitiers*, 50–1; Wolff, 'Civitas et burgus', 200.
40 Stoob *et al.*, *Urkunden Mittel- und Niederdeutschland*, 13–19; Frölich, 'Kaufmannsgilden', 17–19; Fink, 'Rhein und Maas', 173.
41 Planitz, *Deutsche Stadt*, 89; Monier, *Institutions judiciaires*, 90–1, 102; Strait, *Cologne*, 21–2.
42 Ebel, 'Lübisches Recht', 266–70; Barry, *Archaeology Ireland*, 118–20.

given to Sens, Beauvais, Compiègne and Dijon.[43] The seven great cities of Flanders received identical charters between 1165 and 1177. The common features included abolition of the judicial duel and a diminished role of arbitration and increased competence of courts in adjudicating disputes. Fines were raised and the number of capital crimes increased. A new 'count's justiciar', who would be called 'bailiff' in the thirteenth century, convened the aldermen and enforced their judgements.

Magdeburg, Bremen and Lübeck were the most important town law families in Germany. Lübeck furnished law books to the roughly one hundred towns in the Baltic east that received its customs. Freiburg was given the law of Cologne in 1120 and had judicial recourse to Cologne, and the version used at Freiburg was given to other plantations in south-western Germany.[44] In Poland during the eleventh and particularly twelfth century lords gave charters both to new villages and to existing settlements, usually in the form of a personal grant to the prince's advocate or to a group that already had privileges, such as the colonies of foreign merchants living in the suburbs around fortifications. The advocate began as an official of the prince but quickly became an officer of the new urban community. These charters generally involved a grant of one of the German town laws, most often that of Magdeburg.[45]

Contrary to the French practice of affiliation of town law families, before 1216 only the London and Winchester laws were used as models for more than two other English cities, but eventually fifty-nine boroughs would be granted the liberties of another. Sometimes this was third-hand. Oxford received the liberties of London; then Lynn in 1204 was given the liberties of 'our free boroughs', specified in a different charter of the same year as being those of Oxford. There is less similarity between Norman and English urban charters than one might expect. Only five of twenty-five clauses in Henry II's charter of 1151 for Rouen are found in his charters of 1154–57 for London, Chichester, Wallingford, Oxford and Lincoln.[46]

Freedom and freedoms in the medieval city

Virtually all cities of the continent north of the Loire received charters before 1200. Some confined themselves to personal liberties for the

43 Dollinger, *Histoire de l'Alsace*, 113; Baldwin, *Government of Philip Augustus*, 61.
44 Blockmans, 'Vers une société urbanisée', 65; Nicholas, *Medieval Flanders*, 121–2; Clarke and Simms, 'Comparative history', 698; Müller, *Freiburg*, 31–2; van Uytven, 'Stadsgeschiedenis', 214.
45 Knoll, 'Urban development of medieval Poland', 73–5.
46 Ballard, *British Borough Charters*, cvii–iii, cxx–xxi, 25, 31–2.

inhabitants that ended some of the lord's rights. The princes guaranteed security of property, gave procedural safeguards and renounced violence and extortion. Most charters guaranteed citizens the right to trial in the home city except in cases involving their property outside its corporate limits. Punishments were specified, and the peace of the town applied to merchants going to or from its fair or market. The head tax was abolished in many, and most French, Flemish and German charters fixed ground rents in perpetuity, at least those owed to the town lord and often to all landowners.[47]

The characteristic marks of burgage tenure – the legal freedom of the burgess and his ability to inherit and alienate his tenure – were present in most boroughs of Norman England, enjoyed by most but not all inhabitants. The status was being equated by the late eleventh century with paying ground rent (landgable) to the king.[48] But the fixing of ground rents has conveyed an erroneous impression of stability in urban rental markets. Most medieval law distinguished ownership of the land from ownership of the buildings on it. The person who paid ground rent to the town lord and accordingly was the person of record in the written document was often not the actual occupant, who leased it from him. Furthermore, persons who owned improved urban land might be owed both a ground rent on the land and a market rent on the buildings on it. In 1137 the burgesses of Vézelay complained that the count of Nevers had been 'hiring out the stalls of the money-changers and merchants more dearly than [his] predecessors [had] done'. He responded that his predecessors had increased these charges and also rents for houses to take account of the growth of the town. He also 'ought to have this right, especially since we compel no one to hire our facilities, and even the burghers themselves have been accustomed to hire out their own houses . . . at increased rates, without us making an objection'. Landowning burgesses and lords alike thus benefited from rising land values in the city. Land and buildings could be sold as well as rented separately. The actual sale price usually bore little relation to the ground rent retained. A seller who needed cash would have a high price and a small rent; one who wanted an investment income would ask a smaller price and keep a larger ground rent. Subletting could also generate income. As migrants streamed into the cities in the twelfth century, lords of urban properties subdivided tenements to get more rent from them.[49]

Confusion has also arisen about the nature of urban liberty. Although

47 Chédeville, 'Cité à ville', 163; van Uytven, 'Stadsgeschiedenis', 206.
48 Miller and Hatcher, *Towns, Commerce and Crafts*, 31–2.
49 Hilton, *English and French Towns*, 45; Urry, *Canterbury*, 134–5; Hugh of Poitiers, *Vézelay Chronicle*, 323; Keene, 'Property market', 207–9.

many urban charters abolished specific obligations of the inhabitants to their lords, the earliest of them did not give legal freedom after residence for a year and a day in the corporate area of the city. Many cities thus housed serfs, particularly in Germany, where *cerocensuales* and ministerials made up so much of the population. The legal maxim 'town air makes a man free' originated in the efforts of the founded towns of northern Spain to entice settlers in the tenth and eleventh centuries. It appeared in southern France in 1107, then in the urban charters of Louis VI. In Flanders it appears in Philip of Alsace's charter for Nieuwpoort in 1163; other Flemish charters permitted lords to seize runaway serfs in the cities. Henry II's charters for Nottingham and Lincoln contain it. In Germany it is first found around 1160 in the charters of component settlements of Brunswick, then Bremen in 1186, Lübeck in 1188 and generally in the thirteenth century. The year and a day term also applied at Lübeck for unchallenged possession and sale of land. Neither legal freedom nor citizenship after a year and a day was universal. Marseilles required five years' uninterrupted residence as a taxpayer. Some cities in Italy later required thirty years' residence for those who were not children of citizens.[50] Much of the early population of the cities was seasonal and migratory, making rigid distinctions between and burgesses extremely suspect. In 1203 Pierre de Verfeil was a serf at Verfeil during the farming season, but during the winter he made leather bottles at Toulouse and was considered free there.[51]

URBAN GOVERNMENT IN SOUTHERN EUROPE

The urban consulates of Italy

Italian urbanisation affords many contrasts with its northern counterpart. The impact of the church on city politics was more uniformly significant in Italy than in the north before the twelfth century, for the bishop was the lord of many cities of northern Italy before 1100. But although the church always wielded immense patronage, the Italian cities were almost entirely under secular control by 1200, while ecclesiastical institutions were still very important in the northern cities.

50 van Caenegem, 'Constitutionalism', 96–8; see also the comments of Mitteis, 'Stadtluft macht frei', 190–2, who sees the right of asylum as the origin of the maxim; Monier, *Institutions judiciaires*, 93, 121; Godding, *Droit privé*, 229, 246, who sees this as a protection against the seller's lineage later contesting the possessor's title; Keutgen, *Urkunden*, no. 25, pp. 18–19; Keller, 'Italienische Stadtverfassung', 55; Lesage, *Marseille angevine*, 36.
51 Wolff, *Histoire de Toulouse*, 73.

The older Italian cities had secular governments long before there is evidence of them in the north. The doge (duke) of Venice replaced a Byzantine tribune as leader of the city in the late seventh century. From the ninth century judges from the old tribune families limited the doge's power. Twelfth-century Venice was divided into territorial sixths, three on each bank of the Grand Canal. Each was governed by a council of wise men who constituted a small city council after 1206.[52] Rome had fourteen defence districts called 'regions' (*rioni*) by the seventh century. Each had its own banner, militia and leader or representative. By the twelfth century officers of the regions chose fifty-six senators who functioned as a city council. The patrician of Rome was the chief executive officer of the Senate, which fought the pope for power. In 1155 rebels led by Arnold of Brescia demanded that the pope abdicate temporal power in the city to the patrician. The emperor quashed this movement, but in 1188 Pope Clement III and the city agreed that the pope would be the secular lord, but the city government could declare war and received subsidies from him for the maintenance of the walls. In the late twelfth century a single senator was made chief executive.[53]

While the earliest constitutional documents for the northern cities were given personally to members of a sworn association, those for Italy were territorial associations that were formed to limit their lords' power and establish urban governments. The charter given to 'all our faithful persons and inhabitants of the city of Genoa' in 958 by King Berengar made an immunity of the city area and indeed of the house of every Genoese. Breach of the city peace was punishable with a fine to the royal fisc. The king surrendered his rights to hospitality and quartering troops. A short-lived privilege of 996 for Cremona had a similar immunity stipulation, as did the imperial charter for Lucca of 1081. By contrast, the earliest sworn associations in Italy were not city-wide but rather joined specific elements of the population, most often knights or valvassors. Piacenza, for example, had conflicts in 1090 between a group described as 'infantry' or 'the people' against the 'knights'. A communal oath was sworn in 1080 at Pisa, where the bishop called it into being as a union of bishop, viscount and consuls against an external threat.[54]

The connections between commune, sworn association and the magistracy of the consulate are clearest in Genoa. By 1130 each of seven military companies based on geographical districts of the city was being led by two 'consuls of pleas'. The plaintiff's company judged legal actions

52   Barel, *Ville médiévale*, 26.
53   Hubert, *Espace urbain*, 75–93, 130–6; Krautheimer, *Rome*, 152–6.
54   Ennen, *Frühgeschichte*, 238–41; Opll, *Stadt und Reich*, 376; Fasoli, 'Città italiane', 303.

between persons in different companies. All able-bodied males of the district between ages 16 and 70 had to enter a company. This is similar to the role of the Cologne ward associations within the overall sworn association of the city. The Genoese companies had the same role that the sworn association of citizens had in the north, handling militia, courts and finance.[55]

Thus residents of most Italian cities had some voice in local affairs even before the communal movement, although the town lords were powerful. With the emperors less often in Italy, Henry IV and Henry V had to agree to keep their castles outside the walls at Lucca, Cremona and Mantua, renouncing the palaces inside the walls to the town. In 1055 Henry III granted the 'citizens' of Mantua the 'good and just custom' that all 'cities of our empire' possess. Henry IV gave charters to the 'citizens' of several north Italian centres that opposed countess Matilda. In trying to gain allies against the popes, the emperors thus tacitly recognised the existence of citizens' organisations, which presupposes some kind of government.[56]

In the late eleventh century the same groups that had united to extend the bishop's control outside the city when he was fighting the counts were also joining to limit his temporal authority inside it.[57] Although this movement was initially led by the semi-urban nobility who had controlled the eleventh-century cities, persons who combined landowning with merchant activity are found increasingly among the groups that took control of the political institutions of the commune by the late twelfth century.

At first the general assembly of all citizens was the chief legislative body, but since such mass meetings were too large for ordinary business, administration was delegated to 'good men' or 'upright men' in the eleventh century. These were *ad hoc* committees without specific government functions. The first reference to 'citizens' as a body at Padua dates from 1077, when they are represented by 'good men', including an advocate as judge.[58]

During the twelfth century, however, virtually all Italian cities developed true governments with 'consuls'. These officers came from the same social group as the 'good men' but represent a later stage, when the aristocracy had institutionalised its control. Pisa had consuls by 1081, Arezzo and Genoa by 1098, then Brescia, Milan and Bergamo between 1100 and 1110. Henry V's charter of 1119 to the 'people' of Piacenza stipulated that he would not make peace with Piacenza's enemies without

---

55 Ennen, *Frühgeschichte*, 281–4.
56 Haverkamp, 'Städte in Herrschafts- und Sozialgefüge Reichsitaliens', 180–6.
57 Racine, 'Città e contado', 134.
58 Rippe, 'Dans le Padouan', 147.

the consent of the 'consuls of the city'. This amounted to a military alliance in which the emperor recognised the independence of the consuls and gave the regalia (royal prerogatives) to the commune.[59] Lucca and Bologna in 1124 and Mantua in 1126 complete the list of early consular regimes. Most other cities in northern Italy had them by the period of the first Lombard League. Although the consuls and the 'good men' had essentially the same functions as leaders of the citizen commune in most cities, at Pistoia the consuls were the bishop's officials and were thus similar to the *scabini* of the northern cities. The connection between consuls and good men could be very close: in negotiations with Rome, Siena used twelve good men in 1124, consuls in 1125.[60]

We can say that the cities had consuls before we can be certain what governmental functions they actually exercised. Lucca may have issued as many as 3,700 documents in the twelfth century alone, but only 1 per cent survive. They are mainly from church archives and concern land conveyance, undoubtedly a bias in the documents that does not show conditions as they actually were. In the early twelfth century the consuls of Lucca had only arbitral jurisdiction, not coercive power. Three 'consuls of pleas', evidently a subgroup of the consuls and called 'truce officers' in some documents, are found by 1136. It is unclear when the consuls of Lucca gained the power to judge actions.[61]

Scarcely do we hear of consuls than multiple boards of consuls appear. Como and Cremona had 'consuls of the commune' and 'consuls of justice'. 'Consuls of the commune' were distinguished from 'consuls of pleas' at Genoa from 1161. Verona had consuls of justice and consuls of the merchants in the 1170s. Milan had consuls of justice and consuls of the commune. Pisa had a Senate of forty members that is hard to distinguish in the twelfth century from the consulate. They were chosen by the consuls and later by special commissions. Evidently they consulted with the consuls, especially on maritime questions, but they had no independent authority. Pisa had separate consuls of justice by 1156; at first these were a delegation of the main body of consuls, but they were definitely independent by 1158. Beginning as divisions of the consulate of justice but quickly achieving independent standing, courts of appeals and of foresters (for quarrels between residents of the *contado* and citizens) developed in Pisa by 1176, together with a court of arbiters to handle civil cases involving 200 *lire* or less.[62]

59 Haverkamp, 'Städte im Herrschafts- und Sozialgefüge Reichsitaliens', 184–9.
60 Opll, *Stadt und Reich*, 239–40, 257–8, 269, 398, 368–9, 471.
61 Keller, 'Inizi del comune in Lombardia', 57; Tirelli, 'Lucca', 216–19.
62 Ennen, *Frühgeschichte*, 270–1; Volpe, *Medio Evo Italiano*, 219–21; Volpe, *Studi sulle istituzioni comunale a Pisa*, 140–1, 146–9, 150–1.

In some places vestiges of the authority of bishop or count remained. In 1117 the commune and archbishop had separate consuls at Milan. The last written document that shows the viscount of Pisa exercising jurisdiction is from 1116, but he continued to control the weight, ovens, wine trade and occupational organisations until at least mid-century. The viscount even led tower fights against the consuls in 1153.[63]

Given that the bishops had been lords of the Lombard cities in the eleventh century and that their temporal authority was considerable everywhere, they bore the thrust of the growing power of the communal governments. By 1138 the consuls of Milan were adjudicating legal actions involving the local abbeys, and the consuls of Pisa similarly heard cases involving church property. The municipal government of Florence became the financial guardian of the local churches. A statute of 1225 forbade anyone to take property from any church of Florence without permission of the commune, even if the pope had authorised the alienation. The city government also intervened in disputes within the cathedral chapter and between the chapter and the bishop. The consuls of Lucca guaranteed a peace between the bishop and one of his vassals in 1138.[64] Predictably, the change occurred earliest at Milan. The volume of 'Acts of the Commune of Milan' opens in 1117 with the consuls, archbishop and 'people' annulling an alienation of lay property to the bishop of Lodi. The transfer may appear more striking to modern minds than to contemporaries, for most consuls were still the archbishop's vassals in the twelfth century, although this would change in the thirteenth. The 'Garden of the Archbishop' where the consuls had met when they were the archbishop's court was being called the 'Garden of the Consuls' even in the twelfth century.[65]

Appointment and distribution of officials reflected the factional and geographical division of the cities. Nobles and commoners named an equal number of consuls at Orvieto. An outsider called the 'rector' was often mentioned from 1171 at Orvieto, but never in the same year as the consuls, who were involved in the family-based factions. As in the north, wards that were based on public buildings or more often city gates were administrative units. The consuls of the commune were chosen by gate-based districts at Milan in 1158 and 1175. Each gate in turn had its own 'good men', who are sometimes called consuls. They led the militia and enforced the policies of the consuls of the city within the gate. The wards (*populi*) of Genoa were keeping written records of

63   Racine, 'Evêque et cité', 137; Volpe, *Studi sulle istituzioni comunale a Pisa*, 3–4.
64   Keller, 'Inizi del comune in Lombardia', 50; Hyde, *Society and Politics*, 99; Dameron, *Episcopal Power and Florentine Society*, 121–2; Tirelli, 'Lucca', 214–15.
65   Volpe, *Medio Evo Italiano*, 219–21.

their actions even in the twelfth century, as were the quarters of Pisa, which replaced the old gate-based wards shortly after 1164 with other territorial divisions.[66] The consuls of Florence, who are first mentioned in 1138, represented the parishes and neighbourhood associations. They were joined after 1150 by consuls representing professional associations, beginning with the consuls of the knights, then those of the merchants. By 1200 the major guilds had their own consuls. The gates at Piacenza were keeping tax lists before 1200 and had their own consuls by 1221. The gates became involved in the *popolo* organisation, which we shall discuss in Chapter 8; they were composed of smaller societies of *popolani* within the neighbourhoods and were the base of recruitment of the *popolo* militia.[67]

Most Italian cities had separate organs to handle merchant affairs before 1200. They were similar in some respects to the English merchant guilds. Consuls of the merchants were functioning at Pisa, Piacenza and Milan by 1150 and virtually everywhere by 1200. Bologna's first reference to a merchant guild is from 1194. Florence had 'consuls of the merchants' in 1182, but this organisation soon subdivided into the three oldest of the 'major guilds': the Calimala (importers of undressed cloth, to be finished by Florentine artisans) by 1192, the bankers and money-changers in 1202, and Por Santa Maria (mercers, who sold cloth and other goods) in 1216.[68] The merchant aristocracy of Pisa was more open than was often true elsewhere, with diverse sources of merchant capital, but it had a sense of common identity against the crafts. 'Consuls of the merchants' are mentioned in 1161 and 1163, elected by the consuls of the commune to handle commercial litigation. They were initially businessmen, but within a few years, as a body of merchant law evolved, professional jurists held the office. The consuls of the merchants were also considered officials of the commune. Those of Piacenza in 1154 acted with the consuls of the commune in negotiating a commercial question with Genoa. In 1165 at Rome the 'consuls of the merchants and seamen' likewise acted with the Senate to make a trade pact with Genoa.[69]

Although at Pisa and Genoa the consular aristocracies of the twelfth century included both military and merchant families, who were often related, nobles dominated most early Italian consulates. In Milan in 1130 seven consuls were captains, with seven valvassors and six burgesses. The popular party, supported by the clergy and some nobles, forced a

66 Volpe, *Studi sulle istituzioni comunale a Pisa*, 6, 135; Previté-Orton, 'Italian cities till c. 1200', 233.
67 Waley, *Orvieto*, 10; Racine, 'Porte', 180–2.
68 Hyde, *Society and Politics*, 73–4.
69 Volpe, *Studi sulle istituzioni comunale a Pisa*, 239–46.

consular regime on the bishop and the countess at Lucca. The first consuls at Pisa seem to have had a major programme of containing feuds by limiting tower construction. Although we know little of how the early consulates conducted business, by the 1140s texts show those of Lucca, Genoa and Pisa acting by majority vote.[70]

Even in the eleventh century the collective self-consciousness of the larger Italian cities was shown by intercity warfare, coming much earlier than it can be documented north of the Alps. These struggles were initially led by the bishops. Pisa and Lucca, whose episcopal dioceses were roughly coterminous with the city's *contado*, fought such a war in 1004. Pisa fought Lucca for control of the Apennine passes, Genoa over foreign commerce and the territorial ambitions of both in Sardinia. Furthermore, urban leagues are found considerably before the famous struggle of the first Lombard League against the emperor. In 1094 Piacenza, Milan, Lodi and Cremona allied with Henry IV's son Conrad against his father.[71]

The movement for municipal independence in Italy: the communal movement and the first Lombard League

The considerable degree of autonomy that the north Italian cities achieved in the second half of the twelfth century was born out of the multi-faceted wars involving Milan and its allies and opponents, the emperor Frederick Barbarossa as their nominal overlord, and the popes. Between 1002 and 1152 the German kings spent only twenty-two years in Italy, and half of this time was by Henry II (1002–24). When they did come, the fact that they had surrendered their castles in many cities to citizens' organisations forced them to stay in rural castles, for the cities by now were independent enough to be dangerous.[72] City governments had developed with very little oversight, since the bishops were rapidly losing power to the consuls. When Barbarossa made it plain at the Diet of Roncaglia in 1158 that he intended to enforce his rights and have the cities governed by his appointed officials, he intruded on areas that the cities had been controlling. Had he enforced the Roncaglian decrees fully, it would have given him an additional income of 100,000 pounds.[73]

Milan, the largest city of northern Italy, was a natural leader of the resistance, but the other cities feared Milan as much as they did the usually

70 Tabacco, *Medieval Italy*, 185–8; Ennen, *Frühgeschichte*, 273–6; Gouron, 'Diffusion des consulats méridionaux', 30–1; Keller, 'Mehrheitsentscheidung', 2–41; Lansing, *Florentine Magnates*, 9–10.
71 Volpe, *Studi sulle istituzioni comunale a Pisa*, 9; Volpe, *Medio Evo Italiano*, 222.
72 Haverkamp, 'Städte im Herrschafts- und Sozialgefüge Reichsitaliens', 178–9.
73 Fuhrmann, *Germany*, 143–6.

distant emperor. While other cities were coming into conflict with the empire or local potentates by trying to conquer a rural *contado*, Milan did it by subjugating other towns. It had been expanding at the expense of Lodi and Como since the beginning of the twelfth century. Milan's problems with Cremona went back at least to the 1040s, when Milanese landholders began taking castles in the *contado* of Cremona in fief from the bishop of Cremona. The bishops, who were facing threats at home, probably felt that they had no choice, but their supposed allies quickly became the vanguard of Milan's expansion against Cremona. At the very beginning of the conflict with Barbarossa in 1159 the emperor took Imola under his protection and released it from 'all bondage to other cities and persons'. Although the Lombard League was only formalised in 1167, with rectors who acted on its behalf as a unit, the war erupted when Milan was outlawed for ignoring an imperial summons to answer the charges of Lodi, Cremona and Pavia in 1154.[74] Other larger cities also controlled places that would have been cities by north European standards in the twelfth century: Florence subjugated Fiesole in 1125, and Ravenna was the master of Forlì.[75]

Two other problems complicated the issue. The cities had been opposing the bishops who were their lords, but Frederick's attempt to impose an antipope caused Pope Alexander III to ally with the north Italian cities. Secondly, some cities had appointed *podestàs* as administrative and military officers over the consuls even before the war. The earliest were the 'lord of the city' at Siena in 1151, the 'rector of the city' of Verona, and Guido de Sasso, who was rector or *podestà* at Bologna in the early 1150s. Most of them were from native families of the city in which they served. But at Roncaglia the emperor claimed the right to appoint civic officials and after the submission of Milan in 1162 began sending *podestàs* to cities that opposed him. The cities resented them, for they were often foreigners from towns inimical to the host city. By the 1170s the Lombard cities were again appointing their own *podestàs*, but the emperor reimposed them in Tuscany after 1183.[76] We shall see in Chapter 8 that the *podestà* was an important figure in the transition between consular regimes and the multifarious network of councils and societies that ruled the Italian cities in the thirteenth century.

The issues were thus far more complex than simply cities against

---

74 Opll, *Stadt und Reich*, 317–23; Mazzi, 'Milano', 373; Menant, 'Relazioni feudo-vassallatiche cremonese', 236–7; Volpe, *Medio Evo Italiano*, 80, 223, 227.
75 Haverkamp, 'Städte im Herrschafts- und Sozialgefüge Reichsitaliens', 200–1.
76 Fuhrmann, *Germany*, 169; Opll, *Stadt und Reich*, 215, 291–2, 400, 431, 468; Haverkamp, 'Städte im Herrschafts- und Sozialgefüge Reichsitaliens', 218; Dameron, *Episcopal Power and Florentine Society*, 75, 100–1.

emperor. Bergamo first sided with the emperor against its rival Milan but joined the urban coalition in 1165 after the emperor imposed his *podestà* on the city. Como, which had been paying tribute to Milan since 1127, naturally sided with Frederick. Cremona also supported the emperor initially but was alienated when he demanded a ground rent and direct lordship over the villages of the *contado* of Crema, which Frederick himself had helped Cremona seize in 1159. Pavia, Milan's most powerful rival, was the emperor's most faithful Italian ally. Pavia received a charter in the summer of 1164 that gave the inhabitants free choice of consuls and listed the customary rights of the city: high and low justice, fines, free trade and freedom from toll throughout Italy except where customary rights prevailed. Pavia was thus given rights that the emperor claimed to exercise directly elsewhere.[77]

The conflict lasted intermittently between 1159 and 1183, but there was little fighting after a plague forced the imperial army to retreat to Germany in 1167. By the treaty of Constance of 1183, the cities had to take an oath to Frederick and supply provisions ('hospitality') for his army during his Italian campaigns, but he allowed them to exercise his rights of governance and purveyance (requisition of provisions) in return for money payments. This amounted to giving them the regalia, placing the cities on a plane with princes who exercised powers delegated from the ruler.[78]

The developing sense of corporate identity, both of individual centres and on the part of the cities as a group, is an especially noteworthy aspect of the struggle against Barbarossa, particularly at Milan. Milan had had a civic consciousness for centuries. Landulf, the author of an eleventh-century *History of Milan*, linked the city to the tradition of its patron saint Ambrose and expressed pride that its bishop had resisted the impiety of the emperors. In describing the conflict of Lodi against Milan in 1075, Landulf called Lodi the 'hereditary enemy'.[79] Milan was twice destroyed by Barbarossa, and in 1162 its inhabitants were resettled, but they soon returned.

The legends of patron saints of particular cities also took shape in the twelfth century: Ranieri at Pisa, Petronio at Bologna, John and Miniato at Florence, Jacobo at Perugia, Ercolano at Pistoia. Many had been early bishops of the city. The cities were turning what had formerly been purely religious devotion into a civic cult. Before 1200 the occupational guilds were taking control of Florence's chief churches. The cult of St

77 Opll, *Stadt und Reich*, 204–7, 235–6, 254–6, 372–5.
78 Haverkamp, 'Städte im Herrschafts- und Sozialgefüge Reichsitaliens', 219.
79 Racine, 'Evêque et cité', 133–4. See also Hyde, *Society and Politics*, 18.

John was centred on the baptistery, which was controlled by the Calimala guild. The major guilds controlled the leper hospital by 1192. The Calimala established a brotherhood, the Works of St John, for the maintenance of the cathedral. Tithes from some of the bishop's rural communes were diverted into the brotherhood's treasury by 1217, and in 1228 the Calimala took over the Works of St Miniato from the bishop.[80] The crusades also fostered the civic identity of the participating cities. Genoese sources speak of the liberation of the cities in the east and the removal of the relics of St John and the Golden Chain of Caesarea to Genoa. Several poems laud Pisa's fights against the Muslims.[81]

The cities' victory inspired symbolic and real moves toward communal autonomy. In 1179 the consuls of Piacenza decided to move the meeting place of the general assembly to the new cathedral. This required appropriating land to clear a public square, which became the second marketplace, near the main east–west road across the southern part of the city. The larger square may have been needed to accommodate the expansion of the public assembly to include craftsmen; the first reference at Piacenza to consuls of the merchants and of the trades is from 1184. Other Lombard cities built their first town halls about the same time, almost always near or even adjacent to the cathedral.[82]

Urban consulates in France

The earliest references to consuls in France are in the lower Rhone valley, beginning with Avignon in 1129, Arles in 1131, then, further west, Béziers in 1131 and Narbonne in 1132. Thus consuls appear in the French Midi about thirty years after they became common in Italy and may have been imitations; the fact that Narbonne had a consulate is known from a Genoese document. Montpellier had consuls by 1141, but the word was then avoided until the king of Aragon granted a consulate in 1205. Consulates continued to expand westward. Toulouse had *capitularii* in 1152; since the city councillors were later called capitouls, the smaller towns of the region used that name. Consulates only developed in northern and central Provence after 1220.[83]

At Nîmes in 1144 and Avignon in 1166 all consuls were knights, as

80 Dameron, *Episcopal Power and Florentine Society*, 119.
81 Dameron, *Episcopal Power and Florentine Society*, 121–2; Cardini, 'Intellectuals and culture', 15–16.
82 Opll, *Stadt und Reich*, 532; Fuhrmann, *Germany*, 143–8; Racine, 'Place civique', 302–5, 312.
83 Faber and Lochard, *Montpellier*, 84–5; Gouron, 'Diffusion des consulats', 32–7; Ennen, *Frühgeschichte*, 276.

were twenty-one of twenty-eight known by name at Arles between 1135 and 1157. In some places, particularly the small communities, the nobles had a fixed number of consuls. Most consulates thus arose during factional struggles within the aristocracy rather than as a movement for citizen emancipation from the lord. Except in Provence the sworn association was unimportant in the origins of town governments in southern France. The twelfth-century consuls were judges, more like the *scabini* than the *jurés* of the northern cities. They were not representatives of a sworn association of persons, but rather were a territorial government, called 'consuls of the city'.[84]

The spread of consular government paralleled the use of written Roman law in the cities. Far from being a coherent body of state law, Roman law contains provisions that could favour either local autonomy or seigniorial despotism. Some consular towns had extensive liberties, while others were controlled by their lords. The burgesses of Le Puy, Lyon and Romans tried to avoid the imposition of a consulate, which would have restricted their liberties. When the royal government was trying to force cities to accept consulates in the fifteenth century, it was to limit local autonomy.[85]

The example of Toulouse

Toulouse may have been the most independent city north of the Alps before 1200. It tried to conquer the environs and forced its prince to impose the city's decrees throughout his domains. Distinctions between burgesses and knights are not mentioned after 1119. Most knights were valvassors, similar to the group who dominated the north Italian cities in the eleventh century. Like the German ministerials, some were still unfree in the eleventh century, but in the twelfth the wealthier burgesses, who could afford warhorses, were marrying into knightly families. The municipal elite was dominated by landowners rather than merchants. Citizens (who lived in the old City) and burgesses (residents of the bourg-Saint-Sernin) had formed a single organisation with a common treasury before 1147, represented by 'good men'. In 1147 the community forced the count of Toulouse to renounce military service except near the city and some taxes that were becoming lucrative as the population grew. By 1152 Toulouse had a 'common council of the city and the suburb of Toulouse', formed of six 'chaptermen' (capitouls), four of them judges and two advocates. They were probably appointed by the

---

84   Chédeville, 'Cité à ville', 178–9; Tabacco, *Medieval Italy*, 185–8.
85   Gouron, 'Diffusion des consulats', 54, 68–70 and map.

count, but they did not act in his name. By 1180 there were twenty-four capitouls, twelve each for City and bourg, eight judges and four advocates, legislating, exercising criminal and civil jurisdiction, and handling administration, foreign policy and defence. The capitouls thus linked functions that remained distinct in the northern cities until later. After 1180 the chapter was assisted by a larger Common Council. Between 1190 and 1204 the capitouls bought land for a city hall at the border of City and bourg, symbolically linking them.[86]

The cities of Europe were on the eve of their greatest expansion in 1200. The interregional trade that had made the cities commercial centres continued to grow, and they also produced more and better industrial goods. The cities continued to be dominated by mixed oligarchies of landowners and merchants, but the commercial element became increasingly prominent. By the mid-thirteenth century it was in control virtually everywhere outside Germany and Italy, where the rentier element remained more powerful. Yet the Mediterranean and north European cities also display common features that are sometimes obscured by terminological differences.

---

86 Discussion based on Wolff, *Histoire de Toulouse*, 76–7, 94–103; Mundy, *Toulouse*, xi–xiii, 8–13, 24–5, 30–9, 46–58, 66–8, 76–7, 100–3.

PART THREE

The Maturing of Medieval Urbanisation, c. 1190–c. 1270

CHAPTER SIX

The Expansion of the Cities in the Thirteenth Century

Industrialisation, long-distance trade and urbanisation

Throughout the twelfth century the cities of Europe were cult centres, focuses of local government and farm markets. Some also had long-distance commerce, mainly in luxury items of small bulk and high value. Raw material trade was more localised. The aristocracy of the early medieval cities was land-based, often ministerial, deriving its prestige from lineage, its wealth from offices, privileges, rents and the sale of farm products.

By the thirteenth century, however, much of the long-distance trade of the larger cities was in manufactured items, particularly woollen cloth. Western Europe probably had a positive balance of trade in the thirteenth century, with a negative balance toward the Muslim and Greek east more than compensated by a positive balance toward the Slavic east and Scandinavia. In addition to the trade in cloth and oriental luxuries, interregional grain trading now expanded. Many cities imported their food from a considerable distance. Thus, even as the economy as a whole became more productive, the cities remained consumers in the neo-Roman model.

The expanding long-distance trade of the cities was tied to the increased supply of bullion for coin. Long-distance trade had always been based on money and controlled by persons with access to mints or serving those who did; but now coin was becoming more common in local trade, giving impetus to city markets.[1] Some Italian and German cities minted their own coins. The florin was an important aspect of the rise of Florence as a banking centre in the thirteenth century. It was equal to the pounds of Siena and Pisa when first minted in 1252, but by 1311 its value against its competitors had nearly trebled.[2]

1   Britnell, *Commercialisation of English Society*, 41–2, 102.
2   Waley, *Siena*, 207.

The changes of the thirteenth century would have been inconceivable without a considerable improvement in the delivery of goods and services. Most shipping was centred in cities by 1200. There is considerably more evidence of southern French, Spanish and Italian merchants at London from around 1175 on, and of the English in the Mediterranean from the 1160s. By 1200 a large Mediterranean market had developed for northern woollen cloth. Silver was in short supply at the time in the Near East, so Europeans got a good deal in exchanging woollen cloth for spices and other luxuries.[3] The Champagne fairs had originated mainly for Flemish and northern French trade. But when Italian merchants began frequenting them after 1180, joined by the Germans in the thirteenth century, they became a clearing house at which merchants from all regions of Europe exchanged goods and coin initially, then instruments of credit. The Italians bought raw wool and semi-finished cloth from the northern centres at the fairs and sold Mediterranean dyes that were needed for the finest cloth and Oriental luxuries. Commercial techniques that were developed at the fairs transformed long-distance trade, bringing imported crafts and raw materials to a wider market.

Merchants of individual cities usually rented a house together at the fairs. A 'German Street' is mentioned at Provins by 1211, dominated by Cologners. Some Italians stayed permanently. Renier Acorre of Florence became the richest man of Provins in the thirteenth century. The Cahorsin Bernard de Montcuc came to Troyes at the beginning of the thirteenth century, married a prominent local woman and was mayor of Troyes three times in the late 1230s.[4] The numerous Genoese and Lombards who came to Barcelona at the turn of the thirteenth century kept ties with their natal cities and fostered Barcelona's integration into the trading network already established by Genoa and Pisa. They did not, however, obtain their own law or quarters of the city, but rather intermarried with local families.[5]

Most other large cities had colonies of foreign merchants that lived apart from the native population. A large group of bankers of Piacenza lived in Genoa, many of them involved in the Champagne trade, much of which went through Genoa as the Italian port best situated for overland trade to France. Piacenza had a 'consul of the merchants' at Genoa by 1154, suggesting a guild. Milan had a resident colony in Genoa even in the twelfth century, with two 'prefects of the [Milanese] merchants

3   Nightingale, *Medieval Mercantile Community*, 56.
4   Hirschfelder, *Kölner Handelsbeziehungen*, 31; Chapin, *Villes de foires*, 227, 113, 120–3, 60–3.
5   Bensch, *Barcelona*, 221–32.

who are living at Genoa'. In 1203 they negotiated an agreement concerning trade and road freedom with various towns on the Milan–Genoa route. Virtually all Italian cities had citizens and churches with lands in the territory of some other city.[6] By 1278 Marseilles had a merchant office at Naples overseen by a consul.[7] Although most merchant colonies were given the right to their own courts and law only from the late thirteenth century, some individuals covered themselves legally by becoming dual nationals. Simo de Sungham of Lynn owed a debt in 1294 'to Jacopo of Spain, whom certain *jurati* of Lynn said was a burgess of Lynn' but nonetheless was subject to the French king. Cities considered the goods and rights of their citizens, wherever they were located, to come under the law of the home city. Not surprisingly, this was a frequent occasion of intercity wars, first in Italy but later in the north.[8]

The fact that much of the foreign trade of most large cities was controlled by the trading partner rather than by natives caused resentment, but foreign merchants paid dearly for their privileges and were easy to control and tax.[9] The most conspicuous foreign groups were in the cities of Poland and Russia, where they sometimes supplanted the native elite. Kraków and the other Polish centres remained small until German colonists settled in them. By virtue of having privileges from the prince, the Germans were in a strong position to represent the newly chartered cities with the lords. Before the Germans of Kraków were granted a settlement charter in 1257, German urban law had been given to several other settlements on the site. Whereas in the west charters were generally given early in the city-forming process, in Poland as in England, they postdated and in a sense confirmed the development of the urban agglomeration. These syndicates either bought out the prince's property, incomes and judicial rights in the cities, often for a fixed fee, or (as in the case of Kraków) aided him financially in the venture and were given control of the local government in return. In some places this also meant relocating the city centre or establishing new villages that eventually overshadowed the parent town. The two major prior centres on the site of Kraków, the citadel on the Wawel hill and the merchant-craft settlement of Okól just north of it, yielded in significance to a new city that was laid out in a grid plan north of Okól, with a central market and main streets leading to Okól and Wawel. The German patriciate of Kraków bought out the local nobles and became the elite

6   Hyde, *Society and Politics*, 73–4; Volpe, *Medio Evo Italiano*, 224–6.
7   Lesage, *Marseille angevine*, 88.
8   Owen, *Making of King's Lynn*, 454–5.
9   Williams, *Medieval London*, 12–14, 71.

of the late medieval city. At Gdansk, by contrast, the German settlers who came in large numbers in the thirteenth century and formed a separate community under their own law did not absorb the old Slavic city, which had been the commercial centre of Pomerelia since the ninth century.[10]

Diversification and domestic demand

The market for high- and medium-quality woollen cloth grew enormously as distribution mechanisms became more sophisticated. Leather-workers and furriers continued to have a strong export market well into the thirteenth century, but both declined after 1250 because of a shift in taste towards wool and silk; towards window glass rather than oil-soaked leather or parchment; towards glass and earthenware instead of leather-lined wooden bottles; and towards metal armour instead of tough leather. Wool and fur clothing became fashionable. The fate of the tanners at Winchester is typical. Even in the mid-twelfth century they were being displaced from the centrally located Tanners' Street by clothing workers. By 1300 most of them were in the eastern suburbs.[11]

As woollen textiles became the driving force of industrial urbanisation, the Flemish cities became enormous. Textile workers comprised at least 50 per cent of the populations of Ghent and Ypres. By the thirteenth century Ypres was as close to a purely industrial city as medieval Europe was to know. The fact that it hosted one of the 'five fairs' of Flanders, which gave it access to interregional markets, may explain much of its success. Provins, too, used its fairs to its long-term advantage. It had a population of some 2,000 households in the mid-thirteenth century, nearly half of them supported by woollen and linen clothmaking.[12]

The expanding industries had a plentiful supply of labour in the cities, much of it cheap and some of it highly skilled. But this was not solely a reaction to increased demand outside Europe for western services and manufactures. Internal demand grew more rapidly than did foreign. Much

10   Knoll, 'Urban development of medieval Poland', 74–5, 87; Carter, *Trade and Urban Development in Poland*, 58–66; Zbierski, 'Development of the Gdansk area', 316–17; Gieysztor, 'Chartes de franchises', 105.
11   Keene, *Medieval Winchester*, 287. There are some exceptions. Textiles and leather-working were of comparable importance in York in the twelfth century, but textiles declined sharply in the thirteenth. The city's merchants preferred to buy cloth made in the rural environs to that of the local weavers. Over three-quarters of the persons admitted to the freedom of York during the reign of Edward I (1272–1307) were in the leather trades, provisioning and metalworking. Not a single weaver obtained the freedom. Tillott, *City of York*, 43–4.
12   Chapin, *Villes de foires*, 60–70.

of the luxury manufacture was exported to destinations inside Europe. Wine and woollen cloth were the chief items of long-distance trade within Europe in the thirteenth century, and not all of the cloth was luxury woollens. The fairs made it possible to market medium grades profitably. Reims lacked heavy 'grand drapery' but exported substantial quantities of cheaper woollens and linens, which were made both in the city and by farmers of the environs whose products were marketed by merchants of Reims.[13]

Thus while urban luxury manufacturing had previously been directed mainly towards princely courts, after 1200 it was increasingly aimed at the urban well-to-do. Cities in different regions in effect fed off one another, even as some tried to stifle competition from neighbouring cities and particularly rural areas. Rural competition increased for various reasons, including the spread of the fulling mill and the fact that city governments were increasing taxes on weavers' looms. In England the growth of rural clothmaking was also speeded by the fact that merchants of the cities often patronised rural industries, even financing fulling mills, for they could then sell the rural cloth on urban markets.[14] Thus, although the largest textile centres were protectionist and tried to prevent or hinder the distribution of goods made elsewhere that might compete with their own citizens' specialities, most cities simply taxed the imports and let them be sold. This is particularly true of smaller centres, which lacked a large enough labour force and distribution mechanism to be able to manufacture and market highly specialised goods. The concentration of manufactures in the city was fed by interregional demand within Europe.

Trade, manufacture and the wealth structure.
Distribution of goods

Although craftsmen became the largest element of the population of many cities in the thirteenth century, most wealth still came from trade and distribution. Some city elites actually made more money by exporting wool in transit and importing cloth made elsewhere for sale locally than by manufacturing cloth. Although Segovia, Cordoba and Seville all became important cloth producers in the thirteenth century, more Castilian wool was exported through the cities than was made into cloth locally. Linen generated far more income than woollens at Provins in 1298.[15]

---

13 Desportes, *Reims*, 93–7, 114.
14 Miller and Hatcher, *Towns, Commerce and Crafts*, 111–14.
15 MacKay, *Spain*, 75; Chapin, *Villes de foires*, 86–8.

Despite the growth of urban industry, no one made a large fortune solely in manufacturing. It was always an adjunct of trade, for the cities depended on imports: food and the raw materials such as wool, leather and metals that were necessary for manufacturing. The larger the cities became, the more wealth could be made in supplying them. Just as the weaver of Ghent could not go to York to sell his cloth, he could not travel to Yorkshire to buy the fine wool that was used at Ghent in export textiles. Professional merchants organised convoys and made agreements with foreign suppliers and their governments to obtain these goods and bring them to their home cities, where they supplied them to craftsmen at considerable profit. Venice is justly renowned for importing eastern luxuries, but the most important single element in Venice's eastern prosperity was provisioning the city of Constantinople itself. Even the major long-distance trading and banking centres had a substantial underpinning of local trade, particularly in food and locally used items such as low- and medium-grade cloth.[16]

The food trade was especially critical. The rapid population growth since the early eleventh century was reflected first in the clearance and drainage of farmland, then in the expansion of the cities. But only in Flanders and north Italy did the urban index (the size of the largest city as a percentage of total population of the region) increase. Rather, the cities grew as part of an overall increase in population that freed more people from subsistence occupations for other work. However, rural population continued to grow considerably after the late twelfth century, by which time most of the best farmland was in cultivation. More people were therefore being forced off the farms and into the cities after 1175 than before.[17]

Securing a reliable food supply thus first became a critical problem for the cities in the thirteenth century. Feeding a city required the surplus production of a vast agricultural area, even in years of good harvests, and a crop failure could be catastrophic for a large city. Barcelona, whose impoverished rural environs could not feed the enormously growing city population in the thirteenth century, was dependent on Sicilian grain even before its lords, the kings of Catalonia, occupied the island in 1282. The rulers thereafter gave export licences, amounting to monopolies to feed the home city, to the wealthy financiers of Barcelona whose money was largely financing the kings' imperialist designs. The high cost of food led to revolt at Piacenza in July 1250. Grievances leading to troubles at Parma in 1255, Bologna in 1256, Milan in 1258, Siena in 1262 and

---

16 Barel, *Ville médiévale*, 417; Lane, *Venice*, 68–70.
17 Duby, *Early Growth*, 257–70; Nicholas, *Evolution*, 293–4.

Florence in 1266 included complaints about food speculators and demands that food should not be re-exported once it was inside the city.[18] The Italian cities tried initially to force their *contadi* to provide cheap grain for the urban market. Siena was requiring its *contado* communities to furnish quotas of grain to the city by 1223, and border patrols stopped grain from being exported. By 1262 Siena required its citizens in the *contado* to bring grain into the city for sale. After 1250 the captain of the *popolo* in Florence regulated the grain supply, including fixing prices in the city. In 1258 Florence forbade grain exports from the *contado*. In 1274 the city established the 'Six of the Grain', with their headquarters at Orsanmichele, to oversee grain distribution in the city and manage supplies in the *contado*. With conditions tightening in the late thirteenth century – there were eight grain shortages in Florence between 1276 and 1305 – oversight of the *contado* was intensified, and officials were appointed in each rural parish after 1275.[19]

After 1268 Pisa, too, forbade grain exports from its *contado*. The *canova*, the municipal grain office, imposed production quotas on rural communes, then forced the peasants to sell at an artifically low price. Grain production naturally declined in the *contado*, as farmers switched to other crops that the city did not regulate. Pisa was selling grain at a loss to its citizens by 1291 and thus turned to major foreign suppliers. Pisa's policy of keeping grain cheap in the city provided a labour force for its expanding cloth industry by forcing farmers into the city, but at the cost of depressing the *contado*, forcing local merchants out of the grain market, and saddling the government with a permanent debt. As depression deepened in the *contado*, some cities tried to force farmers to stay on the land. Bologna enticed more than 150 families of clothworkers, mainly in silks, from Florence, Lucca, Milan, Mantua, Brescia and Cremona by giving them contractual guarantees of favourable treatment. Shortly afterwards it forbade workers from its own *contado* to emigrate into the city and forced those who had come within the past five years to return, for the *contado* was becoming depopulated. In 1256 Perugia also prohibited the export of wheat outside its *contado*, but its overall policy was less exploitative, for the city made serious efforts to drain swamps in the *contado* and bring more farmland into cultivation.[20]

Urban networks in the north tended to develop on the edge of prosperous farm regions that lacked major cities; thus the grain of Picardy,

18 Mollat and Wolff, *Popular Revolutions*, 36–7; Bensch, *Barcelona*, 333.
19 Dameron, *Episcopal Power and Florentine Society*, 143–5.
20 Barel, *Ville médiévale*, 194–5; Waley, *Siena*, 106–8; Herlihy, *Pisa*, xi, 113–28; Blanshei, *Perugia*, 14–16; Haverkamp, 'Städte im Herrschafts- und Sozialgefüge Reichsitaliens', 236.

Walloon Flanders and Artois fed the great Flemish cities. The cities built canals in the rural areas and acquired extraterritorial jurisdiction over them. This enabled them to obtain grain more cheaply in bulk at a distance than nearby, where poor roads and the need to buy on village markets hindered exchange. Many cities thus became parasites on their immediate environs; the notion that cities grew because the surplus of their rural environs fed them may work for the period of their origins but not for the thirteenth century. Merchants who had access to distant markets, especially for grain and wine, but also for meat and animal by-products, vegetables and the ingredients of beer, thus had the growing populations of their home cities at their mercy. The domestic and regional markets, which were burgeoning in both size and purchasing power, were the basis of more urban merchants' wealth than overseas trade.

Urban networks and demographic patterns

The cities of the Muslim east remained enormous by western standards. Cairo and Cordoba had populations of some 250,000 around 1300. Baghdad was comparable, but this was a great decline from its early medieval height. Aleppo, Damascus and Tunis had 50,000–100,000 inhabitants in the early fourteenth century.[21] The Muslim cities, however, had been large for centuries and did not sustain the tremendous growth of those in the west. Between 1000 and 1300 most cities with a population of more than 20,000 at least doubled in size. Of eighteen cities that would have a population of 100,000 or more by 1800, only Amsterdam, Madrid and Copenhagen had under 5,000 in 1300. The fact that more large cities were providing commercial and financial services meant easier access not only of the rural groups to the cities but also of the cities to one another. Italy and Sicily had the largest cities of Europe, with Milan, Genoa, Venice, Naples, Florence and Palermo probably having populations of 100,000 by 1300. Paris, the largest city of the north, probably had 25,000–50,000 inhabitants in Philip Augustus's time, growing to 200,000 by 1300. By 1300 Montpellier and Rouen and its suburbs had some 40,000 inhabitants, Toulouse 35,000, Tours 30,000; Orléans, Strasbourg and Narbonne 25,000; Amiens, Bordeaux, Lille, Tournai and Metz 20,000; Marseilles 18,000; Arles 15,000; Arras, Avignon, Beauvais, Bourges, Dijon, Douai, Lyon and Reims 10,000–20,000.[22] The English cities grew more slowly. Their textile industries developed precociously in the twelfth century, but they became largely commercial in the thirteenth, for textiles declined as England imported most of its heavy

21 Hourani, *History of the Arab Peoples*, 110–11.
22 Baldwin, *Philip Augustus*, 345.

woollens from Flanders. Industry became directed toward producing consumer goods for a mainly local market. London may have had over 50,000 inhabitants in 1300, but York, the second largest English city, had only 10,000 inhabitants by that time. Even this was double its population as suggested by the Domesday Book.[23]

Such raw figures conceal considerable change. Pisa grew from about 11,000 in 1164 to 38,000 in 1293, and not even this was enough to prevent its loss of position to Florence, which was smaller than Pisa in 1200 but more than twice its size by 1300.[24] Most great successes of the thirteenth century were industrial centres and places such as Siena and Lucca with important banking facilities. Politics and the patronage of the royal court continued to have a great impact on London and Paris, but local churches and lords did not: they were generating less demand for goods and services now than did the wealthier townspeople, and, in contrast to them, no longer gave access to broader currents of trade.

Educational institutions were a new element in city populations. The medical and law schools of Montpellier attracted students.[25] Oxford and Cambridge reversed position in the thirteenth century. Cambridge had a stronger base than Oxford in the regional market and grew as a county town; with more competition within its region, Oxford lost the considerable commercial importance that it had enjoyed in Henry II's time. Both suffered from disputes between scholars and townspeople. The university's privileges and royal pressure forced the mayor of Cambridge in 1231 to appoint 'taxers' jointly with the university to fix rents payable by scholars, and after 1268 the university and city government jointly supervised the assize of bread and ale. Burgesses in litigation with outsiders were normally judged in the town court, but those who fell foul of scholars were judged in the court of the university chancellor.[26] Probably one-tenth of the population of thirteenth-century Paris consisted of scholars. A cessation of lectures in 1253 was a serious enough blow to the city to cause the king to force the university authorities to yield to the church's demands.[27]

Urban regions

Flanders and northern Italy continued to contain the major concentrations of cities, with the Rhine and Danube valleys a distant third. The Italian

23 Tillott, *City of York*, 40.
24 Herlihy, *Pisa*, 36–7, 43–4.
25 Faber and Lochard, *Montpellier*, 63, 111.
26 Lobel, *Atlas* 2: 7–8.
27 Baldwin, *Scholastic Culture*, 28–9, 39–40.

cities were enormous, and the secondary centres reflected the size of the chief cities of the regions. Perugia's lay population of about 34,000 in 1295 made it one-third the size of Florence and comparable to Padua, Verona, Siena and Mantua; yet it was as large as Bruges in 1340 and London in 1377. Padua grew from 15,000 in 1174 to 35,000 in 1320, but half the population lived in the suburbs outside the late-twelfth-century wall.[28]

Yet these figures are deceptive, for cities were market centres of regions. Although France had large cities, it had a low urban density. Metz became great as the only significant city of Alsace. Reims' sphere of influence was on the northeast, where there were no other large cities; its expansion northwest was blocked by the market network of Laon.[29] Flanders had three cities with over 40,000 souls in the late thirteenth century, giving it a higher urban density even than Tuscany. North-western France and Flanders became a virtual 'industrial corridor' whose textiles were marketed through the Champagne fairs, overland to the Rhineland, and the regional gateway port of Bruges. Although the cities grew more rapidly than the rural areas in these regions, elsewhere population increased at about the same rate in town and countryside, creating regional economies that were less dependent on luxury exports and food imports than were Italy and Flanders.[30]

Most scholarly discussion of 'urban' regionalism has included both towns and cities and thus cannot be applied strictly here. There appears to be an inverse correlation between the size of the region and the number of persons in the chief cities. Larger regions thus tend to be loosely structured and economically underdeveloped. The largest city is often on the region's edge, especially on the side toward significant cities outside the region, serving as economic gateways to the interior.[31]

Except for London, Metz and Paris, most large medieval cities developed in regions of high urban density. Although one would naturally expect a saturation of markets in places with many large cities, such as Tuscany, the local community provided demand for its own manufactures. Although most large cities also expanded into markets outside their immediate hinterlands, London and Metz did not: London because demand from the royal court was so large, and Metz because it dominated its environs so completely that it had no reason to seek distant markets. It might, in any case, have had trouble, given its isolation, in

28   Blanshei, *Perugia*, 30; Hyde, *Padua*, 32–3.
29   Le Goff, 'Apogée', 191; Desportes, *Reims*, 421.
30   Bairoch, *Cities and Economic Development*, 153–7; Russell, *Medieval Regions*, 38; Nicholas, *Medieval Flanders*, 117, 130.
31   Hohenberg and Lees, *Making of Urban Europe*, 58, 62–70.

obtaining industrial raw materials that would have made its products competitive in a wider market.

But a high concentration of cities is possible only if transport facilities are sufficiently developed to make possible substantial imports, at least of food, from outside the immediate region. Cities develop either at the end of transport routes or at their intersection. Changing the track of a road or diverting a navigable waterway could affect the urban hierarchy of a region. This may give one large city, usually a gateway, an advantage over others; but in a region of numerous smaller centres of comparable size, it can also mean that all grain will be consumed locally with little surplus left that might provision a major city. The Beauce, for example, supported Chartres and Blois but exported little grain until the sixteenth century.[32]

The region and population replenishment

Preindustrial populations have extremely high death rates – as much as 6 per cent even in normal years. Cities thus can grow only if immigration compensates for or exceeds natural losses. Recent migrants made up one-quarter to half the population of most growing cities. Pirenne thought that most inhabitants of the cities, particularly the merchants, were uprooted wanderers who came from a great distance, but demographic studies show conclusively that this was not so. The city evolved as a natural creation of its immediate environment, generally with a population of emancipated peasants or sometimes serfs. Even as late as the fifteenth century most immigrants came from the immediate environs of the city, although the larger cities attracted newcomers from a larger area.

Migration figures are fragmentary for the thirteenth century, but some cases are instructive. Most immigrants to York at that time came from rural northern England. Of ninety-eight notaries in Cinzica, the commercial sector of Pisa, sixty-five were recent immigrants in 1293, and other evidence suggests rapid influx from the *contado* after 1284. Unskilled labourers would have been more mobile and less recorded in documents than notaries. Nearly three-fifths of the citizenry of Arles in 1271 came from Provence and another one-fifth from Auvergne and eastern Languedoc. Labourers made up 32 per cent of documented immigrants at rapidly growing Montpellier. Most were from surrounding villages, while merchants came from further away. Metz and Arras attracted immigrants

---

32   Bairoch, *Cities and Economic Development*, 142–3; Chédeville, *Chartres et ses campagnes*, 455–6; Chédeville, *Histoire de Chartres*, 90.

from within a radius of 40 km in the thirteenth century. Half the taxpayers at Reims in the early fourteenth century came from less than 13 km away, while 60 per cent were from under 30 km.[33]

Most peasants thus did not migrate further than the nearest large city, and this set up cultural spheres of roughly 35–60 km in diameter. Relatives in the city attracted their cousins, and communities or colonies based on common profession, language or ancestry developed. But the larger the city, the wider its attraction and accordingly the more diverse its population was likely to be. Urban regionalism thus involves not only interaction between regions but also within them. Distance determined population concentration. Cities were more evenly distributed in the Middle Ages than now, for services and production were less specialised and specifically urban. Thus a village was within walking distance of its fields, while market towns were close enough to one another to permit a round trip and attention to business in a single day (about 10 km). The smaller cities were a full day's journey apart (35–50 km).[34]

Urban privilege and the regional market

The military power of the enormous cities veiled their vulnerability to any external stoppage of labour and supplies. Once large the city could only maintain itself by obtaining privileges that its neighbours did not enjoy. Individual cities either seized or were granted the sole pre-emptive right to buy and market specific goods within a given radius of the town. Inhabitants of the privileged locality were exempt from commercial taxes on goods that they did not consume personally, but transients had to stop, pay toll and often transfer their cargoes to local merchants or brokers. Such privileges, called staples, thus strengthened the cities' role as regional markets, in effect forcing the concentration of market activity that might otherwise have been diffused. They centralised sales of goods and facilitated tax collection.

Virtually all cities had a staple: either over a specific rich trade (wine at Bordeaux), or one involving a strategic commodity in a wide area (the grain staple of Ghent), or a coastal/intermediary trade in many items (Bruges). The staple was not established until the city was already thriving, but it contributed materially to its continued expansion. Some staples cushioned the city against the decline of the industry or trade on which

---

33   Tillott, *City of York*, 40; Herlihy, *Pisa*, 36; Faber and Lochard, *Montpelier*, 110; Stouff, *Arles*, 97; Le Goff, 'Apogée', 196–7.
34   Russell, *Medieval Regions*, 12, 26–8, 30–4; Weber, *The City*, 100–2.

its fortunes had initially been built. Except when the staple was comprehensive, the result, as with the fairs, was only a short-term increase in the demand for labour in the city. Thus much of the increase in business provided jobs for part-time workers, many of them recruited from the rural environs.

This is especially true of the wine staples, for the trade was seasonal since wine spoiled quickly. Most of Bordeaux's port traffic came in a single month after harvest. The wine staple generated immense wealth for Bordeaux's patricians but little permanent population increase. Wine growers had to use the city to reach the English market, but they paid taxes that citizens did not. Bordeaux's share of other markets was so small that its economy collapsed when the English left in the fifteenth century.[35] Barcelona, by contrast, obtained in 1227 a monopoly of shipping in the Mediterranean as long as it had ships and seamen available. Since foreign merchants were restricted to loading and unloading their own merchandise, local merchants and brokers controlled sales. This gave year-round employment and contributed largely to Barcelona's growth.[36]

Most staples served two functions: ensuring that the city had enough food and strategic raw materials, and concentrating large-scale exchange there. The earliest staples were imposed by town lords. Mainz originally had a staple only on wood and coal, both of which were monopolies of the archbishop. Thereafter the city's tolls became increasingly important; not only did they provide income for the archbishop and eventually the city, but also, because the goods were held for several days, citizens were able to buy what they needed before re-export was allowed. Salt, the main food preservative, was highly regulated. Passau had a staple on the salt trade between Bavaria and Bohemia. Venice's various monopolies gave it a virtually complete staple on the northern Adriatic. It sold to the Salt Offices of local governments, which in turn monopolised sales.[37]

Grain staples were especially critical. All ships loading grain in Venice's far-flung dominions were required to bring the cargoes home. Venice also competed successfully with the mainland cities for grain supplies, for it could offer high prices to farmers. The mainland Italian cities both imported from overseas and forced the peasants of their *contadi* to sell on the city market; but they also exported whatever was not needed. The smaller cities of northern Europe became obligatory

35 Renouard, *Bordeaux sous les rois d'Angleterre*, 34, 54–8.
36 Bisson, *Crown of Aragon*, 76.
37 Brandl-Ziegert, 'Sozialstruktur', 54–5; Lane, *Venice*, 58–63; Falck, *Mainz in seiner Blütezeit*, 102.

sales depots for nearby farmers, then sold to merchants of the larger cities. The major cities were not fed by merchants haggling with farmers or even by pre-emptive purchases on the rural markets. Rather, they bought from smaller suppliers who had already made the initial purchase or collected the grain as rent, the great rural magnates and the churches, particularly those centred in the home city. The needs of the largest cities for raw materials and particularly for food created demand that led to the smaller cities developing their own staples, and this in turn fostered their prosperity.

CHANGES IN THE CITY PLAN. THE WALLS, INNER CITIES AND SUBURBS

As population grew, mainly through immigration, and the cities increasingly used their gates as control points for trade, most cities of the continent walled their suburbs in several stages between 1150 and 1325. Piacenza went from a walled area of 45 ha in the tenth century to 65 ha in the second wall (1139–56) to 75 ha in the enclosure of 1218–32. Population doubled from 7,500 to 15,000 between the tenth century and 1200, then again to 30,000 by 1300. Pisa nearly quadrupled its walled area, entirely north of the Arno, to 114 ha around 1150, then brought the total agglomeration to 185 ha after 1300 by fortifying the densely populated suburb of Cinzica, south of the river. Florence grew even more spectacularly. Its sixth wall, built between 1284 and 1333, enclosed 650 ha, some of it unoccupied. Some Italian walls did not enclose the inhabited suburbs until after 1300, when the northern cities had reached their maximum extent. Perugia only began to replace its early medieval wall in 1256 and completed the expansion between 1327 and 1342. Tardy fortification, combined with the fact that Italian cities were dominated by towers and other high buildings that could accommodate many inhabitants, explains why the Italian cities had fortified areas comparable to the northern but larger populations. One could walk east–west across Siena in five minutes or less, north–south in fifteen minutes; yet it had a population of 30,000 in the thirteenth century. Genoa is an extreme case. Its medieval wall was extraordinarily small, enclosing only 150 ha. The artisan suburbs were only fortified in the fourteenth century. With space thus at a premium in the central city, Genoa had no public square before 1450. The same principle applies to the cities of the French Midi; the 'Common Cloture' of Montpellier enclosed only 45 ha, and the Narbonne wall only 37 ha. By contrast, the wall of Lille enclosed 80 ha at the end of the thirteenth century, that of Metz 160 ha in 1226.[38] Apart from the planned expansion of some north Italian cities after 1260, most cities walled the suburban areas only after they had substantial settlement. Since the older walls were not torn down when new suburbs were fortified, most cities in the north and some in Italy had what amounted to separate fortified quarters. Particularly in cities that experienced heavy artisan immigration, the areas outside the walls became craft 'ghettoes'. Most eventually incorporated these populated areas within their walls. Bordeaux already had major suburbs on the south outside its second wall by 1260, but a third wall was only commenced in 1302.[39]

Polynuclear cities faced the seigniories of powerful lords as the suburbs were walled. Novgorod was troubled by noble factions whose lands were concentrated in one of the five separate boroughs that made up the city, three on the 'St Sophia Side', two on the 'Merchants' Side'. As at Kiev, Novgorod's constituent settlements continued to elect their own officials throughout the Middle Ages, and these posts became bastions of boyar strength that was reflected in the mayoralty and council of the united city.[40] Although Ghent bought out the rights of several lords in the central city and the immediate environs, two suburban abbey villages remained independent through the Middle Ages. One, which sheltered a large concentration of weavers, received a partial fortification in the 1320s, the other not until the 1380s, in each case under pressure from the government of Ghent.[41] Brunswick had five settlements that were distinct topographically and legally until the end of the thirteenth century: two were around churches, one around Duke Henry the Lion's palace, while the Old City comprised the Old Market and Kohlmarkt settlements and was populated by merchants and artisans. In the twelfth century Henry established the Hagen as a suburban area under urban law, then founded a 'New City' between it and the Old City. Immigrants turned the Hagen into a weavers' quarter, while the Old City became commercial. The New City received a planned layout around 1200.[42]

Since expansion was generally unilateral rather than concentric, along the major road leading into the town or less frequently along a river,

38   Herlihy, *Pisa*, 33, 37, 42–3; Braunfels, *Urban Design*, 49–50; Blanshei, *Perugia*, 22; Waley, *Siena*, 1; Heers, *Espaces Bologne*, 72–3, 76–7, 130; Faber and Lochard, *Montpellier*, 122; Haverkamp, 'Städte im Herrschafts- und Sozialgefüge Reichsitaliens'.
39   Renouard, *Bordeaux sous les rois d'Angleterre*, 89.
40   Langer, 'Medieval Russian town', 28–9; Birnbaum, 'Lord Novgorod', 178–9; Birnbaum, 'Kiev, Novgorod, Moscow', 35–6.
41   Nicholas, *Metamorphosis*, 70.
42   Puhle, *Politik der Stadt Braunschweig*, 4–6.

the original nucleus of the city became topographically peripheral. Rarely if ever were the Roman *forum* or the main Roman streets still in the centre of a thirteenth-century city. Perugia's steep topography forced uneven expansion along five main roads, which gave the city a star shape.[43] Hill sites had a severe defence problem as population grew. Thirteenth-century Siena had thirty-six gates but a discontinuous wall. At Marseilles only the north side of the port was densely inhabited. The wall was incomplete, and access to the port was controlled by a chain stretched across the harbour.[44]

Urban fortification was less developed in England, where the cities were under less threat of attack. Although the king gave some cities 'murage' to help finance the building or maintenance of defences, most did not have a complete walled circuit apart from the primitive Alfredian defences around the centre. Some cities had earth walls, and even as large a place as Coventry only converted them to stone in the fifteenth century. Most had a palisade and ditch, with gates that functioned as toll stations but were of minimal defensive use. Even in the thirteenth century some English cities rented apartments in the gatehouses and towers in the walls as dwellings, a practice that only became common later on the continent.[45]

Reims: a case study of planned topographical expansion

Lords founded villages, some of them outside their major cities, and tried to encourage merchants and craftsmen to settle in them. Edward I tried to found a textile suburb at Bordeaux in the 1280s, but it failed due to the hostility of the city government. Count William VI founded Peyrou west of Montpellier and tried, albeit unsuccessfully, to entice leather artisans and grain merchants to settle there.[46]

At Reims (Plan 7), however, the city lord planned an industrial suburb that was linked successfully to the organic city. Reims had grown rapidly in the twelfth century. The eastern half of the City contained little but churches, while the market, divided into sectors for cloth and grain, was on the site of the Roman *forum*. The street plan was haphazard: the Mercerie and Epicerie [Mercers' and Spicers' Streets] were between the market and the abbey, while the goldsmiths were nearby, and the rue des Monniers [Minters' Street] led off the market. Enough room

---

43   Heers, 'Paysages construits', 297; Blanshei, *Perugia*, 21–2.
44   Waley, *Siena*, 2; Baratier, *Histoire de Marseille*, 80.
45   Lobel, *Atlas* 1: 6–7; Turner, *Town Defences*, 54, 41–7; Platt, *Medieval Southampton*, 36–7; Keene, *Medieval Winchester*, 43–4.
46   Faber and Lochard, *Montpellier*, 49–51, 63, 81–2, 85–93, 118–19.

remained within Reims' Roman wall to accommodate growth until 1160.

But between 1160 and 1210 the inhabited area doubled, taking Reims to the limit of its medieval development. Archbishop William of the White Hands opted for growth in the marshy area controlling the Pont Vesle at the market end of the Roman *decumanus*. A new wall enclosed everything as far east as the abbey of Saint-Remi. The new settlement, called La Couture [the Cultivation, suggesting an agrarian origin], had a main street called Nouvelle Couture [New Cultivation] that was wide enough to be used as a fair. The charter for La Couture gave fixed ground rents and a mayor chosen by the archbishop from the citizenry, with competence to judge all civil actions and misdemeanours.

On the other side of the rue de Vesle, which led from the gate, the archbishop converted his garden into an industrial suburb with a main artery called 'rue du Jard-aux-Drapiers' [Drapers' Garden Street]. Demand for land was so high that the new settlement established here in 1205, Venise, had fixed ground rents that were 50 per cent higher than in La Couture. A wall was begun in 1209. The plan to lure weavers to Reims was only partially successful. The city had a substantial cloth production, but little of it was exported, and many of the workers were part-time farm labourers. While Jard-aux-Drapiers became densely settled, Venise still had vacant lots with many gardens a century later.[47]

The street plan and social geography

Although many streets were named after trades in the early cities, by the thirteenth century this no longer meant that all or even most practitioners of the craft after which they were named lived there, except for some cities in southern France. Some streets were named after a prominent building; for houses too had names, usually that of the owner, colour or other physical peculiarity. A name might also be influenced by the building's use and very often by the design of the sign hung outside the front door or by a wooden or stone sculpture. At Mainz the Himmelgasse [Heaven Street] was not inspired by celestial preoccupations but named after the house 'zum Himmel'. Most street names were unchanged through the central and late Middle Ages; Canterbury had some changes, due to a tendency there and throughout England to name streets after their destinations rather than structures in the street.[48]

---

47 Desportes, *Reims*, 53–80.
48 Keene, *Medieval Winchester*, 55; Bonney, *Durham*, 61; Falck, *Mainz in seiner Blütezeit*, 68–70.

Cities that developed along a single street displayed little occupational segregation. Most of them were ports or had their expansion blocked by a castle or natural barrier. English Street was the main thoroughfare at Southampton; the only east–west artery was East Street, leading from English Street to the walls. Most of the great merchants lived in English Street, but stall-shops were found along the entire length. The smiths were in the north end, the butchers more dispersed. Outside Eastgate the suburb of St Mary's had some shops and the properties of many of the wealthy folk of the town. Particularly on the west, properties might front on English Street and extend back to one of the side streets paralleling it toward the castle, or to an obstacle such as the castle wall. The burgage tenements at Southampton were more rectangular than was common; elsewhere they were characteristically trapezoidal, with a short front on the street side but extending back toward a long side in the rear. Sizes of plots were not standardised. Lanes and alleys divided the properties and served as their service entries.[49]

As the cities became more densely populated and industrial, occupational concentrations gave way to more dispersed settlement, with small concentrations of trade brothers living throughout the city. Butchers and fishmongers were generally on the downwind side of markets and cities because their trades were odiferous. As industrial processes were closely regulated, several unlinked concentrations of settlement might evolve particularly in cities that developed export specialities, most often textiles. Frequently a street in the old city where textile artisans had lived in the early stages of city formation became aristocratic, as the old families living there controlled the marketing side of their trades; but the original street name was retained. The mass of migrants streaming to the cities in the thirteenth century lived in suburban tenements, as space for housing became scarce in the old city centres. Thus most weavers at Reims lived in the suburbs after the great industrial expansion of the turn of the thirteenth century, not in the rue des Teliers [Weavers' Street] in the central city.[50]

The tendency to occupational segregation was always strongest in southern France. The most rigid example in the twelfth century was Montpellier, but the situation present there by 1204 became general in Languedoc during the thirteenth century, as the city governments tried to control the unorganised trades by enforcing divisions into quarters and streets dominated by a single trade. Topographical organisation by trades became the feature that most distinguished the social geography

---

49 Platt, *Medieval Southampton*, 43–7; Aston and Bond, *Landscape of Towns*, 98.
50 Desportes, *Reims*, 97–102.

of the cities from the rural villages by the end of the thirteenth century. Yet occupational segregation applied less rigidly to the larger crafts; for instance, textile workers were too numerous to be confined to a single quarter.[51]

The land market and urban rent

Given the ties of landownership with citizenship and the rapidity of population renewal, the urban land market was very mobile, particularly in places with partible inheritance that facilitated alienation of property. Although the boundaries of tenements as legal units owing ground rent to the town lord or municipal government were rather stable, they could be subdivided and the parts incorporated in a neighbouring tenement. Many tenements took their legal-description name from an early owner-family, and the name persisted for centuries.[52]

Since sales were initially made by oral contract, with the occasional written record simply as confirmation, we know little of the mechanics of the real estate sale market before 1200, apart from purchases by members of wealthy lineages. Purchase price was rarely stated in writing. In most English cities conveyances were being entered by the late thirteenth century on the general court roll of the city, not on a separate roll of deeds.[53]

Information about rents is better. Most English cities had three types. The simple ground rent or landgable was not attached to buildings but to the plot itself. It bore no relationship to the size of the tenement. Freehold rent was connected to tenure in freehold and accordingly was owed even if the tenant's legal interest in the property ended. Leasehold rents had a much higher monetary value to lords than the other two. In Durham and Cambridge rents were high and lease terms short in the city centre, lower on the peripheries.[54]

Our best information about the urban land market in the thirteenth century is from northern Italy. Although the bishops of Florence were concentrating on their rural holdings by this time, they still held considerable property in the city, most of it centrally located between the second and third walls. In 1255 the bishop started selling 'little houses'

---

51 Gouron, *Métiers en Languedoc*, 130.
52 Tillott, *City of York*, 37; Nicholas, 'Poverty and primacy', 37–41; Bonney, *Durham*, 71–3.
53 Keene, *Medieval Winchester*, 8–18. Some deeds at Winchester were initially put on rolls of persons burned at the stake; the 'stake rolls' became a registry of deeds in the fifteenth century.
54 Bonney, *Durham*, 111–15.

in the Cafaggio, the area around the Baptistery, evidently in response to pressure from the new *popolo* regime that had recently assumed power in the city. The Cafaggio became an area of small shops. Most of the Cafaggio contained houses and shops and other business property that was put up for short-term (1–2 years) money rents. The bishops let out some properties in Cafaggio on longer leases (5–6 years) and lower rents on condition that the holder build a shop or make other improvements. In 1297 the bishop sold the Cafaggio and the next year a major street running through it to the city.[55]

Rents were generally for long terms in the early thirteenth century, but this changed rapidly after 1250. Into the thirteenth century the sale rather than rental of emphyteutic (perpetual rent) single-family dwellings dominated the Florentine land market. Properties were generally called *domus*. But the rapid immigration to the city in the thirteenth century created a high demand for property. Thus emphyteusis, which could not be changed easily to take advantage of market conditions, was gradually abandoned, and the sources speak more often of *casa* than of *domus*; both mean 'house', but *domus* were conveyed with the land. Under emphyteusis the buyer would normally build a house on the property and have the right to alienate it for the entire term of the lease. As population grew, from the early thirteenth century there are also more references to properties that are smaller, and the terminology often implied that a building was to be constructed. Business property was becoming especially valuable with the commercial expansion of the cities. Ground-floor shops at Florence by the end of the thirteenth century normally rented for more than the upper storeys. In the many cases where the owner was non-resident and often did not practise a trade – as with the urban nobles – investing in land and rents made economic as well as social sense.[56]

Rome developed a genuine property market for the first time in the thirteenth century, mainly in areas owned by the churches, which were renting them for increasingly short terms. Rome displays a reverse pattern from Florence in that until around 1270 the sale of land along with houses was unusual but became more normal thereafter. Rental contracts in perpetuity and for three lives constituted 80 per cent of the total number of transactions in the twelfth century, followed by longer-term contracts. But perpetual rents were only one-sixth of the new contracts that were made between 1275 and 1300, as short-term rents of one to

---

55   Dameron, *Episcopal Power and Florentine Society*, 153–9; Sznura, *Espansione urbana di Firenze*, 56–7, 61–3.
56   Sznura, *Espansione urbana di Firenze*, 24–5, 30, 134–5.

five years became the norm. They were much higher than perpetual rent but in contrast to it had no entry fees, and the owner rather than the tenant was responsible for maintenance of the property. The rise in property values and prices that became perceptible in the second third of the twelfth century at Rome lasted until the end of the thirteenth. It was especially rapid on 'prestige buildings' such as towers and palaces.[57]

The property market was thus very profitable in the thirteenth century. The Mozzi, an important family of the first *popolo* of Florence, based much of their prosperity and social standing on their acquisition of 1600 *libre* of rent on houses and lands in the rapidly developing suburb of Oltrarno.[58] Recent immigrants and many established persons from the middle and lower social orders rented houses or apartments. Migrants and other poor and marginal persons often sought the cheap housing that was typical of areas of poor drainage, although by now these were generally suburban. The urban wealthy not only bought land for prestige, but they also began speculating on both ground rents and market rents. The former were often fixed, but the latter were extremely profitable as population growth stimulated the demand for housing. Negotiable and heritable, they were relatively safe investments that could provide income for family members who were not following the family business, such as those entering holy orders. In 1295 Hermann von Stein willed the rental income from a moneychanging table to his two granddaughters to support them in a nunnery. The table itself would go to the cloister when the second child died. The nunnery was also buying rents on shops.[59] At Reims the trade in rents was most active in the poorer quarters just inside the walls. The normal price amounted to 5 per cent interest in perpetuity. The proprietor of a house could encumber it to the entire amount of its value, and the buyers could lose if the house were torn down or collapsed.[60]

The market square

Activity was concentrated on the market square. Virtually all large cities had multiple markets by the thirteenth century, permanently or semi-permanently used and differentiated by the commodity sold on them. The period of greatest growth of multiple urban markets in England was the first three-quarters of the thirteenth century, when the provincial centres

57 Hubert, *Espace urbain*, 299–300, 323–6, 337, 342–3, 350–3.
58 Sznura, *Espansione urbana di Firenze*, 106–7.
59 *Nürnberger Urkundenbuch*, 547–8, 523–4, 553–4, 562–3.
60 Desportes, *Reims*, 602–9.

were growing as London stagnated.[61] Domesday York had a 'Market-shire', which evidently included the separate areas occupied by the modern Shambles, Pavement and the Thursday Market. All were held on Sunday until 1322, after which they were staggered throughout the week. The Thursday and Pavement markets were for general merchandise, while the others were for specific goods. Metz had several markets even in the twelfth century.[62] Commercial property on the central market was the most valuable in the city and was taxed at a higher rate than residential areas nearer the walls. Winchester, whose High amounted to a street market, even taxed 'baker women' on the High more severely than those on side streets. Merchants built houses and storehouses around the main market, and some, particularly those of ministerial origin, owned some of the market land.[63]

Access to the market square was a problem, particularly in Italy. Since most public squares there were separate from the main market, market-places were smaller than in the north, were irregular in form and were broken by noble towers. Genoa's three major markets in 1186 were dominated by the residences, towers and shops of aristocratic families whose clienteles vied for control of the area. Although Florence tried to control building on the Grain Market and the New Market, where the halls of four of the seven great guilds of the city were situated, it left the Old Market in total chaos, with at least eleven tiny alleys entering it.[64] Italian market squares had covered arcades for shops, but these were narrow enough to keep access free. Balconies (*loggia*) extended from the palaces over the street and hindered passage, just as the superimposed upper storeys of houses did in northern Europe. Siena regulated the height of buildings and even demanded architectural uniformity of windows on the main square.[65]

Although towers for residence and defence are associated more in the popular imagination with the Italian magnates than with northern city dwellers, the merchants of Ghent had towers in the twelfth century and were notoriously bellicose. Those of Regensburg had about fifty residential towers in the Italian fashion, some as high as nine storeys. Itinerant peddlers and prefabricated stalls caused chaos everywhere. 'Masters of the streets', whose duties included preventing stands and porticoes from projecting too far onto the streets and squares, are documented at Rome from 1233 and functioned in most major Italian centres by 1300.

61 Miller and Hatcher, *Towns, Commerce and Crafts*, 163–6.
62 Tillott, *City of York*, 484–5; Schneider, *Metz*, 202–3.
63 Vance, *Continuing City*, 160–1; Keene, *Medieval Winchester*, 49.
64 Hughes, 'Urban growth', 7; Heers, 'Paysages construits', 305–6.
65 Krautheimer, *Rome*, 284; Heers, *Espaces Bologne*, 86; Racine, 'Palais publics', 144; Heers, 'Paysages construits', 300–4.

In addition to street inspectors Siena had special guardians of the main square, who were to keep both the square and streets leading to it clear of debris. In 1269 the council of Cologne gave the Holy Ghost confraternity the income of four butcher's shops, located 'on the Meat Market outside the Butchers' Hall, extending directly eastward into the area between the shops and the ducking stool'. Expansion had been so rapid that there were too many butchers to be accommodated in the meat hall, so the city was renting open-air stalls for meat sales.[66]

Public buildings on the market

The first public buildings apart from churches and secular lords' castles were being erected after 1200. They were usually built on the main market in the northern cities, but the Italian cities more often cleared land, much of it confiscated or destroyed during the factional conflicts, for a public square distinct from the market.

The cities centred major commercial transactions, specifically those involving imports and potential exports, on the market square, where they could be taxed and checked for quality. Topographical segregation by occupation was strongest among the small craftsmen, who used the same building as home and workshop. In trades such as textiles, which produced for an export market, and foodmongering, where quality control was an important concern, the authorities tried to centralise sales in halls or central markets. The oldest surviving public hall in England today is almost certainly the Exeter guildhall, which is first mentioned in 1160, but it does not seem to have been used as a market. Northampton's combination market- and guildhall may go back to 1138. Bury St Edmunds had a hall by 1169 and Gloucester by 1192. By 1300 Cambridge had a guildhall and a gaol on the market, and many 'rows' (streets) named after trades leading away from the square. The city court of York met at the guildhall or at the tollbooth on Ouse Bridge, which became the centre of the city's financial administration in 1246.[67] Two types of shop, and accordingly of market mechanism, thus developed: prefabricated, portable benches and permanent residence shops along side streets, and non-residential sale and inspection halls on the major markets.[68]

Outside the great textile cities, butchers, fishmongers and grain merchants were the most prominent trades selling at municipal halls and

66 Nicholas, *Medieval Flanders*, 121; Braunfels, *Urban Design*, 119; Stoob *et al.*, *Urkunden*, 236.
67 Lobel, *Atlas* 2: 10; Tittler, *Architecture and Power*, 12–13, 30; Tillott, *City of York*, 34.
68 Gouron, *Métiers en Languedoc*, 116–17.

regulated markets before 1300. Montpellier had a grain market by 1168, and Ghent's grain hall dates from the twelfth century. Virtually every city had at least one municipal butchery. In 1222 Toulouse had three groups of butchers who inherited their stalls in the hall. Narbonne initially had one butchery, but by 1302 there were separate ones for bourg and City. Montpellier had two triperies by 1297; but the butchery was separate, linked by a street to the Grain Market. Butchers of pigs, sheep and cattle had separate organisations at Montpellier, but they evidently sold in the same place. The fish markets were usually close to the butchery.[69]

The Cloth Hall on the main square, where inspections and sales were centralised, was the most prominent public building in many northern cities. The Flemish cities had them long before building separate city halls. In 1260 the Council of Soest charged the 'fraternity' of 'clothmakers' with appointing sworn inspectors, who would charge a fee for affixing the town seal to cloth of appropriate quality. Sales and fee collection were done in a hall that the city had bought from a prominent burgess, which the weavers were renting from the city.[70]

Only the largest cities had a central merchants' hall in the thirteenth century. It was usually on the main market and contained the city weight, toll station, regulators' chambers and staple offices. It was combined with the cloth hall in some cities. Dresden required everyone, 'man or citizen', who had a booth in the 'Cloth Hall, called Merchants' Hall [*Kaufhaus*] in the popular tongue', to pay a fee for bridge maintenance. Only merchants operating from booths in the Cloth Hall could cut cloth in the city. Sales in the cellar were restricted to cloth woven and prepared in Dresden itself; but the finest grades, 'cloth from Ghent and other coloured cloth', could be cut and sold in the upper storey.[71]

Some guilds already had their own halls, but this was unusual. They were usually along the quais or on secondary markets rather than the main square. The earliest were for guilds that exported heavily, such as the cloth halls, or imported, such as the twelfth-century guildhall of the shippers of Ghent, the earliest surviving urban stone hall in northern Europe. In 1265 Erfurt bought a ruined building on land vacated by fishermen and converted it to a bakers' hall. In 1240 the count of Dortmund and his wife sold to the city government for a perpetual rent their 'house on the marketplace of Dortmund', a two-storey structure that was already divided into rented butchers' stalls and shoemakers' shops. The

---

69   Gouron, *Métiers en Languedoc*, 118–24.
70   Stoob, *Urkunden*, 260–1.
71   Möncke, *Quellen*, 130–3.

city government thus acquired lordship over choice business property on the market. At Metz the trades were less centralised. Drapers, tanners and bakers had two halls, while there were several butcheries and merceries, all on the main market squares.[72] After rebuilding the wooden Krämerbrücke [Mercers' Bridge] in stone, the Council of Erfurt gradually bought out the churches that owned the shops on it and tried to restrict shops outside the halls to the bridge.[73]

The first city halls

The first city halls in the north were built in the thirteenth century, then were reconstructed or replaced in the fourteenth or fifteenth. Most governments still conducted public business in rented chambers or the homes of magistrates. City halls were usually massive rectangular structures near or on the main market, close to or even physically joined to the merchants' hall or cloth hall. Work on them continued for decades. Some city halls, such as those of Bristol and Saint-Omer, were converted merchants' guildhalls. Most city halls included the belfry and balconies from which crowds could be addressed, taxes 'cried' (auctioned orally to the highest bidder), and ceremonies conducted. The city hall of Dortmund, built shortly after 1232, had a wine cellar; the ground floor was the cloth hall; the courtroom and council chamber were on the first upper storey, while the top floor was used as a ballroom. The city halls of Lübeck, Bruges and Ypres also served as cloth halls. That of Lübeck was a complex of interlinked buildings.

From this basic type the city halls became increasingly complicated, usually including a chapel, writing offices and archives, and eventually finance chambers. Even in the twelfth century the city governments were often putting the oral arrangements made before the *échevins* into written form. In 1184 the count of Ponthieu ruled that in the absence of the corroborating oral testimony of the *échevins* of Abbeville, a contract was valid only if a written transcript could be shown. This usage spread quickly from Picardy to most regions of the northern continent. Multiple copies in the form of chirographs (handwritten documents) became the norm; for unless the contracting parties had affixed their own seals to a written record or employed a notary to do so, the city had to keep one copy to prove the validity of the engagement. This necessitated a

---

72 Nicholas, *Medieval Flanders*, 149; Stoob, *Urkunden*, 262, 219; Schneider, *Metz*, 203–5.
73 Mägdefrau, 'Volksbewegungen in Erfurt', 330; Möncke, *Quellen*, 72–5.

city archive, as did the increasingly sophisticated financial and diplomatic records that the cities were keeping by the thirteenth century.[74]

Thus in 1265 the council of Rostock established the court and city hall on the central market square and designated the church of St Peter as the municipal archive. The prison might be in the city hall, an adjacent tower or in the town wall. The city halls became foci of municipal pride and accordingly a threat to the town lord; when emperor Frederick II abolished the independent council of Worms in 1232, he also had the city hall destroyed. Some patrician houses at Bruges were modelled on the designs of city halls, but more often the hall borrowed from the styles of the palaces of wealthy citizens. Coats of arms were painted or sculpted on their façades and often on their portals.[75]

The city hall helped shift the urban focus toward a new centre. Since the main market was generally in one of the first suburbs to be brought within the fortification, often at its junction with the old city wall, the city hall was not as peripheral as the prince's castle or the bishop's headquarters. The city hall of Montpellier was built in 1205, just off the square in Condamine, the main merchant quarter and the first of several suburbs that were eventually brought within the wall. The building's main entrance was on the vegetable market, near the pilgrimage route and Notre-Dame-des-Tables, the main church of Montpellier, where public assemblies and ceremonies were held.[76]

Urban renewal in thirteenth-century Italy

While in the northern cities the changes of the thirteenth century were intensifications of tendencies present earlier, accentuated as artisans streamed into the suburbs, civic strife caused a revolution in urban morphology in Italy.

Most Italian cities had inherited a Roman wall and a quadrilateral plan in the centre, then developed in a radial pattern in the suburbs from the ninth century.[77] Neighbourhoods could be ethnically based, particularly in ports. Some parishes had their own squares with bell towers and shops.[78] But except at Venice most neighbourhoods crystallised around the towers of magnates. The Italian cities remained polynuclear until city halls and central markets took over the social and economic functions of the towers.

74 Bedos-Rezac, 'Civic liturgies and urban records', 34–9.
75 Lobel, *Atlas* 2: 9; Isenmann, *Deutsche Stadt*, 54–5; Rossiaud, 'Crises', 578–82; Paul, 'Rathaus und Markt', 92–5; Stoob *et al.*, *Urkunden*, 197; Chapin, *Villes de foires*, 189.
76 Le Goff, 'L'Apogée', 202; Faber and Lochard, *Montpellier*, 126–32.
77 Racine, 'Palais publics', 138–9.
78 Lane, *Venice*, 11–14.

This was perhaps due to the collapse of the centres after the decline of the Roman cities, as well as to magnate power. The feuds of magnate extended families with their clients and retainers were a serious threat to public peace in both city and *contado*.[79]

The military pretensions of the magnate families centred on their towers, 140 of which were destroyed in Rome in the 1250s. Central Bologna had at least 194 towers in the early thirteenth century. They were tall, often windowless to the third or fourth storey. Living space was in the tower complex but not in the central fortification. Access to the street from the interior courtyards was through guarded gates. Magnate complexes in Genoa included a central courtyard where the family could meet, a church, houses, tower, bathhouse and shops that the family rented out or used directly. The noble complexes thus provided the necessities for the lineage and its clients. The main buildings were usually at the intersection of two streets, controlling both. Although other property was subject to partible inheritance, the central house and tower generally descended to the eldest son, who thus preserved the cohesion of the lineage.[80]

These family-based towers became centres of the factions that vied for power during the thirteenth century. They hindered the complete integration of newcomers into the city and had a military strength that could defy the city government. But so many of them were destroyed and confiscated during the factional conflicts of the thirteenth century that public squares could be laid out, either by a town lord or a newly victorious *popolo*. In 1301 the White faction of Lucca destroyed more than one hundred houses of Blacks in a single quarter of town. More often the destruction was done by the commune, which systematically destroyed the property of exiles. When the Guelfs returned to power at Florence in 1267, they demanded compensation for property destroyed during their exile: more than 700 residences in the city and *contado*, including forty-seven palaces, 196 houses and fifty-nine towers in the city.[81]

But there was more to urban renewal and street planning at Florence than using confiscated property for public squares and buildings. The 'old city' of Florence (Plan 11) was the Roman, Carolingian and Matildine city. By the period of the poet Dante Alighieri (1265–1321) it had nostalgic, symbolic significance. Expansion beyond this core had been slow; at the beginning of the thirteenth century there was still

79 Waley, *Siena*, 100.
80 Brentano, *Rome Before Avignon*, 69; Heers, *Espaces Bologne*, 32–8; Hughes, 'Urban growth', 9–11.
81 Heers, *Espaces Bologne*, 100–1; Braunfels, *Urban Design*, 47.

much vacant land in the eastern part of the second wall, that of 1173–75. As the city acquired land by purchase, confiscation and expropriation, usually piecemeal and along the major thoroughfares, streets as public space were laid out, with much more regular traces than those of the 'old city'. When the project of another wall was put forward in 1284, the intention was to build a single street around the wall and straighten the major arteries within it. This project was never completed; if it had been realised, the area north of the Arno would have had 'an integrated system of bridges, streets and squares that welded the two parts of the city around the river: traffic could then have flowed within the urban nucleus without getting into the tortuous and obstructed [side] streets' . . . The whole notion suggests a concept of the city as a whole, well-governed and functional.[82]

Few Italian cities had a hall before the thirteenth century. The rulers of Florence met in private houses until about 1250, usually rotating the sessions to avoid allegations of favouritism.[83] The first Italian city hall may have been at Rome, where a palace of the commune is mentioned in 1151. By the thirteenth century the civic centre was the Palace of the Senators. The city halls of Brescia and Verona were built after Frederick I's wars with the Lombard League, Parma's in 1196. Padua in 1200 began a 'palace of the commune', which had separate buildings for the *podestà* and the council of the elders. It added a 'Palace of the Regions' from 1218, which also served as a market where each trade had assigned sectors. The city halls of Bergamo, Cremona, Como and Milan were built between 1200 and 1233. In Lombardy the city centres were unitary, for the halls were so close to the cathedral as not to constitute a separate pole of attraction.

The Tuscan cities built halls only from the mid-thirteenth century, during the struggles of the *popolo* against the magnates. Volterra's was finished in 1257. The Palazzo Vecchio [old palace] of Florence was built around 1200 but destroyed in 1235. A new one was begun in 1251, using the confiscated tower of the Boscoli family as a nucleus. Florence built a separate palace of the captain of the *popolo*, later called the Bargello, on land purchased for the purpose. The palace of the *popolo*, later called the palace of the priors and eventually that of the *Signoria*, was begun in 1299 on a site left vacant by the destruction of the palace of the Uberti family. The palace of the priors at Perugia was only begun in 1293, and others were still later.[84]

---

82 Sznura, *Espansione urbana di Firenze*, 41–5, 51, 77, and quotation p. 90.
83 Lansing, *Florentine Magnates*, xi; Heers, 'Paysages construits', 285.
84 Heers, 'Paysages construits', 285–98; Blanshei, *Perugia*, 25.

Tuscan public squares, in contrast to those in Lombardy, were dissociated from the cathedral and linked instead to the new city halls. At both Siena and Florence the cathedral was at some distance from the town centre established by the new square. Bologna also built a public square in a way that would isolate the cathedral from the main currents of activity.[85] The Tuscan city halls were so distant from the cathedral that they created a second pole of settlement. The halls were often built on land that the city seized in the political controversies, particularly when separate palaces were built for different agencies of government. At some distance from these structures were the palaces of political organisations, such as that of the Ghibellines at Cremona in 1206 and the palace of the Guelfs at Florence in 1256. Most of these groups were military societies led by captains, and their palaces were fortresses and arsenals.[86] The Nine of Siena began a major reconstruction of the public square, the *Campo*, after 1295 and built the city hall, commissioning Ambrogio Lorenzetti's fresco 'The Effects of Good Government' in the 1330s to adorn it. The programme also included straightening the streets, particularly the access routes to the cathedral and the public square. Residential streets were linked to wells and to the main roads.[87]

The earliest Italian city halls were always built in a fortress style, usually of stone or brick at a time when most domestic building was in wood. Most had a loge on the ground floor for assemblies and a large room for the magistrates on the first storey. This was usually well supplied with windows, and had a balcony from which officials could address mobs or promulgate decisions. The city hall had a tower that gave more security to the formal government of the communes, which began increasingly to take action against the magnates. Florence had 'tower officials', later called 'officials of the five cases', in charge of fortifications, gates, walls, excises and especially confiscated rebel property that could be used for civic purposes. The city ordered private towers to be reduced to a height of 29 metres. Pisa forbade nobles to buy or build towers near the city hall. Once the towers were in city control or regulated, the governments took measures of varying effectiveness against new ones. By 1337 Pisa had an official in charge of demolishing towers.[88]

85   Krautheimer, *Rome*, 206; Racine, 'Palais publics', 139, 143; Racine, 'Place civique', 314; Heers, 'Paysages construits', 300.
86   Racine, 'Palais publics', 136–40.
87   Balestracci, 'Development to crisis', 203–6.
88   Racine, 'Palais publics', 133–8; Lansing, *Florentine Magnates*, 17; Heers, 'Paysages construits', 313.

The example of Bologna (Plan 13)

The Italian cities were trying to get as many paths and alleys into the public domain as possible, making narrow passageways into real streets and linking them to main thoroughfares. Lucca and Bologna in the late thirteenth century required inhabitants to pave alleys and forbade blocking them. Siena, created from a union of bourgs that were linked by bad roads, built a new wall with great circular streets inside and outside it, confiscated land and laid out the avenues as regularly and broadly as possible. Florence also planned such boulevards by 1258, but twenty-five years later the city still had not bought the needed property. Florence did demolish houses confiscated from political exiles and used the vacated space for new public buildings (see Chapter 8).[89]

Bologna lost about one-quarter of its population through the exile of the Ghibelline party in 1274, and the losses were not compensated by immigration of Guelfs from other cities.[90] Thus a vast amount of land in the central city fell vacant for the communal authorities to revamp the street plan and building code to facilitate access and order. This is illustrated by a book of property boundaries in Bologna from 1294. North of the centre of the medieval city the Roman *decumanus* led into the broader Via Maggiore [Main Street], which, in turn, gave access to the main market. The Via Maggiore had many small shops but was dominated by noble palaces and towers that were so large for the narrow streets that they were virtually impossible for the authorities to assault. The newer sections of the city had more regular and wider streets. After the final victory in 1282 of the Guelf faction, led by the Geremei family, properties confiscated from their rivals, the Lambertazzi, were razed to make room for the new main square, the Piazza Maggiore. New towers were forbidden and the old ones torn down or lowered.

Bologna's city hall, the New Palace [Palazzo Nuovo], anchored a new Piazza del Comune [Communal Square] near the Piazza Maggiore. From 1288 statutes forbade people to obstruct this square except for vegetable and poultry sellers. All porticos under the city hall were to remain clear so that grainmongers could go there when it was raining. The government also tried to standardise heights and styles of new and reconstructed buildings, but, except for periods of massive confiscation, the process of acquiring public land was gradual; there were still many private buildings around the squares in 1294 and some irregular property dimensions. Thus the construction of central public squares in Italy

89 Heers, 'Paysages construits', 282–4.
90 Haverkump, 'Städte im Herrschafts- und Sozialgefüge Reichsitaliens', 237.

often followed the city hall by a generation or two. They served the multiple councils and hosted public assemblies.[91]

The city also planned to extend the wall around the suburbs, but actual work only began in 1326. Although the suburbs had some settlement, there was considerable vacant land, much of which became the property of the commune. The new wall was to enclose an enormous market square, the Campo del Mercato, just outside the wall of 1192 on the north. The city government divided the vacant suburban land into regular plots determined by the track of existing roads, then gave them at ground rent to immigrants. Magnates were forbidden to settle in the suburbs, which made the outskirts more attractive to craftsmen. Since the new plan in the suburbs was juxtaposed to the old in the centre, not superimposed on it, there was little conflict. However, since the new squares were built on whatever land was available for razing after political conflict, many Italian city centres were curiously unfocused.[92]

The economic revolution of the central Middle Ages thus was accompanied by a demographic expansion that caused important changes in urban morphology. This process was accompanied by social change, as wealthy merchants sought political power commensurate with their economic importance. By 1275 most urban elites outside Germany contained merchants as well as landowners. Many cities were also more independent of their lords than before. We shall examine these social and political mutations in the coming pages.

91 Heers, *Espaces Bologne*, 41, 49, 67–9, 94–5, 145, 155; Racine, 'Palais publics', 142–3; Heers, 'Paysages construits', 297.
92 Heers, *Espaces Bologne*, 97, 78–81; Heers, 'Paysages construits', 322. Suburbs of organic centres elsewhere were more likely to have a rectangular plan than the central city. Seville shows this clearly. Ladero Quesada, *Ciudad medieval*, 49.

CHAPTER SEVEN

The North European Cities in the Thirteenth Century

Citizenship: the nature of the urban community

Towns conferred the privileges of citizenship on their burgesses. Citizens acquired the status through inheritance from their parents or by a voluntary act that usually culminated in taking an oath. Simple residence without these criteria normally did not make one a citizen. The law of Magdeburg as adapted for the Polish cities, which was probably the most liberal in this regard of the great urban customs, extended the freedom of the city to all who could prove by written record (*litterae genealogiae*) or by witnesses that they were of legitimate birth and were Roman Catholics. An oath was also required. Roman law clearly distinguished citizenship from residence. City courts protected citizens outside the corporate limits, where many of them had to spend considerable time working or travelling to markets. This became a major point of contention, particularly since city courts almost always punished non-citizens more severely than citizens. Many penalised citizens who sued in courts outside the town, and some burgesses of cities outside the royal domain in France escaped their home governments' jurisdiction by placing themselves directly under the crown. They became 'merchants of the king' with royal protection in specific instances, or 'burgesses of the king' who were subject to him in all matters.[1]

Citizenship in the English cities, called freedom of the borough, had been limited in the eleventh and twelfth centuries to persons who owned property in the city and paid tax to the king. By 1230, however, it

---

1 Riesenberg, *Citizenship*, 143–4, 180–6; Renouard, *Bordeaux sous les rois d'Angleterre*, 82; Carter, *Trade and Urban Development in Poland*, 65.

could also be acquired by inheritance from one's parents, by enrolling as the apprentice of a burgess, and by paying an entry fee. In the latter case the newcomer had to find someone who would pledge his good behaviour. Burgesses were members of the merchant guild in cities that had these organisations.[2] On the continent a husband/father normally conferred citizenship on his wife and children as belonging to his household, which continued after his death through the wife. When the sons left the household during the father's lifetime, they might have to acquire citizenship for themselves, although usually for a smaller fee than that charged to outsiders. Daughters and the widow could become citizens through (re)marriage. No one could take the oath of citizenship who was not of free birth and free of pending legal actions that could compromise the town.

While citizenship on the continent hinged on membership of the sworn association, in England it was originally based on owning a house and land. Until the early thirteenth century buying a house made one a citizen in the English cities.[3] To keep citizenship beyond the reach of outsiders some cities prohibited alienating real estate to them. New citizens were sometimes given a year in which to buy property in the town. Zürich sequestrated the personal effects of the new burgess until he could buy a house.

However, as the cities became crowded and prices of real estate escalated, many residents could not afford houses and some cities denied them citizenship. More often, though, non-houseowners were allowed to become citizens, but an elevated status was created for landowners. Thus 'burgess' and its cognates *bourgeois* and *poorter* developed a double meaning in the thirteenth century. They were citizens everywhere, distinguished from mere 'residents'; but 'bourgeois' could also refer to a privileged group within the citizenry, the elite, defined by specific criteria, often the fact that they owned land in the city outright as opposed to paying ground rent on it.[4]

Citizenship was further restricted to those who paid taxes to or with the city. In England the 'free borough' was initially a place with its own courts, return of writs and other privileges that included fiscal autonomy by the late thirteenth century. In most German cities the tax register and citizen list were the same. The charter of Provins of 1230 defined the commune's territory as Provins and several settlements of the environs,

2 Tait, *Medieval English Borough*, 259; Williams, *Medieval London*, 44; Owen, *Making of King's Lynn*, 39; Nightingale, *Medieval Mercantile Community*, 46.
3 Tait, *Medieval English Borough*, 258.
4 Isenmann, *Deutsche Stadt*, 93.

called the 'vilois'. All persons within this area who paid tax to the count of Champagne were considered members of the commune.[5]

Some cities gained extraterritorial jurisdiction over persons who enjoyed citizenship but resided outside the city. Such 'external burgesses' (*bourgeois forains, Pfahlbürger, buitenpoorters*) were already complicating city-country relations in the thirteenth century. They included nobles, peasants and sometimes burgesses of small towns that were in the sphere of influence of a major city. The immunity of the city gave them protection and increasingly tax advantages. External burgesses were generally required to live in the city for a certain time each year, often three forty-day periods. Siena required them to own a house in the city or suburbs, although they could rent these properties out. External burgesses were much disliked by territorial authorities. The imperial Statute in Favour of the Princes of 1231 ordered the German cities to expel them, and the public peace of 1235 prohibited them entirely, but this proved impossible to enforce.[6]

Particularly in Germany the spread of external citizenship was linked to efforts by cities to cement political alliances with nobles, often against the town lords. In a case very similar to the early pacts of Italian cities with magnates, in 1263 Cologne gave Count William IV of Jülich land worth 100 marks yearly, then conferred citizenship on him, his heirs and his 'people' [retainers]. He promised to protect burgesses of Cologne who lived on his lands when they became involved in legal actions. The city reciprocated in cases at the city court that involved the count and 'his people'. The count promised military aid to the magistrates in case of disturbances in Cologne.[7]

The cities and their lords

Nowhere north of the Alps did cities manage to gain *de facto* autonomy of the sort common in Italy except in a few cases of divided lordship within the same community. Montpellier played off its two lords, the king of Aragon and the bishop of Maguelone, against each other.[8] Other polynuclear cities amounted to competing settlements of rival lords. In 1332 the burgesses of Old Hildesheim burned one of the newer settlements and massacred the inhabitants. In England the earl of Arundel

---

5 Tait, *Medieval English Borough*, 197–205; Erler, *Bürgerrecht und Steuerpflicht*, 22–3; Chapin, *Villes de foires*, 177.
6 Waley, *Siena*, 73; Keutgen, *Urkunden*, no. 122, p. 79.
7 Stoob, *Urkunden*, 278–80.
8 Faber and Lochard, *Montpellier*, 104.

was lord of Lynn, but the bishop of Norwich levied tallage and controlled the waterways until 1449.[9]

Although most cities were governed by a council, the lord generally kept some rights of appointment, particularly of police and judges in criminal courts, and he had the right to nominate or confirm the choice of council members. Since most city oligarchies desired more independence than this, and even these concessions were usually given unwillingly by the lord, conflicts were inevitable. The issue at stake was generally not autonomy but rather the extent to which the lord could keep control. Lords maintained at least a skeletal administration virtually everywhere. The German and Flemish cities still had bailiffs who were responsible to the lord, usually chosen (when the position was not hereditary) from among the ministerials. Many city governments bought out these offices and either deprived them of power or turned them into sinecures for powerful families. When a lord's representative, such as the Flemish bailiff, had jurisdiction over more than the town area, he often had a deputy for the town: a *schout* at Bruges and Courtrai, a mayor at Aalst.[10]

Lords continued to have important financial rights in the cities. Although the city controlled justice, police and defence at Troyes, the count of Champagne received immense incomes from market tolls, the wine tax, fisheries and waterways, justice, rents on guildhalls and other real estate and even mills and ovens. Cities were also expected to give 'boon' offerings to their princes. The council of Provins once bought one hundred pigs at enormous cost as a present for the king, who was not even their town lord, then on further reflection decided that this offering was not consistent with royal dignity. As princes' financial machinery became more sophisticated, their right to demand aid became a serious burden for many cities.[11]

The kings of England and France kept firm control over their cities. William I's castles and those erected by the Capetians as they conquered previously Angevin areas were bastions of royal authority that stifled the cities' pretensions to independence. Royal governments began categorising cities in the thirteenth century. 'Commune' began to yield in France to 'good town', while the English government distinguished boroughs from other types of settlement. Germany had 'imperial cities', which acknowledged the emperor rather than another layman or a bishop as

9 Stoob, *Forschungen*, 192–9; Owen, *Making of King's Lynn*, 34–6; Le Goff, 'L'Apogée', 194, 200.
10 van Uytven, 'Stadsgeschiedenis', 222.
11 Chapin, *Villes de foires*, 136, 170–2, 220, 177.

lord, and 'free imperial cities', which gained emancipation from their lords without formally acknowledging the emperor.[12]

The French king was the direct lord only of cities in the royal domain, but he had more general rights as lord of the land. Thus, hearing complaints of peculation, Louis IX ordered all town governments in France to have their accounts audited at Paris, although this was widely ignored in practice. As the domain expanded, some places became the chief cities of bailiwicks, adding an army of bureaucrats to the supply/demand nexus. A network of secondary cities thus developed that was similar to the county towns of England.[13]

In contrast to the English kings, the French monarchs encouraged some local rebellions against town lords, then used them as an excuse to intervene. Reims and its archbishop quarrelled in 1233 when the prelate forbade the magistrates to borrow money and annulled their sale of rents to bankers of Arras. After the cathedral chapter was expelled in a riot in 1234, the archbishop tried to revoke the *échevinage* on grounds that it was prejudicial to the liberties of the church. The king supported the archbishop on the issue of rents, adding that the right to impose a *taille* could only be granted by the king. Troubles sputtered on until 1258, when the king ruled that the archbishop could not make statutes without the approval of the *échevins*, released some imprisoned citizens, and restored the privileges of the bourgs. Cases involving the *échevinage* itself had to go to the royal court. The king was the only real winner in the conflict, and from this time Reims definitely fell behind Arras as a banking centre.[14]

The thirteenth century brings more examples of how changes in princely favour could promote the rise or decline of a city. Duke Henry II of Brabant had favoured Louvain, but Brussels became the chief residence of Henry III. Louvain developed more industry than Brussels, but the princely market combined with commercial ties with the Flemish cities gave Brussels an eventual base of supremacy. The centralisation of English royal administration at Westminster ended the pre-eminence of Winchester. Henry III (1216–72) was the last monarch who still visited Winchester frequently. This hurt the purveyance trades in Winchester at precisely the time when its fairs started declining. Winchester thus became a secondary centre, ranking fourteenth among English cities in tax capacity in 1334.[15]

Most serious conflict between cities and their lords in the thirteenth

12   Martin, 'English borough', 30; Maschke, *Städte und Menschen*, 145.
13   Bur, *Histoire de Laon*, 110; Hallam, *Capetian France*, 158–9, 206.
14   Desportes, *Reims*, 155–73.
15   Martens, *Histoire de Bruxelles*, 73; Keene, *Winchester*, 99–103.

century occurred in Germany, where lords were weaker than the western princes. Cologne feuded with its archbishop over finances and the mint. Cologne acquired rights of high justice when the burgrave pawned his office to the city council. An arbitration in 1258 condemned electoral malpractice by the *Schöffen* and Rich Club (see p. 145) and gave the archbishop the right to try citizens who had been arrested outside the city. Then the prelate allied with the weavers against the lineages (aristocratic families), imprisoned some patricians and deposed the burgomaster. This alliance continued until 1279, when new conflicts erupted after the archbishop redeemed the office of burgrave.[16]

The German emperors were also losing power during the thirteenth century, but their patronage was still important for the prosperity of some cities. The emperors were often the rivals of local authorities. In 1219 Frederick II placed Nuremberg under his bailiff and thus annulled the claims of the bishop of Bamberg to rule the city. Nuremberg was the only great city of southern Germany where the prince did not share the power of the bailiff with the bishop.[17] More in Germany than elsewhere the cities used the financial embarrassment of their princes to gain concessions. Philip of Swabia bought the loyalty and financial help of Speyer in 1198 with a charter giving important tax concessions. Cologne was so powerful that even though Philip took the city in 1207, he still had to agree to control of the fortifications by the citizens, and to toll reductions in the environs. Although Augsburg had a seal, city hall, council and burgomaster by 1257 and acquired the imperial bailiff's office in 1272, the city only received a law code in 1276 in return for paying a debt for the emperor.[18]

The town lords were thus more powerful even in the cities of the thirteenth century than has often been thought, but those of Europe pale beside the town rulers of the east. Muslim cities were governed by the bureaucracy of the caliph or the local emir. There were no separate town lords or municipal governments. The ruling dynasties originated in the countryside, but all ruled from a palace with a garrison that was generally centrally located in a city. Muslim cities were thus more affected by the political and military reverses of princes than western cities were, at least before the fifteenth century. The second echelon of civil administration consisted mainly of local citizens, and the quarters that were so important in the Muslim cities were controlled almost entirely by natives.[19]

16 Ennen, 'Erzbischof und Stadtgemeinde', 42–4.
17 Bosl, *Mittelalterliche Stadt in Bayern*, 15–16.
18 Töpfer, 'Bürgerschaft von Bischofsstädten', 13–33; Bosl, *Augsburger Bürgertum*, 21–8.
19 Lapidus, *Muslim Cities*, 1–16, 20; Hourani, *History of the Arab Peoples*, 130–2.

The urban churches in the thirteenth century

Many cities had arisen in the shadow of a bishopric that functioned both as town lord and nucleus of settlement. The churches were a rarely challenged part of the political life of the cities throughout the twelfth century. This continued to be true in some English cities. The churches of York owned more land in 1300 than in 1200. The English churches have been called with some exaggeration the 'principal feudal presence in the towns'.[20]

Once charters were granted, however, the churches became increasingly peripheral in the political life of most cities. As bishops spent increasing amounts of time on their rural properties, their churches' function as centres of demand diminished. Many churches gradually sold or bargained away their rights in the cities. The suburban abbey of Sainte-Croix at Bordeaux collected a tax on wine sold in taverns at Bordeaux until surrendering it to the city government in 1304 in return for having the abbey included in the new city wall.[21]

Personnel and patronage were critical, for the churches were still immensely wealthy. The greater prelates had several residences, not all within their dioceses. Regensburg housed eighteen abbeys and residences of the Bavarian dukes and of several bishops. Powerful families were identified unofficially with particular churches and embroiled the churches in their feuds. Gaillard Lambert, dean of Saint-Seurin of Bordeaux, used the chapter's resources to further the financial interests of his family, the Colom, in their feud with the Soler for control of the city.[22]

Immunity districts, over which the churches had sole jurisdiction, created a legal mosaic that hindered city growth and made law enforcement difficult. Even at Winchester the bishop owned more property than the king. Winchester was divided formally into two jurisdictions in 1231, centring on the mainly suburban seigniory of the bishop and on the city. Even London still had nineteen sokes in 1275, most of them held by churches.[23]

Thus conflict was endemic. The cathedral chapter of Exeter disputed the city's right of access across the cathedral close and its efforts to seize malefactors on the scattered tenements of the bishop's fee. The disagreements began in the thirteenth century and were only settled in a complicated arbitration in 1445 that validated the claims of the church

---

20 Tillott, *City of York*, 49; Stevenson, 'Monastic presence', 99–106; Hilton, *English and French Towns*, 48.
21 Renouard, *Bordeaux sous les rois d'Angleterre*, 129–30.
22 Strobel, 'Regensburg', 71–3; Renouard, *Bordeaux sous les rois d'Angleterre*, 141–2.
23 Keene, *Winchester*, 72–3; Hilton, *English and French Towns*, 48.

rather than the city. As late as 1469 the city councillors of Chartres, which by then had decayed to the point where royal commissioners noted that 'the said city outside the cloister is built for the most part of small wooden buildings roofed with straw', complained that the cathedral church was locking the gates of the cloister at night, dividing the city and preventing people from leaving.[24]

Most quarrels involved not corporate privilege but rather the churches' practice of giving sanctuary to malefactors or undesirable activities. Responding to complaints, Pope Alexander IV in 1260 prohibited holding taverns or selling wine in cloisters. In 1281 the king had to expel rebels at Provins from monasteries where they had taken refuge. The feud of the Borluut and van Sint Baaf families of Ghent between 1294 and 1306 was exacerbated by the fact that the abbot of St Peter, whose village bordered the city on the south, was the brother of a Borluut ally and sheltered in his church's immunity district murderers fleeing the justice of the aldermen. The bishop of Winchester was lord of the London suburb of Southwark, which was known for its taverns, violence and particularly brothels.[25]

The corporate property of the churches and of individuals in holy orders was not taxable by lay jurisdictions. In 1283 the Franciscans of Strasbourg pledged not to entice laypeople to give property to the friary to the detriment of their heirs. The tax issue was delicate for transactions that churches or their personnel conducted outside their immunities. The council of Augsburg in 1291 agreed that the business that officials of the churches had in the city on behalf of the church was tax-exempt, but their personal business was not.[26]

The new mendicant orders, the largest of whom were the Dominicans and Franciscans, are generally credited with filling a spiritual void for townspeople as the monks and the secular clergy became associated with a political and social establishment. The mendicants lived mainly from charity and endowment income and usually did not become major landlords or control courts. Founded in the early thirteenth century, the mendicants had chapters in most major cities by 1250. Since the central cities had little vacant space by this time, their earliest houses were near the wall or even in the suburbs, but they were often able to move into the city centres by purchasing real estate through third parties or receiving donations. The archbishop of Bordeaux gave the Franciscans a centrally located cemetery, while the Colom family, who dominated the

---

24 Attreed, 'Arbitration', 212–31; Billot, *Chartres*, 88–90.
25 Keutgen, *Urkunden*, no. 381, pp. 475–6; Chapin, *Villes de foires*, 216; Blockmans, *Middeleeuwse vendetta*.
26 Stoob *et al.*, *Urkunden*, 113; Keutgen, *Urkunden*, nos. 379–80, pp. 474–5.

city at the time, gave land both to them and to the Dominicans. In Paris the Franciscans and Dominicans rented houses initially, but both had obtained larger properties by 1234. St Louis also patronised the smaller mendicant orders, giving a house near the walls to the Brothers of the Sack in 1261.[27]

City and countryside. Urban administration in the environs

The cities had a symbiotic relationship with the countryside, depending on it for population replenishment and food and providing it with markets, other services and manufactured goods. It is true that city people were at risk when they ventured outside their walls. As late as 1238 Cologne was reminding the archbishop of his duty to protect its burgesses throughout his diocese, but the city government was already making mutual protection treaties with other towns and lords.[28]

Virtually all cities on the continent gained control over a territory surrounding the walls, called the ban mile, distinct from the more distant regions of the territory. Some French cities expanded into the countryside early but were stopped by the territorial power of the local lords, as the English cities were by the king's jurisdiction. Arles' statutes were valid for the town and its 'district', an area of 25–30 km including several annexed villages, but the count of Provence recovered much of it in the late thirteenth century.[29] Yet even within the ban mile the rights of local lords and privileged villages were respected. Ghent's ban mile was almost exactly six modern kilometres, but this included several villages. Seigniorial enclaves and chartered villages within this area, called 'free towns of law', were untouched by the city's jurisdiction. In England the ban mile of a city was often determined by the bishop's original lordship, a radius of seven leagues at Winchester. In 1377 a Hampshire jury prohibited new markets and buying and selling within this area but exempted those already chartered.[30]

By the early thirteenth century some lords and rural communities feared encroachments by the cities. In 1226 the count of Toulouse enlarged the ban mile (*salvetat*) of the city by one league in all directions, giving it a radius of about eight miles from the city centre. The council of capitouls had jurisdiction only over actions in the area involving citizens of Toulouse, and even this infringed the territorial competence of the rural villages and their lords. Furthermore, many wealthy

27 Renouard, *Bordeaux sous les rois d'Angleterre*, 150–3; Cazelles, *Paris*, 51–5.
28 Stehkämper, 'Absicherung der Stadt Köln', 359.
29 Stouff, *Arles*, 165–6.
30 Nicholas, *Town and Countryside*, 59–66; Keene, *Medieval Winchester*, 68.

Toulousans were landlords who held serfs, but the town law guaranteed such prerogatives. In this way Toulouse enticed some lords of its environs to become external burgesses.[31]

The cities had obvious economic and strategic interests in the rural areas. Arles was on the flood plain of the Rhône and was often inundated. By the thirteenth century the city government was requiring that marshes in its environs be drained and canals be bridged. The city owned land outside its corporate limits and required property owners to maintain levees and roads along their properties.[32] Tudela, which was severely dependent on the Ebro and its canals, controlled diversions of the river by villagers upstream. As burgesses of Bruges and Ghent bought peat bogs in northeastern Flanders in the thirteenth century, their city governments built canals to transport the fuel and gained extraterritorial jurisdiction over them.[33]

Urban leagues

The interests of cities and citizens beyond their walls led to conflict with rural powers and to regionally inspired efforts to cooperate against common threats. We have discussed the conflicts of the first Lombard League with Frederick Barbarossa. Although neighbouring cities were generally political and economic rivals, some had a collective regional consciousness even in the twelfth century. By 1127 the cities of Flanders had a corporate personality with '*scabini* of Flanders', jointly designated by the city governments. In the thirteenth century magistrates of the five great Flemish cities met regularly to advise the count. The cities of Aragon were in the *cortes* of the kingdom from 1214. Interurban leagues in the form of regional peace associations were common in Spain by the late thirteenth century.[34]

The power of urban leagues shows the increasing significance of cities in the political calculations of princes during the thirteenth century. The most important urban leagues in the north were in Germany, where they must be seen in the general context of the territorial peace that the weakened emperors were trying to foster. A decree of 1231 forbade urban confederations, but it was impossible to enforce. A Wendish urban league, comprising Lübeck, Kiel, Wismar, Rostock, Stralsund, Hamburg and

31 Mundy, *Toulouse*, 125–36.
32 The Rhône was also a political weapon. Arles and Tarascon upriver tried to flood each other out by diverting canals in the late Middle Ages. Stouff, *Arles*, 37–9, 55–7.
33 Leroy, 'Tudela', 189; Nicholas, *Town and Countryside*, 131–3, 291–3.
34 Nicholas, *Town and Countryside*, 152; Bisson, *Crown of Aragon*, 80; MacKay, *Spain*, 101; Powers, *Iberian Municipal Militias*, 80–1.

Lüneburg, existed before 1230. It was a forerunner of the most famous German urban league, the Hanse of north German cities.[35] The first Rhenish league was established in 1254. In 1255 the 'consuls and judges' of more than seventy towns of upper Germany informed the emperor of a peace declaration at their general assembly and worked closely with him against peacebreakers who would not heed the courts. The alliance was expanded to some cities of the Danube. Regensburg joined in 1256, receiving a congratulatory message promising assistance from the magistrates of Nuremberg for this action.[36]

The city militia

All cities had citizens' militias to defend their numerous privileges beyond the walls, and some used them for aggression. Even in the eleventh century the *fueros* given to the Spanish towns required citizens to serve in the royal army and the settlers of the environs to help defend the town wall. Most early charters in the north limited burgesses' military obligation to home guard duty or at most restricted service on the lord's behalf to areas within a day's journey of the city, compared to a three-day limitation in the Aragonese charters. Perhaps reflecting this difference, urban militias fought well for Alfonso VIII in 1212, while those of Amiens, Beauvais and Arras serving Philip II of France performed badly in 1214.[37]

The communal oath required mutual assistance and included an obligation to assist in the common defence, but the northern charters said nothing of the towns maintaining their own troops. The Flemish cities had militias by 1127, but they did not have to serve the count since the cities did not owe feudal military service to their lords. Wealth determined individuals' liability in most cities. A chronicler describes an assembly of the militia of Magdeburg in 1277: summoned by the city bell, the rich came in splendid colours, including raiment for their horses, the 'middle group' armed with strong horses, and the 'commoners' with clubs, swords and pikes.[38]

Most cities thus had a militia for emergencies, but they were were small and poorly equipped. In England the Assize of Arms of 1181, which required men between the ages of fifteen and sixty to maintain

35 Wülfing, 'Städtische Finanzpolitik', 50–1; Puhle, *Politik der Stadt Braunschweig*, 13. We shall discuss the Hanse more fully in a different context.

36 Engel, 'Königtum und Städtebürgertum', 103; *Nürnberger Urkundenbuch*, 225.

37 Powers, *Iberian Municipal Militias*, 15–19, 23, 208.

38 Uitz, 'Kommunale Autonomie in Magdeburg', 305; for Bruges, see Nicholas, *Town and Countryside*, 272–3; Lyon, 'Communes feudal system', 243.

weaponry appropriate to their wealth, applied to the towns. The cities also furnished materiel for the royal armies, often deducting the costs from the farm of the borough. The English cities, however, did not have militias to use beyond the walls. A royal ordinance of 1252 did oblige them to maintain a night watch during the summer. Most, including London, Norwich and York assigned defence obligations on the basis of ward boundaries that in turn were sometimes centred on towers.[39]

From the late thirteenth century and particularly after guild regimes came to power, most cities based military liability on guild or parish organisations, a change that circumvented the patrician domination of the military that was the inevitable result of basing liability on wealth. Provins levied a special tax for a night watch of a mere three guards in 1293. By 1315 the city was divided into twelve districts for night watch, and the number of guards was raised to four by 1319. Even this was only for the first three nights of each fair, not continuous guard duty; and the watchmen were hardly a deterrent to crime, since they paraded about with torches, accompanied by minstrels.[40]

URBAN SOCIAL STRUCTURES

Formation and definition of urban elites

Wealth and its sources are important elements of social prestige and the establishment of an elite. No two cities are exactly alike, for cities function at the intersection of supply of and demand for different goods and services. Thus differences in the wealth structure and social ethics of each city become clearer at the upper levels of the social and economic scales than lower, where a pattern of shopkeeping and artisanry seems typical in both northern and southern Europe.

Although contemporaries called the elites that governed the cities of northern Europe 'lineages', modern historians have generally preferred 'patriciates'. Lineages included both blood relations and persons who were 'adopted' into the group. *Alberghi* shared power at Genoa. Five lineages controlled offices at Siena and Metz, six at Antwerp, seven at Louvain and Brussels and seven or eight at Arras. They usually lived around a church, tower or market. Family affiliation is thus crucial: in the thirteenth century most urban magistracies filled vacancies by cooption, most

---

39 Young, *English Borough*, 92–7; Turner, *Town Defences*, 83–5.
40 Chapin, *Villes de foires*, 195.

often of a son, son-in-law or nephew. But wealth was also essential for political influence.[41]

Even before 1200 merchants were trying to gain political power alongside the older landowning elite. The Overstolz family of Cologne were ministerials who built their fortune in land deals, then married into other wealthy houses. They became *Schöffen* in their third generation in the city and drapers in the fourth. Other patricians of Cologne were already knights in the thirteenth century; the Raitze eventually married into the regional nobility and left Cologne. The older patrician families entered commerce gradually, and later than the newer merchant families who used landownership to gain access to the patriciate. In 1233 the patrician Ludwig von der Mühlengasse gave his son Heinrich several mills along the Rhine, along with outstanding obligations owed by bakers; a few years later he loaned money in connection with his grain business. Mathias Overstolz was a patrician draper; yet he gave a bakery and mill in ground rent to a baker who was to operate the business jointly with Overstolz. By the late thirteenth century the Overstolz were leasing stalls in the meat hall from a butcher.[42] The patriciate of Reims also combined ministerial lineages with newly rich families. Blanchard le Sec (d. 1220) made most of his fortune as a moneychanger at the Champagne fairs; but his ancestors had been ministerials of the cathedral chapter, and contemporaries always used terms of greater respect for him than for newcomers who had married into money.[43]

The size of the ruling group varied but was always family-based. The Rich Club of Cologne consisted of eighty-four families in the twelfth century, adding thirty-five more in the thirteenth. The Venetian patriciate had some 200 families. In 1293 the ruling elite of Florence included 147 families, of whom 114 were from the rural nobility, thirty-three from business. The patriciate at Carcassonne had fifty families in 1304; that of Huy had forty, of whom fifteen controlled most offices. Ghent had 108 *poorter* (landowning) families, but thirty-nine individuals could be on the three city councils at one time. The elite of Arras had fifty families in the thirteenth century, while that of Metz had 221, dropping to 150 at the end of the fourteenth. Strasbourg had seventy-four patrician families before 1250, with sixty-seven new ones by 1300. Regensburg had sixty before 1250, adding seventy between 1250 and 1350. Between 1244 and 1312 fewer than forty families furnished *échevins* at Saint-Omer, which meant that the politically responsible group there

41 Strait, *Cologne*, 76; Barel, *Ville médiévale*, 126.
42 Berthold, 'Auseinandersetzungen in Köln', 249–55; Strait, *Cologne*, 97, 105.
43 Desportes, *Reims*, 133–45.

around 1300 consisted of about 300 individuals. There were about sixty families in the lineages of Louvain in the mid-fourteenth century. At Liège all the aldermen between 1214 and 1312 came from nine families. There was movement into the elite as the older lines became extinguished. But although most families either died out or left the city for their rural estates after about three generations, some patrician families had extraordinary longevity. The Juden and Lyskirchen of Cologne lasted over five centuries, and eighteen others were in the city for more than 250 years.[44]

As commerce increasingly became a source of wealth for the urban elites, older perquisites of office sustained the ministerial families. One distinction is found in virtually all episcopal cities of the Rhine and Danube: even when there was otherwise no deep gulf between the largely-rentier and largely-commercial patriciates, ministerial families controlled the coinage and had a corporate existence as *Münzerhausgenossen* (mint associates). This privilege was expanded into a monopoly of money exchange and the trade in precious metals. The importance of this monopoly for ministerial families cannot be overstated. The mint associates were the most closed and preserved element of the patriciate: at Mainz in the fifteenth century all four grandparents had to come from families eligible to be mint associates in order to qualify a young person for membership.[45]

Mainz had three privileged legal standings, reflecting the discrete elements of the local elite. The ministerial families were under 'service law'. They held offices and incomes in fief from the archbishop, advantages not open to the merchant patricians. The originally ministerial mint associates had a separate status. Thirdly, the merchant families had a monopoly of clothmaking and cloth cutting, enshrined in the 'shop law' (*Gadenrecht*). They evidently had shops that were demolished when the archbishop rebuilt the west façade of the cathedral in 1239. In exchange he gave the drapers space for forty-eight new shops where the shoemakers had previously had theirs. He also restricted cutting cloth to the persons named in the charter and their heirs. Thus the merchant patrician families were descendants of those who had *Gadenrecht* in 1239.[46]

Some early texts had distinguished ministerials as subjects of the

---

44 Mollat and Wolff, *Popular Revolutions*, 29–31; Barel, *Ville médievale*, 92, 109 n. 1; van Uytven, 'Stadsgeschiedenis', 209.

45 Falck, *Mainz in seiner Blütezeit*, 95–8; Mollat and Wolff, *Popular Revolutions*, 31; Bosl, 'Regensburg', 184–9; Möncke, *Quellen*, 98 for a monopoly on the sale of silver given to this group at Nuremberg.

46 Falck, *Geschichte Mainz*, 196–7.

town lord from citizens, but this ended gradually in the large cities in the thirteenth century. At Strasbourg a legal distinction initially existed between ministerials and citizens, who were to be represented separately on the city council in 1214. Although the ministerial element in the patriciate continued to be very powerful even after the bishop's rule ended in 1262, the word 'ministerial' itself disappears. It was replaced in the second half of the century by a distinction between burgesses who had been dubbed knights and those, often of the same lineages, who remained citizens.[47]

The urban elites in France, England and the Low Countries were more diverse than those in Germany. Many in the largest cities were of foreign extraction, although the process of assimilation usually required several generations. Richard Renger, who was mayor of London between 1222 and 1229, was descended from Berengar, a servant of the earliest Norman bishops of London. The London aldermanic group was characterised by long lineage, royal and ecclesiastical office-holding and increasingly by purveyance to the court, massive landowning in the city and the home counties, moneylending, advowson (the right to appoint the holder of a church living) and control of private courts. Although most entered commerce, some did not and were similar to the rentiers of the continental cities.[48]

Barcelona illustrates these themes even more graphically than London. Barcelona was a small farm market in the eleventh century, but its environs were so mountainous and infertile that continued growth became impossible in the twelfth century, particularly as continued wars with the Muslims diminished the supply of coin. Unlike the Italian cities, Barcelona thus never controlled a *contado*. The rural nobles withdrew to concentrate on their country properties as Barcelona declined between 1096 and 1140. Thus while rural and urban nobilities were intertwined in thirteenth-century Italy, the elite of Barcelona consisted of lesser landowners, whose properties were mainly in the city and particularly its growing suburbs. Barcelona was granted its first formal city council only in 1249. Although most families who occupied the conciliar seats before 1291 were landowning families whose ancestors were in the city by 1140, they lacked the consciousness of lineage that was characteristic of the rural nobles and were more willing than they to expand into trade and to accept newcomers who had mainly commercial wealth. Fourteen of the twenty-four families who filled most seats on the council during these years were involved in *commenda* contracts.

47 Schwind, 'Reichsministerialität', 87–8; Dollinger, *Histoire d'Alsace*, 119.
48 Williams, *Medieval London*, 50–5.

The patriciate of Barcelona was thus active economically in both land and commerce.

Rapid growth began in Barcelona in the late twelfth and particularly in the early thirteenth century, for its location made it a natural port. Much of the wealth of the elite of Barcelona became based on urban rents that rose as immigrants streamed into the city. Investors speculated in the land of the five new villages that were planned before 1225 outside the Roman City and another two that had been added by 1300. They lured craft groups to settle in these suburbs. While rents rose substantially in the craft suburbs, they soared along the waterfront, which was being opened to development as Barcelona's maritime interests grew in Sicily and North Africa. Thus the elite of Barcelona gained most of its money initially from agriculture, then from real estate development as the city expanded topographically, and finally by lending money to the crown, which gave them access to lucrative royal offices and later to contracts and commercial concessions. Far from developing as a sworn association in opposition to the city lord, the patriciate of Barcelona rose by cooperating with him.[49]

Lineage, political privilege and economic advantage were thus intertwined, but no early patriciate can be defined solely in terms of wealth generated by long-distance trade, as Pirenne and his disciples thought. The Lanstier family of Arras is first mentioned in 1111. By 1270 banking was their major although not sole source of income, and the funds for it evidently came at least in part from textiles. The *échevin* Mathieu Lanstier (as the patriarch was always named) was accused in 1304–5 of forcing people to marry his relatives, compelling butchers to buy animals from him at more than market value and manipulating rents. While the Lanstier show the expansion of a landed family into moneychanging, moneylending and industry, Arras also furnishes the example of Jean Beauparisis, the *nouveau riche* business partner and perhaps evil genius of Mathieu Lanstier. He had a meteoric rise in the thirteenth century, farming taxes and, with the connivance of his friends in high places, selling grain and other goods to the city at more than the market value. He died in 1312 holding enormous mortgages, urban and rural properties, and simple loans.[50]

Three criteria or institutions are thus important for understanding the formation and composition of northern urban elites in the central Middle Ages: land and specifically rents; family; and wealth, often in long-distance and wholesale commerce, but rarely exclusively in local

---

49 Bensch, *Barcelona*, esp. 36–7, 89–91, 177–81, 190–3, 206–20, 301.
50 Lestocquoy, *Dynasties bourgeoises d'Arras*, 98–106.

or retail trade. The elites were not entirely political: some rich families never held offices, and landownership was yielding to commercial wealth in importance. The fact that urban government was family-based explains much of the zeal of newly rich urban families to buy land, which gave a more secure property basis to hereditary privilege than did movable property.

Land became the basis by which the family's political influence could become hereditary and extend over several generations. The Selby family of York made their fortune in long-distance commerce in the thirteenth century, then invested in rural and urban real estate. Their political involvements began when evidence of their commercial activity becomes less direct in the sources.[51] Ownership of real property thus explains the stability of the ruling group. In the rare instances when the urban upper order was largely merchant, it tended to be open to newcomers and not to display much persistence across generations. By investing in land the wealthy became a hereditary elite.

Despite differences between landowners and merchants and between old and new families and money, the urban patricians had a group consciousness in the thirteenth century. They intermarried with other patrician lineages. Those of merchant origin imitated the rural nobility and tried to marry into it. They surrounded themselves with clienteles and became involved in vendettas. Officeholding and the fact that a family was eligible to fill a seat on the council created a common bond that transcended disparate origins. In 1271 the Erfurt council freed persons who assumed municipal office from most obligations of citizenship, including some taxes and night watch. Most importantly, they were not bound to answer in court during their term of office.[52]

These general features seem characteristic of Spain as well as the north. The Castilian kings relied on 'urban knights' for defence of the cities and increasingly for administration. Although early texts use 'good men' and 'urban knights' indiscriminately, a distinction was developing by the late thirteenth century, and by 1330 there was little mobility between the two. By 1256 the urban knights had to own armour, helmet, weapons and war chargers and appear for muster once a year. They had to own and live in houses inside the city for at least six months a year. In return, they were freed from direct taxes, a privilege of noble status; but they were not nobles and accordingly were subject to the jurisdiction of the city council. Castilian sources thus distinguish between 'warriors' and 'taxpayers'. The knights were eventually exempted from

51 Tillott, *City of York*, 46.
52 Stoob, *Urkunden*, 280–1.

taxes on their property outside the city and even obtained tax exemption for their servants. In 1293 Sancho IV made the knights of Valladolid part of the nobility, exempted them from the town courts and made misdeeds against their persons punishable by a high fine. Thus the knights became a network of lineages who monopolised power.

Although some Iberian drapers and merchants enjoyed wealth that was comparable to the knights, they had no political power. Descendants of foreign merchants who settled in Burgos during the twelfth century, such as the Bonifaz, were urban knights in the thirteenth. They controlled long-distance trade. The other knights of Burgos were local, evidently persons whose income qualified them for the status. But not all urban knights were merchants, and some had occupations that were low-status elsewhere, including shopkeepers and one butcher and a muleteer. The butcher and a goldsmith made enough profits from their artisanry to invest in land. Landownership was the key, as in the north: the urban knights dominated the land market at Burgos both in terms of number and value of sales.[53]

The elite of Metz

The 'paraiges' (lineages) of Metz are the most thoroughly studied urban political lineages of northern Europe. They display some similarities to the *alberghi* of Genoa, but in contrast to them were not artificial clans: they were genuine unions of families, based on bilateral kinship. Texts call members of paraiges 'citizens', distinguishing them from 'burgesses' and 'foreigners'. By the late fourteenth century there were about 150 heads of families in the five patrician paraiges, and this number was considerably lower than their high point in the thirteenth.

The three oldest paraiges were recognised legally by 1215, taking their names from quarters of the city. Port-Sailly was the most important in the twelfth century but yielded in the thirteenth to Outre-Seille and Porte-Moselle. By 1234 the paraiges had excluded the bishop from municipal government in all but name and divided offices and incomes among themselves. In 1254 two other paraiges were admitted on an equal basis with the other three: the Jurue were divided into four branches by 1244, of unequal antiquity, but all lived in the Jurue quarter of the city. The Saint-Martin had existed by 1161 and also had four branches by 1311. All paraiges held rural land, although there were distinctions: the Port-Sailly were primarily rural landholders, advocates

53 Discussion based on Ruiz, *Burgos and Castile*, 6–15; Powers, *Iberian Municipal Militias*,
    74, 99; Gonthier, *Cris de haine*, 27.

and ministerials, while the Saint-Martin owned more vineyards and were the only paraige admitting knights.

The five paraiges were not unchallenged. As early as 1244 the city council, the Thirteen [*échevins*], included three commoners and ten patricians. The commoners included most of the city's financiers. They were controlled by a small group of families that would eventually be almost as exclusive as the older paraiges. Especially after 1273 their representative to the Thirteen were all aristocratic. Although the 'commons' were not recognised as a sixth paraige until just before 1350, they had actually functioned collectively much earlier.[54]

Other cities confirm the example of Metz. The patriciate of Louvain was divided into two lineages from 1265: the proximity of rural property to the urban lands of the van den Blanckaerden and van den Colveren meant that the entire city grew up around these two lineages, which functioned as political factions. The artificial grouping of the patricians of Brussels and Antwerp into seven and six lineages was probably because these cities had seven and six *schepenen* respectively.[55]

THE MERCHANT GUILDS IN THE THIRTEENTH CENTURY

The corporate structure of the medieval city was extremely complex. Although most patrician regimes tried to keep craftsmen from forming occupational organisations, they had corporations of their own, generally merchant guilds or 'greater' as opposed to 'lesser' guilds. Guilds of rentiers and moneychangers and the mint associates of the German cities appealed to the patricians.

The merchant guild continued to dominate most English cities. In the thirteenth century references multiply both to guild members pledging mutual assistance when they were outside their native city and to inter-urban associations of long-distance merchants. Members of the merchant guild of Lincoln pledged to support one another in external litigation 'as though they were children of the same parents'. The Flemish 'Hanse of London' grouped merchants who traded in London from twenty-two Flemish communities, dominated by Bruges and Ypres. Most of its several hundred members were drapers, wool merchants and hostellers, but some were craftspeople.[56]

---

54 Discussion based on Schneider, *Metz*, 114–45, 248.
55 van Uytven, 'Stadsgeschiedenis', 209; Heers, *Family Clans*, 44; Martens, *Histoire de Bruxelles*, 70.
56 Holt and Rosser, *Medieval Town*, 12; Nicholas, *Medieval Flanders*, 166–7.

Although not all English cities had a merchant guild – London is the most conspicuous case – most of the larger ones did. Only its members could buy and sell on the city market without paying toll. They fixed prices and wages and enforced the royal assizes of bread and ale, issued economic regulations and toll rates and punished violations. Food merchants dominated the merchant guild at Leicester, with bakers the most numerous single group. The merchant guild initially consisted of burgesses who owned land inside the town and thus were the equivalent of the later Flemish *poorters* and French *bourgeois* in the narrow sense. Later membership of the guild could be acquired through inheritance or purchase by non-residents, usually merchants of the county, and persons who did not own land. Over time priority was given to eldest sons, who were admitted free; younger sons paid more, but still less than outsiders. Widows could be in the guild until they remarried; daughters could either be members or pass it on to their husbands or sons. Craftsmen who sold their own products were admitted, and as industry grew in the cities they were probably in the majority in most English merchant guilds.[57]

Merchant guilds on the continent were more oriented toward long-distance trade than the English, but they too controlled local markets by monopolising imports. Although Saint-Omer had had its merchant guild since the eleventh century, a separate Hanse (the word simply means association) was founded around 1215 as a privileged fraternity for long-distance traders. Only its members could trade beyond the Somme and in Britain, and they were forbidden to engage in manual labour, retail sales or brokerage. Members could not trade in France or England on behalf of a person not in the association. Members had partnerships with non-members; but if the non-member wanted to conduct business in England, he had to join. Entry fees were high, but the real barrier was the need of enough money to finance long-distance trade. The Hanse had about five hundred people in the early thirteenth century, three hundred after entry fees were raised sharply in 1263; but this still suggests that 10–15 per cent of Saint-Omer's population was being supported by the Hanse's trade. The Hanse drew most of its members from the trades; but since its statutes prohibited manual labour or selling retail, these people were evidently guild entrepreneurs. For example, the bakers in the Hanse were grain merchants, although this doubling of function was technically forbidden.[58] Kraków is unusual in

---

57 Simmons, *Leicester*, 36–7; Clune, *Medieval Gild System*, 16–19, 32–3.
58 Derville, *Histoire de Saint-Omer*, 56–7; Nicholas, *Medieval Flanders*, 174–5; Wyffels, 'Hanse', 8–9, 14–16.

having craft guilds before a merchant organisation, but its merchant guild was just as exclusively formed of foreign traders as those of the Low Countries. It was formed only in 1410 as a defensive measure when the King of Hungary tried to exclude from his kingdom the merchants of Kraków, who at the time controlled much of Hungary's export of copper and import of salt.[59]

Merchant guilds controlled the governments of their cities in fact if not in law. At Bruges, Saint-Omer and Tournai income from the merchant guild went directly into the municipal treasury. The oldest urban statute of Schleswig (1200–50) may have been modelled on St Knut's guild, a Danish national organisation of long-distance merchants. The guild included only merchants, not the entire citizenry, but it was involved in peacekeeping and justice in the city, and it may have controlled the market and mint.[60]

The Merchants of the Water in Paris are the most famous long-distance merchant organisation that took over the functions of a city administration. Beginning with a royal grant of monopoly on navigation between Mantes and the Paris bridge in 1171, they gradually extended their competence from handling navigation questions to controlling goods in transit throughout the region, then levied fines and collected taxes. In order to trade in Paris a foreigner not only had to join the organisation but also to become the business partner of a merchant of Paris, with the Parisian buying half the contents of the foreigner's boat. In 1220 Philip Augustus gave the Hanse of the Merchants the right to measure and 'cry' wine (announce the price in taverns). Wine could not be discharged at Paris except by citizens in the Hanse. Salt and then grain measurers were appointed by the *échevins* of Paris under the jurisdiction of their chief, the provost of the merchants. In the 1260s the *jurés* of the Water Merchants became the four *échevins* of Paris. The *échevins* and provost sat at the Parloir-aux-Bourgeois, often assisted by a council of twenty-four.[61]

Crafts and craft organisations

All cities had basic craftsmen who baked bread, brewed beer, cut meat, made shoes, wove coarse cloth, cut it into wearable clothing, tanned leather, and made iron goods for the local and regional markets. Some

---

59 Carter, *Trade and Urban Development in Poland*, 91.
60 van Uytven, 'Stadsgeschiedenis', 217; Hörby, 'Königliche Dänische Kaufleute', 45–6; Hoffman, 'Schleswiger Knutsgilde', 51–4.
61 Cazelles, *Paris*, 197–202, 208–11.

also developed specialities, either in a manufactured item that was not made elsewhere or by controlling something made or grown in the environs and not available and thus in demand elsewhere. This meant that cities relied less on their immediate environs and more on other cities as trading partners, as the developing urban network was strengthened. The enormous growth of the cities provided a market for countless service occupations, particularly in the construction and transport sectors.

The earliest craft guilds with corporate regulations in northern Europe were foodmongers and leather- and clothworkers. A market ordinance from pre-Habsburg Vienna mentions separate statutes for wine and beer measurers, bakers, butchers and sellers of chicken, geese, cheese and fish. The shoemakers, furriers, cordwainers, weavers and tanners corrected violations of their statutes on the advice of the city council. In contrast to this regulation of commerce among the craftspeople, 'the better burgesses by whose counsel the whole city is ruled', clearly a merchant guild, had the right to buy and sell freely on the market.[62] The craft guilds thus had jurisdictional and financial rights over their members and in some circumstances over outsiders. They enforced industrial regulations, and in some places monopolised supplies in the commodities that they traded. They also controlled access to the labour market. Initially their rights of jurisdiction and economic regulation were exercised on behalf of the city government, and their monopoly privileges were developed over its objections.

The line between craftsman and merchant was more blurred in the Italian guilds than in the north, but common to both is the fact that if a craftsman sold the products that he made, he was both manufacturer and retail merchant. Many such trades were found exclusively in local markets. Others, particularly those with complex technology and interests in more distant markets, included both craftsmen and merchants and thus had a considerable range of economic types and wealth. Thus many 'craft' guilds were complex organisations. The first reference to a guild at Reims is to the wool drapers in 1278, but by then it already included all the trades involved in clothmaking.[63]

Thus, although the cities were more market- than manufacturing-oriented, the two branches of the economy were not clearly demarcated. Upwardly mobile merchants imported the raw materials that craftsmen worked into finished products. Particularly in the textile trades, merchants often became involved directly in the industrial process by 'putting out'

62   Keutgen, *Urkunden*, nos. 324–5.
63   Desportes, *Reims*, 97–102.

the work to spinners, fullers, weavers, tenterers, dyers and other specialists. But already in the thirteenth century some craftsmen were becoming entrepreneurs by hiring additional employees and particularly by becoming dealers in raw materials: in 1283 Constance ordered weavers to confine themselves to weaving and forbade them to buy linen with the intent of reselling it and thus acting as brokers.[64] Such practices became increasingly common.

Particularly in cities with large numbers of artisans, the elite saw them as a revolutionary element and tried to prevent them from forming associations. Several English cities issued ordinances around 1200 to control the weavers. London deprived weavers and fullers of citizenship unless they abjured their crafts an paid a large fine. The city government in 1202 obtained a royal charter dissolving the weavers' guild, which the weavers promptly had annulled by offering King John more money. The depression of the English cloth industry in the thirteenth century, after considerable expansion in the twelfth, is reflected in fewer references to craft organisations there.[65]

The fears of the authorities were hardly groundless. In 1245 there were strikes called *takehans* at Douai; the same word was used at Rouen when the weavers agitated at the 'workmen's market', where those who did not have their own establishments went to hire themselves out for short-term jobs. Craft guilds were forbidden at Arras in 1253 and at Douai throughout the thirteenth century. Although informal organisations of textile artisans existed in the cities of Flanders, they did not have corporate organisations that were legally recognised by the authorities until 1302.[66]

The authorities were more successful when strong charitable fraternities existed independently of the occupational organisations. In 1293–4 the king of Norway prohibited guilds of pilots, goldsmiths, ironsmiths, England traders, craft journeymen, 'workers', brewers and serving girls at Bergen, thus admitting tacitly that such organisations existed. These guilds were probably already trying to set maximum prices and wages, for in 1281 the royal governor of the city did just that for the cobblers and other trades that twelve years later were forbidden to organise. Purely charitable guilds could still meet socially in individual homes. The policy worked; later sources suggest that there were no craft guilds in Bergen as late as the 1380s. Even in heavily industrial Walloon Flanders there is

---

64   Möncke, *Quellen*, 124–5.
65   Brooke and Keir, *London*, 276–85; Salter, *Medieval Oxford*, 58–9; Bridbury, *Medieval English Clothmaking*, 6; Miller and Hatcher, *Towns, Commerce and Crafts*, 107.
66   Mollat and Wolff, *Popular Revolutions*, 37; Mickwitz, *Kartellfunktionen*, 100; Sosson, 'Körperschaften', 81–90; Nicholas, *Medieval Flanders*, 202–3.

no record of occupational guilds before the beginning of the sixteenth century.[67] Most guilds originated as charitable associations of persons in the same occupation; but as the Bergen example suggests, they turned to economic demands. The authorities realised that this was happening, and Saint-Omer even tried to forbid pious confraternities. The weavers and linen workers of Huy in 1234 and the fullers and shearers of St Truiden in 1237 had occupationally-based charities. There were revolts at Liège in 1254 and at Huy in 1255. In that year the coppersmiths of Dinant made the transition to a genuine guild, receiving the right to choose their own officers and to make industrial regulations subject to the prince's confirmation. Within a few years the guilds in the prince-bishopric of Liège were largely independent.[68]

Craft associations were also discouraged in cities with a large ministerial element. Some German cities distinguished between the *Gilde* ('guild', a patrician organisation, often but not necessarily a merchant guild) and the *Zunft* ('craft', a trade association). Frederick II's charter of 1219 for Goslar forbade organisations and guilds except the mint associates, who were largely ministerial. In 1223 he relented to the extent of permitting organisations of weavers and construction workers, on the excuse that merchants had an interest in cloth manufacture. Merchants were thus distinguished not only from crafts but also from the 'guild'.[69]

Despite official hostility, the German cities developed craft organisations early. The felt hatmakers of Cologne were granted a privilege in 1225, the wool weavers in 1230. The goldsmiths were a 'fraternity' before 1259 and the clothiers in 1247, but the terminology is deceptive. The brotherhood had no common religious observances. Like the drapers of Reims, the clothiers of Cologne were a composite organisation of retailers and clothmakers, including linen workers, cutters, woollen workers and tailors, among others. The brothers were to buy and sell among themselves, thus creating a cartel. The Cologne guildsmen were also entering the magistracy. After an uprising in 1259 a weaver, a fishmonger, a brewer and a baker became *Schöffen*. At Dortmund the guilds also had representatives on the Council from 1259 along with the patricians in the aristocratic Reinold guild, which was similar to the Rich Club of Cologne.[70]

Some craft organisations were thus quite complex in the thirteenth

67 Blom, 'Gilden in Norwegen', 14–16; Sosson, 'Körperschaften', 81–90.
68 Derville, *Saint-Omer*, 62; van Uytven, 'Stadsgeschiedenis', 210–11.
69 Frölich, 'Kaufmannsgilden', 36.
70 Berthold, 'Auseinandersetzungen in Köln', 258; Epstein, *Wage Labor and Guilds*, 86–7; Czok, 'Bürgerkämpfe', 315, 320.

century. Trades that later would be under a single administration still had separate branches, generally with certain seats on the guild council reserved for each and with the deanship rotated. The butchers of Montpellier had distinct organisations for butchers of pigs, cattle and sheep. The knife makers of Passau shared an organisation with the swordsmiths by 1259, although they were later separated. The oil merchants of Florence included cheesemongers, salt merchants, grain merchants, and butchers of pork and dry or fresh meats and fish.[71]

The butchers' purchases of live animals involved them in large-scale marketing operations and frequently in rural landowning. They sold hides to tanners, shoemakers and others who manufactured goods with animal by-products. They were generally among the earliest guilds to receive corporate recognition. Leatherworking also encompassed several specialities that were sometimes under a single organisation. At Regensburg the cordwainers were probably identical to the 'new shoemakers', who in turn were divided into two groups. The older and core group, who lived in three streets, possessed 'Three-Street Right': they chose the master and were free of the fee that those not enjoying Three-Street Right paid for exemption from the obligation to sell on the local market.[72]

At Metz eight diverse trades (mercers, pursemakers, cordwainers, brewers, haberdashers, clogmakers, glovemakers and cloth preparers), lacking separate organisations but jointly called 'the free guild', had privileges in the twelfth century. The guild master, whose office was an episcopal fief, parcelled out stalls and shops and judged most civil cases arising between practitioners of the eight trades. Each craft had the right to trade outside the city and chose two inspectors to make sure that work was done properly. The free trades and some others, notably the butchers, had the right to levy tolls on the raw materials of their trades and keep part of the proceeds. Apart from these eight, the barbers, cultivators, knife polishers, coppersmiths, carders, needlemakers and smiths had confraternities by 1215. Several other guilds, including weavers, coopers, cutlers, bakers and chamois dressers, are mentioned later in the thirteenth century but did not originate in a fraternity.[73]

Elsewhere conglomerated guilds usually linked different specialities within the same overall area of endeavour, such as construction work or clothmaking. Particularly in the case of textiles, where several specialists contributed to a single final product, the advantage was held by

---

71   Faber and Lochard, *Montpellier*, 134; Brandl-Ziegert, 'Sozialstruktur', 50–1; Epstein, *Wage Labor and Guilds*, 211.
72   Le Goff, 'L'Apogée', 252; Mickwitz, *Kartellfunktionen*, 124–5.
73   Schneider, *Ville de Metz*, 207, 227–34.

the wealthier element within the guild, whether called merchant, draper or clothcutter. At the beginning of the century the merchants generally produced as well as sold, but this was less invariably true by 1250, when workers might become dependent on the purveyors of the raw material for the trade. As early as 1272 the provost of Paris distinguished lesser weavers, who worked for others, from greater weavers, who gave work to them. There were merchant/drapers in virtually all guilds, even that of the fullers, the least prestigious textile craft in most cities. The drapers of Provins had their own hall by 1256, where their cloth was sold each Monday. By 1291 a distinction existed between drapers of the 'great houses' and those of the 'lesser houses', who were now being allowed to diversify their textile types without hindrance from the great drapers.[74]

Guilds of woollen workers were thus among the most complex, and inclusion in a conglomerate organisation hurt the relative position of some trades. The German weavers were largely independent operators in the early thirteenth century but fell increasingly under the influence of wool merchants who provided the raw material and made the weavers wage-earners. In Magdeburg in 1183 and 1214 native woollen weavers were forbidden to practise cloth cutting. Thus conflicts arose between the clothcutters, who had members on the city council, and the weavers, who did not.[75] The drapers' guild of Chartres was similar to the Italian wool guilds, encompassing all aspects of cloth production. Its four principal trades (wool combers and carders, weavers, makers and finishers, and dyers) controlled the fullers. The individual trades were forbidden to form their own guilds.[76]

In both France and Germany town lords kept firm control over guilds when the city government was weak. We have seen that before 1200 the king or other city lord gave corporate privileges to occupational organisations in several French cities, generally including limited monopolies under the supervision of the lord's officials. In the 1260s, evidently at the instigation of the Provost of the Merchants, Etienne Boileau, the regulations of 102 crafts of Paris were put into written form, including entry fees, apprenticeship requirements, and industrial standards. The document is incomplete; the butchers are absent from it, although they are known to have had corporate privileges. They were strictly regulated by the king. Louis IX gave some guilds 'according to his pleasure' to various court officials, who took the profits of fines and

74 Geremek, *Salariat*, 17, 19; Chapin, *Villes de foires*, 60–70.
75 Möncke, *Quellen*, 14; Mägdefrau, 'Volksbewegungen in Erfurt', 334.
76 Epstein, *Wage Labor and Guilds*, 90. Compare the situation at Toulouse: Le Goff, 'L'Apogée', 290, 284–5.

other incomes and issued regulations. The Provost of the Merchants controlled the guilds that were not directly under a courtier, regulating admission of new masters and apprentices and quality control. In some cases he appointed guild *jurés*, usually on the advice of the guild masters.[77]

The northern urban guilds were already trying to monopolise the labour market. In 1251 the council of Stendhal granted the weavers a fraternity, called *ininge*. The 'fraternity' was in fact an occupational guild, for whoever did not belong to it could not prepare cloth. A strong preference was already being shown for sons of masters, and the weavers were trying to force residents of the city who were not yet guild members to join: sons of 'brothers' paid an entry fee of 2s., while outsiders who joined before St Nicholas' day paid an entry of 3s., but 6s. thereafter. The guild already had its court to handle petty squabbles between members. The fraternity also fined workers for cutting cloth of insufficient breadth. In 1197 the archbishop of Magdeburg gave the armourers the right 'to choose masters by common counsel who had the right to keep anyone from working who had not previously acquired their communion, commonly called *ininge*'.[78]

URBAN GOVERNMENT IN THE THIRTEENTH CENTURY

Government through councils

During the thirteenth century the cities of northern Europe gained more rights of self-determination, but except in Germany none became completely independent even in fact, much less in law. In France and particularly England municipal liberties were curtailed by the power of the kings. In Flanders the cities were more independent, while in Italy the cities had very little control from lords. The landowners who had controlled the cities in the twelfth century gradually yielded some share of power to wealthy merchants and in a few cases to craftsmen. Nevertheless, most annually rotating city councils, far from being an expression of urban autonomy, were actually established by the town lord as a means of breaking the older oligarchy.

Virtually all cities moved in the thirteenth century to government by a council, but this did not mean a radical change in the elite, which was

---

77 Baldwin, *Philip Augustus*, 346–7; Cazelles, *Paris*, 86, 90; Epstein, *Wage Labor and Guilds*, 137; Hilton, *English and French Towns*, 78–81.
78 Stoob *et al.*, *Urkunden*, 254–8.

still dominated by landowners. The efforts of wealthy merchants to enter government met with little success until after the 1280s. The newly rich in Nuremberg formed a circle of 'Honourables' who were sometimes consulted but in the last analysis were politically powerless beside the patrician council.[79] The attempt to differentiate old from new elites can be deceptive. The patriciate of Ghent consisted of persons who owned land in the city. Yet this group made most of its money in the thirteenth century from two sources other than rent: provisioning the city with food and industrial raw materials, and controlling the production process and export of luxury woollen cloth.[80]

Italy had pioneered government by consuls in the twelfth century, but they did not evolve there into councils with fixed numbers and terms of office. Councils were delayed in the north, where the cities were more often governed by *scabini*, the assessors of the town lord's court, or *jurés* representing the sworn association of the community. After about 1190 the Italian and northern cities took divergent routes. While conciliar regimes gradually became the norm in the north, in Italy the lord's *podestà* took over the functions previously exercised by the consuls. The Italian cities only developed councils, and under arrangements much more complex and overlapping than was normal in the north, after the civic conflicts of the thirteenth century had limited the *podestà*'s power in favour of that of the *popolo*.[81]

The Low Countries

The change to conciliar regimes was accompanied by such officials as the *scabini*, who had initially exercised purely judicial functions, branching into public administration. The Flemish cities were powerful enough simply to assume control of a court that had previously been the prince's. Thus the originally seigniorial *scabini* (Flemish *schepenen*) became real councils, but this was unusual elsewhere. Ghent, Courtrai, Saint-Omer, Arras and Lille had both *scabini* of the lord and *jurés* of the sworn association of the city in the twelfth century, but *jurés* are rarely mentioned after 1200. The councils were always oligarchical, but the degree to which penetration by outsiders was possible varied. The *schepenen* held office for life in the twelfth century but were replaced at Ghent by an annual magistracy in 1212. This yielded in turn in 1228 to a cooptive body of thirty-nine, grouped into three thirteen-member

79   Möncke, *Quellen*, 13.
80   Nicholas, 'Structures', 512–23.
81   Opll, *Stadt und Reich*, 20.

bodies (*schepenen*, councillors and 'vacationers') who rotated offices among themselves. The council of Ypres was made annual but cooptive in 1209. Thus the patriciate of the city chose the council without the intervention either of the commoners or of the Flemish counts.[82]

In Brabant the *jurés* had a more active role alongside the *schepenen* than in Flanders. In 1235 the duke of Brabant gave Brussels an annual magistracy of seven *schepenen*, whom he chose from the ministerials who owed him military service, and thirteen *jurés* who were chosen by cooption from among the burgesses. In the eastern Low Countries the *jurés* became the city council. At Liège the *scabini/échevins* took the oath of office before the cathedral chapter of Saint-Lambert, while the *jurés* did so in the city hall. The two groups were both wealthy, but the *échevins'* families were older. In the fourteenth century some *échevins* functioned simultaneously as *jurés* or even as burgomasters.[83]

Low Country cities that had burgomasters generally had two. The title 'deputy' or 'regent' was preferred at Ypres and Lille, 'port masters' at Leiden and later Amsterdam. Burgomasters are found at Liège in the twelfth century, and in all cities of the prince-bishopric, as well as in Utrecht and Brabant, before 1300. As in some German cities, the burgomaster might simply be the *schepen* ranked first in dignity, as at Ghent after 1301, or so designated by his colleagues. Different colleges of the magistracy might choose one burgomaster, such as *schepenen* and councillors at Bruges, Louvain, Maastricht and Utrecht, or the patricians and the guildsmen. The burgomaster originally controlled finances but yielded early to special receivers or paymasters, often imposed by the prince as a means of controlling the city. By 1300 the burgomaster's functions were largely diplomatic and ceremonial.[84]

France

The evolution of conciliar government was slower in northern France than in Germany and Alsace. At Metz a council of thirteen *jurés*, first mentioned in 1205, was the first major urban institution that did not originate in the bishop's palace. It was similar to institutions of peace found elsewhere, handling criminal cases and directing foreign policy and administration. Although the Thirteen limited the *échevins* and the mayors, they were recruited from the same families as they. By 1228 the Thirteen had a 'master', a role which was rotated among their

---

82 Monier, *Institutions judiciaires*, 105–11; van Uytven, 'Stadsgeschiedenis', 227–8, 231–2; Nicholas, *Medieval Flanders*, 134.

83 Martens, *Histoire de Bruxelles*, 64–70; van Uytven, 'Stadsgeschiedenis', 228–30.

84 van Uytven, 'Stadsgeschiedenis, 232–3.

number at four-week intervals. The *échevins'* chief function became to act as the repository of local custom and its principles.[85]

The communes: mayors, *jurés* and public administration

Urbanisation had been linked to the grant of communes in the twelfth century, but after 1223 communal charters did little more than confirm existing arrangements. Legal writers of the thirteenth century endowed existing communes with juridical characteristics after the fact. Although communes had had no specific form of government in the beginning, Philippe de Beaumanoir saw them as privileged societies whose laws were enshrined in a charter rather than custom. The commune enjoyed the right to be governed by a mayor and a council of *jurés*. It had to have a seal to certify expressions of its corporate will; Reims and Lyon, which were not communes, did not have seals. The commune had a bell to summon or warn the inhabitants and a chest containing the city charters. Communes normally lacked a royal provost or bailiff. These officers tended to protect the towns to which they were assigned from peculation and exploitation by the local lord and the oligarchic councils. Thus the king usually appointed a provost or bailiff when he ended a commune.[86]

The mayor was the chief executive in the communes of northern and southwestern France. The Establishments of La Rochelle, which were extended to other cities in the south, imitated those of Rouen in having a hereditary college of one hundred peers who then nominated three persons from whom the prince would choose the mayor. At Poitiers the hundred peers elected the mayor directly, along with thirteen *échevins* and twelve councillors who met under the mayor's presidency.[87] Bordeaux had a variation of the Rouen system, with a mayor elected annually by fifty *jurats*. The *jurats* had both civil and criminal jurisdiction. No mayor could return to office before a three-year 'vacation', but in fact mayors were being re-elected in the 1220s. Mayor and *jurats* together constituted the *jurade*, which was similar to the *Signoria* of the Italian cities. Thirty 'councillors' chosen by the *jurade* and a guard of three hundred citizens completed the magistracy. Outgoing *jurats* chose their own successors. The *jurade* could legislate subject to royal approval, collect taxes and conduct diplomacy.[88]

The cities of Champagne illustrate the development of communal

---

85 Schneider, *Metz*, 104–12, 151–6.
86 Petit-Dutaillis, *French Communes*, 82–7, 91.
87 Dez, *Poitiers*, 56ff.; Petit-Dutaillis, *French Communes*, 96.
88 Renouard, *Bordeaux sous les rois d'Angleterre*, 39–42, 103–4; Lodge, *Gascony under English Rule*, 156.

institutions. Troyes had a sworn association by 1153 and a mayor by 1187, but only in 1230 did the count of Champagne give Troyes and Provins virtually identical charters granting a mayor and elected representatives, which by then were necessary for a place to enjoy the legal standing of a commune. The two cities gained their own government and the right to administer justice in exchange for paying 300 livres yearly to the count, but he still judged' the capital offences of murder, rape and theft. The count could try no cases involving burgesses unless they concerned him personally. He or his representative chose thirteen men from the community each year, who would elect one of their number as mayor. The other twelve became *jurés*. The count kept lucrative seigniorial rights. Unless the mayor and *jurés* certified that the count lacked enough mills and ovens to satisfy the city's needs, the burgesses had to use his facilities.

The charter of 1230 was the apogee of municipal independence at Troyes. Fiscal problems provoked the count to revoke the communal government in 1242, although the personal liberties of the burgesses were unaffected. Provins, which was less under the prince's eye, developed genuine civic government under a patriciate. Its commune lasted until the mid-fourteenth century. A new charter of 1252 provided for a mayor, twelve *échevins* chosen by the count, and forty *jurés* as parish representatives. Courts were held in the three loges that served as centres of the city government; their judges often served simultaneously as *échevins*, with a clerk who kept the city accounts. The mayor had a clerk and sergeants and supervised the night watch, the town crier and the keepers of the municipal fields and vineyards.[89]

The conciliar regimes were so inefficient and the level of violence between rival lineages so severe that Bayonne, La Rochelle, Compiègne, Senlis and Rouen had to appoint non-citizen 'rectors' or mayors, with functions similar to the Italian *podestàs*. A sort of circuit of mayors developed; just as some Italian nobles made a career of being *podestàs*, some in France were mayors of several cities in the course of a career.[90] The feud at Bordeaux between the Soler and Colom lineages so disrupted the city from the late 1240s that the English king as town lord took over the mayoralty and reduced the power of the *jurats*. When the French controlled Bordeaux briefly after 1294, they found the city so factionalised that using local people in government was impossible.[91]

89　Petit-Dutaillis, *French Communes*, 89; Chapin, *Villes de foires*, 141–3, 147–56, 166–83.

90　Mollat and Wolff, *Popular Revolutions*, 34; Petit-Dutaillis, *French Communes*, 93.

91　Renouard, *Bordeaux sous les rois d'Angleterre*, 112–13, 117, 123–6; Lodge, *Gascony under English Rule*, 157.

While regimes of mayor and council tended to degenerate into corrupt oligarchies, the strictly consular regimes had so many positions in
government that they encouraged factionalism and inefficiency. Nîmes
from 1272 had eight consuls and a council of twenty-seven, chosen according to both geographical and occupational criteria. Six represented
the aristocratic 'burgesses' of the area of the Roman arena, where most
knightly families lived. Twelve were chosen from the city at large,
while nine represented the 'scales' or orders into which the population
was divided. There was some internal logic to this division, versions
of which would be found in several cities of northern Europe in the
fourteenth century. It grouped trades according to their relationship to
the market and to raw materials, but no single group had more seats
than another. One seat went to the moneychangers, apothecaries, grocers and all who sold goods by weight, while another went to clothing dealers (merchant drapers, furriers, and tailors). This group in turn
was distinct from those who made the raw materials from which the
clothiers made their finished products (weavers, curriers and tanners).
Herdsmen and butchers, who worked with animals, were a 'scale', as
were blacksmiths and all who worked with hammers; carpenters and
stonecutters as construction workers; manual labourers; and jurists, physicians and notaries. The retiring consuls and councillors chose their successors. After 1283 two of the burgess representatives had to come from
'scales'. Montpellier had a similar arrangement from 1252.[92]

Political struggles at Toulouse involved the usual issues of ward rivalries, rich versus poor generally, and newly rich versus old and often
landed rich specifically. Combined with these, however, was the Cathar
heresy, which was strong in the bourg, while the City, the home of the
older aristocratic lineages, was orthodox. The bishop founded a 'White'
confraternity, mainly of doctrinally orthodox patricians living in the
City; a rival 'Black' organisation, with ties to the Cathars, was formed
in the bourg. Although the City was larger and richer than the bourg,
in contrast to the norm elsewhere, each furnished twelve of the twenty-
four capitouls. In 1248 a social division was superimposed on this geographical basis when the count ordered that half the capitouls be chosen
from the 'great' and half from the 'middle' families. Toulouse received
its final medieval constitution in 1283, after which twelve retiring
capitouls named eighty-four persons, two from each ward, from whom
the royal vicar would select new capitouls.[93]

92 Mollat and Wolff, *Popular Revolutions*, 41–2; Faber and Lochard, *Montpellier*, 100–2.
93 Wolff, 'Civitas et burgus', 206–7; Mollat and Wolff, *Popular Revolutions*, 38–42;
     Mundy, *Toulouse*, 74–6, 82–3, 98–9, 104–14, 149–51.

Toulouse shows that neighbourhood organisations formed the basis of much city government. Streets in Paris were grouped into parishes, which were grouped for tax purposes into *questes*. Paris began with four quarters, which were initially military associations but quickly became the basis of tax assessment. Philip Augustus added four more without changing the name. Leaders called *quartiniers* were chosen by the citizens, with subordinates variously called *cinquanteniers* and *dixainiers*. We know little of the practical functioning of the quarter governments at Paris, but at Metz from 1197 the inhabitants of each parish chose two *ammans* to validate and eventually to write contracts.[94]

City governments in Languedoc tried to govern through craft organisations by requiring practitioners of the same trade to live in a single street or quarter. This led to confusion of street and trade. The consuls of Narbonne in 1278 ordered the population to swear in groups of fifteen to twenty persons, each chosen to represent simultaneously his craft and his street. At Carcassonne in 1327 the consuls of the trades were simultaneously 'consuls of the streets'. Whenever the consuls of the city were elected by geographical sectors rather than by guaranteeing certain seats for each trade, as at Montpellier and Nîmes, the fact that the professions were grouped by street still guaranteed *de facto* representation for the larger trades.[95]

Germany

The first city council (German *Rat*) in the Empire that was independent of a lord's tribunal was chosen at Utrecht in 1196, followed by Speyer and Worms around 1200, Lübeck in 1201, Erfurt around 1212, Soest in 1213, Strasbourg in 1214 and Cologne in 1216. Northern Germany thus gained councils ahead of the south, where they were unusual until after 1250. As in France, councils evolved as foils to the *Schöffen/ scabini* but came from the same social milieu as they. Since the council rotated annually, while *Schöffen* served for life, some served simultaneously as councillor and *Schöffe*.[96] In some of the largest cities of northern Germany, however, and in the planned foundations in the south that grew into genuine cities, a single council was created without a preexisting body of *Schöffen*. The places that were given the law of Lübeck had no *Schöffen*; political, economic, legislative and judicial power resided in a council chosen by cooption, not by choice of the citizens, whose

94   Cazelles, *Paris*, 16–18; Schneider, *Metz*, 101, 161–7.
95   Gouron, *Métiers en Languedoc*, 126–7, 137.
96   Isenmann, *Deutsche Stadt*, 133; Berthold, 'Auseinandersetzungen in Köln', 249.

members served for life. It thus resembled the *Schöffen* of the older cities more than their councils. Two-thirds of the members were the 'sitting council', while one-third, the 'old council', had a year off to take care of their private businesses.[97]

Bishops were generally hostile to councils, but the emperors were more receptive. Conflicts over government in the north German cities became quite complex, often under the stimulus of outside events. Although crafts rarely had the direct right to representation in government until after 1270, the rise of craft associations often accompanied the assumption of power by a city council at the expense of the town lord's *Schöffen*. The council regulated the trades, but the *Schöffen*, who were judges, never did. The wool weavers, shoemakers, smiths, hatmakers, painters, bakers and butchers of Erfurt, for example, had guilds by 1248–9 but were subject to the council and were without political voice until 1283.[98] The Cologne crafts had risen with the patricians against the archbishop in 1257, but when they were left out of power by the settlement, they changed sides. In 1259 the prelate deposed the old *Schöffen* and named a new college drawn from all elements of the population, including patricians, ministerials and at least one brewer and one weaver. But after 1261 the issue shifted to municipal autonomy against perceived encroachments by the archbishop. From 1263 the magistrates were mainly patrician again, and 'fraternities' disappear from charters. The guilds continued to fight the patrician regime, aided by hostility within the ruling group between the ministerials and the newer merchant group.[99]

While most cities with a resident bishop had a large ministerial element on the council, most of whom had expanded into commerce, merchants of more recent lineage were prominent in cities that were not seats of bishoprics. Cologne and some other north German cities excluded nobles from the conciliar elite. This was not true in southern Germany, with its smaller cities and larger noble element; but except at Zürich, which had a council by 1223, conciliar government only came to southern Germany after 1250. Although a few craftsmen gained access to the council in the north German cities, this was delayed in southern Germany until later in the century.[100]

Just as mayors and *jurés* functioned together in the French communes, so burgomasters normally presided over the council in the north German cities. In Cologne a 'master of the citizens', in effect a burgomaster,

97 Ebel, 'Lübisches Recht', 258–61.
98 Mägdefrau, 'Volksbewegungen in Erfurt', 329; Mickwitz, *Kartellfunktionen*, 68.
99 Berthold, 'Auseinandersetzungen in Köln', 268–75.
100 Rabe, 'Stadien der Ratsverfassung', 1–9, 14–17.

was the leader of the Rich Club by 1174. In south Germany some larger places had burgomasters in the mid-thirteenth century, but most did not get them until the fourteenth, often in conjunction with the introduction of the guild constitution as the basis for membership in the council. The first references both to guild masters on the council and to a burgomaster presiding over it at Ulm is from 1292, nearly half a century after the place received its seal. In Soest, Hildesheim, Hamburg, Lübeck, Schwerin, Wismar, Erfurt and Regensburg the first burgomasters were presidents of the council. The emperor did not generally exercise as much control over appointing the burgomasters as the French kings did with the mayors.[101]

England

The powerful English kings intervened directly in borough affairs, issuing statutes for the realm that took precedence over those of local lawmakers. Municipal officials had to enforce royal economic legislation, such as the assizes of wine, bread and ale, wool and grain embargoes and royal confiscations of the property of foreign merchants. After 1283, when the Statute of Acton Burnell required expansion of municipal record-keeping, collecting unpaid debts required a complicated confiscation and reimbursement procedure done by the city officials. The kings often fined city administrations for actions that their own charters permitted. The privilege of citizens not to be tried outside the home town was a particularly important issue, especially in cases involving city relations with royal officials or justices.[102]

King John (1199–1216) gave virtually identical charters to most of his cities. Most of them granted the farm of the borough and ordered the burgesses to choose two bailiffs and four coroners, set down general principles, and left the rest to the individual communities. Although the early town charters gave the cities the right to elect judges to keep the pleas of the crown, their place was quickly taken by the royal circuit justices. The charters do not mention mayors. John's grant of a mayor to London in 1215 was the first one recognised formally, although Henry fitz Ailwin was mayor of London in practice between 1192 and 1212. The next officially recognised mayor was Nottingham's in 1284, although many other cities had *de facto* mayors. The kings appointed local men to control some cities, such as 'Richard the Burgess', who

---

101 Eggert, 'Städtenetz und Stadtherrenpolitik', 118; Rabe, 'Stadien der Ratsverfassung', 11–12.
102 Young, *English Borough*, 14–15, 122–4, 130–3.

used the title 'Mayor of Gloucester' for twelve years between 1228 and 1240.[103]

The first charters do not mention councils either, but most cities developed them in the thirteenth century. Most were called 'aldermen'. English councils were weaker than those on the continent, and nowhere is there an equivalent of the dichotomy of the lord's court of *scabini* with the *jurés* representing the sworn association of inhabitants. How the burgesses of Ipswich fleshed out their government can be followed beyond the charter that John granted on 25 May 1200. The officials required by John's charter were elected at a meeting on 29 June 1200; twelve 'capital portmen' were also chosen as a city council on the grounds that this was the norm in other boroughs. For future elections four electors were named from each parish. The new government then met on 13 July to transact business. It established procedures for collecting tolls, set money aside to pay the farm of the borough, appointed other officers and suggested that a burgess be elected to serve as alderman of the merchant guild. This council adopted a town seal.[104]

Ties between the merchant guilds and embryonic city governments continued to be close in England. At Winchester only members of the guild were citizens. The mayor of the city was the chief officer of the guild. Non-citizens enjoyed full civil liberties, including landownership, but they could not participate in public affairs. The heads of the merchant guilds were initially called aldermen; but as the French notion of a commune gained influence in England, the term 'mayor' became more common. At Lincoln the last reference to the alderman as head of the government is from 1217. At Southampton the merchant guild and city government gradually merged, with an 'alderman' remaining chief of both.[105]

However, in most true cities the city court, the 'portmanmoot', began taking over the jurisdiction of the merchant guild from the late twelfth century, although the guild remained more powerful than even the government in the smaller towns. Though initially separate, the city court and merchant guild of Leicester had the same hall and officers by 1280. In the fourteenth century the guild became more powerful, assuming control of city finance, while the portmanmoot declined into a court for minor actions.[106]

103 Keene, *Medieval Winchester*, 68; Chew and Weinbaum, *London Eyre of 1244*, ix; Holt, 'Gloucester', 154; Platt, *English Medieval Town*, 159; Williams, *Medieval London*, 4.
104 Platt, *English Medieval Town*, 157–9.
105 Keene, *Medieval Winchester*, 70; Hill, *Medieval Lincoln*, 194–5; Platt, *Medieval Southampton*, 54–6.
106 Simmons, *Leicester*, 27–9; Martin, 'English borough', 33, 37, 44.

The special case of London

London was the only English city with a size and social structure comparable to the greatest continental centres, and the complexity of its government is instructive not only for general questions of public administration but also for the extent to which even a powerful city had to accept royal intervention. King John issued three charters for London; the third, for which the city paid 3,000 marks, fixed the farm of the borough at £300 and acknowledged that the burgesses might elect the royal sheriff, but this office declined as the central court of twenty-four aldermen became more important. Magna Carta confirmed the ancient liberties of London without specifying what they were. The mayor of London was one of the twenty-five barons who were to force the king to comply with the charter.[107]

The aldermen were the city council. They were essentially law-men of each of the twenty-four wards, which often had boundaries taken over from ancient sokes or formed by streets or markets. The Lord Mayor was the chief alderman. The aldermen were judges, but they also led the ward-based militia. The office was not salaried, but it had so many perquisites that it was very attractive. By 1249 most aldermen were being elected in theory by the 'discreet men' of the ward, but in fact some aldermanries became property and passed to descendants.[108]

The Husting (portmote) was the general court of the city. It initially heard all cases except pleas of the crown, but business increased so much that by 1244 separate actions were held in alternate weeks for pleas of land and common pleas. In 1221 the Mayor's Court was established to handle debt cases between natives and aliens, and it was soon hearing actions between citizens. Over time it came to handle other types of cases, including some on appeal. By 1300 the Husting dealt with land cases, the Mayor's Court personal actions, particularly commercial matters. London also had lesser courts, notably those of the sheriff and the chamberlain, who heard cases concerning apprenticeship and the franchise.

The English kings had more trouble controlling London in the thirteenth century than their French counterparts did with Paris. London had not shared the general urban growth that the early thirteenth century had brought to most places. English foreign trade was falling into foreign hands, and, in particular, Flemish clothiers and wool merchants were taking over what had been an active English trade. London still

---

107 Brooke and Keir, *London*, 49–55.
108 Williams, *Medieval London*, 27–8, 30–3; Brooke and Keir, *London*, 51–2.

paid the highest amount in John's 'taxation of merchandise' of 1203–4, 16.8 per cent of the total, but it was followed closely by the northern ports where Flemish goods arrived, and which were near the fairs and the wool and wheat areas. While in 1213–14 the aids and tallages (taxes owed by the cities and demesne lands of the crown) of the eight richest provincial towns were 125 per cent of London's, this figure had risen to 285 per cent in 1269.[109] Thus after Henry III cashiered the city's liberties in 1239 in a quarrel over appointing the sheriff, the council was led by a radical faction allied with the king's baronial opponents. When the Londoners claimed in 1255 that they owed only aid but not tallage to the king, although written records proved the contrary, the royal government tried to incite the 'popular' faction in the city against the aldermen by accusing them of peculation.

All city leaders of London were royalist at the beginning of the baronial movement, but this changed when Montfort appealed to the popular party. The royal courts set aside normal procedures and seemed to be acting favourably on any action brought against a London magistrate. Sporadic violence escalated into a complete breakdown of order in 1263. The pro-Montfort radicals among the patricians took control in 1264 and revived the ancient folkmoot. The mayor referred all questions to this court, and the crafts, now released from dependence on the aldermen, brought their industrial ordinances there for confirmation. Montfort's death brought the end of this 'commune'. Edward I intervened more directly in London's affairs than his father. The aldermen were restored in 1270. The royal alliance with those elements of the London moneyed group who supplied the court became especially close from 1274, when the wine merchant Henry le Waleys became mayor. He opposed the royal bailiff Walter Hervey, who allied with the fishmongers in hope of establishing a new royalist coalition among the trades.[110]

EARLY CITY FINANCES

Most cities owed money to their lords at regular intervals by 1200, and this, together with the enormous fines that were levied on rebellious communities, shows that the cities had considerable money and the machinery for collecting it. Yet, although they would eventually develop tax structures to finance a myriad of services for their populations, we have little

109 Nightingale, *Medieval Mercantile Community*, 59–66.
110 Discussion based on Williams, *Medieval London*, 82–3, 205–15, 220–6, 233–9, 243–6.

knowledge of how these functioned before 1300. Most city taxes were based on property or consumption of goods rather than on personal status, although some German governments evidently levied a mortuary duty.[111] The English kings held that the townspeople were serfs and accordingly subject to tallage. Most urban charters permitted the lord to demand taxes from the city as a corporation but not from individual citizens. In 1168 the Exchequer assessed individual burgesses, but in the other instances the cities assessed and collected the aid themselves. They also paid for new charters and confirmations, all of which implies a collection mechanism, but we do not know how it functioned.[112] The French cities paid *tailles* to the crown. The cities of the old Capetian domain were taxed heavily, while some areas that the crown acquired after 1185 were exempt from the *taille* or had only a limited liability.[113]

Municipal finances were relatively sophisticated in Walloon Flanders and Artois. Several cities used direct taxation, requiring all who were liable to tax to declare their assets. Amiens, Senlis, Douai and most German cities used oral statements, but Arras and Saint-Quentin had written declarations, made by the taxpayers queuing before the *échevins* in parish meetings. At Arras the *taille* was collected from 1213 at a uniform rate, not adjusted according to wealth as would be common later. In principle the government determined in advance what the town budget would be and divided it among the taxpayers. This sometimes meant very high rates, and the public – and the poets who were so vocal at Arras – accused the rich *échevins* of falsification, rigging the tax assessments for their friends and stealing from the city treasury. Arras had much larger budgets in the late thirteenth century than did the Flemish cities. Extrapolations from an inquest of 1289 suggest that 84 per cent of the city's income came from the *taille*, the rest from sales taxes and fees, particularly on wine. This schedule is informative but incomplete, for no figures survive for cloth, fees at the halls, wool, and rents on real estate owned by the city. Evidence from other cities suggests that these sources did not generate much revenue until later.[114]

By contrast, direct taxation was rarely used in the Flemish cities and was really a forced loan when it was utilised. The Flemish centres in 1228 began levying sales taxes on the major consumption goods: food, beer, peat, wool and other industrial raw materials, and, most lucratively, wine. The Flemish counts forced their cities to pay dearly for the

---

111 Opll, *Stadt und Reich*, 139; Erler, *Bürgerrecht und Steuerpflicht*, 18, 20, 93–5; Falck, *Mainz*, 170–2.

112 Erler, *Bürgerrecht und Steuerpflicht*, 20; Ballard, *British Borough Charters*, lxxx–lxxxiii.

113 Baldwin, *Government of Philip Augustus*, 158–9.

114 Lestocquoy, *Dynasties bourgeoises d'Arras*, 51–7.

right to tax, but in 1291 the impecunious Duke John I of Brabant had to sell to Brussels his incomes from use fees assessed at the local weighing balance and crane and gave the city the income from the sales tax on goods passing through the gates. These levies were controversial, for they were generally farmed at great profit to the city patricians and bore heavily on the poor. Ibn 'Abdun called the tax collectors of Seville 'the worst of the creatures whom Allah put on earth, equal to the wasp that he created to injure and be of no use'.[115] The patricians of Arras leased the wine tax at profits of up to 100 per cent. The excises were an issue in the demands of the Flemish commoners for reform in the late thirteenth century, but by 1300 they had become the main ordinary revenue of the cities.[116] Other expedients were makeshift. The governments of the great Flemish cities were hopelessly in debt to the bankers of Arras. By 1275 Ghent owed 38,500 livres, while by 1299 Bruges owed 110,000 livres to a single family, the Crespins.[117]

The French royal domain and the south

Most French cities developed a central treasury as they became more unified territorially in the thirteenth century, although tax assessment and often collection were still done by parish or quarter. By mid-century the royal tax burden and the need for services to keep pace with a burgeoning population forced many French cities to put in place a mechanism for direct taxation. As in Germany this was generally done by the taxpayer making a personal declaration of income, which made cheating easy.

As the cities plunged from one ill-conceived financial expedient to another, the kings began to intervene directly in their affairs. In 1256 Louis IX ordered the mayors of Rouen to render annual accounts in the presence of three persons chosen by the 'notables of the city', probably the peers. In 1260 thirty-five French communes were ordered to present their accounts of the preceding year – a demand that shows that they were already keeping records – to the royal court. In 1262 Louis required councils in the communes of France and Normandy to rotate on 29 October; the new governments were then to present their accounts at Paris on 17 November. These orders were not enforced for long. The normal procedure became an audit by a commission of notables chosen from the town and presided over by a royal

115 Lévi-Provençal, *Seville musulmane*, 66.
116 Nicholas, *Medieval Flanders*, 186; Martens, *Histoire de Bruxelles*, 82.
117 Nicholas, *Medieval Flanders*, 183–5; van Houtte, *Economic History*, 54.

official. Towns with consuls usually handled the audit without royal intervention.[118]

The finances of thirteenth-century Provins, a medium-sized city with an international fair and an export textile industry, have been examined carefully. Although the government borrowed from the Italians who came to the fairs, Provins seems to have been untypical only in its solvency. The city's charter of 1230 based municipal finance on the *jurée*, a tax on movable and immovable property that was based on sworn personal assessments. Payment of the *jurée* made one a member of the commune and thus included subjects of the count of Champagne who lived outside the city. In 1268 the count declared clerks, vassals, knights, Jews and foreign merchants excluded from the commune and accordingly exempt from the *jurée*. In 1273 the count replaced the *jurée* with a sales tax on various items, particularly cloth and taxtile raw materials, including dyes.

Municipal accounts for Provins survive for most years between 1274 and 1331. Judicial fines were the most regular source of income. Small sums came from fees. From 1295 a tax to support the night watch usually yielded 150 livres, and after 1310 the farm of the public baths brought 100 livres. The largest expenses were 250 livres paid to the count for the right to have a city court and 400–500 livres for gifts to the king, count and other potentates, messengers and other diplomatic travel. The wages of the mayor and city clerk cost about 80 livres and those of the city guards 150 livres. Paying other city officials and renting loges, buying candles, parchment and other accessories of bureaucracy added 100–150 livres. The entire cost of municipal administration was thus less than payments and presents that the city had to make to the prince, a theme too often overlooked in investigating the extent of municipal autonomy. Provins, typically for the French and English cities, thus had to cover most of the expenses associated with city government, but many of the incomes were kept by the count or the king. Although Provins 'officially' ran a surplus in most years, this was only because obligations were covered by foreign loans at high interest rates, mainly from Italian merchants at the fairs and at Arras.[119]

In addition to taking direct loans from bankers, city governments were already borrowing by issuing life rents: the investor paid a lump sum to the city and in return received a fixed payment annually for his lifetime. By the mid-thirteenth century the leading French cities owed

118 Mollat, *Histoire de Rouen*, 93; Glénisson and Higounet, 'Comptes villes françaises', 41; Mollat and Wolff, *Popular Revolutions*, 34.
119 Discussion based on Chapin, *Villes de foires*, 66, 125–6, 177–8, 210–18, 292–5, 303–9.

thousands of livres: in 1232 alone Troyes sold nearly 1000 livres to thirty-eight burgesses of Reims.[120]

England

Royal control of municipal finances was especially stifling in England. The charters fixed the amount of the 'farm of the borough', the tax that the cities owed each year to the Exchequer, and the right to have municipal rather than royal officials collect it was prized. Most cities had one or two chamberlains as receivers. But the farms were high, and inflation, which was never as serious in England as on the continent, scarcely diminished their real value. York's farm was set at £160 in 1212, but the city had trouble meeting it from the beginning. Edward I in 1292 seized the city government for debts of over £300, some going back twenty years or more: for York's income, given by royal assignment, was inadequate to pay the farm, yielding only £123 4s. 9d. in 1292–3. Three-quarters of it came from tolls and a royal charge on wool entering and leaving the city.[121]

In addition to the farm, the cities paid tallage an average of once every three years during the reigns of John and Henry III. The amount was set in principle by the king, although the city governments usually negotiated it downward. In 1206 John ordered the barons of London to elect twenty-four citizens to see to the collection of tallage, which had hitherto been borne 'by the ordinary townspeople rather than the wealthy minority'. Some boroughs offered a sum for the entire community, but the king might insist on a per person assessment. Apart from the fact that royal officials assisted municipal officers in collecting the tallages, we know little about the actual mechanics of collection. In London the mayor and sheriffs delegated it to the aldermen and between four and six collectors per ward.[122]

In contrast to the situation on the continent, few English cities were authorised to levy indirect taxes on goods entering the city. The only exception was murage, which was first granted in 1220 but only to those cities with particular defence needs, usually to help finance a wall. The earliest grants were for a single year, but this was soon lengthened, and seven-year terms were common by 1300. The cities collected murage by a variety of expedients, from municipal employees to tax farmers. Although the cities were not supposed to use murage receipts for expenses

---

120 Mollat, *Histoire de Rouen*, 86; Desportes, *Reims*, 125–31.
121 Tillott, *City of York*, 35.
122 Brooke and Keir, *London*, 50–1; Young, *English Borough*, 43–6.

other than fortifications, the kings themselves began making assignments on murage and other revenues, for instance directing the city government to pay a royal official or creditor. The cities themselves also diverted the money to other uses. By 1233 they were giving exemption from murage to their trading partners. The result was frequent controversy at the city gates when someone tried to claim that he was a burgess of an exempted community. Exemptions from murage eventually became so widespread that some boroughs tried to get permission to levy property taxes, shifting emphasis from trade goods entering the city to the property of the burgesses themselves.[123]

The English cities had a heavy burden of enforcing royal legislation, but the kings were unwilling to give them the money to do it effectively. At least half London's expenditure recorded in the chamberlains' accounts of the early fourteenth century was for royal demands, not local administration. London was unusual in financing most of its obligations by direct taxation, most often on movable property, assessed by juries in the wards. Offices such as the Bridge Trust had independent administrations. In 1257 the king ordered an inquest into charges of peculation and favoritism in collecting tallage in London. The problem seems to have been that individuals had received royal exemptions from tallage, not that the assessment was unjust in itself or that the aldermen had been dishonest. This fact did not deter the rebels of 1263, even though the ultimate cost was loss of the city's liberties to the crown.[124]

Germany

Urban public finance was more sophisticated in the German cities than in France and England, probably because the cities were dealing with local lords whose authority was being eroded, rather than with increasingly powerful national monarchs. There is no evidence of a German equivalent of the English 'farm of the borough' except for Frederick II's privilege of 1219 to Nuremberg, which allowed the burgesses to pay taxes as a community rather than individually. Town lords initially collected ground rents, but by 1300 most had surrendered this to city governments, which in exchange took over some responsibilities that the lord had previously exercised, such as street repair.[125]

As in the west, the most reliable and least popular sources of income were sales taxes on goods entering the city. They were similar initially

---

123 Young, *English Borough*, 60; Turner, *Town Defences*, 30–9; Allmand, 'Murage', 223–9.
124 Williams, *Medieval London*, 88–92, 198–9; Young, *English Borough*, 46–7.
125 *Nürnberger Urkundenbuch*, 113; Stoob *et al., Urkunden*, 220.

to murage, for they were instituted in the late twelfth and early thirteenth centuries to pay for extending the walls.[126] Many German cities also levied direct taxation, to which all citizens were liable. Those who were below a given level of wealth paid a flat rate assessed by the council, while wealthier citizens paid in proportion to their incomes.[127] A text of 1291 illustrates the procedure at Augsburg, which was probably typical. Each year the council chose three 'tax masters'. The job was unpopular; persons chosen could not refuse to serve, but a three-year vacation between terms of service gave some relief. The tax was assessed on all property. Money that was owned or loaned was taxed at 10 per cent, annuities at 20 per cent, and other property that was not convertible to money was taxed according to the judgement of the masters. Everyone paid the tax, but according to their 'status'. Those whose payments were late were fined one-third of the tax amount. Foreigners were also taxed; if guests had deposited money with innkeepers, they were either to declare it, or the landlady would be assessed tax on it. Landlords were punished for concealing guests' property.[128]

The cities of northern Europe thus underwent important changes before 1270, but the composition of most urban governments did not reflect the extent of social transformation or physical expansion. The Italian cities changed much more obviously, but careful analysis of developments both north and south of the Alps shows striking parallels. We thus turn to urbanisation in Italy.

126 Berthold, 'Auseinandersetzungen in Köln', 266; Haverkamp, *Medieval Germany*, 288; Keutgen, *Urkunden*, no. 116, p. 76.
127 Erler, *Bürgerrecht und Steuerpflicht*, 22, 31–2, 39.
128 Keutgen, *Urkunden*, no. 211, pp. 266–7.

CHAPTER EIGHT

The Commercial Cities of Thirteenth-century Italy under 'Popular' Oligarchies

The Italian cities had councils and undertook concerted political activity earlier than those of northern Europe. They had much large populations than all but the greatest northern cities. While charters were the basis of urban liberties in the north, the Italian communities simply assumed powers that were not being exercised by their town and regional lords, the emperor and the bishops.

During the thirteenth century some differences sharpened. Although industry did develop in some Italian cities, it did not do so to the same extent as in the north; Florence, which is so often taken as the proto-type of the Italian city, was unusual. The trade at the Champagne fairs, however, solidified the Italians' position as the leading merchants of the west. They bought undressed cloth in the north and brought it to Italy for finishing or re-export. They were the only source of the dyes used in the finest woollens made in the northern cities, and of alum, the mordant used to fix the dyes.

Overseas trade continued to be the main source of commercial wealth for Venice, Genoa and Pisa, the coastal emporia, but banking and finance became increasingly significant in the interior cities. Papal patronage was important for their burgeoning wealth. The bankers of Perugia had a guild by 1260, when they and the merchants were asked to establish a mint. They financed military operations in southern Italy and handled papal funds, then declined in the fourteenth century as they lost papal contracts.[1] Banking was also important in Siena, mainly for old families with lands in the *contado*. Sienese bankers were at the Champagne fairs by 1216. They loaned to French prelates and the English kings. But although they also dealt in commodities, especially cloth at the fairs and

---

1 Blanshei, *Perugia*, 17.

English wool, the basis of their wealth was the popes' business, transferring funds from northern Europe to Italy. Sienese bankers also loaned money to their own city government. The Salimbeni family had a high assessment in a tax of 1285, but the city owed them so much that it is likely that no money changed hands; indeed, the Salimbeni bank administered this tax on behalf of the government.[2]

Although annually rotating councils were initially imposed on most northern cities by lords who hoped to break the previously dominant oligarchy of the landowners, over time the councils became the focal point of moves toward local autonomy. The conciliar regime in Italy, however, atrophied in the wake of ferocious civil strife, much of it exacerbated by political elements extraneous to the cities themselves.

The Italian urban family

The Italian cities, like those of the north, were ruled by elites that consisted almost entirely of landowners into the early thirteenth century. The wealth of the oldest families even of Venice, the most commercial of the large centres, came from landownership and possession of the lagoons.[3] During the thirteenth century wealthy merchants began demanding a political voice. But in contrast to the north, the merchants of the north Italian cities developed an organisation, the *popolo*, through which they acted collectively.

Family consciousness was strongest among the magnates, who had rural lands and social ties. In Tuscany and Liguria the great lineages had rural branches that were older than the urban ones. Although most residences were for nuclear families, aristocratic lineages tended to group theirs around defensive towers. Of 1,000 citizens of Pisa who swore peace with Genoa in 1188, only 130 had family names drawn from the city and countryside of Pisa. The others were foreign, mainly German, indicating their continued dominance of the Pisan aristocracy. Fifty-three of the 130 were grouped together in a single line in the text and were mainly of merchant and urban origin. Thus even at coastal Pisa the merchant family nuclei were less important politically at the end of the twelfth century than were the old lineages. Noble *consorterie* (unions of lineages), with a base in both city and *contado*, dominated the city through their towers.[4]

Although some adult sons moved into separate domiciles near their

2 Waley, *Siena*, 26–35.
3 Romano, *Patricians*, 22–4.
4 Volpe, *Studi sulle istituzioni comunale a Pisa*, 276–9.

parents, others remained in the central home. Even after the father's death brothers often lived together, held some joint property or remained business partners. The father dominated the lineage, for sons were normally emancipated only as adults. They were expected to adopt his feuds as their own. The lineage held property in common and shared liabilities. If the father was on the losing side in a factional conflict, the entire property of the lineage could be lost; if only a son was considered culpable, his share alone was lost, and property owned by females was unaffected. At Florence the magnates did not begin dividing family property into individual shares until after 1293. Bologna shows the same predominance of aristocratic impartible (indivisible) inheritance.[5]

All nobles and many merchants of Genoa were in unions of lineages called *alberghi*, which had between a few dozen and several thousand members. *Alberghi* admitted nuclear families to membership, but not individuals. Descent was always in the male line. Marriage was exogamous, for since the *albergo* was considered a family in law, however lacking in blood ties its members may have been, endogamy was incest. Yet the Genoese *alberghi*, like the paraiges of Metz and the lineages in the German cities, were closer to factions or political parties than to lineages in the modern sense. The *consorterie* of Florence were similar to the *alberghi* but were more numerous and had smaller memberships.[6] From 1216 there is some evidence at Pisa of societies of knights, with captains. Pisa had between fifteen and twenty *consorterie*, each with between twenty and thirty adult males and based on a tower.[7]

CITY GOVERNMENT IN ITALY DURING THE EARLY THIRTEENTH CENTURY

The executive: senator, doge, *podestà*

Although the Italian consular regimes seem to have served as models for the city councils of northern Europe which developed later, the evolution of councils was delayed in the north Italian cities by the rise of executive authorities that were stronger than the mayors and burgomasters of the northern cities. Rome was a peculiar case, given the great power both of its noble lineages and of the pope as city lord. Its governing body was the Senate, a body of varying size. About 1252 one or two

5 Lansing, *Florentine Magnates*, 57–61; Hughes, 'Urban growth', 4, 7, 18–20; Heers, *Espaces Bologne*, 52–3, 105.
6 Heers, *Family Clans*, 35–45, 70–90.
7 Volpe, *Studi sulle istituzioni comunale a Pisa*, 395–7.

Senators became the leaders of the city government. Some Senators were foreign protectors, such as Charles of Anjou and Richard of Cornwall. The Senator had some similarities to the north Italian *podestà* but, like the northern mayor, usually was a native of the city. He was the head of an inchoate administration that included scribes, notaries and peace-keepers who functioned in specific regions of the city.[8]

Venice also had a singular form of government. The doge (duke), a descendant of the Byzantine governor of the city, held office for life. He was the most powerful urban magistrate in Italy until 1172, after which each new doge had to accept the principle that he would never act against the advice of his councillors. Thereafter, on the death of each doge a committee suggested restrictions to be imposed on his successor in his oath of office. Although by 1268 the doge was chosen by majority vote in a committee of forty-one, this was at the conclusion of a ten-stage process, five of which involved commissions chosen by lot. The use of lots is found earlier in Venice than in the other Italian cities and tended to blur factionalism in Venetian elections.

The base of Venice's government was theoretically the General Assembly, but the most powerful body was the Great Council, with a total membership of some three to four hundred at this time. It chose all magistrates and the members of the other councils, legislated and acted as a court. Since it was so large, most ordinary business was delegated to other councils. The Forty was the supreme court of appeals, but it also prepared legislation on finance and coinage for approval by the Great Council. The Forty was eventually overshadowed by the Senate (*Consiglio dei Pregadi*), which was originally a committee of sixty concerned with maritime affairs. The *Signoria*, the executive organ of the Venetian state, was composed of the doge's six-member council (one for each of the six geographical sectors of the city), the three leaders of the Forty and the doge himself.[9]

The regimes of consuls declined at the turn of the thirteenth century in most north Italian cities and were replaced by multiple councils. Changes in the nature of the *podestà*'s position were instrumental in this development. Even in Tuscany the *podestàs* were rarely imperial appointees by this time. It was once thought that from the beginning they were outsiders who could provide impartiality in the ferocious party conflicts, but research into the family origins of the early *podestàs* shows that they were more often natives of the city where they served. Only when this proved unsatisfactory did the cities start appointing foreign

---

8   Brentano, *Rome Before Avignon*, 95–6, 101, 110–11, 117–22.
9   Lane, *Venice*, 92–7, 111.

podestàs. Quarrels among magnates who held consulships led to the imposition of *podestàs* by the city governments themselves in the late twelfth century. When alternating offices between factions did not make peace at Florence, the first citizen *podestà* was named, evidently from the Ghibelline faction. A regime under which consuls and a *podestà* served in alternate years continued until 1207, after which Florence named foreign *podestàs.*[10] Thus the *podestà* who was external and above local conflicts took years to accomplish. At first the *podestà* was not always a single figure; at one point Milan had three simultaneously.[11]

At Pisa the consuls became increasingly divided between factions for whom commercial wealth was more important and those who were cultivating their ancestral ties with the landed nobility. The consuls used their offices to pursue vendettas. The construction of a bridge led to violent conflict in 1183, involving patronage by consular families and access to the towers and the quarters that they controlled. Elections to the consulate usually returned persons in the same group of families, but every consulate contained one or two members of the Visconti family, who were descendants of the imperial viscounts of Pisa. The office of *podestà* was alternated between the Visconti and their rivals, the Gherardesca, who seem to have abolished the consulate in the 1190s. After 1201 the Visconti and their allies controlled the office and restored the consuls, who were now called 'rectors'. Although initially the consuls had been a council for the *podestà,* the two were independent of each other by 1217. The older consuls of the sea and of the merchants continued to function. Foreign *podestàs* came to Pisa only when the Visconti used the office to wreak vengeance on the Gherardesca. The last Visconti *podestà* left office in 1228, and the commune always appointed outsiders after 1233. At Lucca too the *podestàs* were more the result of infighting among the consuls than of the appearance of a separate force, for evidence shows some families serving as both *podestà* and consuls. This suggests that the interests of the great magnate families were shifting more towards the city in the late twelfth century.[12]

The *podestà* was closer to the Flemish and French urban bailiffs than to a mayor or burgomaster. He took over the executive and administrative functions of the consuls, presided over the city court, promulgated its verdicts and kept order. While a foreigner was usually *podestà* in the city itself by the 1230s, residents of the city often served as *podestàs* in *contado* communities. The position was initially so lucrative that some

10   Raveggi, 'Famiglie di parte Ghibellina', 283–8.
11   Based on Introduction to *CD* by Emilio Cristiani, 2–3.
12   Volpe, *Studi sulle istituzioni comunale a Pisa,* 284–7, 293–6, 324, 344–6, 361–3, 392–4; Tirelli, 'Lucca', 187–8.

aristocrats became 'career *podestàs*', going from one city to another. After foreign *podestàs* became the norm, alliances between cities were sometimes secured by a citizen of one becoming *podestà* in the other. This changed as the *podestà* lost power to the captain of the *popolo*, and some cities had to make several offers or even give the job to a native.[13] The position was particularly attractive to members of the older landed aristocrats among the consuls, such as the Porcari of Lucca, for it was the only urban office that could help them retain their power in the *contado*. The fact that the *podestàs* held office in different cities – the Porcari served in Lucca itself, Pisa, Florence and Genoa – helped them solidify their rural clienteles.[14]

The rural power base of so many *podestàs* may in turn explain some of the hostility directed towards them by the *popolo* societies. Some cities experienced problems when the rise of the *popolo* placed their governments at odds with their own knights who were strengthening the city's control of the *contado*.[15] As the Ghibelline party of Florence became identified more with the rurally-based faction of the aristocracy after 1250, they tried whenever they controlled the city government to keep the commune from intervening in the *contado*, while the Guelfs, who were more city-based than the Ghibellines, concentrated increasingly on subjugating the countryside politically as well as economically.[16]

Siena's complex procedure for choosing the *podestà* illustrates how the need to guarantee impartiality led to short-term magistracies and excessive bureaucracy. Three electors chosen by lot from the city council nominated four persons, subject to confirmation by the entire council. By the early fourteenth century the Nine, who ruled Siena after 1287, were sending emissaries to selected communities to enquire about possible candidates. Then they, the consuls of the knights and a college of sixty other persons designated the new *podestà*, who had to be at least age thirty and a knight. Most successful candidates were persons with legal training from Lombardy or Emilia. The *podestà* had to reside in a different sector of the city from his predecessor and could not go more than one day's journey outside the city. He was not permitted to receive gifts from or even to eat with Sienese citizens. The salary was high, varying with the social status of the appointee, but the *podestà* was expected to come with his own retainers, including judges and police, and pay them from his salary. Late thirteenth-century Siena had one

---

13 Lansing, *Florentine Magnates*, 10; Hyde, *Padua*, 211; Blanshei, *Perugia*, 54; Haverkamp, 'Städte im Herrschafts- und Sozialgefüge Reichsitaliens', 229.
14 Tirelli, 'Lucca', 192.
15 Haverkamp, 'Städte im Herrschafts- und Sozialgefüge Reichsitaliens', 234–5.
16 Dameron, *Episcopal Power and Florentine Society*, 124.

non-Sienese policeman for every 145 inhabitants. The *podestà* had to remain in the city for a stated time after his six-month term expired while his regime was investigated and audited.[17]

Councils

Virtually all Italian cities were divided geographically into groups of parishes for purposes of administration. At a time when membership on most city councils in northern Europe was based on lineage or affiliation to a merchant guild, the consuls of the Italian cities and later the councils that limited the *podestà* were apportioned by districts. These were initially units for raising the city militia, but some became identified with the trades whose practitioners resided in them. Many districts were centred on a prominent feature, particularly a tower. Each of the seven divisions of Genoa, called *campagne* (companies), extended across the city and was responsible for defending a space at the port and a share of the wall on the hill side of the city. By 1219 Bologna had four gate-based quarters, each with its own militia, standard and captain. Each quarter chose two of the eight 'elders' who were heads of the city government. Each of the nearly one hundred parishes (*cappelle*) also had its own organisation and officers. Venice was divided into sixths, within which the parishes (*contrade*) had their own organisations and 'heads' (*capi*). Siena was divided into *popoli*, most of which took their names from parish churches, but representation on the councils was based on larger divisions called *terzi* (thirds).[18]

A bewildering network of councils ruled most Italian cities in the early thirteenth century. Their membership was rotated more frequently than those in the north, and most of them were so large that they could handle administrative business only through subcommittees. While most northern councils ranged in size from a dozen to one hundred members, the Great Council at Pisa included captains of the knights, consuls of the 'order of the sea', consuls of the merchant order, consuls of the four guilds (tanners, furriers, smiths, butchers), consuls of the captains of the ports of Sardinia, and four hundred 'good men' chosen from the quarters of the city. Bologna by 1176 had nine consuls and a fifty-member council. From 1194 the 'merchants' named four consuls and the moneychangers three. In 1248 this 'merchant guild council' became the general council of the city. The Great Council of Padua, despite being limited to those

17 Waley, *Siena*, xvii, 42–5; Larner, *Age of Dante and Petrarch*, 200, after Bowsky, 'The Medieval commune'.
18 Hughes, 'Urban growth', 6; Heers, *Espaces Bologne*, 60–1; Lane, *Venice*, 98; Romano, *Patricians*, 15–18; Waley, *Siena*, xvi.

with a minimum tax assessment of 50 *lire*, had at least 1,000 members by 1277, or one-tenth of the adult male population. Political activity was limited to those who could qualify for the Great Council.[19] While disorders in the northern cities arose because there was little government beyond a city council whose membership was tightly controlled, in Italy the proliferation of factions led to frequent rotation and overlapping to give all interested parties a share of offices and perquisites. Most cities of northern Italy had a commune that included all citizens; but after about 1250 a *popolo*, various *consorterie*, guilds, *rioni* [regions] and Guelf and Ghibelline parties were added to this basic structure, each with its own records, councils, and in some cases militia. Since a goal of *popolo* governments was more stringent control of the *contado*, offices also proliferated there.[20] Much depended on going before the magistracy at a time when one's friends were being rotated onto it.

The numerous overlapping councils of the early thirteenth century thus provided too much direction at the top, but the *popolo* regimes after 1250 compounded this by a proliferation of bureaucracy and lower-level administrators. Using Perugia as one example, the following organisations constituted the city government by the mid-thirteenth century: the Special Council of fifty, the General Council of one hundred and the Great Council of five hundred, each with an equal number from each of the five districts of the city; the Special Council of the previous six months; the two-hundred member Council of the *Popolo*; the Council of the [Guild] Rectors; and the military companies. By the 1280s they had merged into two chief councils, those of the *Popolo* and of the Commune. The Great Council was the nucleus of the Council of the Commune. By the end of the century half its members were magnates, half *popolani*, and half each were from the city and the suburbs. This council quickly became a figurehead, as real power went to the Council of the *Popolo*, consisting of the Special Council, General Council, Rectors, and a smaller 'True Council of the *Popolo*' of two hundred (forty per district, with twenty each chosen by the Special Council and General Council).[21]

The administration of the *contado*

Contado boundaries in Italy added another political dimension to urban politics, for the cities were really city-states, administering and taxing their rural environs. The emperors had tried to limit city influence in the *contadi*

---

19 Barel, *Ville médiévale*, 120–1; Heers, *Espaces Bologne*, 58–9; Hyde, *Padua*, 210.
20 Tabacco, *Struggle for Power*, 258; Herlihy, *Pistoia*, 231–7.
21 Blanshei, *Perugia*, 53–6.

during their wars against the Lombard League, but the confusion after Henry VI's premature death in 1197 enabled the cities to recover their old rights. A Guelf League was quickly formed in an arrangement that included a clause recognising the suzerainty of the signatory cities over their *contadi*. This is the first theoretical statement of the subjection of the Florentine *contado* to the commune.[22] We have seen that sometimes the *contado* included relatively large subject towns that in turn had their own *contadi*, creating legally defined regions within regions. In the Po valley a score of city-states contained 1–2,000 sq km, and Milan, Florence, Bologna and Parma were even larger. The city was not always centrally located within the boundaries of the *contado*. Siena was in the northern quarter of its *contado*, only 15 km from the Florentine state. Siena had to garrison castles on the frontier, often depopulating villages when the military situation demanded it. This unfortunate location undoubtedly contributed to Siena's eventual loss of independence to what had been a less powerful neighbour in the thirteenth century.[23]

The administration of the *contadi* of some Italian cities can be followed closely from the thirteenth century. Lucca established a separate court for the *contado* at the beginning of the century. Most cities derived much of their income from their *contadi* in the thirteenth century, rather less so thereafter. Even by 1093 Florence was levying an 'aid' in its *contado* in addition to taxes collected by the commune for the margrave. Between 1156 and 1183 both the emperors and the city levied the *fodrum* (a head tax that the prince collected on his Italian trips) separately. In 1197 Arezzo abolished the imperial tax but doubled the rate of the communal *fodrum*; Florence in 1198 went the other way, abolishing the communal tax but pocketing the proceeds of the imperial levy.[24] The peasants in the *contado* of Orvieto were paying ground rent and hearth taxes to the commune by 1216. The commune also owned large amounts of land in its *contado*, including some entire villages. Florence compiled a census of its *contado* between 1230 and 1233, then imposed a hearth tax.[25]

The cities handled defence and built roads. As Siena gained control over its *contado*, the magnates who were also powerful in the city built strongholds along the main road. These private residences housed the government offices of the *contado* villages. The need to keep rural roads in repair and control traffic across them provided work for many city

22 Dameron, *Episcopal Power and Florentine Society*, 75.
23 Chittolini, 'Italian city-state', 591; Waley, *Siena*, 104–8.
24 Dameron, *Episcopal Power and Florentine Society*, 75–7.
25 Wickham, 'Rural communes and the city of Lucca', 2; Dameron, *Episcopal Power and Florentine Society*, 123.

dwellers. Residents of the city were commonly *podestàs* of *contado* communities, usually as absentees who made only occasional visits, as part of the patronage network that so enriched the Italian urban aristocracies. Some and perhaps most cities exploited their rural areas economically. Although industrial protectionism to safeguard the export markets of urban artisans did not generally become part of city policy toward the rural areas until after artisans had gained representation in city governments in the late Middle Ages, the *contadi* were administered initially for defence against semi-rural nobles and to ensure the grain supply. By the late thirteenth century all Italian cities regulated the grain trade, usually forcing farmers of the *contado* to sell on the city market. Padua's *contado* contained some of the best farmland in Italy, with a surplus for export that was the basis of the city's trade. The city government tried to restrict new markets in the *contado*, prohibited the export of many strategic goods, and tried to enforce the principle that surplus goods were to be brought to Padua itself for sale.[26]

City finances in Italy

Most Italian cities had used direct taxation regularly since their quarrels with Frederick Barbarossa. In 1081 Lucca received a guarantee, later confirmed by Henry V and Lothar, of privileges previously granted by margraves and other potentates. Henry IV in 1081 transferred to the cities to which he gave privileges the right to keep part of the *fodrum*. Henry V restricted the amount of tax owed to the emperor at Bologna, which presupposes that the commune had a collection apparatus in place.[27] The *fodrum* continued to dominate city finances until around 1200. Pisa began in 1162 to combine it with property taxation. In each tower district the consul chose five or more persons to compile lists of inhabitants, from whom he exacted an oath. Sworn assessors then set the amounts. Two fragmentary documents illustrate the municipal finances of Lucca in the twelfth century, but taken together they show a sophisticated system. A reference to three 'justiciars of the commune and debt of Lucca', who were vassals of the cathedral church, in 1179; and the fact that in 1184 Lucca agreed to give Florence half the revenues from the hearth tax, indicate that Lucca and probably Florence had such a levy.[28]

The finances of Pisa are the clearest of the Italian cities for the twelfth

26   Balestracci, 'Development to crisis', 200–1; Waley, *Mediaeval Orvieto*, 151; Waley, *Siena*, 3, 37; Hyde, *Padua*, 43–9.
27   Haverkamp, 'Städte im Herrschafts- und Sozialgefüge Reichsitaliens', 190.
28   Tirelli, 'Lucca', 196–7.

century. Ordinary revenues consisted of the *contado* tax and direct taxes in the city on movable and immovable property, with the assessment determined by a board of five consuls per gate. Frederick Barbarossa also confirmed Pisa's use of various indirect taxes, including the tax on goods passing through the gates, the salt tax, taxes on measures and regulation of the coinage. These were ordinary revenues. For emergencies, Pisa used forced and voluntary loans, for example the tax on the inhabitants of Cinzica in 1162 to wall their quarter. The commune also borrowed from the 'societies' and levied regular imposts in the second half of the twelfth century for new bridges, wall repairs, towers, port improvements, and galleys for war against Genoa.[29] Genoa in 1154 repaid a loan of 8500 pounds to the commune of Piacenza in 1154 (part of the value was in spices and dyes), a fact that reveals much of the financial and accounting capacity of both city governments.[30]

By the end of the century the cities were starting to use proportional property taxes, determined by the payer's oath (*estimo*). Siena was the first in 1198, but by 1250 Vercelli, Milan, Florence, Bologna, Genoa and Turin were using the *estimo*. This soon became a formal tax declaration, supplemented by an oath that the *estimo* was a true statement of assets. Although the 'poor' (*miserabiles*) were not actually taxed in some communities, they had to furnish declarations before being categorised as poor.[31]

In the early communal period direct taxation was used mainly for military campaigns. Since knights were the major component of the militia and provided their own equipment, they and their lands were exempt from taxation. But as more revenues were needed in the thirteenth century, most cities switched from extraordinary aids based on ability to serve with a horse to some version of the money-based *estimo*, which made the full tax exemption of knights anachronistic. Thus in the early thirteenth century Pisa divided its public debt into two parts, distributed on the basis of social status: the corporations of knights and of the *popolo* were each responsible for half.

The basic tax at Pisa became the *libra* (the silver pound), which was paid in proportion to the property's assessed value in pounds. The amount that the city needed was divided into the yield that was anticipated from the *estimo*, and the result was the tax rate. In the city the *estimo* was the basis of the *libra*, while in the *contado* the number of hearths was the basis, although the city allowed *contado* communities also to devise

29   Volpe, *Studi sulle istituzioni comunale a Pisa*, 5–6.
30   Hyde, *Society and Politics*, 73.
31   Erler, *Bürgerrecht und Steuerpflicht*, 18, 20, 93–5; Racine, 'Palais publics', 135; Blanshei, *Perugia*, 28.

local *estimi* if they wished. This tended to shift taxation unfairly toward the *contado*, although to equalise the burden each section of the city was linked for assessment to a section of the *contado*. Milan did something similar in 1240. The *libra* was not efficiently administered, in part because real property was disproportionately burdened, since in contrast to liquid capital it could not be hidden.[32]

Perugia, Florence and other cities also used the *libra* as the basis for direct taxes and forced loans. *Libre* were levied when the city had to raise money fast. Citizens' declarations were recorded in *catasti*. The earliest *catasto* extant at Siena, that of 1260, divided property into land, movable goods and credits. Each levy of the direct tax at Siena, the *dazio*, required a new assessment in principle, which was done by fifteen assessors in each district. *Dazi* were occasionally levied on the *contado* only.[33]

Most Italian cities did not have centralised treasuries but tended to rely on independent organisations, especially for long-term projects and public works. Examples are the 'Bridge Works' and the 'Works of the Church of Santa Maria Maggiore' for constructing and maintaining the cathedral at Pisa. The city could earmark revenues for a public project; the first tax on imported grain at Pisa was used for the cathedral. Siena is unusual in having two central financial offices by the mid-thirteenth century, the Biccherna to control direct taxes and the Gabella for indirect. The Biccherna was managed by a chamberlain, usually a monk, and four provisors who held six-month appointments.[34]

Most Italian cities realised windfall profits from disposing of the property confiscated from political enemies. But as population grew and administration became more complex, they, like the northerners, had to borrow. We have seen that Pisa and Genoa incurred substantial debts even in the twelfth century. Venice first used the forced loan in 1207, and in 1262 the various loans were organised into a permanent debt that paid 5 per cent interest. The forced loan amounted to a direct tax at Venice, for other forms were not used. To meet emergencies Venice used voluntary loans, repaying them quickly from the yield of the next forced loan. Shares of the forced loans were based on the *estimo* principle, originally the amount of taxable income above 100 *lire*, later raised to 300 *lire*. Forced loans used the same assessment base as the *dazio* at Siena and thus were often hard to distinguish from direct taxes there as well.[35]

32 Herlihy, *Pisa*, 70–86.
33 Waley, *Siena*, 170–5.
34 Waley, *Siena*, 58–9, 177.
35 Luzzatto, *Economic History of Italy*, 124; Waley, *Siena*, 170–5.

City governments also relied increasingly on indirect taxation. Into the thirteenth century most indirect revenues were tolls and fees that were collected by private families and churches. At Pisa private 'toll companies' administered some indirect incomes as tax farms. At Siena such companies operated the mint and city monopolies on the sale of iron, grain, salt, oil and fish. In 1203 the commune, the count palatine of Grosseto and eight entrepreneurs established the 'company of the salt toll of Grosseto and of Siena'. It was to create a salt monopoly by buying all salt mined in the *contadi* of Siena and Grosseto and selling to consumers. Similar operations appear elsewhere in Tuscany about this time.

Merchants, crafts and guilds

The Italian craft guilds appeared earlier than those of the north, but only the richer and more prestigious of them played a political role before the 1270s. Pistoia had 'rectors of the trades' by 1177. Bologna had craft organisations in the twelfth century, guild officials (*mistrales*) by 1219 and written guild ordinances by 1228. Venice, with its large luxury trade and specialised crafts, also had some guilds by the twelfth century, mainly of newly rich groups that were not engaged in maritime activity, such as tailors, jacket makers, goldsmiths and jewellers, dyers, coopers, cordage makers, and barber-surgeons. In 1173 the city instituted three Justices (the 'Old Justice') who controlled weights and measures, policed the markets and regulated the crafts. Venice also had at least fourteen religious fraternities (*scuole*) affiliated with occupational groups that soon began regulating the members' professional activity. The doge initially appointed the guild leader, the *gastaldo*, but from 1249 he had to have the consent of a majority of the guild members. Some guilds were choosing their own *gastaldi* by the 1280s. They and other guild officials were usually chosen by lot or by a group named by the outgoing guild council. But the Justices could legislate for guilds without the guild's approval, and they could veto any guild legislation or activity.[36]

Most Italian guilds were composites of several occupations. Even after the changes of the late thirteenth century not many Italian cities had more than twenty-five legally recognised corporations, and most had fewer. As in the north the wool guilds are the most common example of a composite. Metalworkers' guilds were also prone to subgroups. In the early stages some of them linked gold-, silver- and ironsmiths, others armourers and burnishers. At Piacenza the smiths had six sub-guilds.

36   Lane, *Venice*, 104–7; Mickwitz, *Kartellfunktionen*, 25, 63.

Leatherworkers, who were very important to the urban economies even after the expansion of woollen manufacturing, formed specialised guilds earlier than textile artisans and ironworkers. At Pisa the statute of the tanners, redacted before 1234, is the oldest surviving guild regulation. By this time, however, they included three groups (tanners, cordwainers and makers of shoes from cow leather), each with two captains.[37]

The craft guilds were subject in principle to the city government. Those of Siena legislated for themselves but were required in 1262 to submit their statutes for inspection three times yearly. Craft guilds had only a consultative, not official role in the government of Siena. As in France, the Italian guilds helped the authorities regulate their members' activities. Officials of the commune swore to investigate any 'sinister agreements and ordinances, written or verbal, made by guilds'. The two major guilds, the merchants and grocers (dealers in spices, wax, parchment and paper as well as food), had a corporate status as the 'two *mercanzie*', and their rectors supervised the crafts. The authorities were particularly suspicious of butchers and bakers. The bakers were forbidden in 1287 to have a guild, but this caused problems; for the excise on baking could not be farmed by the bakers unless they had an organisation. By this time the authorities at Venice also feared guilds. From the 1260s the Great Council required insertion in all guild statutes of a clause forbidding activity contrary to the honour of the doge, his council or the commune.[38]

The *popolo* at Florence did not initially have a guild structure, but one was superimposed on it after 1250. The oldest guild (*arte*) of Florence was the Calimala (cloth importers and finishers), which is attested in the late twelfth century. It was joined in 1206 by the moneychangers, in 1212 by the Lana (wool manufacturers), and in 1218 by Por Santa Maria (the mercers' guild, which handled general merchandise and the sale of native and foreign cloth except French; it was named after the main shopping street). Judges and notaries, physicians and apothecaries (who included spice importers) and the fur importers and manufacturers joined the four oldest to form the seven greater guilds. The older lineages of these guilds were closer to the nobility than to the rest of the population, but the organisation into *arti* was definitely a sign of greater power of the popular party. The college of priors was opened in 1282 to five 'middle' guilds (butchers, shoemakers, blacksmiths, builders including carpenters and masons, and haberdashers); and in the 1290s to nine 'minor' guilds (wine retailers, innkeepers, oil and cheese sellers, tanners,

---

37 Mickwitz, *Kartellfunktionen*, 50–3; Herlihy, *Pisa*, 137–9.
38 Waley, *Siena*, 19–21; Lane, *Venice*, 106.

armourers, ironworkers other than blacksmiths, girdlemakers, bakers and woodworkers other than carpenters).[39]

In other cities of northern Italy the gap between the major guilds and the others was not so great as in Florence, and merchants and money-changers were sometimes more powerful. Most cities had composite craft guilds that included several aspects of the productive process, as did the Florentine, and a directorate of merchants that amounted to a guild that supervised the craft organisations. Piacenza had statutes of a *Mercandanzia* (merchant association) before 1258, but not all guilds were included in it. Parma's crafts were ruled by 1211 by the '*podestà* of the merchants' from his office in the 'merchants' hall'. But these were crafts whose members sold their products. The *Mercandanzia* was formed of fifteen guilds in 1215, and another thirteen were included by 1261. These guilds were represented in the city council at Piacenza by the beginning of the thirteenth century. At Rome the cloth merchants supervised five smaller guilds that in turn had their own statutes.[40]

Until 1268 Pisa recognised two major 'orders' of merchants: the inland merchants and the 'order of the sea'. Together they had a guaranteed seat in the Great Council of the commune and exercised judicial powers. The crafts, by contrast, were called 'arts' and were subject to the court of the merchants. Four (the tanners, ironworkers, furriers, butchers) had corporate privileges before 1234. By 1267 the vintners, shoemakers, notaries and hot water tanners had guilds. The ironmakers declined into insignificance. The vintners' statutes claimed control over Pisa's inland waterway system, against the claims of the merchants' 'court of the sea', and also seized control of carting operations in the Arno valley. As Pisa grew, specialities became more marked, and small groups acquired their own guilds. Thus the shoemakers broke away from the tanners and the notaries from the judges. The furriers were eventually divided into three guilds. Leatherworking had initially been more important at Pisa than woollens, but this changed during the thirteenth century. By 1268 the woolworkers were recognised as a third 'order'. By 1277 Pisa was thus ruled by three 'orders' or major guilds (merchants, sea, and wool) and seven 'arts' or minor guilds (tanners, ironworkers, butchers, furriers, vintners, shoemakers, notaries).[41]

The organisation of the crafts at Perugia, in Umbria, was probably similar to the smaller Tuscan centres, with more emphasis on geography

---

39 Schevill, *Medieval and Renaissance Florence*, 153–8; Tarassi, 'Famiglie di parte Guelfa', 308–10.

40 Heers, *Espaces Bologne*, 61; Fasoli, 'Oligarchia', 27; Mickwitz, *Kartellfunktionen*, 47–9; Brentano, *Rome Before Avignon*, 52–4.

41 Herlihy, *Pisa*, 60–2.

and numbers of guildsmen and less on a prestige hierarchy within the guild than is true of Florence. The earliest craft organisations mentioned are the fishmongers in 1258 and the horse traders and stone workers in 1260. By 1277 the wool guild, shoemakers, barbers, and a single organisation that included the spurriers, tavernkeepers and innkeepers were legally recognised as craft associations. Judges and notaries had a corporate organisation but were outside the guild structure politically. Two lists from 1286–7 have forty and thirty-six guilds respectively, and one of 1323 with forty-four guilds became final. The individual organisations had rectors whose numbers varied with the numbers in the guild. They represented districts reflecting the geographical distribution of the membership. Sixty members were required for status as a 'great guild', while a guild with thirty members had the right to elect a chamberlain. Rectors had to be aged at least 20 and have a minimum tax assessment of 50 *lire*, chamberlains aged 25 with a 60 *lire* assessment.[42]

The Italian craft organisations were more successful than those of the north in gaining a monopoly over access to the workplace, forcing those who wished to work to join them. The guilds controlled supplies of the raw materials needed in their trades. The smiths' guild of Venice had a central depot where members had to buy coal, and it eventually rationed coal among them. By the early thirteenth century the millers of Piacenza could force labourers to join their union as a condition of working. The statute of the oil and cheese merchants of Venice of 1263 declared that 'if anyone practises the art and is not in the guild's organisation, the *gastaldus* is to set a date by which time he must join, and he must pay the guild the required fee. If he refuses to join, the *gastaldus* is to inform the men of the trade that they may not buy from or sell to him'. The barbers were given a similar privilege in 1270.

But these cases are unusual. Even in such a specialised trade as butchering Padua expressly permitted open competition. The guilds of Bologna also remained open, not even charging entry fees, although journeymen smiths who worked for the same master longer than four months had to join the guild. The obligation to join the guild as a condition of working arose on the initiative of the guildsmen, not of the government. The guilds sometimes used subterfuges to restrict access. In 1244 the government of Siena raised questions about the long apprenticeship required for barbers and bakers. Statutes prohibiting forcing labourers to join guilds were repeated so often, however, that city authorities were clearly fighting a losing battle.[43]

---

42 Blanshei, *Perugia*, 17–18.
43 Mickwitz, *Kartellfunktionen*, 24–5, 32–5, 42, 54, 60.

Most crafts of northern Europe would not have the right to fix prices until the fourteenth century, but some Italian guild statutes were already doing it by 1250. This bothered the authorities more than the guilds' efforts to stifle competition. When the tailors of Venice tried to fix prices and establish a cartel in 1219, they were forced to accept new statutes. It was probably to combat such cartels that Bologna in 1256 prohibited guilds in the food trades, extending this by 1288 to clothiers and barbers. In 1254 at Parma the oil sellers specifically and other guilds generally were forbidden to fix prices. The government of Pisa in 1286 and shortly afterward that of Bologna compromised by forbidding craftsmen and merchants to act in collusion to raise the prices of goods; but in exchange, although the guilds could not restrict entry, persons desiring to work had to swear to comply with the guild's statutes.[44]

While the city authorities disliked guilds gaining monopolies and encouraged outsiders to compete with guildsmen, they discouraged competition within the guild. If one cloth merchant of Rome was showing a customer his cloth on the market, no other merchant might do so until the first merchant's goods were rolled up and carried away. Textiles of different merchants were not to be compared. Bologna forbade fighting over sale- and work places among the tailors in 1247, the carpenters in 1265, the furriers in 1248 and the smiths in 1252. A carpenter had to share jobs with his colleague if the latter made a claim before a contract was concluded. Cheesemongers were forbidden to entice customers away from each other.[45]

MUNICIPAL GOVERNMENT UNDER THE *POPOLO*

Factionalism led to the formation in many cities of the *popolo* as a political institution that sometimes functioned alongside or even in opposition to the commune, whose leader was the *podestà*. This arrangement, which is often taken from the Florentine example as typically Italian, is actually peculiar mainly to Tuscany, where Florence, Prato, Pistoia, Lucca and Siena had them. In the Veneto, only Padua was dominated by a *popolo*; in Lombardy, only Cremona and Brescia; in Emilia, Parma and Bologna; and in Umbria, Perugia. Although 'popular' elements participated in governments at Forlì, Ravenna and Rimini, they dominated in no city of Romagna but rather shared power with the nobles.[46] Simply

---

44   Mickwitz, *Kartellfunktionen*, 74–5; Lane, *Venice*, 106.
45   Brentano, *Rome Before Avignon*, 53; Mickwitz, *Kartellfunktionen*, 45–6, 93.
46   Fasoli, 'Oligarchia', 25; Larner, *Age of Dante and Petrarch*, 122.

because the word *popolo* is most conveniently translated as 'people', some have argued ahistorically that the *popoli* were democratic movements. Actually, *populus* was used in Italy – as later in southern France – not for a social class, but in the Roman meaning of 'every member of the community'. In the twelfth century *populus* was sometimes equated with *cives* (citizens), including all members of the commune who owed military service; only simple residents, serfs, persons older than sixty and those in holy orders were excluded.[47] Because of the problem in rendering *popolo* into contextually accurate English, the Italian word has been left untranslated in the present work.

The *popoli* included both wealthy and poorer persons, who were forged into a single political unit only with difficulty. Notaries and lawyers were *popolani*, which may help to explain the bureaucratic character of *popolo* governments. Military societies, based on parishes, were at the base of the *popolo*, not guild organisations, which were superimposed upon them later. At Lucca armed, voluntary, parish-based 'societies of concord of infantry' are mentioned by 1197.[48] The *popoli* linked groups that were threatened by magnate feuds that disturbed the peace. The magnates were also diverse. Although all citizens were required to serve in the militia, the wealthier were expected to equip themselves more elaborately, with the top group required to do service on horseback. Only a small proportion of the persons called *milites* in the Italian sources were actually dubbed knights, a title of great prestige but involving considerable expense. Only eighty knights are known by name from Padua between 1256 and 1328, but several hundred '*milites* for the commune' did mounted military service for the city. Most members of the Great Council at Padua in the thirteenth century were in this group. They were not knights in the social sense, and many of them were actually in the *popolo*.[49]

Two broad groups can be distinguished within the *popolo*. Wealthy merchants, bankers, moneylenders and professional people such as physicians and notaries held land and were wealthier than some magnates, but they were denied admission to the councils on grounds of lineage. A second group consisted of prosperous artisans and shopkeepers who did not want offices for themselves but desired a more equitable distribution of taxes, better financial administration, and an end to the favouritism that the courts showed the magnates. All members of the *popolo* wanted an end to factional conflict. The two groups were usually united in one association, although in Milan there were two: the *Motta*

---

47   Rogozinski, *Power, Caste*, xvii–xviii; Volpe, *Medio Evo Italiano*, 130.
48   Tirelli, 'Lucca', 171.
49   Hyde, *Padua*, 92–5.

(the rich), and the *Credenza di Sant' Ambrogio* (craftsmen and shopkeepers). But the text of 1214 that shows this division also shows that merchants were in the noble party. The *podestà* distinguished both groups from the captains and valvassors and their party. He ordered that consuls of justice and consuls of the commune be chosen in equal numbers from both sides. The consuls of the merchants were to be chosen solely by the merchants, but each side would name three, which meant that the merchants in the noble party would name that society's consuls. The two groups of *popolani* were called *popolo minuto* and *popolo grasso* (literally lesser *popolo* and fat *popolo*) at Venice and Florence.[50]

Diverse organisations preceded the establishment of the *popoli*. The knights of Perugia had organised themselves as cavalry and common citizens as infantry by the late twelfth century. The groups were flexible; some *popolani* became wealthy enough to buy horses, and some magnates were in the infantry. Organisations were calling themselves *popoli* by the early thirteenth century, and our consideration is complicated by the fact that groups representing the craftsmen, many of whom were in the *popolo*, were entering the city councils. At Mantua the leaders of both neighbourhood associations and of professional groups were in the city government by 1201, and by 1206 the 'popular' element included more than half the city council. At Modena a *popolo* rose in 1229 against the earlier elite and issued its own statutes; but not until 1250, the year of the 'first *popolo*' at Florence, did captains of the 'regions' and of artisan associations enter the general council and establish a council of 'ancients' and a general society of the *popolo*. Cremona had a 'society of the *popolo*' by 1209, and the town council had 'consuls of the neighbourhood and of the artisans and societies'. In 1210 the bishop granted the *popolani* one-third of the city offices.[51]

The *popolani* cannot always be distinguished from the magnates in the early records. An arbitral judgement of 1222 gave half the public offices at Piacenza to the '*popolo* and to the knights who follow it' and the other half to the 'knights of Piacenza and those of the *popolo* who follow the knights'. Neighbourhood associations, not social groups, were the basis of the *popolo* in Piacenza, but the *popoli* were led by newer families whose wealth was in trade. From the mid-thirteenth century, just as ministerials were being excluded from the citizenry in some German cities, Italian statutes excluded the old 'magnate' families from the *popolo* and generally limited their political rights.

---

50 See analysis of Larner, *Age of Dante and Petrarch*, 113–14; Lane, *Venice*, 103; Keller, *Adelsherrschaft und städtische Gesellschaft*, 34–5.
51 Blanshei, *Perugia*, 52–3; Tabacco, *Medieval Italy*, 228; Larner, *Age of Dante and Petrarch*, 114–15; Fasoli, 'Oligarchia', 25–9.

This exclusion was quickly extended to commercial wealthy families who had compromised themselves by participating in feuds, going about armed on horseback, or engaging in other behaviour that caused them to be branded as 'magnates'. The magnates were placed under a special law in penal matters, in some cases also in civil, in addition to suffering political disenfranchisement. The ordinances of the *popolo* of Perugia in 1260 suppressed all societies except guilds and those of judges and notaries and penalised sedition, fines being twice as much per offence for knights as for *popolani*. Becoming the vassal of another was made a capital offence. Later statutes elaborated these principles. Magnates were forbidden in 1266 to enter the main square of Perugia armed, and tournaments were forbidden in 1294. Carrying party insignia into the market without the priors' permission became a capital offence in 1315, and the next year magnates, anyone of knightly parentage and judges were forbidden to enter the town hall or the homes of priors unless specifically authorised by seven of the ten priors. Penalties varied according to whether the deed was committed with or without weapons, the status of the perpetrator, whether the crime was done at night or by day, and the location of the deed. Fines were five times as high for deeds in the town square, the market, magistrates' houses, the city hall, the law courts or five designated major streets as elsewhere. Much higher penalties were levied for crimes committed in the city than in the *contado*. Fines were four times as high for persons from the *contado* or foreigners hitting a Perugian than vice versa. To discourage nobles from forming clienteles of armed *popolani*, the high fines for nobles applied to *popolani* who associated with nobles. From about 1250 the *popoli* were changed by purges of nobles and confiscations; they were more socially homogeneous in 1300 than in 1250 without being wholly so.[52]

Thus it is unwise to make fine social distinctions. The wealthier *popolani* were as captivated by the military mystique as the nobles. References to chivalry, dubbing, mounted fighting, and personal participation in military campaigns abound. The commune of Orvieto granted knighthood to some newly wealthy individuals, who transmitted the status to their entire families. In 1322 Orvieto had forty-eight noble families, twenty-seven of them residing permanently in the city, the rest in the *contado*.[53]

Furthermore, *popolo*-dominated governments might brand as 'magnates' individuals or families who had no blood tie to nobles simply because they wanted to disenfranchise them. In 1286 Florence defined magnates

52 Fasoli, 'Città italiane', 307–8; Blanshei, *Perugia*, 62–5.
53 Waley, *Siena*, 77–85; Waley, *Mediaeval Orvieto*, 37–8.

as lineages that had included a knight within the past twenty years, persons who had already posted surety as magnates, and for good measure those who were considered magnates according to the opinion of the *popolani!* The 'Sacred Ordinances' of Bologna of 1282–92, which became the model for anti-magnate legislation at Pistoia and Florence, named ninety-two persons from forty families as 'rapacious wolves' and required them to post huge bonds with the *podestà* and swear to obey the captain of the *popolo* in all matters.[54]

The *popolo* usually had a territorial organisation. Officials were elected by district within the city. The captain of the *popolo* was initially a powerful military leader of the *popolani* against the knights. At Pistoia he had to be aged at least 30 and non-Tuscan. He served a six-month term, during which he was to defend the privileges of the *popolo*. He was to support the *podestà* and help him enforce laws but also to keep him, as the leader of a commune that included both magnates and *popolani*, from encroaching on the *popolo*'s liberties. At Florence the 'first *popolo*' in 1250 divided the city into twenty district-based military companies (*gonfaloni*). The *popolo* of Bologna had twenty 'societies of arms' in 1274. They pledged mutual assistance, chose officers, recruited members and held property corporatively, including meeting halls. The *popolo* also had a standard-bearer (called the standard-bearer of justice at Florence after 1293) and generally a council of eight to twelve members, frequently called the 'elders of the *popolo*', who represented the *popolo* in its dealings with the *podestà*. Although the captain yielded as the leader of the *popolo* of Florence after 1293 to the standard-bearer, he continued to be important for his police function. Florence had separate statutes of the *podestà* and the captain until a unified code was issued in 1355.[55]

Guelfs and Ghibellines

Factions thus developed, but nowhere was social 'class' in anything close to the modern sense the basis of allegiance. The ruling group in most cities became a sort of official, politically correct club that excluded its opponents from power or exiled them. Another element of the urban political turmoil in Italy was the formation of Guelf and Ghibelline parties in Florence. Initially the Guelfs were those who favoured the Welf candidate for the imperial throne, while the Ghibellines were the partisans of the ruling house of Hohenstaufen. This was a real political

54 Lansing, *Florentine Magnates*, 13–16; Heers, *Espaces Bologne*, 61–7.
55 Herlihy, *Pistoia*, 217–18; Lansing, *Florentine Magnates*, 193; Heers, *Espaces Bologne*, 61–7; Hyde, *Society and Politics*, 115.

issue for most of the thirteenth century. The emperor Frederick II (1212–50) appointed rectors and vicars in cities where his partisans were strong, including Florence. As conflicts with the emperors and between cities became endemic, the party designations spread beyond Florence, and personal rivalries determined allegiance.

The Guelfs and Ghibellines in Florence were rooted in neighbourhood factions. According to legend, they originated in the hostility arising from a murder in 1215: Buondelmonte dei Buondelmonti, who was betrothed to an Amidei, was enticed to marry a Donati maiden by her mother. The jilted girl's family avenged the stain on their honour by assassinating him. The city split along factional lines, with the Buondelmonte leading the Guelfs and the Uberti the Ghibellines. But the hostility between emperor and papacy was only a cloak for pre-existing family rivalries; the chronicler Giovanni Villani details the families of each party and the sectors of the city in which they were strong.[56] Recent studies have confirmed much of this story. The Uberti were indeed the nucleus of the Ghibelline faction. They were one of Florence's oldest lineages; they had already been fighting the consuls in 1177. The other oldest Ghibelline families were also of this group, basing their position on antiquity of ancestry, rural property and some commercial interests. Ghibelline faction militias originated just after the imposition of the foreign *podestà* in 1207, but they were led by newer families of commercial wealth who hoped to gain social status and a coat of arms. Many of them became knights in the second half of the thirteenth century. The most powerful were the Lamberti, one of whom in the 1230s always held two offices: one of the three consuls of the knights and one of the two consuls of the Calimala guild.[57]

The Guelfs were more diverse, including both old aristocratic and new banking families. The Guelf families were generally younger than the Ghibelline, but some of them also served as consuls until 1207, when the regime of the foreign *podestà* became fixed. Some Guelf lineages, including the Buondelmonte, were even more ancient and had lands in the *contado*. The newer Guelf families, who were becoming more influential, were somewhat stronger than the Ghibellines in the Calimala guild in the early thirteenth century, but they too had rural land and were in tower societies. The means of social and political advance *par excellence* continued to be dubbing as knights and the acquisition of towers. The Guelfs thus ended by identifying completely with the older aristocracy. Many families, both Guelf and Ghibelline, that held office in the first

56 Villani, *Chronicle*, 121–5.
57 Raveggi, 'Famiglie di parte Ghibellina', 281–2.

half of the thirteenth century were proscribed as 'magnate' in 1293 (see Chapter 9).[58]

Given the diverse composition of the early *popoli*, including both nobles and commoners, it is hardly surprising that both Guelfs and Ghibellines were councillors of the first societies that called themselves *popolo*. The Ghibellines dominated in the early thirteenth century, but this began to change after 1246, when the imperial vicar installed a government that restricted local autonomy, with the assent of Ghibelline magnates. When the *popolo* took power in 1250 and expelled the vicar and his supporters among the great families, it was difficult for the Ghibellines to remain in the *popolo*.[59] After 1260 the Ghibellines were mainly older families who reacted against the measures of the 'first *popolo*', which ruled Florence between 1250 and 1260, and with personal animosity against individual Guelf lineages.[60] But allegiance outside Florence often depended on whether the pope was considered a greater threat than the emperor (in which case the city would be Ghibelline) or whether a rival city was Ghibelline (in which case its neighbour would be Guelf). In the 1250s Orvieto, which was controlled by the popes and accordingly Guelf, fought Siena, which as a rival of Guelf Florence was Ghibelline, only becoming firmly Guelf after 1271.[61]

The *popolo* at Florence

Florence had the most successful *popolo* of northern Italy and was the most militantly Guelf city of the region. Villani gives the classic account of the civic strife leading to the establishment of Florence's first *popolo* in 1250. The story becomes inextricably intertwined with the attempt of the emperor Frederick II and his successors to subjugate the cities of Tuscany and Lombardy. Villani was an unabashed Guelf. Meeting to counter a perceived threat from the Uberti in 1250, the *popolo* organised itself under thirty-six captains, seized power from the *podestà* and elected the first captain of the *popolo*. With a council of the *popolo*, he established twenty military companies of *popolani*. He had charge of the *popolo*'s bell and chief banner. This 'first *popolo*' abolished the 'knights' society' and limited the height of private towers. The Bargello was built as the headquarters of the *popolo*.[62]

Guelfism thus became strongest in Florence, the most rapidly growing

---

58   Tarassi, 'Famiglie di parte Guelfa', 302–10.
59   Raveggi, 'Famiglie di parte Ghibellina', 289–90.
60   Lansing, *Florentine Magnates*, 180–4.
61   Ascheri, 'Siena', 163; Waley, *Mediaeval Orvieto*, 35, 115–19.
62   Villani, *Chronicle*, 150–1; Lansing, *Florentine Magnates*, 12.

city of Tuscany, but the Ghibellines were not expelled en masse until 1258, in response to the danger that Manfred, Frederick II's son, would reconstitute his empire and end the *popolo*. Typically, those who were exiled went to Siena, which was in Ghibelline hands, and used it as a base. They returned in 1260, defeating the Florentines at Montaperti and exiling the Guelfs in their turn. Most Guelfs went to Lucca. There was no proscription of those who wanted to stay in Florence, although the houses of Guelfs who left were destroyed. Guelf exiles conducted a running war from sympathetic cities that had received them. Even before Manfred's death thirty-six 'good men' became the chief magistracy of the Guelf party. Ordinances gave each of the seven major guilds a 'college of consuls' and their own militia standards. When the Ghibellines tried to overthrow the Thirty-Six in 1266, the Guelfs seized the city and exiled all Ghibellines. The old families still dominated, with only a few of the most influential *popolani grassi*. Most of the later governing families of the *popolo*, who were oriented more toward commerce and banking than land, only emerge after 1280.[63]

The final Guelf victory in 1266 unleashed such massive destruction that much of the city was in ruins. Property confiscated from exiled Ghibellines went in equal thirds to the commune, to individual Guelfs to compensate them for their losses during Ghibelline rule, and to the Guelf 'party', which sold it and invested the money. The party was strong enough to be loaning money to the commune by 1277, and it had accounts with the great bankers. In 1267 the Guelfs drafted ordinances for their party, which had a common treasury, three captains from the six districts of the city who were rotated every two months, a privy council of fourteen, and a larger council of sixty magnates and *popolani*; the *popolo*, far from being a socially homogeneous group, thus excluded all Ghibellines but not all magnates. Three magnates and three *popolani* were called priors of the Guelf party and became its chief executive.[64]

The Guelfs generally controlled Florence after 1266 and relentlessly branded anyone who offended a member of their ruling group as 'magnate' or 'Ghibelline', giving the two terms an identification in history that was not always warranted. Yet the *popolo* was less revolutionary outside the Guelf cities of Tuscany. While *popolo* and commune had clearly distinguished organisations at Florence, the distinction was blurred elsewhere. The *popolo* was called the *comunanza* at Padua, where it was formed in the early thirteenth century as an alliance against the magnates

63 Tarassi, 'Famiglie di parte Guelfa', 312–13, 316–18.
64 Villani, *Chronicle*, 164–83, 217–28; Schevill, *Florence*, 133–41; Holmes, *Florence, Rome*, 19–23.

and nobles who controlled the commune. As in the Tuscan cities the *comunanza* was governed by twelve elders chosen by indirect election for two-month terms. Meeting at least twice a week, they reported misdeeds committed against members of the *comunanza* to the *podestà* as leader of the commune and initiated most legislation passed by the Great Council of the commune. Membership in the *comunanza* was a prerequisite for membership on the Great Council and other public offices.[65]

Even in Tuscany the separation of *popolo* from commune was less rigid outside Florence. After the Nine were established as an executive at Siena in 1287, the General Council of the Commune, called the Council of the Bell, comprising one hundred from each of Siena's three districts and the consuls of the *Mercanzia* and the wool guilds, continued to be critical. From 1262 at least half of its three hundred members had to be members of the *popolo*, with the proviso that brothers could not serve on the council simultaneously and that officeholders could not be councillors. Considerable public activity was left open to magnates and others who were not *popolani*. Although the *popolo* had kept its separate council, it rarely met after this. The Council of the Bell transacted most public business and eventually would have to ratify acts of the Nine. Delegations from the council met with 'wise men from magnate families'. The relative weakness of the *popolo* at Siena left most justice in the hands of the *podestà* and other officers of the commune.[66] Thus the Italian cities underwent significant social and institutional changes after 1250, but lineage and family-party affiliation rather than occupational or economic group were the basis of most political infighting.

The *popolo* and the guilds

The *popolo* was thus led through the 1260s by families whose wealth was largely in landholding and who had combined this with officeholding in the early stages of the commune, although generally at a later stage than the magnates. Commerce and banking were important but decidedly secondary for them. The earlier magnate group had begun in rural landholding; some but not all of them then had expanded into merchant activity. Crafts and manufacturing were not always officially represented in the structure of the *popolo*, although they provided much of its physical force during conflicts. There are exceptions. At Perugia the guild rectors elected the captain of the *popolo* and consuls of the guilds, the most powerful magistrates.[67]

65   Hyde, *Padua*, 211–13.
66   Waley, *Siena*, 49–55, 62.
67   Blanshei, *Perugia*, 57.

We shall see in Chapter 9 that power was reordered within the *popolo* of Florence on a guild basis after the Guelf regimes were restored in 1266. This happened even earlier in some cities. In 1245 the 'small council of the *popolo*' at Bologna was led by twenty-five elders, but it had yielded by 1256 to a 'great council of the *popolo*' that included thirty-three each from the merchants and moneychangers, and from each professional society eight 'officers', two 'councillors', and two to four 'wise men', giving a total of over three hundred persons. The captain of the *popolo* and a 'council of the consuls of the guilds' ruled Perugia between 1255 and 1270, gradually assuming power at the expense of the council of the commune. At the end of the century separate guild councils, including a general assembly, were controlling the *popolo*, gradually pushing aside the older councils that were dominated by the merchants and bankers. After 1303 'priors of the guilds' and the standard-bearer of the *popolo* and of the guilds became leaders of the commune.[68]

The cities of Italy thus show important contrasts with those of the north in the thirteenth century. However, some of them are differences less of type than of degree, such as the level of guild organisation, the extent to which landed elements still dominated and the respective role of council and single-person executive. During the half-century after 1270 urban Europe underwent fundamental changes that would diminish the regional contrasts and fix lines of development for the next two centuries. We shall examine those changes in a Europe-wide context.

---

68   Heers, *Espaces Bologne*, 58–9; Blanshei, *Perugia*, 7, 52. Guilds were also at the basis of the *popolo* of Orvieto. Waley, *Mediaeval Orvieto*, 39–41.

PART FOUR

A Half-Century of Crisis

Merchant as Craftsman, Magnate as Guildsman: The Transformation of the Medieval City, c. 1270–c. 1325

The social and political structures of most cities were transformed in the half-century after 1270. More than the generation after the 'Black Death' of 1348–9, this period was transitional for the medieval cities of Europe, north and south alike. Except in Languedoc, occupational guilds came to share power with the older oligarchies of landowners and merchants and occasionally overthrew them. The most famous episodes are the guild revolutions in Flanders, which corresponded in time and to some extent in character to the second *popolo* and the Ordinances of Justice in Tuscany. However, changes no less profound that fit the broad social patterns suggested by the Flemish and Italian examples occurred elsewhere. After 1325, as before 1270, moneyed elites ruled the cities; but their bases had been broadened, corporate affiliations had been redefined, and the composition of city councils reflected wider participation.

Economy and demography

By the late thirteenth century Europe's population was outstripping its agricultural resources. While earlier the growing demand for industrial goods had both concentrated manufacturing in the cities and provided jobs there for newcomers, the cities and rural areas alike were reaching demographic saturation by 1270. Some rural districts in places as diverse as Tuscany and the English Midlands reached population densities in the late thirteenth century that were higher than they would become again before the nineteenth. The peasants' purchasing power diminished as heirs divided estates into units that were too small to sustain a household. The demand for land buoyed lords' rental incomes, but they were hurt by the grain policies of cities such as Pisa.

Increasing numbers of peasants therefore moved to the cities which, as their markets became saturated, could not provide jobs for them. After 1270 large cities were characteristically surrounded by an economically depressed countryside and thus became dependent on massive imports from an increasingly wide area. The demographic problem was most severe in Italy. By 1300 at least 16 per cent of the population of northern Italy lived in cities of over 10,000 souls.[1] Cities planned for continued expansion, but in fact the population of most cities peaked and started to decline during this half-century, earlier in Italy than in the north. As Bruges' population reached its height at the turn of the fourteenth century, the city bought several seigniories and extended its walls into areas that would remain thinly populated into the modern period.[2] Other cities planned suburbs. Siena laid out an octagonal scheme for Talamoni. Arezzo divided its suburbs into tenements of standard size and required landowners to sell to immigrants, who could not buy in the crowded centre, at a price set by city surveyors.[3]

The problem was exacerbated by a shift in climate toward longer, colder winters and thus shorter growing seasons. Severe famines and plagues began in the 1290s in Tuscany. In the winter of 1295–6 the council of Siena spent 24,000 gold florins, about one-third of the ordinary budget of the commune, on grain purchases alone. Cities that had not previously set grain quotas for *contado* communities and required them to sell at a fixed price on the city market were doing so by 1303. By the 1340s Siena was pawning *contado* villages to get money to buy grain.[4] In northern Europe a series of bad harvests after 1310 culminated in a total crop failure and famine in 1315, then a plague the next year. Population in Flanders declined by between 5 and 10 per cent. The plague of 1315 at Reims affected mainly the poor, but another in 1320 had a more general impact. The population of the city dropped from about 20,000 in 1300 to 14,000–16,000 by 1328. As climate worsened, local scarcities and epidemics continued to drive population down.[5]

1   England, even if Derek Keene's controversial figure of 100,000 for London is correct, was no more than 3 per cent urban. Britnell, 'England and northern Italy', 168.
2   Nicholas, *Town and Countryside*, 57–8.
3   Balestracci, 'Immigrazione e morfologia urbana', 90–3.
4   Bowsky, *Finances Siena*, 31–42.
5   Nicholas, *Medieval Flanders*, 206–8; van Houtte, *Economic History*, 60–1; Desportes, *Reims*, 209–12, 234–48.

As markets declined, craft organisations restricted admissions of new masters who were not sons of incumbent members of the trade, most often by raising entry fees. The oil merchants' guild of Florence began recording the names of all sons and daughters of masters in 1308. Children born after their father had become a master were admitted to the guild without a fee, as were outsiders who married masters' daughters (the woman could not practise the trade herself but passed the presumptive right to it to her husband and children). New members paid a large entry fee, which was raised substantially in 1345. Extended families were limited to one shop under this favoured treatment; the brother of a deceased master could succeed him only if he had not set up his own shop during the brother's lifetime.[6]

Taking Europe as a whole, urban economies may have become marginally more industrial in this half-century, but the great generator of wealth continued to be long-distance trade. In this area two extremely important changes must be noted. First, merchant convoys began sailing directly from Italy to the northern ports from 1278, bypassing the Champagne fairs. The fair cities reverted to being local market centres, but the change made the fortune of Bruges. In a series of enactments beginning with privileges given to German merchants in 1282 and soon extended to other national groups, the counts of Flanders centralised foreign trade at Bruges, which quickly assumed the fairs' place as the entrepôt for Italian, German, and English trade with Flanders.[7]

The onset of this change coincided almost exactly with the English embargo on trade with Flanders between 1270 and 1274, which resulted in a long-term structural modification of the commerce of northwestern Europe. Flemish merchants ceased visiting England in large numbers, even after peace between the two was re-established. After 1313 English wool was normally sold through a staple on the continent, first at Saint-Omer, then at Bruges but eventually at Calais. The Flemings' place in England was taken by the Germans and the Italians. The latter were visiting north European ports in much larger numbers after 1278. They increasingly centred their operations in London and depended on London merchants to buy the wool that they were exporting in considerable quantity to provide for the growing Italian urban woollen industries. They also needed them to market the edible spices and dyes that the Italians were bringing increasingly into the northern markets. The English capital thus grew after 1270, while the provincial towns that

6   Epstein, *Wage Labor and Guilds*, 211.
7   Nicholas, *Medieval Flanders*, 182, 204–6.

had depended on the fairs and the wool trade with Flanders declined. While English foreign trade continued to have a large foreign element, the foreigners now depended on native merchants, mainly Londoners and their business partners in the county towns.[8]

Just as had happened with the fairs, the centring of international commodity exchange at Bruges made it important in banking and finance. Arras, which had been the leading banking city of the northwest, was hurt by the decline of the fairs, for much English and Flemish trade to Champagne had passed through Artois.[9] Paris, the capital of an increasingly invasive national monarchy, also picked up considerable banking activity from the fairs. Montpellier, which had become the payment site for exchange contracts initiated in Marseilles, Barcelona, Piacenza and the Levant even before 1260, was still handling the transactions of Italian bankers with the Champagne fair network as late as the 1340s. Montpellier's banks compensated for the decline of the Champagne money markets by expanding partnerships in Spain and by transmitting funds for the popes and even university students travelling between Italy and the north.[10]

Banking and finance took on increasingly critical importance in the economy just as international trade was growing in volume and value. Although the Italians had access to plentiful supplies of gold and silver, mint outputs in northern Europe were higher in the late thirteenth century than they would be again before the sixteenth. The money supply began declining in the late 1290s. The problem was critical by the 1320s, and the inadequacy of the bullion supply reached crisis proportions in the late fourteenth and fifteenth centuries. This had two corollaries. First, once Europeans had become accustomed to the greater flow of goods that began in the late thirteenth century, it could only be continued by adjustments between banks, which were now in the cities rather than the fairs. Secondly, trade could not be one-sided; for an import needed a corresponding export, since payment in coin became more difficult. This made international trade more truly reciprocal. It also made monetary manipulation much more serious and gave enhanced power and prestige not only to groups such as the mint associates of the German cities, but also to guilds whose merchant aristocracy was involved in international trade and now became increasingly occupied with moneylending and credit. Great merchants, such as drapers, were

---

8   Nightingale, *Medieval Mercantile Community*, 81–7, 95, 104; Miller and Hatcher, *Towns, Commerce and Crafts*, 225.

9   De Roover, 'Comptes communaux Bruges', 87; Lestocquoy, *Dynasties bourgeoises d'Arras*, 84; Barel, *Ville médiévale*, 212.

10 Reyerson, *Montpellier*, 114–20.

moneylenders, both to private citizens in their native towns and beyond, and to princes.[11]

The changes contributed to a shift in the balance of economic and political power among the Italian cities. The elite of Siena had the greatest concentration of banking families in Italy in the thirteenth century; it was a much more commercial group than the ruling element of Florence. However, they were heavily involved in the Champagne fairs, which became moribund during this half century. They also suffered from the removal of the papacy, much of whose credit was with Sienese banks, to France after 1305. The bankers thus turned to land as a safer investment, and the change was essentially accomplished between 1290 and 1320. By the fifteenth century Siena was half to one-third of its thirteenth-century size, a satellite of Florence, and its elite consisted of landowners. Even its banking families had much more money invested in land than in trade or manufacturing. Much of the commerce on the market of Siena itself fell into the hands of Florentine merchants.[12] Perugia also suffered from the loss of papal business. Florence, whose expansion toward industry brought it increasingly into the English trade in wool, took up the slack. Financiers of Florence and, for a time, Lucca dominated the Italian credit market in the late Middle Ages, and this decisive shift occurred essentially during this critical half-century.

The development of larger and more seaworthy ships facilitated transport of bulk cargoes. Not only were much larger quantities of eastern luxuries entering the north European market through Italy than previously, but grain was now being transported to the cities not only overland and by small barge, but also by large boat. The famine in Flanders in 1315–16 was alleviated by grain brought on the galleys from Italy. The trade in grain and forest products sustained the commerce of the German Hanse cities with densely urbanised northwestern Europe, which could not feed itself. The diverse economies of Europe had always been interdependent in respect of luxuries and some manufactures, but now this was becoming true of basic foodstuffs.

Standards of living became higher as more and finer goods became commonly available, but a concomitant of the increased dependence on imports was the episodic nature of much urban employment. As long as the cities drew most of their industrial raw materials from the immediate environs and worked for a domestic demand market, work

11   Nightingale, *Medieval Mercantile Community*, 85, 115; Miller and Hatcher, *Towns, Commerce and Crafts*, 232–8.
12   Pinto, ' "Honour" and "Profit" ', 89–90.

was relatively stable through the year. But as clothmaking in particular became more specialised and used products imported from a great distance, much work became seasonal, dependent on the arrival of cargoes of dyes or wool. Workers might have nothing to do for part of the year, either relying on savings or taking assistance. Those who owned their own shops were likely to survive short-term declines in demand, but those whom the shopowners employed could not.

The cities were thus increasingly vulnerable from many different perspectives, but there is an element of strength in this weakness. Derek Keene's suggestive analysis corroborates our thesis that this half-century was transitional. For a city to function well it is not enough for it to have a population large enough to support specialised occupations. Individuals within the community must have confidence that others with different specialities will act in such a way that the interdependence will be actual rather than theoretical. After 1300 there is considerable evidence that this was happening, and thus the 'broad correspondence between population size and specialization' was realised. Large cities thus have a more diverse occupational pool, much of it generated by demand internal to the city itself, and a broader economic potential and more resilience than smaller places. Faced with an external disaster such as the loss of a major market, a large place can build on the other specialities present within its population to develop new markets. What had been a demographic reality before 1300 – large cities had so many basic factors of production that they could weather major disasters – now became economic reality.

Despite the accumulation of some large fortunes, productive units were largely individual until around 1300, centred around the worker's household and concentrated on a particular aspect of production. Thereafter, while the household unit of production remained the most common, many productive units became larger despite the population decline. There is more evidence of several trades being practised in a single workshop, most demonstrably in textiles but also in other branches of the artisanate. As mastership increasingly became a family prerogative, production also became more geared toward 'networks'. The same person engaged in many different forms of productive activity, sometimes simultaneously, sometimes in succession. Keene uses the example of Mark le Fayre of Winchester, who in a business career of about fifty years was a wine importer, cloth exporter and owner of a tavern, inn and shops. He put out cloth, bought and sold it, and sold dyes. He owned a dyehouse in Winchester, a country estate, and a house in Southampton.[13]

---

13 Discussion based on Keene, 'Continuity and development', 1–16.

Although these changes were accompanied by the rise of newer families into the economic elite, these families were still kept off the councils in most cities. We have seen aspects of this in the distinction between ministerial and merchant elements of the patriciates in Germany. The urban elites in France and the Low Countries also invested in land increasing amounts of capital acquired through trade, particularly after the mid-thirteenth century. Although the elite of Southampton was more purely commercial than most, many families even there remained only for two or three generations in the city, then were lured away by rural landownership. By 1275 burgesses of Erfurt owned so much land in the environs that rural courts were objecting to their claim that deeds committed on their estates should be judged by the city court. Large-scale land investment by burgesses of Metz, much of it through mortgage foreclosures by city financiers, quickened noticeably from 1262 and especially 1285. At Ghent and Bruges, whose elites did not have a large ministerial element, there is little evidence of rural land investment before 1260 except for peat bogs. Thereafter, as the landed nobility became weaker, city people rushed to buy land, which was a secure form of investment and conferred social status.[14]

Political changes accompanied these structural modifications. The hostility between the English and French crowns became a series of wars punctuated by truces during these years. Kings were beginning to use economic warfare, such as embargoes that deprived a vulnerable area of strategic imports or an export market. Since the cloth produced in Catalonia was of such low quality that Flemish and French textiles were imported, the French tried after 1293 to put political pressure on Aragon by hindering cloth exports.[15] Secondly, princes manipulated the economy by controlling coinage. Inflation caused by coin debasement became serious in the late thirteenth century except in England. As demand for luxuries remained high and military expenses rose, the town lords' money supplies declined in real terms, for they were often fixed in nominal terms in rents or at best grew with increased use of the facility in question. Particularly in Germany the lords had to surrender their rights in return for money. Churches were particularly vulnerable. Debasing the coin caused prices to rise but permitted princes to pay off old debts in a coin that was worth less than when the debt was incurred. The

14 Platt, *Medieval Southampton*, 63; Mägdefrau, 'Volksbewegungen in Erfurt', 337; Schneider, *Metz*, 346–58, 365–73; Blockmans, *Gentse Stadspatriciaat*, 400–19; Nicholas, *Town and Countryside*, 268–71, 289–93.
15 In this case it backfired, for within two decades the Catalans had created an industry independent of French imports and were competing with them on international markets. Carrère, *Barcelone*, 431–5.

situation created a volatile capital market that presented opportunities for financiers.

Most conflicts covered in this chapter concern the city councils, specifically eligibility for membership as the nature of the elite changed, and the accountability of the council members. The outlines of other features of urban administration, notably poor relief and public works, become clearer, but rarely was there a revolutionary departure in this area from previous practice. The late medieval urban types were being forged in the half-century after 1270.

ENGLAND

Since the English cities were less industrial than those of the continent, Britain is unusual in the impotence of its craft organisations. Although several cities had them in the twelfth century, they atrophied with the decline of English urban industry in favour of continental imports and rural manufactures. Cities with structured craft organisations were thus unusual until some revived in the fourteenth century.[16]

England had proportionally fewer seigniorial towns than France and Germany. English abbots were particularly stingy with municipal liberties. There were riots against the abbey of Bury St Edmunds in 1264. The burgesses sometimes harassed the monks physically. A single alderman was the mayor, chosen by the abbot from a slate of three presented by the 'Aldermen's Guild' from 1292. In that year the burgesses were also given the right to elect bailiffs and keepers of the gates. In 1327, when many of the monks were away, the burgesses seized the abbey, imprisoned some monks and raided the abbot's treasury. They extracted a charter that gave the town an independent government and reduced the abbey's fiscal exactions, but the abbot was restored by the sheriff and revoked the charter in 1329.[17] Winchester escaped political turmoil, but the decline of royal patronage diminished demand for the city's goods. Winchester was the chief town of Hampshire, which was average or below average among English counties in wealth and population. Although the St Giles fair was at its peak in the thirteenth century and cushioned Winchester's decline until after 1250, most trade there originated in London. The metropolis was stifling the other cities of the south by the thirteenth century, and it was close enough to attract immigrants from Hampshire who might otherwise have gone to Winchester.

16   Hilton, *English and French Towns*, 76–7.
17   Gottfried, *Bury St Edmunds*, 131–3, 215–31.

Winchester's decline into a poor county town illustrates an important point concerning the social composition of urban elites. Among the London patricians those of foreign extraction were generally of northern French or Italian ancestry, whilst those of smaller communities such as Winchester were natives of the rural environs. A good example is the Inkepenne family, which migrated to Winchester from the village of Inkpen, just over the Berkshire border. The merchant Roger de Inkepenne became prominent at Winchester just before 1300, was mayor five times and married into a prominent family from the bishop's soke. His older son became a country gentleman, living on his rural estate, while the younger one remained at Winchester as a wool merchant. A rural family thus came to the city, made a fortune there and used it to re-enter rural society at a higher level. The converse did not happen: for few knights of the shire bothered to keep town houses at Winchester.[18]

London: the metropolis as paradigm

With a population of some 80,000–100,000 inhabitants in 1300, London was much larger in relation to its secondary towns than was Paris. Landowners dominated the London elite in the early thirteenth century, but by the 1280s the older 'patrician misteries' controlled the aldermanic court, fulfilling the function that merchant guilds had elsewhere. The great trades for London political families were wine importing, particularly purveyance to the royal court, and drapery, which involved importing cloth rather than manufacturing it. London drapers provisioned the royal wardrobe. The rest of this merchant elite were from luxury trades: goldsmiths (who were often Wardens of the Exchange), pepperers (who were also wool exporters and spice importers through their contacts with the Italians; they would later establish the Grocers' Company), and mercers. Two-fifths of the aldermen of London had positions in the king's government.[19]

The insurrection of 1263 at London had been led by newer crafts that at that time consisted mainly of artisans, but charters were given in 1269 not to them but rather to the cordwainers, girdlers, wool-packers and joiners, all of which had a large merchant element. The changes after 1270 led to a major expansion of London's foreign trade. Cheapside, the main market street, had its highest density of population of any time before the seventeenth century. Merchants led many guilds into areas of endeavour that had only tangential relation to the activity after which

18   Keene, *Medieval Winchester*, 87–8, 220–8.
19   Keene, 'Property market', 202–3; Williams, *Medieval London*, 58–67, 126–30, 168.

the trade was named. After disorders in 1293 Edward I had to ally with the skinners, fishmongers, cutlers and cornmongers, the groups that had led the revolt in 1263. By now many of them were also merchants. The cornmongers, who, with the fishmongers, controlled most bakeries by leasing their facilities to bakers, nearly trebled their seats on the court of aldermen in the early fourteenth century. The fishmongers' involvement in the grain trade would be a foundation of their political importance in the fourteenth century. This was a revolutionary change, for the fishmongers had been a rebel group in 1263, but in less than half a century they became an established liveried company.[20]

As merchants gained control of the older guilds, the 'artisan' movement passed to groups that had been dependants of the earlier craft associations, such as the lorimers and joiners to the saddlers, which were getting recognition as independent trades at the beginning of the fourteenth century. Primarily artisan crafts such as the weavers remained a depressed group, doing piece work for cloth entrepreneurs.

Thus the earliest politically active 'craft' guilds were usually in cities such as London that lacked a merchant guild. They were mainly in the luxury and food crafts as wholesalers or in service occupations. A second group of craft guilds, which were rising to prominence in London in the late thirteenth century, corresponds to the Italian 'middle guilds' in that they were basically craft-oriented in the beginning but had the possibility of engaging in long-distance or luxury merchandising. They often included dependent trades whose practitioners actually manufactured goods. The manufacturing trades in turn broke away in the late thirteenth century and established the guild-based regimes of the late Middle Ages. However, the elite were still the older group of guilds, which would become the liveried companies in London, that engaged mainly in trading rather than manufacturing.

The growth of population, particularly of support personnel in response to the centring of the wool and spice trades in London, threatened many trades with an excess of labour and led them to organise for the first time. In 1274–5 the city ordered that the names of apprentices should be registered to stop persons who were falsely claiming the freedom on grounds of apprenticeship, and this was done by the craft organisations themselves after 1294.[21] The crafts of London became political pressure groups, particularly as they formed into misteries and developed organisations and internal hierarchies. Except in France and the Low

---

20   Williams, *Medieval London*, 160–7; Nightingale, *Medieval Mercantile Community*, 81.
21   Nightingale, *Medieval Mercantile Community*, 81, 100.

Countries, most city councils until the late thirteenth century were chosen by district of the city. As craft-based regimes came to power, they tried to get council elections based on representation by craft rather than ward, or in some places in addition to ward. London was no exception. Since the politically active guilds were economically diverse, including both labourers and merchants, the power struggles thus divided the ruling elite and involved considerably more than pitting one guild or group of guilds against others.

The situation in London was complicated by agitation against foreigners, particularly Italians and Germans, whose privileges were resented. They had been forbidden to visit the fairs since 1285, which in effect gave the London trading guilds control of distributing Italian imports in the counties. Although they were allowed only forty days' residence in the city, this was largely ignored. Edward I, heavily in debt to Italian and Gascon financiers, sided with the aliens and in 1302 gave them the right to live in their own hostels and trade with other foreigners. Five months later the *Carta Mercatoria* of 1303 gave these same privileges to all alien merchants, which meant that foreigners could get into much of the city's retail as well as wholesale trade. Since the foreigners were now able to deal with other non-citizens of London directly, the London merchants who had been their middlemen suffered.

National factions, too, were reflected in political rivalries in the city. After intermittent agitation since 1312, royal commissioners were appointed to investigate allegations of peculation by city officials.[22] Edward II gave a charter in 1319 that confirmed the city's old liberties and added new provisions that the commons demanded. The mayor and aldermen were to serve for a single year, and aldermen could not be re-elected. Although revolutionary, this provision was not enforced until after 1376, and then only briefly. The Common Clerk, Common Sergeant and Chamberlain were to be elected and to have no salaries other than that paid by the city. Persons who did not have the freedom of the city were forbidden to engage in retail trade, and the forty-day restriction on aliens was restored. Four elected auditors handled tallages. Although London was again torn by disorder during the rebellion in 1327, Edward III's charter of that year guaranteeing London's liberties ushered in a period of comparative calm. Several liveried companies,

---

22 At York an inquest of 1305 showed that a confraternity established in part to maintain a hospital was being used as a tax front by the rich, including the mayor. The confraternity was dissolved, but its members were soon readmitted to the government. Hilton, *English and French Towns*, 131, 137.

including the skinners, tailors, goldsmiths and girdlers, received charters in or shortly after 1327. At least twenty-five crafts were recognised legally by 1328, and fifty-one participated in elections to the Common Council in 1377.[23]

Freedom of the city and the crafts

As the London craft guilds became more organised, apprenticeship thus became a major way of gaining the freedom of the city. The *Carta Mercatoria* established the rule that no one could practise a trade unless he enjoyed the freedom of the city. The registers of the craft chamberlains reveal a mass of immigration into London from 1309, coinciding with the drive toward craft independence between 1309 and 1319.

Under pressure from the crown, the city had been admitting foreigners to the freedom by purchase (redemption). The charter of 1319 conceded that 'no man was to be admitted to the franchise until he had been accepted by six men of the mistery he wished to join, or by the commonalty, if he wished to follow no trade'. The individual misteries were thus given the power of admitting men to the freedom by controlling apprenticeship. Newcomers, including aliens, who desired citizenship thus had to join a guild. By the mid-fourteenth century citizenship was rarely obtained without simultaneously entering a craft. Purely artisan occupations lost status except as stepping stones for newcomers. While apprenticeship was a major way for immigrants to become citizens, a citizen's son who became an apprentice could only claim citizenship through purchase and not through patrimony. Probably no more than one-third of London's residents were actually citizens in the fourteenth century. Thus 'citizenship by patrimony withered away as London grew to an intensely commercial capital'. Although most guilds regulated the number of apprentices that a master might have at one time, for the apprentices were masters and citizens presumptive, none limited the number of journeymen. Admissions between 1309 and 1312 show that freedom by apprenticeship was normal in the great liveried companies, while it was generally obtained by redemption in lower-status trades. Immigrants were better able to enrol in them because they could bypass apprenticeship, which was controlled by the masters.[24]

---

23 Williams, *Medieval London*, 159, 168–91, 227–9, 259, 265–91; Mickwitz, *Kartellfunktionen*, 144–5; Hilton, *English and French Towns*, 146–7, 67; Nightingale, *Medieval Mercantile Community*, 117–19, 127, 144.
24 Williams, *Medieval London*, 45–8, 191–5, including quotations; Epstein, *Wage Labor and Guilds*, 120, 112–13, 199–201.

FRANCE

While the cities of Germany, the Low Countries and Italy became more independent of their lords, the monarchy stifled the municipal autonomy that the charters of the twelfth century had seemed to presage for the French cities. Nowhere in France did craft guilds even approach the power of those in regions that lacked a strong central authority.

The special case of Paris

Although Paris was even less independent of the royal government than London, and its guilds were strictly dependent on the Merchants of the Water (see Chapter 7), economic and social trends in Paris illustrate in magnified and thus more easily traceable form developments also present in smaller cities.

The French and English kings were the only princes who were strong enough to collect national taxes in their cities. The kings and most townspeople preferred the *taille*, a direct tax assessed on the wealth of the hearth, to indirect taxes on consumption. The elites, however, preferred excises, since they often farmed them from the government at a profit. This generally meant that taxes were biased against the poorer citizens but not the absolutely indigent, who had to pay the excises when they bought goods but were often exempt from direct taxation. Seven books of the *taille* survive for Paris from the years 1292–1313. Most persons who paid were called 'great people'. They were listed by residence and household. Lombards, 'lesser people' and Jews were placed in separate categories.[25]

Paris had grown rapidly through the thirteenth century and particularly after 1250. By 1292 settlement on the left bank had expanded beyond Philip Augustus' wall, especially on the southeast. Population on the right bank had already grown beyond the area that would later be walled by Charles V (1364–80). A survey of 1328 listed 61,098 hearths in the city and some suburbs. This suggests a population that may have been as high as 275,000, making Paris the largest city of Europe.[26] But the *taille* records suggest that even this enormous figure was down from that of around 1290, for the number of hearths that were taxed declined by 60 per cent between 1292 and 1313. Since the amounts

---

25 Petit-Dutaillis, *French Communes*, 126; Le Goff, 'L'Apogée', 301; Cazelles, *Paris*, 250–2; Herlihy, *Opera Muliebria*, 132.

26 Although these figures have been rejected as impossibly high, recent scholarship corroborates them. See Cazelles, *Paris*, 136–45, for a historiographical discussion.

collected were roughly the same in all seven documents, either the assessors were concentrating on the wealthier taxpayers in the later surveys, or population was declining, or both. Population was extremely
mobile. Tracking persons between *taille* surveys is difficult, but personal names couched in the 'de [place]' form suggest that about 40 per
cent of the males of Paris and 30 per cent of the females were recent
immigrants.[27]

The *taille* records also show that assessments increased considerably
on the Île de la Cité and on the peripheries of Paris in these critical
decades, particularly in the north part of the right bank. Between 1297
and 1300 there were few changes in median tax paid per hearth. The
right bank and the island remained the centres of wealth, and the Île,
containing the bishop's residence and the royal palace on opposite ends,
was the preferred residence of the wealthy.[28]

Citizenship

Just as 'freedom' in the English boroughs meant membership of a guild
or a great liveried company with minimal artisan involvement, so 'bourgeois' at Paris did not mean 'citizen' in the modern sense. It was applied
in the early thirteenth century to all masters practising a trade, but not
to journeymen, and by 1300 it meant only the richer artisans, those
with merchant interests. Although one could be a burgess of any chartered city, the freedom of Paris was a special distinction, requiring
formal application to the king and usually payment of a fee. An aristocracy was also created among the artisans of Paris by grants of the title
'butcher [tailor, etc.] of the king'. They were not royal officials as such,
but merely guildsmen whose clients included the royal court, which
conferred enormous social prestige. The French kings borrowed from
Italian financiers but also patronised the bankers of Paris, particularly
goldsmiths. The royal *Argenterie* was largely a monopoly of Parisians,
and they were also conspicuous in the Chamber of Accounts. The Paris
elite farmed revenues, taxes and offices.[29]

As in virtually all major cities, most great fortunes in Paris came
through wholesale commerce rather than crafts. The Merchants of the
Water were now the city government. The highest-taxed Parisian in
1297 was Pierre Marcel, grandfather of Etienne Marcel, likewise one of
the wealthiest men of the city but a revolutionary in a personal cause

27   Herlihy, *Opera muliebria*, 128–36; Cazelles, *Paris*, 132.
28   Discussion based on maps in Cazelles, *Paris*, 113–15 and commentary 116–17.
29   Cazelles, *Paris*, 90, 96, 112, 102–5; Hilton, *English and French Towns*, 81–2.

in 1358. Speculation in grain was especially lucrative, but the wine and wood trades were also profitable, much more so than wool, fur and leather. Although the food trades were important in the fortunes of the Paris elite, direct supply of grain and to a lesser extent wine from rural estates owned by burgesses was more important for Paris and most French cities than for the English cities, where it was impossible to bypass the market mechanism for wine.

The crafts in the French cities

The kings and other city lords generally kept firm control of craft movements. In 1306 Philip IV suppressed confraternities and executed the leaders of 'various lesser folk, fullers, weavers, taverners, and others of different guilds in alliance with them' who rebelled. In 1313 he ordered the deans of the craft organisations in each 'good town' to have each guild choose two persons to represent it to the authorities.[30]

The French cities that had a large textile industry experienced the same types of struggle as those found in Flanders in these years, specifically a drapers' group that dominated craft organisations and tried to keep craftsmen from selling their products retail. A conflict between the master drapers and the weavers at Reims led to comprehensive statutes for a drapery guild in 1292. Anyone who wished could weave cloth at Reims on condition of swearing to make only products of high quality. Weavers could make textiles of any type they wished, but only if they did not put them out for sale. The eight masters of the guild controlled the quality of all cloth and had the right to deny the seal of the city. Weavers were forbidden to form unions against the master drapers or to appoint their own leaders.[31]

The trend toward greater specialisation that did not always involve subdividing craft organisations is confirmed by evidence from Toulouse. The capitouls collected statutes for nineteen crafts between 1270 and 1325 to buttress their claim to control the guilds against the encroachments of the royal vicar. Like the Paris *Livre des Métiers*, the Toulouse collection is obviously incomplete. The bakers, who controlled the pastrymakers in most cities, are not listed, but the pastrymakers had a guild that was divided into four district organisations. Rectors appointed by the capitouls over each craft were to visit the shops regularly, oversee, inspect, approve or reject finished products and levy fines. They received a portion of the fines as their wage, but the capitouls also reserved a

---

30 Le Goff, 'L'Apogée', 307.
31 Desportes, *Reims*, 346–7.

share of guild fines for themselves, usually spending them on public works or guild costs. Substandard goods were always confiscated and often donated to the poor.[32]

Government and political conflict in France and Iberia

Some French cities experienced serious rebellions in this half-century, but the results were much less revolutionary than elsewhere. The king used many of them to extend his power in the cities. Paris and nearby Rouen coexisted until the king for political reasons violated Rouen's ancient monopolies for the benefit of Paris (Philip II in 1207 had confirmed the Rouennais' control of traffic on the lower Seine, even though it conflicted with his privileges for the Merchants of the Water of Paris).

Rouen was one of the leading textile cities of France, but it was still governed by the twelfth-century Establishments, which had given self-perpetuating power to one hundred peers. Their number was down to some twenty-five by 1291, making an even tighter oligarchy than the more famous Thirty-Nine of Ghent. The *échevins* and councillors provided for in the Establishments went out of existence, and their functions were assumed by the peers. Riots in 1281 provoked royal intervention, and when the citizens refused to pay a *taille* in 1286, the king imprisoned the mayor and several burgesses. After the royal castle was pillaged in a new riot in 1292, the mayor and the city elite, fearing the royal reaction, helped suppress the rebellion and hanged the leaders. Philip IV nonetheless abolished Rouen's commune and revoked the privilege of 1207. This gave control of the entire Seine to the Merchants of the Water of Paris and permitted all merchants to pass freely through Rouen without using the brokerage of local merchants. Paris probably reached its commercial apogee in the early fourteenth century, when there was no competition from Rouen.

The commune and Rouen's old commercial privileges were restored in 1309, including control of the bridge across the Seine and the custom called 'Norman company', which obliged merchants from upstream to discharge goods at Rouen. But new troubles began in 1315, complicated by struggles between guilds and even among the peers. The mayor and a few insiders ignored the others in the elite, controlled finances and never rendered accounts. The commoners sued at the royal court, and in 1320 King Philip V gave Rouen a new constitution, theoretically with broader representation. The old peers were left in place for life; as they died, they were replaced by thirty-six new peers chosen from the 'more sufficient

---

32 Mulholland, *Toulouse*, xvi–xvii, xx–xxi, xxii–xxviii, xxx–xxxi, xli.

commoners' for three-year terms and by district of the city. Close relatives could not serve simultaneously. Twelve 'gentlemen of the commons' chosen by the peers were to advise the mayor and oversee administration. Four receivers, two from the peers and two from the gentlemen, took over finances from the mayor. The procedure for electing the mayor was complex, beginning with a slate of six peers chosen by the commons; eventually three names went to the king, who chose the mayor. The mayor was placed under severe fiscal constraints, and the king authorised an extraordinary tax to relieve Rouen's public debt, which stood at more than 40,000 livres.[33]

In most cities an element of family-party feuding was involved in the struggles of this half-century. The Colom-Soler rivalry at Bordeaux continued, with one branch of the Caillau family on each side. The issues were not ideological; each party wanted to use the resources of the commune for its own partisans and patronage. The formal Councils of Thirty and 300 did not play an active role. Arnaud Caillau, the mayor who led the rebellion that led to the English restoration in 1303, was a Colom partisan and stayed in office until 1308, when he yielded to another Caillau who favoured the Soler. The English government tried to mediate by building a third party, but at different times both the Colom and Soler appealed to Paris. The Colom used a threat of French conquest after 1324 to regain power, but only in a numbing wave of riots and assassinations. Conditions became relatively calm after 1331.[34]

Barcelona in Catalonia was a regular trading partner of the southern French cities and shared their tradition of internecine feuds among the patriciate. Riots erupted in 1257 after Bernat Marquet was murdered and his houses burned. Although this uprising is sometimes portrayed as a city-wide rebellion, it was actually the work of Marquet's competitors in developing the waterfront district of the city. The conspirators were kinsmen of one another but not of the Marquet. The king put the waterfront under a separate administration (this eventually gave birth to the famous Consulate of the Sea) and briefly enlarged the council to provide space for both the Marquet and their opponents. A more broadly-based uprising occurred in 1285, when the commoner Berenguer Oller organised disturbances against the city council. Although most persons condemned after order was restored were from the crafts, some

---

33   Rouen's prosperity was irretrievably compromised when its privileges on the Seine were withdrawn again in 1315. The income of the tax farm of the Viscounty of the Water there declined from a high of 8,847 livres in 1301 to 5,500 livres in 1336. Mollat, *Histoire de Rouen*, 92–8; Petit-Dutaillis, *French Communes*, 130–1; Cazelles, *Paris*, 368–70.
34   Renouard, *Bordeaux sous les rois d'Angleterre*, 349–54.

patricians were also involved. As in the 1257 conflict, they were rivals over land development and the benefits of royal patronage; specifically, one faction claimed that the other had been receiving a disproportionate share of licences to export grain.[35]

Distaste of citizens for their churches explains some agitation in the episcopal cities of France. The kings used the troubles at Lyon as an excuse to intervene. An interregnum in the archbishopric after 1268 led to periodic disturbances that lasted until 1293, when the king confirmed the citizens' right to maintain the walls and gates and prohibited the archbishop and canons from meddling in temporal affairs. By now all parties saw the king as a greater threat than one another. In 1310 the archbishop's men and a party among the burgesses expelled the royal officers. The king ended the rebellion in 1311, and Lyon became the seat of a royal seneschal. In 1320 the Lyonnais were given the right to choose consuls, be free from trial outside the city, defend the city, have an archive, impose *tailles* and be free of the archbishop's taxes. The archbishop and chapter continued to exercise high and low justice, and the only restriction was the possibility of appeal to the king.[36]

The end of the communal movement

Most French communes were terminated or irretrievably weakened between 1270 and 1325. Communal obligations were more burdensome than the privileges enjoyed. Although mismanagement was part of the communes' problem, the king's financial demands were a contributory factor. Louis IX levied frequent aids, particularly for his crusades. He initiated the practice of selling city governments the right to collect specified taxes and borrow. In return, the government did not usually audit their accounts. Noyon had a debt of 16,000 livres by 1278, which it asked the king to pay. Parlement only acted on this suit in 1291, decreeing partial bankruptcy on the pretext that the city's creditors had exacted usury. Noyon was still in debt in 1333, although it kept its commune.

The expansionist foreign policy and fiscal chicanery of Philip IV made the financial burdens of the cities insupportable. Provins had a weaver-led rebellion in 1279 when the mayor simultaneously increased taxes and added an hour to the working day. The king levied crushing fines, with the drapers alone paying 4,000 livres. More high taxes provoked disturbances in 1310 and 1324. In 1320 the city government complained

35 Bensch, *Barcelona*, 336–41.
36 Valous, *Patriciat Lyonnais*, 31–42.

that royal provosts were forbidding local magistrates to function and even alleged that they had confiscated bread in burgesses' homes on grounds that the grain had not been ground at the lord's mill and cooked in his bakery. They also had urged the citizens to exchange their commune for a *prévôté*. The king asked for a referendum in Provins and its dependent villages; and if the results can be believed, the vote was 11.4:1 against the commune in the city, 59:1 in the villages.[37]

The communes were unpopular among their own citizens. Their elites had been narrow from the beginning and became even more so during the thirteenth century, as twelfth-century charters remained in effect for cities that had grown to several times their initial size and population. As patrician lines died out, the surviving lineages often simply governed without choosing successors for them. Perhaps for this reason, the citizens of the communes were blaming their officials and seeking help from the king for problems that the king had caused. Sens became the first commune to surrender its charter voluntarily. When some inhabitants complained to Louis X of maladministration by the mayor and *jurés* and asked for the abolition of the commune, the royal bailiff called a general assembly, which voted to terminate the commune. The provost replaced the mayor, and the commune was suppressed in 1318. Compiègne followed suit in 1319, Meulan in 1320. In each case the royal government drew up terms for liquidating an enormous municipal debt and installing a provost.[38]

Probably no French or Iberian city had social distinctions as severe as those dividing *popolo grasso* from *popolo minuto* in Italy. But a situation comparable to that in Italy, with the typically French features of royal involvement and tax abuse, occurred at Montpellier at the conclusion of our period. Conflicts began in 1323, when the consuls levied a *taille*, and many citizens refused to provide estimates of their assets. The consuls initially refused to let their accounts be audited, then yielded when the *populus*, a wealthy group outside the government, formed a sworn association. The royal procurator allied with the *populares*, and an audit of the accounts of the previous twenty-three years was begun in 1326. A compromise in 1331 provided that public estimates of all the taxpayers' property would be the basis of any new *taille*, but the consuls were given complete authority to levy direct and indirect taxes in the future. The 'popular' syndicate was disbanded.[39]

---

37 Petit-Dutaillis, *French Communes*, 114–15; Mollat and Wolff, *Popular Revolutions*, 47; Chapin, *Villes de foires*, 69.
38 Discussion based on Petit-Dutaillis, *French Communes*, 109–32.
39 Rogozinski, *Power, Caste*, 1–30.

THE LOW COUNTRIES AND NORTHERN FRANCE

The changes illustrated by the English and French examples are also found in the Low Countries and industrial northwestern France. Flanders was dependent economically on two political rivals: England for wool and France for grain. The struggles of wealthier craftsmen for a voice in city government were complicated not only by the ubiquitous thread of personal rivalries among the city elite, but also by issues of loyalty to the count of Flanders and sympathy for the French or English.

English wool was the finest available and was required by local Flemish statutes for export textiles. During an English embargo on wool exports to Flanders between 1270 and 1274, the wool went to Brabant and Italy. The large Flemish cities never recovered their unchallenged supremacy on the international cloth market. Their reaction, rather than expanding into cheaper manufacture, was to concentrate even more rigidly than before on luxury cloth, leaving production of medium- and low-grade woollens to the smaller towns and even the rural villages.[40] Flemish domination was seriously threatened by the growth of the cities of Brabant, particularly Mechelen, Antwerp and Brussels. Conflicts with textile artisans were severe. In 1249 the cities of Brabant agreed not to receive one another's rebellious weavers and fullers, and in 1274 Ghent and the cities of Brabant pledged not to give asylum to each other's rebels. A drapery guild is first mentioned at Brussels in 1282, and in 1289 the duke recognised its complete control of the industry. It set fullers' wages and hindered occupational organisation by fullers and other lower-status clothworkers.[41]

The problems were political as well as economic. Local control of government did not translate automatically into good government. In areas where the prince was weak the council could have virtually total control. That of Valenciennes had high justice over all inhabitants, including nobles, and could enforce its own judgements rather than leaving this to the bailiff or territorial prince. Although the Capetian kings used bailiffs to limit the power of communal governments, the bailiffs of Saint-Omer became largely ceremonial figures under the weak counts of Artois. The *échevins* chose their own successors, and by 1268 they legislated without the bailiff. Fiscal peculation and abuses of judicial power were rampant: a grain measurer who worked before daylight and a bridegroom who hired more than six minstrels for his wedding were

---

40   Sortor, 'Saint-Omer', 1486. In a comparable situation during the 1350s, when the weavers were disenfranchised at Ghent, the city's textiles lost markets to other suppliers and never recovered them. Nicholas, *Metamorphosis*, 135–40, 155–8.

41   Martens, *Histoire de Bruxelles*, 74–7.

both fined the enormous sum of 60 pounds. Parties and factions formed around political families.[42]

Virtually every urban revolt in northwestern Europe was accompanied by allegations of fiscal mismanagement by the city councils. All Flemish city governments were keeping written accounts before 1300 that show them hopelessly in debt to the bankers of Arras. Borrowing often did not even suffice to cover the expenses of the year when the loan was incurred. Nearly 52 per cent of Bruges' receipts in 1281–2 came from borrowed funds. While peculation by aldermen, the fines owed to the Flemish count after Bruges' insurrection in 1280 and the costs of new walls undoubtedly contributed to the problem, sloppy bookkeeping was at the root of the difficulty. Bruges sequestered the property of orphans to prevent their guardians from cheating them; but instead of keeping the money in a separate account, as other cities did, Bruges put it into the general municipal treasury and spent it, all the while paying 10 per cent interest to the children. Thus the debt to the orphans doubled in the late thirteenth century. Loans from Arras accounted for nearly 61 per cent of Bruges' debt in this quarter-century, but the Arras money was being used to pay for the orphan debt and the city's obligations from the sale of rents.[43] Although evidence of greed and dishonesty is widespread, part of the magistrates' problem was that an inadequate tax base was forcing them to borrow. The Crespin and Louchart banking families of Arras had personal fortunes about the size of the Flemish cities' entire budgets.[44] The exponential growth of the cities in the thirteenth century had created problems of police, sanitation, walls, street and bridge maintenance. While bureaucracies multiplied in Italy, city services did not keep pace, and even the bureaucracies were small in the northern cities. Most Flemish cities did not use direct taxation, and indirect taxes on sales were much resented, particularly those that were farmed to syndicates of wealthy patricians. When the rates were raised in Ghent in 1288, the outcry provoked French intervention. In 1301 Philip IV precipitated a financial crisis by agreeing too readily to the demand of the commons of Ghent that they 'be freed from a certain heavy tax which there was at Ghent and Bruges upon articles for sale, especially beer and mead. . . . This greatly displeased the patricians of the town, who were used to making profit from the said exaction'.[45]

42 Platelle, *Histoire de Valenciennes*, 52–8; Derville, *Histoire de Saint-Omer*, 49–51.
43 Sosson, 'Finances communales et dette publique', 239–49, 251–6; Nicholas, *Medieval Flanders*, 185.
44 Barel, *Ville médiévale*, 280.
45 Johnstone, *Annals of Ghent*, 12–13.

Although the Flemish cities were more industrial than those of any other region, artisans were excluded from public office longer there than elsewhere. Craftsmen had confraternities with common treasuries but no specifically professional organisations, and the city councils included no artisans. The narrowest oligarchy was the self-perpetuating Thirty-Nine of Ghent, dominated by merchant-landowners. Unrest became severe in 1279–80, beginning with uprisings at Tournai, Douai and Saint-Omer. The Saint-Omer disturbance was evidently caused by a new excise. Municipal ordinances between 1281 and 1283 ordered 'good people' to take arms and expel the undesirables, presumably artisans who had been banished from Flanders. The *échevins* forbade craftsmen to assemble or go armed to the place where journeymen were hired for short-term employment. Ghent, Bruges and Ypres also suffered uprisings in 1280 and 1281. The rebellions at Ghent and Bruges involved patrician factions and concerned commercial privilege, although craft leaders sat on the Bruges city council for eight months in 1280. At Ypres clothworkers, most of whom lived in the suburbs and neighbouring villages, rose against their employers, who lived in the city. The work-givers included both great merchants and 'drapers' (smaller operators who bought wool and gave work to artisans such as weavers and fullers but were outside the merchant oligarchy). In 1280 the count issued wage scales limiting what the drapers could pay the craftsmen, and these were much resented.[46]

A new element was interjected when Philip IV became king of France in 1285. He evidently hoped to annex Flanders. To embarrass the Flemish count he allied with parties in the cities, generally the land-owning aristocracy that governed them. At various times he appointed royal guardians in the cities, agreed to the commoners' demands that the municipal accounts be audited, and gave trading concessions to Flemish drapers in France. In response the count in 1297 allied with Edward I of England, abolished the Thirty-Nine of Ghent and issued the 'Great Charter', a civil and criminal code that would govern Ghent until 1540. After 1301 the city was ruled by two colleges of *schepenen*, one of which was the chief court and legislative body of the city, while the other functioned as justices of the peace and guardians of orphans' property. They were chosen in equal numbers by the outgoing aldermen and the count.

Factions called Lilies and Claws, after the French and Flemish coats of arms, developed in the cities. Both cut across social lines, although

46   Derville, *Histoire de Saint-Omer*, 63; Nicholas, *Medieval Flanders*, 181–5.

the Lilies were generally wealthier and more likely to be landowners. Personal feuds divided the municipal aristocracies and split families into branches. The feud at Ghent between the ancient lineages of Borluut and van Sint-Baafs, the former Claws and the latter Lilies, began with a dispute over a broken marriage promise, ignited into violence when a verbal slight ruptured a truce and included a brawl in the local cathedral. It was finally settled after twelve years in 1306 in a peace that accounted for nine homicides, numerous mutilations and personal injuries, and was atoned by twenty-seven pilgrimages and huge damage assessments that roughly cancelled out between the sides.[47] When Philip IV made a triumphal entry into Ghent in May 1301, the citizens were 'all clad in new garments, the patricians in two fashions, because they disagreed among themselves'.[48] The king's allies were restored to the city governments, but his troops were ejected in rebellions beginning with the famous 'Matins of Bruges' in 1302. That uprising was led by disaffected Claw patricians and craftsmen such as the Bruges weaver Peter de Coninc.

Although the battle of Courtrai in 1302 has entered popular legend as a triumph of Flemish townsmen over French nobles, the actual result was less than revolutionary. Unpopular though they were, sales taxes became the basis of municipal finance in all Flemish cities, which had to pay substantial fees to the count for permission to levy them. Craft organisations were recognised legally, and many would later claim privileges that went back to 1302. Although no guild had the right to specific seats on a Flemish city council until considerably later, guildsmen served as individuals. After the war with the French ended in 1305, however, the aristocrats were gradually repatriated and again ruled the cities by 1312. Peter de Coninc, far from being a simple craftsman, was knighted for his role in the national struggle. After 1320 the five parishes of Ghent chose captains who led the city government in practice, although the two colleges of *schepenen* continued to rule formally. The weavers, whose support had been instrumental in breaking the power of the old oligarchy in 1297, were forbidden political participation until 1338.[49]

Despite the declining market for Flemish cloth, the power and prestige of the cities were enhanced by the events of 1302. The Flemish counts had been dealing for decades with the '*scabini* of Flanders', who

47 Nicholas, 'Vendetta and civil disorder', 182–3, after Blockmans, *Middeleeuwse Vendetta*.
48 Johnstone, *Annals of Ghent*, 12.
49 Discussion based on Nicholas, *Medieval Flanders*, 181–206, 211–12 and literature cited there.

were really delegations from the councils of the five major cities. After Lille and Douai were lost to the French in 1312, the 'three cities' of Ghent, Bruges and Ypres consulted regularly with the count on policy. The city governments also gained limited jurisdiction over their surrounding areas. They had always been the seats of judicial recourse of the lesser courts of their environs; in 1302 Bruges was given the added right to appoint the members of the councils of the places that had judicial recourse to it. By 1314 the three cities had the right to prohibit the manufacture of woollen cloth within a substantial radius of the city wall, except in places with written charters permitting clothmaking.

The events of 1302 in Flanders were the catalyst of revolutionary developments in other cities of the region. A thread common to most rebellions was the absence of economic or social grievances. Rather, the magistrates were accused of fiscal mismanagement, and the leaders of the opposition were out-of-power aristocrats. To defuse agitation that erupted in May 1305 at Saint-Omer, the two boards of *échevins* established 'twelve *jurés* for the commons' to control finances. After a more serious rebellion in January 1306 the countess of Artois had to choose the popular leader, the wealthy Grart Mainabourse, as mayor and appoint twelve new *échevins* (six guildsmen and six patricians from the Hanse of Saint-Omer). This was as far as the aristocrats wanted to go, but the guildsmen pushed for more, led by 'five workers' (two weavers and one fuller, shearer and butcher). Thirty-two guilds were organised, and legislation issued since 1270 against artisan associations was repealed. The aristocrats retired to the country; and after the *échevins* arrested three of the Five, the guilds contacted the Flemings and Peter de Coninc. On his advice the guilds formed a union and elected eight captains. When the *échevins* recalled some aristocrats and handed the Five over to the bailiff for execution, the commons seized the city hall and released them. The countess initially yielded, abolishing the Hanse, opening commerce to all, and directing the *jurés* to elect twenty-four persons to be *échevins* and *jurés*, albeit with a substantial property qualification for the *échevins*. But she then precipitated new riots by ordering the execution of the mayor and the Five. Order was restored by late August. But although the countess did not reverse the legislative changes that had ended the oligarchy, the old element gradually returned, as in Flanders. The Hanse was re-established in 1312, and *jurés* had no part in the government between 1311 and 1316. After 1316, when the *échevins* of 1306–11 returned and the *jurés* reappeared, the old and new oligarchies gradually merged. Of sixty *échevins* who served between 1325 and 1349, all but five were in the Hanse. The guilds were not in the government formally, but the danger of disorder was enough to give the *échevins* a healthy fear of offending them.[50] The Flemish situation may also have had an impact on the cities of the prince-bishopric of Liège, where the artisans, unlike the Flemish, made almost exclusively small consumer goods for the local market. The archbishop of Liège was the most powerful prince of the eastern Low Countries. Although the city governments had had problems since the 1250s with artisan agitation led by renegade patricians such as Henry of Dinant, the first reference to a guild at Liège is to the tanners in 1288. However, there were twelve craft organisations by 1298 and fifteen in 1308. Most lineages of Liège were related to noble families of the environs, some of whom were external burgesses of the city, and participated in their vendettas.

Following agitation in protest against a sales tax in early 1303, the bishop's *échevins* established a brigade called 'youth of France' to terrorise opposition. This alienated the cathedral chapter, which allied with the guilds. By May the guilds had formulated a political programme that included the abolition of tax farming and sales of rents on the city without their consent. The lineages had to concede representation on the city council to the commoners. Many *échevins* withdrew to their rural estates. In 1312, when the patricians were returning to power in Ghent and Saint-Omer, the exiled Liège magnates, aided by the bishop, assembled at Huy and attempted an armed assault on the city. They joined a force of patricians who had remained in Liège and burned the Butchers' Hall, but then were trapped when the gates were closed. One hundred and thirty-four patricians, including ten of the fourteen *échevins*, were burned to death in the church where they had taken refuge. The next year membership in a craft was made a prerequisite of service on the city council, two generations before this happened in Flanders. But the guildsmen abused their power by excluding the bishop's officials, and civil war continued. A settlement in 1330 established a twenty-four member council chosen by geographical sector of the city, and offices were also divided between 'great' and 'lesser' persons. This system lasted until 1384.[51]

Curiously, while the crafts gained political recognition in most cities of Brabant during these years, control of Brussels was confirmed to one of the most conservative regimes in the Low Countries. Each of seven

---

50 Derville, *Histoire de Saint-Omer*, 64–70.
51 Pirenne, *Early Democracies*, 134–40; Vercauteren, *Luttes sociales*, 37, 61–89; Mollat and Wolff, *Popular Revolutions*, 60.

multi-family lineages provided an *échevin*. After the lineages defeated the other citizens in a pitched battle in 1306, townspeople outside the lineages were forbidden to bear arms. Those with wealth under 100 livres were forbidden even to carry knives unless they were servants of a lineage member. Until 1421 the lineages also monopolised and rotated the two receiverships, ten deans of the drapery guild and ten justices of the peace. They owned most land in the city and controlled charitable foundations. The new city wall of 1357 had seven gates, and each lineage had the key to one. In 1385 a prison was made in each gate for those who had disgraced the reputation of their lineages. The lineages were not closed – having one parent in the lineage was enough – so there was intermarriage with rural aristocrats and newly rich Brusselers. Since the lineages intermarried, until 1375 a person could declare himself first in one lineage and later in another for political advantage.[52]

Everywhere in the Low Countries the cities were becoming intimately involved in deliberations at the duchy or county level. Flanders was in the vanguard, but by 1300 most princes were consulting with town representatives, especially over finances. The first urban league in Brabant was made in 1261–2. The representatives of the nobles and of the cities of Liège, Huy and Dinant allied against the bishop in 1271. From 1316 a commission of eight burgesses and twelve persons representing the bishop, cathedral chapter and nobility generally oversaw policy. Cities were included in regular meetings of the Estates of Brabant after the famous Charter of Kortenberg of 1312, which provided that a council of ten townsmen and four nobles would meet every three weeks to maintain the privileges of the land. This was extended in 1314 into general oversight of finances.[53]

GERMANY

The changes in Germany in this half-century were less revolutionary than in the Low Countries and Italy. The absence of a powerful monarchy had surprisingly little impact on urban development, probably because most cities were geared primarily toward local markets. Italy was unique in having commune and *popolo* as separate corporations, but there are similarities to the distinction between *scabini-Schöffen* representing the city lord, rarely becoming a genuine city council except in Flanders and adjacent areas, and a council representing the sworn

---

52 Martens, *Histoire de Bruxelles*, 130–4.
53 Engel, 'Frühe ständische Aktivitäten', 40–9.

association of inhabitants. Just as in Italy some magnates were in trade and wealthier *popolani* owned land, the landowning and commercial elites overlapped in Germany.[54]

Many German city governments, particularly those that were theoretically under the emperors, already enjoyed considerable freedom of action before 1270. From 1298 the councils of imperial cities were permitted to issue statutes as long as they did not contradict imperial law. But the councils were aristocratic, and Nuremberg was the only major German city that had no significant agitation before 1348 to broaden the composition of the magistracy. There were unsuccessful craft revolts at Magdeburg in 1301, Augsburg and Trier in 1302–3, Speyer in 1304, Strasbourg and Bremen in 1308 and Erfurt in 1310. The issues were more often personal rivalries than general political programmes. Some, such as the Stolzhirsch revolt at Augsburg in 1302–3, were tied to broader party formations outside the city. Disorder erupted at Regensburg in 1302 when the council fined several patricians and declared them ineligible for public office. Between 1327 and 1333 a new series of outbreaks had more success, changing the local regimes, albeit not radically, at Mainz, Speyer, Strasbourg, Regensburg and Ulm. By 1335 most larger cities permitted at least some token representation on the council for the larger or wealthier and more prestigious crafts.[55]

City lords were still powerful in Germany in 1270 but generally not by 1330. There was thus more conflict in Germany than in France as the city councils tried to gain independence of the lords' bailiffs and *Schöffen*. Some were unsuccessful. Except for a brief episode Trier was ruled by its archbishop through the *Schöffen* and *Schultheiss* (bailiff) until the mid-fourteenth century. Although much diminished in function elsewhere, urban advocates were still important in Germany, and the fact that the archbishop of Trier had acquired the advocacy from the local count strengthened him considerably. Agitation in 1302 established a council of nine representatives of the guilds and five of the community, which functioned alongside the fourteen *Schöffen*. Two of the nine guildsmen were weavers, and seven other trades had one representative each: butchers, tanners, bakers, smiths and stonemasons, carpenters and coopers, mercers and furriers. Each of the guilds fits the pattern found elsewhere of craft organisations dominated internally by merchants. This council was gone by 1309, and there is no further evidence of guilds in the government of Trier until 1344.[56]

54 Bechtold, *Zunftbürgerschaft und Patriziat*, 106–12.
55 Mollat and Wolff, *Popular Revolutions*, 66; Haverkamp, 'Conflitti interni', 144–8.
56 Matheus, *Trier*, 84–6; Haverkamp, 'Conflitti interni', 145–6.

Elsewhere, however, financial embarrassment forced town lords first to pawn and eventually to sell their remaining offices and tax and toll rights in the cities. Often these were major offices, but some were seigniorial rights. In 1296 the archbishop of Magdeburg had to pawn his Yeast Office, through which the brewers had to buy yeast for their beer, to the city. It became an important source of income for Magdeburg as the brewing industry grew.[57]

German city government became more professionalised in these years. At Nuremberg by 1302 two members of the Inner Council rotated the presidency of the council every four weeks. Called *Frager*, they amounted to burgomasters, handling ongoing business when the entire council was not in session. Two collectors handled finances, basing collection districts on streets. By 1300 Mainz had a receiver who collected the direct tax (the *Schatzung*, based on self-declaration), auditors, messengers, and an inspector who enforced building codes, resolved surveying disputes and handled street-cleaning. Elsewhere the members of the council normally handled these duties, assigning them yearly among themselves, with a college of at least two per office.[58]

Freiburg-im-Breisgau

The successful urban rebellions illustrate these characteristics. In some cities the crafts formed a corporate body that the council sometimes consulted, such as the 'masters of the crafts' mentioned at Halberstadt in 1289 and the 'Sixteen' at Worms in 1298.[59] In 1293 an Old Council at Freiburg-im-Breisgau, consisting entirely of descendants of the founding families of the city, was joined by a new council of Twenty-Four, consisting of eight each from the nobles, merchants and craftsmen but chosen by a largely patrician electoral college. Also in 1293 the count gave the guilds that were organised in the city at that time the right to issue statutes through their 'masters', whom he named until 1316, leaving the choice thereafter to the members. After 1338 all citizens had to be enrolled in one of eighteen guilds, all of them composites of several occupations, which became the basis of the militia. Trades that were not separately organised at that time could not do so subsequently. Specialisations within the trade and development of new crafts had to occur in the form of 'brotherhoods' within the 'great guilds'.[60]

57   Uitz, 'Kommunale Autonomie in Magdeburg', 309.
58   Bischoff, 'Stadtherrschaft im ostfränkischen Städtedreieck', 100; Pfeiffer, *Nürnberg*, 35; Falck, *Mainz in seiner Blütezeit*, 183.
59   Mollat and Wolff, *Popular Revolutions*, 38.
60   Schulz, *Handwerksgesellen und Lohnarbeiter*, 25; Müller, *Freiburg im Mittelalter*, 53–5.

Magdeburg

Magdeburg used the military needs of its archbishop to force him in 1292 to agree to take taxes only with the consent of the burgesses and cathedral chapter. The originally eight-member council had grown to thirteen by 1293 with the addition of the masters of the five great guilds: drapers, mercers, furriers, bootmakers and tanners. The five masters immediately accused the ministerial patricians of levying a tax on the town with forged imperial letters and pocketing the proceeds, diverting shiploads of grain to their own houses, and usury. In 1294, in return for a loan to redeem the office of *Schultheiss*, which the archbishop had pawned, the council forced him to agree that he would no longer influence the choice of *Schultheiss* or *Schöffen*. The prelate conceded sole competence of the city court for taxes and property transactions. By 1295 the council was trying to get the right to appoint the *Schöffen*. Although the archbishop refused, the *Schöffen*, having made their point, in fact coopted those whom the council suggested.

These political gains corresponded to the rise of the merchants, who dominated the greater crafts, at the expense of the landowners. But they could not limit the ministerial regime further without the support of the lesser guilds, which thus entered the council in 1303. In 1309 the archbishop sold the city a new charter that confirmed old rights and forbade the prelate and cathedral chapter to harbour persons exiled by the city. The archbishop renounced his tolls, including those on beer and wine and one charged on each wagonload of bulk imports. Magdeburg had a grain staple on the Elbe, re-exporting a considerable amount after it had passed the city's toll. For control purposes, transfers of grain were to take place only in the Old City in the future, not in the suburbs that remained under the bishop's jurisdiction, and no toll would be taken from citizens or foreigners on grain that they were exporting downstream. Prohibitions on exporting grain from the city in the future would be declared only by archbishop and council jointly. After new conflicts in 1313, the archbishop retired to his rural estates and spent little time in the city thereafter.

New disorders erupted at Magdeburg in 1330. This time the changes established a permanent regime of aristocratic guilds that were dominated by merchants. The five Greater Guilds, which had had seats on the council since the late thirteenth century, were joined by the Common Guilds (butchers, clothmakers, smiths, bakers, brewers, goldsmiths, escutcheon makers and draymen). Other trades were represented by two councillors whom the guild masters chose. The masters of the Great Guilds were to consult those of the Common Guilds twice per week, and the latter had to obtain the consent of the members of their trades to their votes on the council.[61]

Erfurt

Erfurt had had craft organisations early. Conflicts developed after 1264, when the archbishop, at the request of the aristocratic council, abolished the 'society' of bakers and butchers, who were in the same organisation, and placed inspection for trade violations in the hands of two bakers and two butchers who would be named by the council. He guaranteed freedom to all natives and foreigners to sell bread and meat on the market as long as toll was paid to the archbishop, thus violating guild claims to monopolise the market. In 1283 the number of seats on the council was raised from fourteen to twenty-four, with ten guilds guaranteed the additional seats. Nine more strictly artisan trades had guilds but were kept off the council. The council continued to issue industrial regulations. In 1289 the archbishop had to lease his mint and major offices to the city. Erfurt's municipal statute was compiled in 1306, and by then the council was so independent that it did not bother seeking confirmation from the archbishop.

Erfurt's military involvements strained its resources and led to accusations of corruption and complaints that the council was too narrowly based. Following an uprising in 1310, the council adopted Seventeen Articles. All citizens were liable to tax. Four chief councillors were to be chosen (three by geographical district, one from the guilds) to sit continuously in the city hall, hear complaints and bring them to the immediate attention of the full council. The Four also got the right to settle quarrels among artisans, acting with two 'guardians' of each guild. They were to inform the council immediately if they heard of a conspiracy of craftsmen or commoners. The four chief councillors and ten representatives each of the community and the guilds constituted a council of twenty-four. Although only masters in the greater guilds had the franchise, public participation was rather wide at Erfurt. Before ratifying a diplomatic alliance in 1311, the council held a conference with 185 named citizens, who are not grouped by their guilds in the report of proceedings.[62]

---

61 Gleba, *Gemeinde*, 95–107; Stoob, *Urkunden*, 68–9; Uitz, 'Kommunale Autonomie in Magdeburg', 299–321; Mollat and Wolff, *Popular Revolutions*, 246.
62 Mägdefrau, 'Volksbewegungen in Erfurt', 334, 341–5, 349–63; Möncke, *Quellen*, 64–7, where the singular noun is clear in the text of 1264, 124–5; Stoob, *Urkunden*, 321.

The episcopal cities of the Rhineland

Although most lay lords still exercised substantial powers only in their residential cities by this time, bishops and archbishops were still very powerful. Using Mainz as an example, the episcopal courts had cognisance over most criminal cases, while the city court handled civil actions except those involving church property. Low justice (over misdemeanours) was shared with the archbishop's steward. Often, as at Cologne and Magdeburg, the bishops used military resources from the diocese surrounding the city to fight the council's pretensions to autonomy. This may explain why the burgomasters were stronger in the Rhenish cities than elsewhere in Germany. Although Mainz was the last episcopal city to acquire a burgomaster (between 1286 and 1300), he summoned the council into session and enforced its wishes, conducted foreign policy and was commander in chief of the militia.

In virtually all cities the bishop owned considerable prime business property in the central city, generally letting it out for perpetual rent. His tolls and other domanial rights were burdensome and gave him control over the food trades and important public services. Faced with financial pressures, in 1325 the archbishop of Mainz had to agree in return for a fixed payment that he would not cease to provide these services. Persons who were exiled by the town court would no longer be given refuge in the archbishop's enclaves, and citizens had the right to capture them there and bring them to the archbishop for trial. Such guarantees are found in other Rhenish episcopal cities. These gains of the citizens were accompanied by a growth of corporate consciousness. The council controlled the city's seal after 1277. The Peace Decree of 1300, Mainz's earliest town law apart from the customary law of the archbishop, was read aloud at the annual rotation of magistrates, who swore to abide by it. The separate citizen oath was also repeated periodically.[63]

The mint associates continued to be extremely important in the Rhenish episcopal cities. Much of the agitation for greater representation for merchants and merchant-craftsmen was directed at them rather than at the council *per se*. The mint associates were not always a small group: a list of them from 1266 for Strasbourg has more than three hundred names. At Speyer they had to concede seats on the council to thirteen guilds in 1304, leaving only eleven places for the mint associates and Rhine merchants. This was really a split within the elite, with the out-of-power group using the guilds for political advantage, and the mint associates again monopolised the council seats by 1317. Conflicts

---

63 Falck, *Mainz in seiner Blütezeit*, 149, 163–5, 176–9, 183.

continued until 1330, when several other city governments of the region mediated a settlement: a twenty-eight member council would have fourteen each from the patricians and the guilds, and the outgoing council would choose its successors. Given the domination of the political guilds by merchants, antiquity of lineage was a more serious issue than economic orientation.[64]

Cologne, the largest city of the Rhineland, faced the most powerful archbishop of the area. From 1258 the city council issued charters jointly with him. The fifteen-member council originally had a chiefly financial competence but expanded against the *Schöffen* and the Rich Club and was in control of city government by 1305. After 1321 it became the Small Council, supplemented by a general council of eighty-two members chosen from the parishes. The general council concentrated on finances but under the control of the Small Council. Until 1396 the councillors coopted their successors, usually from their own families. A two-year 'vacation' was required, but a three-year rotation of forty-five persons became standard. For especially important matters the incumbent council would call in the other two groups, and the resulting group was called 'All Councils'.[65]

Thus, although most German cities were governed by councils, efforts to broaden them through guilds amounted to a slight relaxation of the lineage-based elites but rarely gave political rights to craftsmen until later in the fourteenth century.

Urban leagues

Urban leagues were more numerous and powerful in Germany than anywhere else outside Italy. The Hanse of north German cities developed a more western orientation. What had previously been a Hanse of individual merchants, similar to the Flemish Hanse of London, became a 'Hanse of towns' in the late thirteenth century, as Cologne and later Lübeck established their leadership. The 'Easterlings' established offices with resident personnel, beginning in the late thirteenth century in England and Flanders but reaching fuller development later.[66] While the Hanse began as an economic union that turned to politics to gain trade concessions, the other German urban leagues were political and directed against lords who disturbed the peace. From 1304 Erfurt, Nordhausen

---

64 Czok, 'Bürgerkämpfe', 327–9; Haverkamp, 'Conflitti interni', 141–4; Maschke, *Städte und Menschen*, 124–5.
65 Huiskes, *Beschlüsse Köln*, xii–xiii; Howell, *Women, Production, and Patriarchy*, 105.
66 Lloyd, *England and the German Hanse*, 2–3, 21; Dollinger, *German Hansa*, 45–82, 86–9.

and Mühlhausen were in more or less continuous alliance, generally renewed every two or three years. The first Rhenish League of 1254 was succeeded by a second in 1326 that grew from a nucleus beginning with Strasbourg, Basel and Freiburg-im-Breisgau. Some of the treaties provided for collaborative action to secure long-distance routes and mutual aid in prosecuting criminals.[67]

ITALY

The Italian cities also underwent important changes in this half-century. Those of Tuscany show the greatest similarity with developments in the north, but they are only part of a larger movement. In Milan and most of the smaller cities local potentates were beginning to consolidate the power that would eventually make their descendants city lords. The della Torre of Milan began as officers of the *popolo*, first for normal terms and then for more extended periods. By 1294, however, they had yielded to Matteo Visconti, who began his rise with a five-year term as captain of the *popolo*, then was recognised as imperial vicar of Milan in 1294.[68]

Venice also had a revolutionary change, but of a singular nature. The existing members of the Great Council coopted enough newcomers in 1297 roughly to double the size of the body to about 1,100 persons. This is called the 'closing' of the council; although for a few years after 1297 the new regime was comparatively open, new families had great difficulty gaining acceptance as noble thereafter. Membership in the Great Council was hereditary by 1323; to enter it, one had to prove that one's ancestors had held high office in the commune. Membership in the Great Council was a prerequisite to election to any other magistracy or council, notably the powerful Forty. Venice was unusual only in making the elite a legally closed class, for the size of the council actually gave Venice a larger oligarchy than many other cities had. Although perhaps one-fifth of the adult males of Florence were technically eligible for political activity, most did not participate, while Siena was controlled by about sixty leading families.[69]

The new order at Venice was not unchallenged. In the aftermath of a foiled conspiracy in 1310, a 'noble' was defined as someone who was

67 Schulz, *Handwerksgesellen und Lohnarbeiter*, 8; Mägdefrau, 'Volksbewegungen in Erfurt', 354; Stoob, *Urkunden*, 321, 329–31.
68 Tabacco, *Struggle for Power*, 288–91.
69 Lane, *Venice*, 111–17; Mollat and Wolff, *Popular Revolutions*, 77–8; Larner, *Age of Dante and Petrarch*, 122.

or could be a member of the Great Council. When tensions continued, a committee of ten 'wise men' was chosen on 10 July. Their mandate was originally for only two months, but successive renewals culminated in a ten-year term in 1316. The Ten became a permanent institution in 1355, when the last serious threat to the Venetian state occurred, a plot led by the doge Marin Falier to assassinate the members of the Great Council.[70]

Tuscany and Umbria

Factional struggle intensified in the Tuscan cities when the Guelf regimes were restored after 1266. The captain of the *popolo* began yielding to trade-based regimes, but this change was accompanied by the growth of family-based factions that were stronger than any guild and probably stronger than the *popoli* themselves. At Perugia the most powerful body was the Executive Council or Council of the Credenza. It began as the small council of the captain and his advisors, joined after 1266 by four consuls of the merchant association (*Mercanzia*). In the 1270s five consuls of the guilds, with one chosen from each district of the city by the rectors, joined the captain's council and eventually assumed his functions on it. Two were usually merchants, one a banker, with two seats left open to other trades. In 1293 a new court of appeals in criminal cases further eroded the captain's power. Its judge also ruled on the constitutionality of measures ordered by the guild consuls and administered roads and fountains, which had formerly been the *podestà*'s job. In 1303–4 the Executive Council was revised when the Council of the [ten] Priors of the Guilds, two per district, replaced the consuls of the guilds. There were still two merchants and one banker, but now there were seven seats for other professional groups. The term of the consuls of the guilds was originally one year, but the statute of 1303 fixed it at two months. The government of Perugia at the end of the thirteenth century thus had shorter terms of office, more complicated modes of election, and a combination of residence and professional affiliation as the basis of representation.[71]

Changes at Florence too paralleled developments in northern Europe. Conflicts became severe again after 1280 as the Guelfs tried to exclude the Ghibellines totally. The Guelf-dominated *popolo* had divided since 1267, as the bankers such as the Cerchi, Bardi and Mozzi moved toward the older landed aristocracy and knighthood, while other wealthy

70 Ruggiero, *Violence*, 3–8.
71 Blanshei, *Perugia*, 16, 55–7.

persons remained with the *popolo*. The older Guelf families, who had been associated with landholding and with patronage in the local bishopric and cathedral chapter, dominated until 1280; then power shifted to the merchants in the party.[72] The word '*popolo*', which had fallen out of use, was revived. A new government of fourteen 'good men' became the chief executive. It initially included eight Guelfs and six Ghibellines, but the Guelfs were able to expel the Ghibellines in 1282. Florence became officially Guelf; Ghibellinism was an act of treason. The Guelf party, through its councils and captains, had power comparable to that of the *popolo*.

This 'second *popolo*' of 1282 instituted a six-member priorate. Although the Fourteen, rather than the priors, were still the supreme council, the change of 1282 was a fundamental departure: for although there was to be one prior for each of the six districts of the city, the priors were now chosen for the first time from twelve trade organisations: the seven greater and five 'middle' guilds. The priors served for two months and chose their own successors, meeting with the rectors of the twelve politically privileged guilds. The older Guelf lineages held only fifteen of 381 seats in the priorate during the next decade, although they were more active in the lesser councils. Florence was clearly moving away from domination by landholders and toward merchant and banker control at the end of the thirteenth century under the aegis of the second *popolo*. Understanding the significance of choosing the priors through the guilds, however, half the magnate lineages had members in the greater guilds by 1293.[73]

The capstone of the *popolo* constitution of Florence was the Ordinances of Justice of 1293, imitating those of Pistoia a year earlier. Issued by the priors under the prompting of Giano della Bella, a member of the aristocratic Calimala guild, the Ordinances were the culmination of legislation against the magnates. They broadened the basis of political participation by bringing nine 'lesser guilds' into the magistracy. A seventh prior was added, called the Standard-bearer of Justice, serving a two-month term that was rotated among the six districts. With a militia of 1,000, he enforced judgements rendered in the *podestà*'s court. The priorate now became the *Signoria*, the chief executive organ of Florence. Priors had to be guildsmen practising a trade or profession; persons who were enrolled in a guild without practising its trade were excluded. Magnates could not be elected consul of a guild, which was a condition

---

72 Dameron, *Episcopal Power and Florentine Society*, 146–9.
73 Holmes, *Florence, Rome*, 27; Waley, *Siena*, 121–4; Mollat and Wolff, *Popular Revolutions*, 81; Dameron, *Episcopal Power and Florentine Society*, 149–50.

of eligibility for the priorate. Nominations to the priorate were by a complicated procedure involving some choice of guildsmen within the districts, and this territorial element weakened the purely guild aspect of the arrangement. One hundred and fifty-two families were declared magnate, required to post bond and made ineligible for all offices of the *popolo* and guild magistracies. A magnate who killed a *popolano* was to be executed, and the testimony of any *popolano* was to be accepted, even if uncorroborated, against any magnate. Florentine magnates could have themselves inscribed as *popolani*, but few did.[74]

When the priors became Florence's first guild-based magistracy in 1282, trades other than those legitimised in 1293 were still jockeying for position and furnished some priors. Dino Compagni, writing around 1310, refers to 'seventy-two craft guilds, all of which had consuls', although only twenty-one were politically recognised. After 1291 the names of thirty-six priors-elect were placed in a bag, and six were drawn every two months; thus the identity of the priors was determined by other means, but the order of service was fixed by lot. The major guilds furnished 90 per cent of the priors between 1282 and 1293, and almost half came from the Calimala and the moneychangers' guilds. The major guilds may have had about 3,500 members in the early fourteenth century, while the entire group of twenty-one guilds had 7,000–8,000 members. Some five hundred wealthy bankers and long-distance merchants drawn from the five major commercial guilds had their own organisation, the *Mercanzia*, established by the city in 1308, which in turn gave them a collective sense that was stronger than their individual guild affiliations. The twenty-one guilds whose members were made eligible for the priorate in 1293 remained fixed until 1378.[75]

The urban magnates after 1293

Although the *popolo* became more powerful than the formal government of the commune at Florence, magnates still lived in the city and could be members of councils that were defined as communal rather than involving solely the *popolo*. This gave them access to patronage but little power, while the priors, who were technically officers of the *popolo*, were the real executive of the city government.[76] Magnates also remained

74 Najemy, *Corporatism and Consensus*, 10–11, 45–52; Villani, *Chronicle*, 302–3; Schevill, *Florence*, 157–60; Larner, *Age of Dante and Petrarch*, 121; Herlihy, *Pistoia*, 200, 219–20; Mollat and Wolff, *Popular Revolutions*, 133.

75 Schevill, *Florence*, 149–55; Compagni, *Chronicle*, xix; c. 7 p. 37; Najemy, *Corporatism and Consensus*, 20–30.

76 Lansing, *Florentine Magnates*, 220; Herlihy, *Pistoia*, 219.

wealthy and influential at Perugia, despite their civil disabilities. Statutes of 1308–18 defined magnates as those of knightly parentage on the paternal side. *Popolani* were persons in the city or *contado* with enough property to qualify for membership on the council of the *popolo*. Magnate families display a striking persistence; of 398 magnate houses listed in a 'red book' compiled in 1373, 252 were in the tax list of 1285. Sixteen of the twenty richest Perugians of 1285 were magnates. There were no poor nobles, a few of modest wealth, but most were rich. Their total share of the wealth in the central city was actually rising in the early fourteenth century. The tax assessments of most members of the 'Special and General Council,' a part of the council of the *popolo*, show that most were wealthy, but in general they were much less affluent than the magnates.[77]

Magnates were also influential at Siena. Although the city required members of 'houses' to post bond, the first years of the regime of the Nine, the chief magistracy that corresponded to the priors at Florence after 1287, saw the consolidation, not the disintegration, of the domination of banker-landowner families. Magnates were prohibited from serving on the Nine, but in fact they did so and also held other offices. They were especially useful as *podestàs* in *contado* communities.[78] At Genoa the nobles remained more powerful than in the Tuscan and Lombard cities, and they were always distinguished in lists of oath-takers from *popolani*. Although the nobles often had to join guilds, they still had political power through their *alberghi*.[79]

Florence's guild constitution was strained in the struggles after 1295. Factions, rather than the guilds, chose the priors in 1304. After 1310 *balie* (*ad hoc* commissions designated by the *Signoria*) or the outgoing *Signoria* itself often suspended normal electoral procedures and named new priors directly. The system was only changed in 1328 when *balia* elections were ended in favour of a complex four-step electoral procedure that gave scrutiny and veto powers to the incumbent *Signoria*, the captains of the Guelf party and officials of the *Mercanzia*. Anyone approved for inclusion in the scrutiny of 1328 would always be eligible unless removed for a reason; later scrutinies could add names but not delete them. Thus the change was the opposite of a democratic reform; 71 per cent of the priors in 1328 came from the three commercial guilds of Calimala, moneychangers and wool.[80]

77   Blanshei, *Perugia*, 50–1.
78   Waley, *Siena*, 94–6; Bowsky, *Siena under the Nine*, 19–22.
79   Heers, *Family Clans*, 52–8.
80   Najemy, *Corporatism and Consensus*, 79–119. At neighbouring Pistoia elections to offices in the *popolo* were also done by a carefully controlled system of scrutiny for

Feuds and civil discord

The continued influence of the magnates is a partial explanation of the persistence of civil discord in virtually all Italian cities at the turn of the fourteenth century. The feuds are associated especially with the magnate lineages but were by no means confined to them. Most had nothing to do with political issues, but they exacerbated the overall climate of violence and the pervasive notion that private vengeance was more honourable than having recourse to the civil government. Most cities permitted 'lawful' vendetta: this condition was met when the offence was obvious and public, the vengeance taken was appropriate and was taken only on the offender as long as he was alive, although if he died without making peace it could be conducted against his children. Offended persons who waged a vendetta could involve their own kinsmen up to fourth cousins, a very substantial group. The *podestàs* were forbidden to take action against persons who were engaged in a vendetta that satisfied these criteria of legitimacy. Siena allowed persons who were known to have 'capital enemies' to wear armour. Despite efforts to limit vendettas to the principals, a statute of Siena of 1309–10 exempted persons from murder accusations for taking revenge on the kin of known enemies up to the third degree, meaning brothers, first and second cousins.

A Sienese feud evokes memories of the Borluut–van Sint-Baafs vendetta at Ghent. Before 1285 Cione Picchiati was killed by Mino di Pero, who in turn was killed in 1292 by arrangement of Cione's eldest son, Guerra, after a lapse of more than seven years. Guerra and his three brothers fled to the *contado*. Guerra was condemned in absentia to execution and total confiscation of his property, his brothers to fines or imprisonment. Since this condemnation could be enforced in the *contado* of Siena, they went to Viterbo, a city with regular commercial contacts with Siena. After making some money in trade at Viterbo, they contacted the eldest surviving brother of the man they had killed, as head of his family. A pacification was made in exchange for an indemnity, according to the law of vendetta. But the di Pero brothers also had to get pardon from the Nine in 1304 in order to return to Siena.[81]

acceptable candidates under the guise of more random selection. The Standard-bearer of Justice chose forty names from purses by district. The sequence of quarter-by-quarter rotation was continued in subsequent elections over four years until all purses were emptied. The 128-member General Council of the *Popolo* was chosen by a similar method. Herlihy, *Pistoia*, 221–3.

81 Larner, *Age of Dante and Petrarch*, 123; Waley, 'Blood Feud', 41–7.

Guelfs, Ghibellines, Blacks and Whites in Tuscany

The power of party organisations is another element of disorder in the Tuscan cities. Violence continued at Florence after the *popolo* achieved its aims in 1293. Just as the *popolo* had become a separate government within the commune after 1250, so the Guelf party now was a government within the *popolo*. Giano della Bella tried but failed in 1293 to seize the party's property for the commune. Thus the Guelf organisation continued to influence Florentine politics.[82] Ghibellinism as a programme to restore imperial control over the Italian cities was a dead issue after 1273 – political Ghibellinism was a concern only when the emperor Henry VII's descent into Italy in 1312–13 revived it briefly – but the party names were still used for family-based factions. Ghibellinism was associated more than before with rural landholding. Until 1270 the commune of Florence had controlled some parts of the *contado* directly but relied on the bishop or rural lords who were citizens for the rest. But the threat to order from the Ghibelline enclaves was so serious, especially on the peripheries of the *contado*, that the Guelf commune now tried to end jurisdictional enclaves and rule the entire *contado* directly.[83] The Blacks and Whites of Florence in the 1290s were Guelfs and Ghibellines under different names, but there is no trace of a political programme with either group.

The names White and Black had originated in 1286 for parties at Pistoia that had started as rival branches of the Cancellieri family, then involved both the Cancellieri and the Panchiatichi, then spread to the countryside. One branch of the Cancellieri was strongly Guelf; the other was less so and eventually joined the magnates and the Panchiatichi, who were Ghibellines and Whites. The rural clienteles of the families made matters worse. Each party had prominent allies at Florence. As late as 1350, when Giovanni Panciatichi took power in Pistoia, it provoked the Florentine conquest of Pistoia the next year, so hostile were the Florentines to the idea of a Ghibelline ruling there.[84] At Florence the White and Black factions crystallised around the Cerchi and Donati families respectively, both of them magnates but initially Guelf. The Donati were older and poorer, the Cerchi newer and richer. The Whites initially had the advantage and nearly conquered Florence, with considerable help from the *popolo minuto*, which was being victimised now by Guelf party infighting as it earlier had been hurt by the magnates.

---

82 Hyde, *Society and Politics*, 135.
83 Dameron, *Episcopal Power and Florentine Society*, 143–5.
84 Herlihy, *Pistoia*, 198–9, 202–3.

Foreign influence permitted Charles of Valois to enter Florence in November 1301 and exile the Whites. The Blacks in turn split: Corso Donati was murdered in 1308, evidently for suspected Ghibelline sympathies! The Whites made common cause with the Ghibellines and with elements in Florence's neighbouring cities that disliked the Guelf regime, notably Arezzo, where Florence had engineered a Guelf takeover. Henry VII's expedition raised Ghibelline hopes, but the Whites were never restored. The party affiliations affected relations with other towns: after the Black conquest of Florence, Pistoia remained White and Ghibelline.[85]

Urban government under the *popoli* outside Florence

While at Florence the seven priors constituted a guild government of the *popolo* that functioned poorly because of factional discord, this period at Siena witnessed the establishment of a coherent oligarchy, the Nine, who were able to provide a generally effective government without guild involvement until 1355. The *noveschi* ['eligible to serve on the Nine'] families were not numerous, but the oligarchy was still open enough for half of the identifiable members of the Council of the Bell to serve on the Nine at some point. The Nine were chosen by extremely complex procedures at a secret meeting attended by the *podestà*, the captain of the *popolo* and at least three consuls of the *Mercanzia*. They had to be taxpaying Guelf *popolani*, aged 30 or more and citizens for ten years. They had to be out of office for at least one year between terms and could not be on the same Nine with close kin or business partners. Magnates, judges, notaries and physicians were ineligible. In reality a few magnates were chosen for the Nine, but the other prohibitions were more closely adhered to.

The Nine served two-month terms, living in isolation from their families in the city hall. Their powers were limited. They could issue no new ordinances unless backed by a two-thirds majority on the Council of the Bell. The Nine had no fiscal power, which resided with the four Provisors of the Biccherna. They held a public session each Thursday morning to hear petitions. Guelfism was not as important in Siena as in Florence; except during crises, only the most famous Ghibellines were excluded from office. As elsewhere, the new regime severely limited both the *podestà* and the captain of the *popolo*, who lost power first to the Nine, then from the 1320s to the War Captain.[86]

85 Holmes, *Florence, Rome*, 167, 170, 175–81, 194; Compagni, *Chronicle*, introduction, xx; Bk 1, c. 20, p. 23; Bk 2, c. 28–30, pp. 52–7; Bk 3, c. 11, p. 74.
86 Waley, with a two-decade overlap with Bowsky, sees more involvement by the middle group of merchants at Siena, while Bowsky and Holmes emphasise a narrower

Padua, like Florence, superimposed a guild government on the *popolo* during these years. From its inception in 1256 the council of the elders of the *popolo* had eight representatives from the guilds. Although the guilds were numerous and had political influence, they were strictly controlled by the commune, which supervised the election of officials and issued their statutes. In 1293 thirty-six trades that had been involved in municipal government in 1287 made a 'Union of the Guilds', whose officers, led by the *podestà*, took charge of the city militia. In 1295 the *gastaldi* of these guilds declared themselves a corporate body, with monthly meetings, and were recognised by the commune.

The Union made few fundamental changes in the constitution. In 1293 the *podesta's* term was reduced to six months, and around 1300 the number of elders was raised from twelve to eighteen, with the extra members evidently guildsmen. Yet the Union, far from broadening public participation, actually restricted officeholding to guildsmen who were already in the commune, precisely what happened at Florence with the regime of 1293. A growing distinction between major and minor guilds was apparent from the fact that fifteen *gastaldiones* (four of whom were to be notaries, with one notary as president) were the executive committee of the Union. Although Padua was less tumultuous than the other north Italian cities before 1312, Henry VII's descent into Italy unleashed problems. Padua had established a protectorate over Vicenza but now lost it to the lord of Verona, Cangrande della Scala. The Union of the Guilds was suppressed briefly in 1314, then revived and the new office of 'defender of the *popolo*' created, in turn to be superseded by a captain of the *popolo*. The Union and the council of *gastaldi* survived until 1328, when Marsiglio da Carrara of Verona became lord of Padua.[87]

The struggles of this period at Orvieto ended in the Monaldeschi lordship. The city was led by a *popolo* that functioned under a charter granted in 1247. The seven consuls of the major guilds replaced the captain as leader of the *popolo* from 1292, corresponding to the executive council of Five at Perugia from 1270, the priors of Florence from 1282 and the Nine at Siena from 1287. The parties amounted to the factions of the two chief families, the Guelf Monaldeschi and the Ghibelline Filippeschi, but they were united initially against outsiders, joining whatever outside party seemed advantageous. After Pope Boniface VIII, the city's nominal lord, tried to obtain strategic noble lands in Orvieto's

but still relatively open regime. Waley, *Siena*, xv, 48; Bowsky, *Siena Under the Nine*, 24–36, 54–92; Holmes, *Florence, Rome*, 195.

87   Castagnetti, 'Città della Marca Veronese', 65–6; Hyde, *Padua*, 1–3, 243–7.

contado that the city hoped to acquire, some magnates who had ties to the family whose lands were involved refused to support the *popolo's* project of annexing this territory. The *popolo* took complete control of the city government. After the Ghibellines nearly seized the city in 1313, officeholding was limited to Guelfs, but their leaders were magnates. Many of Orvieto's richest persons were Ghibellines whose assets were confiscated; thus the rulers had a vested interest in preventing their return.

The Guelf nobles briefly became a government of the Five, almost always including at least one of the Monaldeschi, but in 1315 the Five fell to a new *popolo* whose executive organ was again the Seven. In 1319 the trades were amalgamated into sixteen instead of the earlier twenty-five guilds, and the Seven thereafter included only four of their consuls, with three from the seventy councillors of the *popolo*. The Guelf party and its four captains (two each from the nobles and the *popolani*) were a state within the state, with the right to veto acts of the Seven. Periodic *balie* supplanted all other councils during emergencies. After 1322 the *popolo* lacked leaders, for the nobles held most wealth at Orvieto and controlled its government until 1334, when the Monaldeschi established a tyranny. Characteristically, many rich *popolani* who had been active in earlier *popolo* governments also held offices under the Monaldeschi.[88]

Divisions were severe at Genoa, where the *popolo* was called the 'Society of the Holy Apostles Simon and Jude'. The city tended to be White/Ghibelline but had some Black/Guelfs, notably the Fieschi and Grimaldi families, who contested the two offices of 'captains of the republic' with the Ghibelline Doria and Spinola lineages between 1270 and 1308. From 1309 six nobles and six *popolani* were named the twelve governors, similar to the priors of Florence. This regime lasted until 1339, when the Guelf nobles were expelled and the Ghibelline Simon Boccanegra became doge for life. Half of all other offices, councils and jobs were reserved for Whites, half for Blacks, in the city and in the governments of the Rivieras and the colonies. Blacks and Whites thus became tradition-linked groups without councils or governors, in contrast to the *alberghi*. This system kept the great houses in power; the Fieschi, Grimaldi and Lomellini controlled most seats in the council of the elders, with the Spinola and Doria not far behind, but the other noble families had much less power. Power among the *popolari* was

---

88 Discussion based on Waley, *Mediaeval Orvieto*, 79–119; Carpentier, *Ville devant la peste*, 36–9, 67–71.

more diffused, but Giustiniani and Franchi were at the top, roughly at the level of Spinola and Doria.[89]

This half-century thus saw the consolidation of the rule of groups within the commune variously called *popolo*, Guelf or Ghibelline party. The internecine conflicts had little permanent impact on institutions of government, since rival elite families competed for the same offices. Each city had a hierarchy, but the common thread was merchant wealth both within and among the guilds. The factions tried to control the councils, not overthrow them. But the traditional institutions of government were clearly unable to maintain order, and as each faction looked for someone to provide a *coup de grace* to the opposition, the confusion of this period helped prepare the way for *signori* who tried, albeit in some cases unsuccessfully, to establish one-person rule in most north Italian cities after 1325.

Municipal finances in Italy

The expenses of Italian governments were growing in the late thirteenth century, particularly on defence and public works. Italian city finances continued to be more sophisticated than those of the north. But although the northern cities were developing more unitary and accountable financial administrations, the proliferation of magistracies in Italy meant that while each of them used up-to-date accounting techniques, it is virtually impossible to calculate an overall financial balance for most cities. Pisa had at least eight public treasuries in the early thirteenth century: the city, the corporation of knights, and six public courts, and the consuls of the guild of overseas merchants and the captains of the customs house probably handled more money than the city treasuries did. In addition, many cities did not finance extraordinary expenses such as public buildings directly, but rather set up independent offices, gave them specific revenues, then allowed them to continue to exist after the purpose for which they had been created had been accomplished. This practice, however, was being restricted around 1300. Privileged corporations and magnates either lost the right to collect taxes or were strictly supervised by the city. In 1317 Florence required all income from all sources to be accounted for with the treasurers of the commune.

89 This is similar to the situation at Ghent in the fifteenth century, when all offices were divided among the three political 'Members' of the City. Heers, *Parties and Political Life*, 65, 212; Heers, *Gênes. Civilisation*, 394–6; Mollat and Wolff, *Popular Revolutions*, 68.

The size of city budgets in Tuscany grew tremendously. Pisa's treasurers handled 2,400 *lire* annually in 1227–32 but nearly 40,000 *lire* in 1288. The city had an income of 717,000 *lire* in 1313. Taking periods of two months, Florence received 4,300 *lire* in 1240, 130,000 *lire* in 1301, and the amounts continued to grow in the fourteenth century despite population decline.[90] The tax burden on the cities and particularly their *contadi* was thus severe. The cities raised some money by converting to cash some old civic duties, such as the *cavallata* (providing a horse or serving mounted in the militia). Profits of justice, pardons sold to criminals and political exiles, naturalisation fees and export licences brought the communes some money. Most city-states had regalian right on mines in their *contadi*, the most profitable of which was salt. The salt monopoly was administered through tax farmers, but other mineral rights were exploited directly. The cities also rented shops, houses and pastures that were in the civic patrimony. Curiously, the vociferous complaints of peculation and tax evasion that disturbed the northern cities were not echoed in Italy.

More Italian than northern cities had used direct taxation in the early thirteenth century, and methods of assessment now became more sophisticated. The *libra* or *lira* continued to be the most common valuation tax. It was usually based on annual rental value, not estimated market value. At Siena the commune appointed assessors, who were usually men with previous experience and preferably eligible for service on the Nine. The assessors' hearings were conducted over a two- or three-month period in parish churches, giving plenty of opportunity for negotiation.[91] After 1250, however, most Italian cities began to shift toward excises. The General Gabella, which handled indirect taxes on consumption and business transactions, became a separate office from the Biccherna at Siena.[92] By 1292 Orvieto was using the *lira* for ordinary expenses and indirect taxes (*collecte*) for emergencies, reversing the earlier norm. The *collecte* were generally based on the market value of goods, except that the town devised a version of what is now called a value added tax on grain. Municipal officials levied taxes at several stages on the grain assigned in quotas to the communities and lords of the *contado*: at harvest, the same amount again when it entered Orvieto and a double tax if it was re-exported from the city. Other taxes were levied when the grain went to the miller, and three times with the bakers: for the shop, the

90 Discussion based on Herlihy, 'Tuscan urban finance', 386–99.
91 Bowsky, *Finances Siena*, 70–83.
92 Bowsky, *Finances Siena*, 2–3, 14–15.

oven and the sale of bread. The result was predictable: guaranteed supply but high cost to the consumer, escalating bureaucracy and depression of the *contado*.[93]

During the late thirteenth and early fourteenth centuries the north Italian cities thus continued under *popolano* governments, but the new *popoli* after 1266 had broader participation than their predecessors. The middle range of guilds gained meaningful political representation, and the lesser trades won at least a token voice, but power remained with a merchant and banking elite. As in the north, the powerful guilds were either strictly merchant or merchants and craftsmen combined into a single organisation. The conciliar regimes became stronger and city lords weaker; but while the older elites continued to dominate the northern municipal councils, officially in Germany and under the guise of a guild regime elsewhere, the newer groups had most power in Italy. In Italy most city councils served for two months and rotated personnel, making continuity at the top very difficult but with some stability provided by the already oppressive bureaucracy. Most council members in the north served for a year, but the city bureaucracies were much smaller than the Italian. In each case the outgoing officeholders normally could not succeed themselves, but a pattern developed of regular return after a given period of absence from the council. During this time the person might serve in some administrative office or a different branch of the city council.

Although the northern cities were making important changes towards more scientific funding and record-keeping during this half-century, they lacked the tax base of the Italian communities. As their magistrates tried to finance essential services, they often borrowed so much that they compromised their governments' solvency and their own political futures. This did not happen in Italy. In both north and south there was increasing reliance on indirect taxation as the basis for public finance, but Italian city finances were less centrally administered than the northern.

Nowhere in the north was the sworn association of townspeople formed into a *popolo* separate from the nobles who still lived in the cities. Some smaller Italian cities came under the domination of a single lord, and the chronic confusion and bloodshed in some larger ones led to one-person rule toward the end of this period, initially for a short term as in the case of Charles of Valois at Florence, then permanently with the Monaldeschi of Orvieto and the Visconti of Milan.

93 Carpentier, *Ville devant la Peste*, 42–6.

A concluding reflection

During the three centuries since the millennium the European city had developed as a type and in a regional pattern that would remain essentially fixed politically, albeit with some important structural changes in the late Middle Ages, until the rise of national capitals in the modern period. In economic terms, the pattern established would last until the Industrial Revolution. The urban map of medieval Europe was largely established by 1000, completely so by 1300.

Around 1000 the Italian cities were city-states based upon bishoprics, with an aristocracy composed of rural landholders who were vassals and rear vassals of the bishops. During the political struggles of the central Middle Ages and with the tremendous expansion of regional and interregional trade after 1100 and particularly after 1200, the lordship of the bishop gave way to a city organisation that, by 1300, had assumed most secular rights that the bishops had enjoyed in both city and countryside. The municipal elite was still as family-based as ever, and landownership was still an important indication of social standing. But wealth was becoming increasingly associated with trade, particularly in the luxurious commodities that the Italians controlled that were needed by the ever-more discriminating palates and the textile manufacturing industries of northern Europe.

The northern cities had broad similarities to those of Italy. They were governed by a simpler system of councils, a more rudimentary but perhaps more coherent financial apparatus, and by family-based elites. The power of the bishop was never as complete in the north as it was initially in the south; but the power of the city governments over the bishop was less complete in the north than in Italy during the thirteenth century. Northern cities developed a more important export manufacturing component in the twelfth and particularly thirteenth centuries than can be found in Italy, but this was rarely accompanied by artisan penetration of the municipal government until the late thirteenth century and often even later. In northern Europe, as in Italy, associations within the city – almost exclusively occupational or devotional guilds in the north but also military societies and the more inclusive *popolo* of some north Italian cities – were important agencies of economic regulation and of social and political control.

We have explored these developments in detail in these pages. What is perhaps most striking is the extent to which the city governments and the urban elites remained rooted in landownership while the cities had become the nerve centres of the interrelated commercial and industrial economies of the west by 1300. Changes after 1325 would be profound but would be alterations of detail, not of governing principle or economic orientation. They did not modify the fundamental institutional or social structures of urban Europe. The firm base that was created between 1000 and 1200 and solidified in the crucible of the demographic and economic expansion and then downturn of the next 125 years would survive the disasters of the late Middle Ages. The European city had evolved to maturity as a governing, service and economic entity by the early fourteenth century.

Glossary

advocate

A person who can represent another. In the context of the medieval cities, it is the deputy of the town lord who handled his affairs in the city, specifically judicial actions. In the late Middle Ages it can also mean the city attorney.

albergo

plural *alberghi* [Italian]. Unions of lineages and nuclear families, creating a family in law.

alderman

Member of a guild council. In England the term also means a representative of a ward on the municipal council. 'Alderman' is also a convenient translation for terms in other languages designating members of the city council, such as *échevins, scabini* and *schepenen* and in some contexts *jurés*.

ban mile

The area outside the city walls within which its *bannum* (public-legal power of command) ran.

bastide

Proto-urban defensive fortification, used generally only for places in southwestern France and along the border of the French royal domain with Gascony.

borgo

plural *borghi* [Italian]. See *bourg*.

bourg

[French]. Initially unfortified settlements near a *civitas*, castle or abbey, eventually walled as the city population and area expanded. The *bourg* was the French equivalent of the German *Wik*.

bourgeois

[French]. In a broad sense, a citizen; in a technical sense, a citizen who owned land within the city.

burgensis	plural *burgenses* [Latin]. Inhabitant of the borough or *bourg*, later restricted to those inhabitants enjoying full rights of citizenship.
burgess	Member of the sworn association of a city. It is the equivalent of 'citizenship' in a city, but the broader modern use of 'citizen' precludes employing it exclusively for urban dwellers.
burgrave	Seigniorial official, 'count of the borough' or 'count of the *Burg*' (fortification).
burhs	Fortifications established by Alfred the Great, his successors and the Danes in Wessex and Mercia during the late ninth and tenth centuries.
cerocensuales	[Latin]. Person paying ground rent in wax to lord.
civis	plural *cives* [Latin]. Citizen.
civitas	plural *civitates* [Latin]. 1) City-state in the Roman Empire, an administrative subdivision of a province. In northern Europe it generally refers to a tribal capital that had been occupied by the Romans. 2) During the Middle Ages *civitas* referred variously to cities that were bishoprics and, in the cases of cities that had been Roman, to the part of the eventual settlement that was within the late Roman wall, as opposed to the suburbs outside it.
cnihtas	Aristocratic landholders in England before the Norman Conquest, some of whom lived at least part-time in the towns.
collegia	[Latin]. Occupational associations of the late Roman cities, persisting in a few cases in Italy into the seventh century.
commune	Association of persons, generally living in the same territory, who have bound themselves to one another by oath to give assistance in matters of common concern, most often peacekeeping. By extension the term came to mean city governments that had a sworn association at their base.
consorteria	Unions of nuclear families into an extended group. The term is also used for businesses that originated in family partnerships.
consul	Member of early city council in Italy and southern France; the term is occasionally used elsewhere

	for members of city councils and for leaders of guilds or merchant associations.
contado	plural *contadi* [Italian]. Countryside, specifically the area around the city that was initially subject to the count but was gradually subordinated to the city.
count	Public official, ruler of a county in most areas by the early Middle Ages, although under the Romans and in some medieval cities the count had a governmental palace and occasionally jurisdiction.
dazio	[Italian] Direct tax.
decurions or *curiales*	[Latin]. Members of city councils of late Roman Empire.
échevins	[French]. Judges and assessors in the court of a town lord. In Flanders and some cities of northern France, the *échevins* became the city council. The term is the same as *schepenen* [Flemish], *Schöffen* [German] and *scabini* [Latin]. In cases where the *échevins* became the city council, the term may be translated 'aldermen'.
emphyteusis	Perpetual lease, in which the face value of the rental payment will not change when the property on which it is assessed changes hands.
estimo	[Italian]. Sworn estimate by the taxpayer of his/her taxable property, initially given orally, but eventually put into writing in most Italian cities. The same principle of self-assessment is also found in the north, particularly in Germany, but oral rather than written declarations were used longer there than in Italy.
farm of the borough	In England, the fixed payment that chartered cities owed to the king. Municipal authorities were responsible for collecting it.
fodrum	[Latin]. Payment initially deriving from a food rent taken by German kings as a seigniorial right over the Italian cities, but eventually passing to the city governments.
folkmoot	Public court in the early English cities.
forum	[Latin]. Market.
guild	Group of persons, generally bound by oath, who enjoy the right to regulate an aspect of their

corporate behaviour that poses special problems or concerns. Guilds assume many forms: they could link persons in the same or in several occupations, be dedicated to a saint and/or to charitable functions, be purely convivial associations, or have any combination of these characteristics.

Hanse [German]. A league, such as an interurban union or a merchant association. The word is often used alone to mean a league of north German cities that controlled most trade in the Baltic and also had offices in Norway, Russia, Flanders and England.

immunity A formal right to be exempt from incursion of officials holding the public *bannum*; and by extension, the territory covered by such a right. A territory under immunity could be governed by its lord without interference from the king.

jurés [French]. Officials of the sworn association of inhabitants of the town, to be distinguished from the *échevins*, who were officials of the town lord. In most cities of northern France and some in the eastern Low Countries, the *jurés* became a city council, sometimes replacing the order board of *échevins* but more often leaving it in existence while depriving it of its most important functions. The *jurés* are the equivalent of the German *Räte*. Somewhat later the council members of occupational guilds, whose function was to advise the guild dean, and of parishes were often called *jurés* or the equivalent word meaning 'sworn person' in another language.

libra [Latin]. *Lira*, plural *lire* [Italian]. Tax assessment based on the pound.

lineage A union of nuclear and extended families that may be linked by blood kinship but often are not.

magnates Persons of noble or aristocratic ancestry. Nonnoble persons were sometimes classified as magnates for political purposes. The term is used chiefly for the Italian cities.

mercanzia [Italian]. Office of the merchants' guild.

messuage House with surrounding land.

ministerials	Serfs, mainly in the cities of Germany and the Low Countries, who performed honourable services such as castle guard for their lord or had responsibilities in his household or bureaucracy, such as in his mint. Some ministerial families held fiefs and achieved knighthood.
mistery	Craft organisation.
murage	Tax levied on goods passing through the city gates, with the receipts intended for building or maintaining walls; used only for England.
pomerium	[Latin]. Central area of Roman city, sacred to the gods.
podestà	[Italian]. Administrative, police and judicial official in some Italian cities from the late twelfth century, eventually replacing the consuls as formal leader of the commune.
popolo	plural popoli [Italian]. Organisation, mainly of prosperous merchants, but with some craftspeople and magnates, that formed a political pressure group in many Italian cities in the thirteenth century. Originally all-inclusive and intended as a militia organisation, it became directed chiefly against the magnates after 1250 and particularly 1270. In some cities the popolo became a separate government for its members.
poorter	[Flemish]. See bourgeois.
port, portus	[Latin]. On the continent, a settlement of traders outside a fortification; in some places the term later referred by extension to the entire city. In England the port was a merchant settlement, sometimes but not always in a fortification, in which the Anglo-Saxon kings tried to centre commercial activity.
purveyance	The right to requisition provisions.
Rat	[German]. City council, formed in distinction to the scabini or Schöffen. Plural form Räte means councillors.
scabini	[Latin]. See échevins.
schepenen	[Flemish]. See échevins.
Schultheiss	[German]. Mayor or other chief magistrate of a village; lord's bailiff in a city.

seigneury	Right of lordship or by extension the territory under such a lordship.
Signoria	[Italian]. Chief governing body of an Italian city, usually a rotating council.
staple	Privilege of having the sole right to manufacture, sell, transport or provide a given commodity or service.
syndic	Proctor or advocate; members of some city councils, particularly in southern France were called syndics.
taille	[French]. Direct tax assessed on the wealth of the hearth.
tallage	Tax owed in England by serfs of the royal domain and by cities.
thegn	Landholding aristocrat in Anglo-Saxon England, but some townspeople had the rank of thegn.
valvassor	Rear vassal (vassal of someone who in turn was the vassal of another person).
vicus	plural *vici* [Latin]. Street, but sometimes with a connotation of trading settlement, particularly in cases where the German *Wik* becomes confounded with the Latin term.
Wik	[German]. Literally 'bay'. Unfortified settlement, often but not always outside a fortification, and generally given over to merchandising and sometimes crafts.

Suggestions for Further Reading

This book represents the distillation of some thirty-five years of professional preoccupation with urban development in medieval Europe. The subject is immense, and no single volume can hope to capture every nuance or exception. Although I have used some original documents in translation for purposes of illustration, the book is intended principally as a synthesis and comparison of scholarly literature. It is thus based essentially on urban monographs, relatively few of which are in English except for cities in the British Isles, and on scholarly articles. These suggestions to aid the student who wishes to explore particular topics in greater depth will concentrate on the limited literature in English, but the complexity of the topic precludes limiting it to that. This essay includes only authors and titles; complete citations can be found in the bibliography.

1. GENERAL TREATMENTS

The history of the medieval city is a chapter in the broader history of urban development. The series that includes the present volume will provide a general survey of urbanisation in five volumes from classical antiquity to the present. One companion volume, Christopher Friedrichs, *The Early Modern City*, has already appeared. The synthesis provided by Max Weber, *The City* remains extremely provocative. More general aspects of early stages of urbanisation are discussed in Gideon Sjoberg, *The Preindustrial City*. Paul Bairoch, *Cities and Economic Development*, takes a suggestive and global approach to urbanisation from the beginning of history to the present. Aspects of city planning and of the role of the city in a larger social environment are given in Lewis Mumford,

The City in History. City planning and architecture are also emphasised in Wolfgang Braunfels, *Urban Design in Western Europe*; Marc Girouard, *Cities and People*; James E. Vance, *The Continuing City*; and Josef W. Konvitz, *The Urban Millennium*. All are stronger on the modern period than on the Middle Ages. The eight-volume *International History of City Development* edited by E. A. Gutkind has much of interest to the medievalist, particularly on city plans. In *The Making of Urban Europe* Paul Hohenberg and Lynn Hollen Lees have provided an analysis of urbanisation that is of interest to medievalists but concentrates on the period since 1500. They analyse the impact of politics and nationality on two urban models: the city as the central place of an economic, administrative and cultural region, and cities in networks, providing links between their own regions and the outside world. Within the regions a hierarchy of cities develops, in a generally discernible rank–size pattern that some geographers, followed too rigidly by the historian and demographer Josiah Cox Russell in *Medieval Regions and Their Cities*, have suggested can be determined by formulas based on population and population rank within the region. Philip Abrams and E. A. Wrigley's edited work *Towns in Societies* has important articles.

Of general works dealing specifically with the early Middle Ages, Henri Pirenne's classic, *Medieval Cities. Their Origins and the Revival of Trade*, was the first significant summary of its topic to appear in English and can still be read with profit, although its interpretations are outdated. Edith Ennen's *The Medieval Town*, a translation of a book originally published in German, is a distinguished work by the doyenne of modern German historians of medieval urban life. It shows the author's intimate familiarity with the scholarly literature, particularly in German, and her interests in urban origins and medieval women. Unfortunately, it shares with most German work a hypersensitivity to juridical questions. Rodney Hilton's *English and French Towns* compares French and English urban life in general terms, focusing on the smaller centres and placing them into a Marxist framework of feudalism. Although it must be used with care and conflates the city with the town, it is a useful survey of the literature. Of general works not in English, Jacques Heers's *La ville au moyen age en occident: paysages, pouvoirs et conflits* reflects Heers's interest in questions of space utilisation and urban topography as well as his scholarly preoccupation with Italy. Yves Barel's Marxist analysis *La ville médiévale* has some useful insights.

Studies on particular topics in a Europe-wide context have value for comparative questions. On the general problem of urban origins M. W. Barley's edited work *European Towns. Their Archaeology and Early History* details archaeological excavations on urban sites throughout Europe;

despite its publication date of 1977, it is very useful. More current is H. B. Clarke and Anngret Simms, *The Comparative History of Urban Origins in Non-Roman Europe*. For founded towns, some of which developed into genuine cities, the best English work is Maurice Beresford, *New Towns of the Middle Ages*. Two general treatments of guilds have been published recently. Antony Black, *Guilds and Civil Society in European Political Thought from the Twelfth Century to the Present*, is theoretical, while Steven A. Epstein's *Wage Labor and Guilds in Medieval Europe* is an ambitious effort that is marred by questionable readings of documents and an uncertain focus. The best comprehensive work on the occupational guilds remains Sylvia L. Thrupp, 'The Gilds'.

2. FRANCE

The only survey of even a single aspect of French urbanisation in English is Charles Petit-Dutaillis's classic *The French Communes*. A fine survey of urbanisation in France is Georges Duby (ed.), *Histoire de la France urbaine*, whose first two volumes concern late antiquity and the Middle Ages. Of topical studies, Irving A. Agus' *Urban Civilization in Pre-Crusade Europe* studies city life in the early Middle Ages from the perspective of the Jewish *responsa* literature. André E. Guillerme, *The Age of Water* gives a provocative thesis concerning hydrographic problems in the cities of northern France. André Gouron, *La Réglementation des Métiers en Languedoc au Moyen Age* is the only general study of the French crafts and occupational guilds for the Middle Ages. Michel Mollat, *The Poor in the Middle Ages* contains considerable material on urban poverty, particularly in but not confined to France, but its major focus is later.

Several good monographs have been published in English on individual French cities, although most that merit further study are in French. Except for John H. Mundy, *Liberty and Political Power in Toulouse*, the English studies generally concern specific topics of urban history rather than providing a comprehensive treatment of one city, for example Richard Emery, *The Jews of Perpignan in the Thirteenth Century*. The studies in French that are most important for English readers are the first two volumes of the magisterial New History of Paris: Jacques Boussard, *De la fin du siège de 885–886 à la mort de Philippe Auguste* and Raymond Cazelles, *Paris de la fin du règne de Philippe Auguste à la mort de Charles V, 1223–1380*. Bronislaw Geremek, *Le salariat dans l'artisanat parisien aux XIIIe–XVe siècles* deals with the labourers and unemployed in the French capital. Elizabeth Chapin, *Les villes de foires de Champagne, des origines au début du XIVe siècle,* concerns the cities and their government as much as the fairs.

Other monographs on the French cities are also useful. Some are edited works, such as Alain Derville, *Histoire de Saint-Omer* and Louis Trenard, *Histoire de Lille.* A series of popular and nicely illustrated studies of individual cities has been published by the Privat firm of Toulouse. Important works include André Chédeville, *Chartres et ses campagnes;* Ghislaine Faber and Thierry Lochard, *Montpellier;* Kathryn L. Reyerson, *Business, Banking and Finance in Medieval Montpellier;* Charles Higounet, *Bordeaux pendant le Haut Moyen Age* and Yves Renouard, *Bordeaux sous les rois d'Angleterre.* Jean Schneider, *La Ville de Metz* is of fundamental importance.

3. ITALY

Early urbanisation in Italy as derived from Roman prototypes is explored in two works of Bryan Ward-Perkins: *Cities of Ancient Greece and Italy* and *From Classical Antiquity to the Middle Ages. Urban Public Building in Northern and Central Italy, AD 300–850.* The ecclesiastical topography of Rome has been studied by Richard Krautheimer in *Rome. Profile of a City* and its conclusions extended and compared to Milan and Constantinople in *Three Christian Capitals.* George W. Dameron, *Episcopal Power and Florentine Society, 1000–1320* is a fine recent study. Ferdinand Schevill, *Medieval and Renaissance Florence* is an older but still very useful study. John M. Najemy, *Corporatism and Consensus in Florentine Electoral Politics, 1280–1400* is an important prosopographical examination of the interaction of parties, guilds and lineages in staffing the city government. Robert Brentano's *Rome Before Avignon* concentrates more on the papacy and on intellectual and artistic developments than on the lay society of the city. Useful summaries that include urban material are Giovanni Tabacco, *The Struggle for Power in Medieval Italy. Structures of Political Rule;* Gino Luzzatto, *An Economic History of Italy;* John Larner, *Italy in the Age of Dante and Petrarch, 1216–1380;* and J. K. Hyde, *Society and Politics in Medieval Italy.* A sophisticated treatment of Rome in the central Middle Ages is Etienne Hubert, *Espace urbain et habitat à Rome.* Readers conversant with Italian should see Maria Ginatempo and Lucia Sandri, *L'Italia della città;* Gioacchino Volpe, *Medio Evo Italiano* and *Studi sulle istituzioni comunali a Pisa.*

On the smaller Italian cities, many of which were quite large by north European standards, a model work is Sarah R. Blanshei, *Perugia 1260–1340: Conflict and Change in a Medieval Italian Urban Society.* Siena is well served by Daniel Waley, *Siena and the Sienese in the Thirteenth Century*, and by the first sections of William Bowsky's two books: *The Finances of the Commune of Siena, 1287–1355* and *A Medieval Italian Commune. Siena Under the Nine, 1287–1355*. J. K. Hyde, *Padua in the Age of Dante*, is an important study of a large city that escaped much of the turmoil of the Tuscan centres. Daniel Waley's older study of *Mediaeval Orvieto. The Political History of an Italian City-State, 1157–1334* can be read with profit.

The early monographs of David Herlihy, *Pisa in the Early Renaissance* and *Medieval and Early Renaissance Pistoia*, deepened our understanding of the urban economy and its symbiotic relation with the countryside. Most of Jacques Heers's many studies remain in French, unfortunately including his monographs on Genoa and his recent study of the acquisition and allocation of public land in Bologna. Two that deal with the nature of the extended family and with the composition of urban factions and their political role in the cities are available in English: *Parties and Political Life in the Medieval West* and *Family Clans in the Middle Ages*.

Venice has been studied by Frederic C. Lane in a survey monograph, *Venice. A Maritime Republic*, but readers should also see Lane's collected papers, *Venice and History*. Richard MacKenney, *Tradesmen and Traders* deals with an often-neglected aspect of Venetian history, those outside the elite, although most of its material is later.

4. SPAIN

Little exists in English on the Spanish cities, most of which were small into the thirteenth century. Heath Dillard, *Daughters of the Reconquest*, uses urban charters to eludicate the situation of women in the frontier towns. The role of the militias of the frontier towns in conflicts with the Muslims is explored by James F. Powers, *A Society Organized for War. The Iberian Municipal Militias in the Central Middle Ages*, but his notion of urbanisation is very broad. Miguel-Angel Ladero-Quesnada, *La ciudad medieval* is part of Francisco Morales Padron's multivolume edited *Historia de Sevilla*.

5. GERMANY, AUSTRIA AND SWITZERLAND

Little on the German cities exists in English, but a notable exception is Paul Strait, *Cologne in the Twelfth Century*. Readers conversant with German can benefit from an immense literature. Several collected works in the series *Vorträge und Forschungen* of the Konstanzer Arbeitskreis für Mittelalterliche Geschichte are useful, particularly *Studien zu den Anfängen des europäischen Städtewesens* and *Untersuchungen zur gesellschaftlichen Struktur der mittelalterlichen Städte in Europa*. Several monographs in the Städteforschung series A published by the University of Münster have been of critical importance for this book. The most comprehensive treatments of early urban development in Germany remain two older classics: Edith Ennen, *Frühgeschichte der europäischen Stadt* and Hans Planitz, *Die deutsche Stadt im Mittelalter*. Carl Haase has published numerous scholarly articles in a three-volume collection, *Die Stadt des Mittelalters*. Of urban monographs in German, readers should see especially Ludwig Falck's two volume *Geschichte der Stadt Mainz*, which takes the story of the city to 1328.

6. LOW COUNTRIES

Given the importance of this region in the urban development of Europe, it is especially unfortunate that until recently little has been available in English except for Pirenne's works. There is a substantial literature in French, but most remains in Dutch. Considerable recent work has been published in English on Ghent, Flanders' largest city, but for a later period than that covered in this book. David Nicholas, *Medieval Flanders*, summarises Dutch and French work on the Flemish cities and provides a bibliography. A promising new series that links history with urban planning is the *Historische Stedenatlas van België* [Urban Historical Atlas of Belgium].

7. ENGLAND

Several syntheses of early city life in the British Isles are useful: R. A. Butlin, *The Development of the Irish Town*; for early constitutional developments, James Tait, *The Medieval English Borough*; Susan Reynolds, *An Introduction to the History of English Medieval Towns*; John Schofield and Alan Vince, *Medieval Towns* and Colin Platt, *The English Mediaeval Town* both discuss urban development from the archaeologist's perspective, an orientation conspicuous also in Platt's *Medieval Southampton*. R. H. Britnell's recent synthesis *The Commercialisation of English Society, 1000–1500* has much of value for urban history. A fine recent survey is Edward Miller and John Hatcher, *Medieval England. Towns, Commerce and Crafts*. Important studies of early medieval England have shown the precocity of urban development there, for example Martin Biddle, *Winchester in the Early Middle Ages*. Helen Clarke and Björn Ambrosiani, *Towns in the Viking Age* deals with early urban development in Britain as well as on the continent. More controversial are Richard Hodges, *Dark Age Economics* and Richard Hodges and Brian Hobley, *The Rebirth of Towns in the West*, which provide a fascinating reappraisal of the Pirenne thesis.

A work of fundamental importance is the ongoing series edited by M. D. Lobel, *Historic Towns. Maps and Plans of Towns and Cities in the British Isles*. Charles R. Young, *The English Borough and Royal Administration, 1130–1307*, discusses the role of the royal government in the early constitutional development of the boroughs. An edited collection of articles useful for this period is Richard Holt and Gervase Rosser, *The Medieval Town*.

Several fine monographs on English cities have appeared within the past decade: Margaret Bonney, *Lordship and the Urban Community. Durham and Its Overlords, 1250–1540*; A. E. Brown, *The Growth of Leicester*; Robert S. Gottfried, *Bury St. Edmunds and the Urban Crisis*; and Gervase Rosser, *Medieval Westminster*. Francis Hill, *Medieval Lincoln* can still be read with profit. William Urry, *Canterbury under the Angevin Kings* provides important insight on changes in English urbanisation immediately after the Norman Conquest. Derek Keene's monumental *Survey of Medieval Winchester* is important both for its methodology and its conclusions.

London's growth so outstripped the other English cities that it became a depressant on them. The capital has been the subject of a vast literature. Christopher N. L. Brooke and Gillian Keir, *London 800–1216. The Shaping of a City* has much of value but is marred by a diffuse style and an unsophisticated effort to compare English and continental developments. The next period is well served by Gwyn A. Williams, *Medieval London. From Commune to Capital*, a riveting account of social change and political rivalries during the thirteenth century. Williams' work should be supplemented by the first chapters of Pamela Nightingale, *A Medieval Mercantile Company. The Grocers of Medieval London*.

Abbreviations

	Thirteenth Century. 2 vols continuously paginated. BAR International Series 255. Oxford: British Archaeological Reports, 1985.
CS	Barbara A. Hanawalt and Kathryn L. Reyerson (eds). *City and Spectacle in Medieval Europe.* Minneapolis: University of Minnesota Press, 1994.
EcHR	*Economic History Review.*
ECI	Renato Bordone and Jörg Jarnut (eds). *L'Evoluzione delle città italiane nell' XI secolo.* Annali dell'Istituto storico italo-germanico. Quaderno 25. Bologna: Il Mulino, 1988.
EHR	*English Historical Review.*
FC	*Finances et comptabilités urbaines du XIIIe au XVIe siècle. Finaciën en boekhouding der steden van de XIIIe tot de XIVe eeuw.* Brussels: Pro Civitate, 1964.
FSE	Werner Besch *et al.* (eds). *Die Stadt in der europäischen Geschichte. Festschrift Edith Ennen.* Bonn: Ludwig Rohrscheid, 1972.
GTG	Hans Conrad Peyer (ed.). *Gastfreundschaft, Taverne und Gasthaus im Mittelalter.* Munich and Vienna: Oldenbourg, 1983.
HFU	Georges Duby (ed.). *Histoire de la France urbaine. 1. La ville antique. Des origines au IXe siècle. 2. La ville médiévale. Des Carolingiens à la Renaissance* (Paris: Editions du Seuil, 1980).
HZ	*Historische Zeitschrift.*
IC	A. H. Hourani and S. M. Stern (eds). *The Islamic City. A Colloquium.* Papers on Islamic History, 1. Philadelphia: University of Pennsylvania Press, 1970.
JMH	*The Journal of Medieval History.*
KRE	*Köln, das Reich und Europa. Abhandlungen über weiträumige Verflechtungen der Stadt Köln in Politik, Recht und Wirtschaft im Mittelalter.* Mitteilungen aus dem Stadtarchiv von Köln, 60. Cologne: Paul Neubner, 1971.
LS	*Das Leben in der Stadt des Spätmittelalters.* Internationaler Kongress Krems an der Donau 20. bis 23. September 1976. Veröffentlichungen des Instituts für mittelalterlichen Realienkunde Österreichs, no. 2. Österreichsche Akademie der Wissenschaften, Phil.-Hist. Klasse, Sitzungsberichte, 325. Vienna: Verlat der österreichischen Akademie der Wissenschaften, 1977.
LUR	*Les Libertés urbaines et rurales du XIe au XIVe siècle. Vrijheden in de stad en op het platteland van de XIe tot de XIVe eeuw.* Colloque International, Spa 5–8 IX 1966. *Actes. Handelingen.* Brussels: Pro Civitate, 1968.

MA	*Le Moyen Age.*
MT	Richard Holt and Gervase Rosser (eds). *The Medieval Town. A Reader in English Urban History, 1200–1540.* London: Longman, 1990.
OT	Thomas W. Blomquist and Maureen F. Mazzaoui (eds). *The "Other Tuscany".* Essays in the History of Lucca, Pisa, and Siena during the Thirteenth, Fourteenth, and Fifteenth Centuries. Kalamazoo, Michigan: Medieval Institute Publications, 1994.
PP	*Past and Present.*
PT	M. W. Barley (ed.). *The Plans and Topography of Medieval Towns in England and Wales.* CBA Research Report #14. N.P.: Council for British Archaeology, 1976.
PTME	Jean-Marie Duvosquel and Erik Thoen (eds). *Peasants and Townsmen in Medieval Europe. Studia in honorem Adriaan Verhulst.* Ghent: Snoeck-Ducaju en Zoon, 1995.
PU	*Le Paysage urbain au Moyen Age.* Actes du XIe Congrès des historians médiévistes de l'enseignement supérieur. Lyon: Presses Universitaires de Lyon, 1981.
SAES	*Studien zu den Anfängen des europäischen Städtewesens.* Vorträge und Forschungen herausgegeben vom Konstanzer Arbeitskreis für mittelalterliche Geschichte, 4. Constance and Lindau: Jan Thorbecke, 1958.
SH	Friedrich Vittinghoff (ed.). *Stadt und Herrschaft. Römische Kaiserzeit und hohes Mittelalter.* Historische Zeitschrift, Beiheft 7 (neue Folge). Munich: R. Oldenbourg, 1982.
SLL	Riccardo Francovich and Ghislaine Noyé (eds). *La Storia dell'Alto Medioevo italiano (VI–X secolo) alla luce dell'archeologia.* Convegno Internazionale (Siena, 2–6 dicembre 1992). Florence: Edizioni all'Insegna del Giglio, 1994.
SMOE	Jean-Claude Maire Vigueur (ed.). *D'une ville à l'autre: Structures matérielles et organisation de l'espace dans les villes européennes (XIIIe–XVIe) siècle.* Actes du Colloque organisé par l'Ecole française de Rome avec le concours de l'Université de Rome (Rome 1er–4 décembre 1986). Rome: Ecole Française de Rome, 1989.
SS	Bernhard Töpfer (ed.). *Stadt und Städtebürgertum in der deutschen Geschichte des 13. Jahrhunderts.* Berlin: Akademie Verlag, 1976.
SSt	Bernhard Töpfer (ed.). *Städte und Ständestaat. Zur Rolls der Städte bei der Entwicklung der Ständesverfassung in europäischen Staaten vom 13. bis zum 15. Jahrhundert.* Berlin: Akademie Verlag, 1980.

Abbreviations

Stoob FS   Helmut Jäger, Franz Petri and Heinz Quirin (eds). *Civitatum Communitas. Studien zum europäischen Städtewesen. Festschrift Heinz Stoob zum 65. Geburtstag.* Cologne and Vienna: Böhlau, 1984. 2 vols Städteforschung 19, 21.

Strayer FS   *Order and Innovation in the Middle Ages: Essays in Honor of Joseph R. Strayer.* Princeton: Princeton University Press, 1976.

TRHS   Royal Historical Society, London. *Transactions.*

TUVC   *Topografia urbana e vita cittadina nell'alto medioevo in occidente.* 26 aprile–1 maggio 1973. Settimane di Studio del Centro Italiano di Studi sull'Alto Medioevo, 21. Spoleto: Presso la Sede del Centro, 1973.

UAB   Schofield, John, and Roger Leech (eds). *Urban Archaeology in Britain.* Research Report 61. London: Council for British Archaeology, 1987.

UGS   *Untersuchungen zur gesellschaftlichen Struktur der mittelalterlichen Städte in Europa.* Reichenau-Vorträge 1963–1964. Vorträge und Forschungen herausgegeben vom Konstanzer Arbeitskreis für mittelalterliche Geschichte, 11. Constance and Stuttgart: Jan Thorbecke, 1966.

USEE   Barisa Krekic (ed.). *Urban Society of Eastern Europe in Premodern Times.* Berkeley and Los Angeles: University of California Press, 1987.

Bibliography

Abrams, Philip, and E. A. Wrigley (eds). *Towns in Societies. Essays in Economic History and Historical Sociology.* Cambridge: Cambridge University Press, 1978.

Abulafia, David, Michael Franklin and Miri Rubin (eds). *Church and City 1000–1500. Essays in honour of Christopher Brooke.* Cambridge: Cambridge University Press, 1992.

Addyman, P. V. 'York and Canterbury as ecclesiastical centres'. In Barley, *European Towns*, 499–509.

Agus, Irving A. *Urban Civilization in Pre-Crusade Europe.* 2 vols. New York: Yeshiva University Press, 1968.

Algemene Geschiedenis der Nederlanden. 2nd ed. Utrecht: Fibula–Van Dishoeck, 1982.

Allmand, Christopher. 'Taxation in medieval England: the example of murage'. In Bourin, *Villes*, 223–30.

Ambrosiani, Björn. 'Urban archaeology in Sweden'. In Barley, *European Towns*, 103–26.

Ammann, Hektor, 'Vom Städtewesen Spaniens und Westfrankreichs im Mittelalter'. *SAES*, 105–50.

Anderson, Bonnie S., and Judith P. Zinsser. *A History of Their Own. Women in Europe from Prehistory to the Present.* 1. New York: Harper and Row, 1988.

Andersson, Hans. *Urbanisierte Ortschaften und lateinische Terminologie. Studien zur Geschichte des nordeuropäischen Städtewesens vor 1350.* Göteborg: Kungl. Vetenkaps- och Vitterhets-Samhället, 1971.

Ascheri, Mario. 'Siena in the fourteenth century: state, territory and culture'. *OT*, 163–97.

Aston, Michael, and James Bond. *The Landscape of Towns.* Gloucester: Alan Sutton, 1987.

Bibliography

Attreed, Lorraine. 'Arbitration and the growth of urban liberties in late medieval England'. *Journal of British Studies* 31 (1992): 205–35.

Bachrach, Bernard S., and David Nicholas (eds). *Law, Custom, and the Social Fabric in Medieval Europe. Essays in Honor of Bryce Lyon.* Kalamazoo, Michigan: Medieval Institute Publications, 1990.

Bairoch, Paul. *Cities and Economic Development. From the Dawn of History to the Present.* Translated by Christopher Braider. Chicago: University of Chicago Press, 1988.

Bairoch, Paul, Jean Batou and Pierre Chèvre. *La Population des villes européennes. Banque de données et analyse sommaire des resultats. 800–1850. The Population of European Cities. Data Bank and Short Summary of Results.* Geneva: Droz, 1988.

Baker, Robert L. 'The government of Calais in 1363'. *Strayer FS,* 207–14.

Baldwin, John W. *The Government of Philip Augustus. Foundations of French Royal Power in the Middle Ages.* Berkeley and Los Angeles: University of California Press, 1986.

Baldwin, John W. *The Scholastic Culture of the Middle Ages, 1000–1300.* Lexington, Mass.: D. C. Heath, 1971.

Balestracci, Duccio. 'From development to crisis: changing urban structures in Siena between the thirteenth and fifteenth centuries'. *OT,* 199–213.

Balestracci, Duccio. 'Immigrazione e morfologia urbana nella Toscana bassomedievale'. *SMOE,* 87–105.

Ballard, Adolphus (ed.). *British Borough Charters, 1042–1216.* Cambridge: Cambridge University Press, 1913.

Baratier, Edouard (ed.). *Histoire de Marseille.* Toulouse: Privat, 1973.

Barel, Yves. *La ville médiévale. Système sociale. Système urbain.* Grenoble: Presses Universitaires de Grenoble, 1977.

Barral I Altet, Xavier (ed.). *Artistes, Artisans et Production artistique au Moyen Age. Colloque international.* Paris: Picard, 1986.

Barley, M. W. (ed.). *European Towns. Their Archaeology and Early History.* London: Council for British Archaeology by Academic Press, 1977.

Barley, M. W. (ed.). *The Plans and Topography of Medieval Towns in England and Wales.* CBA Research Report #14. N.P.: Council for British Archaeology, 1976.

Barley, M. W. 'Town defences in England and Wales after 1066'. *PT,* 57–71.

Barry, T. B. (ed.). *The Archaeology of Medieval Ireland.* London: Methuen, 1987.

Bassett, Steven (ed.). *Death in Towns. Urban Responses to the Dying and the Dead, 1000–1600.* Leicester: Leicester University Press, 1992.

Beaumanoir, Philippe de. *The* Coutumes de Beauvaisis *of Philippe de Beaumanoir.* Translated by F. R. P. Akehurst. Philadelphia: University of Pennsylvania Press, 1992.

Bechtold, Klaus D. *Zunftbürgerschaft und Patriziat. Studien zur Sozialgeschichte der Stadt Konstanz im 14. und 15. Jahrhundert.* Sigmaringen: Jan Thorbecke, 1981.

Bedos-Rezac, Brigitte. 'Civic liturgies and urban records in northern France'. *CS*, 34–55.

Bender, Thomas (ed.). *The University and the City. From Medieval Origins to the Present.* New York: Oxford University Press, 1988.

Benevolo, Leonardo. *The History of the City.* Translated by Geoffrey Culverwell. Cambridge, Mass.: MIT Press, 1980.

Bensch, Stephen P. *Barcelona and Its Rulers, 1096–1291.* Cambridge: Cambridge University Press, 1995.

Beresford, Maurice. *New Towns of the Middle Ages. Town Plantation in England, Wales, and Gascony.* New York: Frederick A. Praeger, 1967.

Berghans, H. P. 'Die Münzpolitik der deutschen Städte im Mittelalter'. *FC*, 75–84.

Berthold, Brigitte. 'Sozialökonomische Differenzierung und innerstädtische Auseinandersetzungen in Köln im 13. Jahrhundert'. In Töpfer, *Stadt und Städtebürgertum*, 229–87.

Besch, Werner *et al.* (eds). *Die Stadt in der europäischen Geschichte. Festschrift Edith Ennen.* Bonn: Ludwig Rohrscheid, 1972.

Biddle, Martin. 'The development of the Saxon town'. *TUVC*, 203–30.

Biddle, Martin. 'The evolution of towns: planned towns before 1066'. *PT*, 19–32.

Biddle, Martin. 'Towns'. In David M. Wilson (ed.), *The Archaeology of Anglo-Saxon England.* London: Methuen, 1976, 99–150.

Biddle, Martin (ed.). *Winchester in the Early Middle Ages. An Edition and Discussion of the Winton Domesday.* Oxford: Clarendon Press, 1976.

Billot, Claudine. *Chartres à la fin du Moyen Age.* Paris: Editions de l'Ecole des Hautes Etudes en Sciences Sociales, 1987.

Birnbaum, Henrik. 'Kiev, Novgorod, Moscow: three varieties of urban society in east Slavic territory'. *USEE*, 1–62.

Birnbaum, Henrik. *Studies in Early Slavic Civilization.* Munich: Wilhelm Fink, 1981.

Bischoff, Johannes. 'Die Stadtherrschaft des 14. Jahrhunderts im ostfränkischen Städtedreieck Nürnberg-Bamberg-Coburg-Bayreuth'. In Rausch, *Stadt und Stadtherr*, 97–124.

Bisson, T. N. *The Medieval Crown of Aragon. A Short History.* Oxford: Clarendon Press, 1986.

Bibliography

Black, Antony. *Guilds and Civil Society in European Political Thought from the Twelfth Century to the Present.* Ithaca: Cornell University Press, 1984.

Blair, John, and Nigel Ramsey (eds). *English Medieval Industries. Craftsmen, Techniques, Products.* London: Hambledon Press, 1991.

Bland, A. F., P. A. Brown and R. H. Tawney (eds). *English Economic History. Select Documents.* London: G. Bell and Sons, 1914.

Blanshei, Sarah Rubin. *Perugia 1260–1340: Conflict and Change in a Medieval Italian Urban Society.* Transactions of the American Philosophical Society, n.s. 66, part 2. Philadelphia: American Philosophical Society, 1976.

Blockmans, F. *Het Gentsche Stadspatriciaat tot omstreeks 1302.* Antwerp: De Sikkel, 1938.

Blockmans, W. *Een Middeleeuwse Vendetta. Gent 1300.* Houten: De Haan, 1987.

Blockmans, W. 'Vers une société urbanisée'. In Els Witte (ed.), *Histoire de Flandre des origines à nos jours.* Brussels: La Renaissance du Livre, 1983.

Blom, Grethe Anthen. 'Der Ursprung der Gilden in Norwegen und ihre Entwicklung in den Städten während des Mittelalters'. In Friedland, *Gilde,* 5–27.

Bocchi, Francesca. *Attraverso le città italiane nel medioevo.* Casalecchio di Reno: Grafis Edizioni, 1987.

Bocchi, Francesca. 'Développement urbain de Ferrare'. *Cahiers Bruxellois* 20 (1975): 64–77.

Bocchi, Francesca. 'Le développement urbanistique oriental de Bologne (Xe–XIIe siècle)'. *PTME,* 135–50.

Bolton, Brenda. '"Except the lord keep the city": towns in the papal states at the turn of the twelfth century'. In Abulafia, *Church and City,* 119–218.

Bonney, Margaret. *Lordship and the Urban Community. Durham and Its Overlords, 1250–1540.* Cambridge: Cambridge University Press, 1990.

Bordone, Renato, and Jörg Jarnut (eds). *L'Evoluzione delle città italiane nell' XI secolo.* Annali dell'Istituto storico italo-germanico. Quaderno 25. Bologna: Il Mulino, 1988.

Bosl, Karl (ed.). *Die mittelalterliche Stadt in Bayern.* Munich: C. H. Beck, 1974.

Bosl, Karl. 'Die Sozialstruktur der mittelalterlichen Residenz- und Fernhandelsstadt Regensburg. Die Entwicklung ihres Bürgertums vom 9.–14. Jahrhundert'. *UGS,* 93–213.

Bosl, Karl. *Die wirtschaftliche und gesellschaftliche Entwicklung des Augsburger Bürgertums vom 10. bis zum 14. Jahrhundert.* Munich: Bayerische Akademie der Wissenschaften, 1969.

Bourin, Monique (ed.). *Villes, bonnes villes, cités et capitales. Etudes d'histoire urbaine (XIIe–XVIIIe siècle) offertes à Bernard Chevalier*. Tours: Université de Tours, 1989.

Boussard, Jacques. *Nouvelle Histoire de Paris. De la fin du siège de 885–886 à la mort de Philippe Auguste*. Paris: Hachette, 1976.

Bowsky, William M. *The Finances of the Commune of Siena, 1287–1355*. Oxford: Clarendon Press, 1970.

Bowsky, William M. 'The medieval commune and internal violence: police power and public safety in Siena, 1287–1355'. *American Historical Review* 73 (1967): 1–17.

Bowsky, William M. *A Medieval Italian Commune. Siena Under the Nine, 1287–1355*. Berkeley: University of California Press, 1981.

Boyer, Marjorie N. 'Working at the bridge site in late medieval France'. In Barral I Altet, *Artistes*, 217–27.

Bradley, John. 'Planned Anglo-Norman towns in Ireland'. *CHUO*, 411–67.

Brandl-Ziegert, Renate. 'Die Sozialstruktur der bayerischen Bischofs- und Residenzstädte Passau, Freising, Landshut und Ingolstadt. Die Entwicklung des Bürgertums vom 9. bis zum 13. Jahrhundert. In Bosl, *Mittelalterliche Stadt in Bayern*, 18–127.

Braunfels, Wolfgang. *Urban Design in Western Europe. Regime and Architecture, 900–1900*. Translated by Kenneth J. Northcott. Chicago: University of Chicago Press, 1988.

Brentano, Robert. *Rome Before Avignon. A Social History of Thirteenth-Century Rome*. New York: Basic Books, 1974.

Bridbury, A. R. *Medieval English Clothmaking: an Economic Survey*. London: Heinemann, 1982.

Britnell, R. H. *The Commercialisation of English Society, 1000–1500*. Cambridge: Cambridge University Press, 1993.

Britnell, R. H. 'England and northern Italy in the early fourteenth century: the economic contrasts'. *TRHS*, ser. 5, 39 (1989): 167–83.

Brogiolo, Gian Pietro. 'La città longobarda nel periodo della conquista (569–in. VII)'. *SLL*, 555–66.

Brooke, Christopher N. L., and Gillian Keir. *London 800–1216. The Shaping of a City*. Berkeley and Los Angeles: University of California Press, 1975.

Brooke, Christopher N. L. 'The medieval town as an ecclesiastical centre: general survey'. In Barley, *European Towns*, 459–74.

Brooks, N. P. 'The ecclesiastical topography of early medieval Canterbury'. In Barley, *European Towns*, 487–98.

Brown, A. E. (ed.). *The Growth of Leicester*. Leicester: Leicester University Press, 1970.

Bibliography

Brühl, C. R. 'The town as a political centre: general survey'. In Barley, *European Towns*, 419–30.

Bullough, D. A. 'Social and economic structure and topography in the early medieval city'. *TUVC*, 351–99.

Bullough, D. A. 'Urban change in early medieval Italy: the example of Pavia'. *Papers of the British School at Rome*, 34 (n.s. 21) (1966): 82–130.

Bunge, F. G. von. *Die Stadt Riga im dreizehnten und vierzehnten Jahrhundert. Geschichte, Verfassung und Rechtszustand*. Leipzig, 1878, reprinted Amsterdam, E. J. Bonset, 1968.

Bur, Michel (ed.). *Histoire de Laon et du Laonnais*. Toulouse: Privat, 1987.

Busch, Ralf. 'Die Wasserversorgung des Mittelalters und der frühen Neuzeit in norddeutschen Städten'. In *Stadt im Wandel* 4: 301–15.

Butler, Lawrence. 'The evolution of towns: planted towns after 1066'. *PT*, 32–47.

Butler, R. M. 'Late Roman town walls in Gaul'. *The Archaeological Journal* 116 (1959): 25–42.

Butler, W. F. *The Lombard Communes. A History of the Republics of North Italy*. London: T. Fisher Unwin, 1906, reprinted Westport, Conn.: Greenwood Press, 1969.

Butlin, R. A. (ed.). *The Development of the Irish Town*. Totowa, N.J.: Rowman and Littlefield, 1977.

Büttner, Heinrich. 'Studien zum frühmittelalterlichen Städtewesen in Frankreich, vornehmlich im Loire- und Rhonegebiet'. *SAES*, 151–89.

Caenegem, R. C. van. 'Galbert of Bruges on serfdom, prosecution of crime, and constitutionalism (1127–28). In Bachrach and Nicholas, *Law, Custom, and the Social Fabric*, 89–112.

Cagiano de Azevedo, Michelangelo. 'Aspetti urbanistici delle città altomedievali'. *TUVC*, 641–77.

Cahen, Claude. 'Y a-t-il des corporations professionnelles dans le monde musulman classique? Quelques notes et réflexions'. *IC*, 51–63.

Cardini, Franco. 'Intellectuals and culture in twelfth- and thirteenth-century Italy'. *CC*, 13–30.

Carpentier, Elisabeth. *Une ville devent la peste. Orvieto et la Peste Noire de 1348*. Paris: SEVPEN, 1962.

Carrère, Claude. *Barcelone. Centre économique à l'époque des difficultés, 1380–1462*. 2 vols. Paris and The Hague: Mouton, 1967.

Carter, F. W. *Trade and Urban Development in Poland: An Economic Geography of Cracow, from Its Origins to 1795*. Cambridge: Cambridge University Press, 1994.

Castagnetti, Andrea. 'Appunti per una storia sociale e politica delle città della Marca Veronese-Trevigiano (secoli XI–XIV)'. In Elze and Fasoli, *Aristocrazia cittadina*, 41–77.

Castaldo, André. *Seigneur, villes et pouvoir royal en Languedoc: le consulat médiéval d'Agde (XIIIe–XIVe siècles)*. Paris: A. and J. Picard, 1974.

Cazelles, Raymond. *Paris de la fin du régne de Philippe Auguste à la mort de Charles V, 1223–1380*. Paris: Hachette, 1972.

I Ceti dirigenti dell'età comunale nei secoli XII e XIII. Comitato di studi sulla storia dei ceti dirigenti in Toscana. Atti del II Convegno, Firenze, 14–15 dicembre 1979. Pisa: Pacini, 1982.

Chapin, Elisabeth. *Les villes de foires de Champagne des origines au début du XIVe siècle*. Paris: Honoré Champion, 1937.

Charles, J. L. *La ville de Saint-Trond au Moyen Age. Des origines à la fin du XIVe siècle*. Bibliothèque de la Faculté de Philosophie et Lettres de l'Université de Liège, fasc. 173. Paris: Société d'Edition 'Les Belles Lettres', 1965.

Chédeville, André. *Chartres et ses campagnes (XIe–XIIIe s.)*. Paris: Klincksieck, 1973.

Chédeville, André. 'De la cité à la ville'. *HFU*, 2: 29–181.

Chédeville, André (ed.). *Histoire de Chartres et du pays chartrain*. Toulouse: Privat, 1983.

Chew, Helena M., and Martin Weinbaum (eds). *The London Eyre of 1244*. London: London Record Society, 1970.

Chittolini, Giorgio. 'The Italian city-state and its territory'. In Molho *et al.*, *City States*, 589–602.

Ciampoltrini, Giulio. 'Città "frammentate" e città-fortezza. Storie urbane della Toscana centro-settrionale fra Teodosio e Carlo Magno'. *SLL*, 615–33.

Cipolla, Carlo M. *Before the Industrial Revolution. European Society and Economy, 1000–1700*. 2nd ed. New York: Norton, 1980.

La Città nell'alto medioevo. Settimane di Studio del Centro Italiano di Studi sull'Alto Medioevo, 6. Spoleto: Presso la Sede del Centro, 1959.

Clarke, H. B., and Anngret Simms (eds). *The Comparative History of Urban Origins in Non-Roman Europe. Ireland, Wales, Denmark, Germany, Poland and Russia from the Ninth to the Thirteenth Century*. 2 vols continuously paginated. BAR International Series 255. Oxford: British Archaeological Reports, 1985.

Clarke, H. B., and Anngret Simms. 'Towards a comparative history of urban origins'. *CHUO*, 669–714.

Clarke, Helen, and Björn Ambrosiani. *Towns in the Viking Age*. New York: St. Martin's Press, 1991.

Claude, Dietrich. *Die byzantinische Stadt im 6. Jahrhundert*. Byzantinisches Archiv, Heft 13. Munich: C. H. Beck, 1969.

Claude, Dietrich. *Topographie und Verfassung der städte Bourges und Poitiers bis in das 11. Jahrhundert*. Historische Studien, Heft 360. Lübeck and Hamburg: Matthiesen, 1960.

Clune, George. *The Medieval Gild System*. Dublin: Browne and Nolan, 1943.

Cogiano de Azevedo, Michelangelo. 'Aspetti urbanistici delle ciltà alto-medievali'. *TUVC*, 641–77.

Cohen, Mark R. *Under Crescent and Cross. The Jews in the Middle Ages*. Princeton: Princeton University Press, 1994.

Compagni, Dino. *Chronicle of Florence*. Translated, with an introduction and notes, by Daniel E. Bornstein. Philadelphia: University of Pennsylvania Press, 1986.

Corfield, Penelope J., and Derek Keene (eds). *Work in Towns 850–1850*. Leicester: Leicester University Press, 1990.

Coulet, Noel. 'Quartiers et communauté urbaine en Provence (XIIIe–XVe siècles)'. In Bourin, *Villes*, 351–9.

Cunliffe, Barry. *The City of Bath*. New Haven: Yale University Press, 1986.

Czacharowski, Antoni. 'Forschungen über die soziale Schichten in den Städten des deutschen Ordenslandes im 13. und 14. Jahrhundert'. *BSS*, 119–29.

Czok, Karl. 'Die Bürgerkämpfe in Süd- und Westdeutschland im 14. Jahrhundert'. In Haase, *Stadt des Mittelalters* 3: 303–44.

Dameron, George W. *Episcopal Power and Florentine Society, 1000–1320*. Cambridge, Mass.: Harvard University Press, 1991.

Darby, H. C. *Domesday England*. Cambridge: Cambridge University Press, 1977.

Deisser-Nagels, Francine. 'Valenciennes, ville carolingienne'. *MA* 68 (1962): 51–90.

Dejevsky, N. J. 'Novgorod: the origins of a Russian town'. In Barley, *European Towns*, 391–403.

Delaney, C. J. 'The present state of Welsh urban archaeology'. In Barley, *European Towns*, 35–46.

De Roover, Raymond. 'Les comptes comonunaux et la comptabilité communale de la ville de Bruges au XIVe siècle'. *FC*, 86–102.

Derville, Alain (ed.). *Histoire de Saint-Omer*. Lille: Presses Universitaires de Lille, 1981.

Derville, Alain. 'Les origines de Gravelines et de Calais'. *Revue du nord*, 66 (1984): 1051–69.

De Soignie, Raphael R. 'The fairs of Nîmes: evidence on their function, importance, and demise'. *Strayer FS*, 195–205.

Desportes, Françoise. 'Droit économique et police des métiers en France du Nord (milieu du XIIIe–début du XVe siècle'. *RN* 63 (1981): 321–36.

Desportes, Pierre. *Reims et les Rémois aux XIIIe et XIVe siècles*. Paris: A. and J. Picard, 1979.

Dez, Gaston. *Histoire de Poitiers*. Poitiers: Société des Antiquaires de l'Ouest, 1969.

Dickinson, Robert E. *The West European City. A Geographical Interpretation*. 2nd ed. London: Routledge and Kegan Paul, 1961.

Dickstein-Bernard, C. 'Activité économique et développement urbain à Bruxelles (XIIIe–XVe siècles)'. *Cahiers Bruxellois* 24 (1979): 52–62.

Diermeier, Ulf. 'Le condizioni materiali dell'esistenza nelle città tedesche del Basso Medioevo: ambiente esterno, reddito, consumi'. In Elze and Fasoli, *Aristocrazia cittadina*, 79–122.

Diestelkamp, Bernhard (ed.). *Beiträge zum hochmittelalterlichen Städtewesen*. Cologne and Vienna: Böhlau, 1982. Stadtforschungen A/11.

Diestelkamp, Bernhard. 'König und Städte in salischer und staufischer Zeit. Regnum Teutonicum'. *SH*, 247–97.

Dilcher, Gerhard. 'I Comuni italiani come movimento sociale e forma giuridica'. *ECI*, 71–98.

Dillard, Heath. *Daughters of the Reconquest. Women in Castilian Town Society, 1100–1300*. Cambridge: Cambridge University Press, 1984.

Doherty, Charles. 'The monastic town in early medieval Ireland'. *CHUO*, 45–75.

Doll, Anton. 'Zur Frühgeschichte der Stadt Speyer', *Mitteilungen des historischen Vereins der Pfalz* 52 (1952): 133–200.

Dollinger, Philippe. 'Der Aufschwung der oberrheinischen Bischofsstädte in salischer Zeit (1025–1125)'. *BHS*, 134–48.

Dollinger, Philippe. *The German Hansa*. Stanford: Stanford University Press, 1970.

Dollinger, Philippe (ed.). *Histoire de l'Alsace*. Toulouse: Privat, 1970.

Dollinger-Léonard, Yvette. 'De la cité romaine à la ville médiévale dans la région de la Moselle et la Haute Meuse'. *SAES*, 195–226.

Doren, Alfredo. *Le Arti Fiorentine*. 2 vols. Florence: Felice Le Monnier, 1918.

Du Boulay, F. R. H. *Germany in the Later Middle Ages*. London: Athlone Press, 1983.

Duby, Georges. *The Early Growth of the European Economy. Warriors and Peasants from the Seventh to the Twelfth Century*. Ithaca: Cornell University Press, 1974.

Duby, Georges (ed.). *Histoire de la France urbaine. I. La ville antique. Des origines au IXe siècle. II. La ville médiévale. Des Carolingiens à la Renaissance*. Paris: Editions du Seuil, 1980.

Duby, Georges. 'Les villes du sud-est de la Gaule du VIIIe au XIe siècle'. *CAM*, 231–58.

Bibliography

Duvosquel, Jean-Marie, and Erik Thoen (eds). *Peasants and Townsmen in Medieval Europe. Studia in honorem Adriaan Verhulst.* Ghent: Snoeck-Ducaju en Zoon, 1995.

Dyer, Chris. 'Recent developments in early medieval urban history and archaeology in England'. In Genecke and Shaw, *Urban Historical Geography,* 69–80.

Dyer, Christopher. *Standards of Living in the Later Middle Ages. Social change in England, c. 1200–1520.* Cambridge: Cambridge University Press, 1989.

Ebel, Wilhelm. 'Lübisches Recht im Ostseeraum'. In Haase, *Stadt des Mittelalters* 2: 255–80.

Eggert, Wolfgang. 'Städtenetz und Stadtherrenpolitik. Ihre Herausbildung im Bereich des späteren Württenberg während des 13. Jahrhunderts'. *SS,* 108–228.

El-Adi, Saleh Ahmad. 'The foundation of Baghdad'. *IC,* 87–101.

Elze, Reinhard, and Gina Fasoli (eds). *Aristocrazia cittadina e ceti popolari nel tardo Medioevo in Italia e in Germania.* Bologna: Il Mulino, 1984.

Emery, Richard W. *The Jews of Perpignan in the Thirteenth Century. An Economic Study Based on Notarial Records.* New York: Columbia University Press, 1959.

Engel, Evamaria. 'Beziehungen zwischen Königtum und Städtebürgertum unter Wilhelm von Holland (1247–1256)'. *SS,* 63–107.

Engel, Evamaria. 'Frühe Ständische Aktivitäten des Städtebürgertum im Reich und in der Territorien bis zur Mitte des 14. Jahrhunderts'. *SSt,* 13–58.

Ennen, Edith. 'The early history of the European town: a retrospective view'. *CHUO,* 3–14.

Ennen, Edith. 'Erzbischof und Stadtgemeinde in Köln bis zur Schlacht von Wörringen (1288)'. In Petri, *Bischofs- und Kathedralstädte,* 27–46.

Ennen, Edith. 'Die europäische Stadt'. In Meckseper, *Stadt im Wandel* 3: 13–28.

Ennen, Edith. 'Europäische Züge der mittelalterlichen Kölner Stadtgeschichte'. *KRE,* 1–47.

Ennen, Edith. 'Die Forschungsproblematik Bürger und Stadt – von der Terminologie her gesehen'. *BSL,* 9–26.

Ennen, Edith. *Frühgeschichte der europäischen Stadt.* Bonn: Ludwig Röhrscheid, 1953.

Ennen, Edith. *The Medieval Town.* Amsterdam: North Holland, 1979, translated from her *Die europäische Stadt des Mittelalters.* Göttingen: Vandenhoeck and Ruprecht, 1972.

Ennen, Edith. 'Das Städtewesen Nordwestdeutschlands von der fränkischen bis zur salischen Zeit'. In Haase, *Stadt des Mittelalters,* 139–95.

Ennen, Edith. 'Zur Städtepolitik der Eleanore von Aquitanien'. *Stoob FS*, 42–55.

Ennen, Edith and Dietrich Höroldt. *Kleine Geschichte der Stadt Bonn*. Bonn: Wilhelm Stollfuss, 1967.

Epstein, Steven. 'Labour in thirteenth-century Genoa'. In Irad Malkin and Robert L. Hohlfelder (eds), *Mediterranean Cities: Historical Perspectives*, London: Frank Cass, 1988, 114–40.

Epstein, Steven A. *Wage Labor and Guilds in Medieval Europe*. Chapel Hill: University of North Carolina Press, 1991.

Erdmann, Wolfgang. 'Forschungen zur Typenentwicklung des lübischen Kaufmannshauses im Mittelalter'. In Friedland, *Gilde*, 105–6.

Erler, Adalbert. *Bürgerrecht und Steuerpflicht im mittelalterlichen Städtewesen, mit besonderer Untersuchung des Steuereides*. 2nd ed. Frankfurt am Main: Vittorio Klostermann, 1963.

Espinas, Georges. *Les Origines du capitalisme. I. Sire Jehan Boinebroke, patricien et drapier douaisien (?–1286 environ)*. Lille: A Raoust, 1933.

Ewig, Eugen. 'Residence and capital in the early Middle Ages (Ostrogoths and Visigoths)'. In Sylvia L. Thrupp (ed.), *Early Medieval Society*. New York: Appleton-Century-Crofts, 1967, 163–73.

Faber, Ghislaine, and Thierry Lochard. *Montpellier. La Ville médiévale*. Paris: Imprimerie Nationale, 1992.

Falck, Ludwig. *Geschichte der Stadt Mainz (Mitte 5. Jahrhundert bis 1244)*. Düsseldorf: Walter Rau, 1972.

Falck, Ludwig. *Mainz in seiner Blutezeit als freie Stadt (1244 bis 1328)*. Düsseldorf: Walter Rau, 1973.

Fagniez, Gustave (ed.). *Documents relatifs à l'histoire de l'industrie et du commerce en France. 1: Depuis le Ier siècle avant J.-C. jusqu'à la fin du XIIIe siècle*. Paris: Alphonse Picard et fils, 1989.

Fahlbusch, F. B. 'Die Wachstumsphasen von Duderstadt bis zum Übergang an Mainz 1334/66'. *Stoob FS*, 194–212.

Fasoli, Gina. 'Oligarchia e ceti popolari nelle città padane fra il XIIIe e il XIV secolo'. In Elze and Fasoli, *Aristocrazia cittadina*, 11–39.

Fasoli, Gina. 'Città e feudalità'. In *Structures féodales et féodalisme dans l'Occident méditerranéen (Xe–XIIIe siècles). Bilan et perspectives de recherches*. Rome: Ecole française de Rome, 1980.

Fasoli, Gina, Raoul Manselli and Giovanni Tabacco. 'La struttura sociale delle città italiane dal V al XII secolo'. *UGS*, 292–320.

Favresse, Félicien. *L'Avènement du régime démocratique à Bruxelles pendant le Moyen Age (1306–1423)*. Brussels: Marcel Hayez, 1932.

Fehring, Günter. 'The archaeology of early Lübeck: the relation between the Slavic and German settlement Sites', *CHUO*, 267–87.

Bibliography

Fehring, Günter P. 'Der Beitrag der Archäologie zum Leben in der Stadt des späten Mittelalters'. *LS*, 9–35.

Fehring, Günter P., and Rolf Hammel. 'Die Topographie der Stadt Lübeck bis zum 14. Jahrhundert'. In Meckseper, *Stadt im Wandel* 3: 167–90.

Ferruolo, Steven. '*Parisius-Paradisus*: the city, its schools, and the origins of the university of Paris'. In Bender, *University*, 22–43.

Février, Paul-Albert. 'Permanence et héritages de l'Antiquité dans la topographie des villes de l'Occident durant le Haut Moyen-Age'. *TUVC*, 41–138.

Février, Paul-Albert. 'Vetera et nova: le poids du passé, les germes de l'avenir, IIIe–VIe siècle'. *HFU* 1: 399–493.

Finances et comptabilités urbaines du XIIIe au XVIe siècle. Financiën en boekhouding der steden van de XIIIe tot de XIVe eeuw. Brussels: Pro Civitate, 1964.

Fink, Klaus. 'Stand und Ansätze ständischer Entwicklung zwischen Rhein und Maas in salischer Zeit'. *BHS*, 170–95.

Finley, M. I. 'The ancient city: from Fustel de Coulanges to Max Weber and Beyond.' *Comparative Studies in Society and History* (1977), 305–27.

Fixot, Michel. 'Une image idéale, une réalité difficile: les villes du VIIe au IXe siècle'. *HFU* 1: 495–563.

Fohlen, Claude. *Histoire de Besançon. Des origines à la fin du XVIe siècle*. 2nd ed. Besançon: Cêtre, 1964.

Font-Rius, J. M. 'Organos y funcionarios de la administración económica en la principales localidades de Cataluña. *FC*, 257–75.

Francovich, Riccardo, and Ghislaine Noyé (eds). *La Storia dell'Alto Medioevo italiano (VI–X secolo) alla luce dell'archeologia*. Convegno Internazionale (Siena, 2–6 dicembre 1992). Florence: Edizioni all'Insegna del Giglio, 1994.

Friedland, Klaus (ed.). *Gilde und Korporation in den nordeuropäischen Städte des späten Mittelalters*. Cologne and Vienna: Böhlau, 1984. Quellen und Darstellungen zur hansischen Geschichte, ed. Hansisches Geschichtsverein, n.s. 29.

Fröhlich, Karl. 'Kaufmannsgilden und Stadtverfassung im Mittelalter'. In Haase, *Stadt des Mittelalters* 2: 11–54.

Frugoni, Chiara. *A Distant City. Images of Urban Experience in the Medieval World*. Translated by William McCuaig. Princeton: Princeton University Press, 1991.

Fuhrmann, Horst. *Germany in the High Middle Ages*. Translated by Timothy Reuter. Cambridge: Cambridge University Press, 1986.

Galinié, Henri. 'Reflections on early medieval Tours'. In Hodges and Hobley, *Rebirth*, 57–62.

Ganshof, F. L. 'Einwohnergenossenschaft und Graf in den flandrischen Städten während des 12. Jahrhunderts'. In Haase, *Stadt des Mittelalters* 2: 203–25.

Gautier Dalché, Jean. *Historia urbana de Leon y Castilla en la Edad Media (siglos IX–XIII)*. Madrid: Siglo XX de España Editores, 1979.

Gelichi, Sauro. 'La città in Emilia-Romagna tra tardo-antico ed alto-medioevo'. *SLL*, 567–600.

Genecke, Dietrich, and Gareth Shaw (eds). *Urban Historical Geography. Recent Progress in Britain and Germany.* Cambridge: Cambridge University Press, 1988.

Geremek, Bronislaw. *Le salariat dans l'artisanat parisien aux XIIIe–XVe siècles. Etude sur le marché de la main d'oeuvre au Moyen Age.* Paris and The Hague: Mouton, 1968.

Gieysztor, A. 'Les chartes de franchises urbaines et rurales en Pologne au XIIIe siècle'. *LUR*, 103–25.

Ginatempo, Maria, and Lucia Sandri. *L'Italia della città. Il popolamento urbano tra Medioevo e Rinascimento (secoli XIII–XVI)*. Florence: Le Lettere, 1990.

Girouard, Mark. *Cities and People. A Social and Architectural History.* New Haven and London: Yale University Press, 1985.

Given, James Buchanan. *Society and Homicide in Thirteenth-Century England*. Stanford: Stanford University Press, 1977.

Gleba, Gudrun. *Die Gemeinde als alternatives Ordnungsmodell: zur sozialen und politischen Differenzierung des Gemeindebegriffs in den innerstädtischen Auseinandersetzungen des 14. und 15. Jahrhunderts. Mainz, Magdeburg, München, Lübeck.* Cologne and Vienna: Böhlau, 1989.

Glénissen, Jean, and Charles Higounet. 'Remarques sur les comptes et sur l'administration financière des villes françaises entre Loire et Pyrénées (XIV–XVIe siècle)'. *FC*, 31–67.

Glick, Thomas F. *Islamic and Christian Spain in the Early Middle Ages.* Princeton: Princeton University Press, 1979.

Godding, Philippe. *Le droit privé dans les Pays-Bas méridionaux du 12e au 18e. siècle.* Académie royale de Belgique. Mémoires de la Classe des Lettres 14, fasc. 1. Brussels: Palais des Académies, 1987.

Goehrke, Carsten. 'Bemerkungen zur altrussischen Stadt der frühen Teilfürstenzeit (Mitte des 11. bis Mitte des 12. Jhs.)'. *BHS*, 208–27.

Goehrke, Carsten. 'Die Sozialstruktur des mittelalterlichen Novgorod'. *UGS*, 357–78.

Goetz, Hans-Werner. *Life in the Middle Ages, from the Seventh to the Thirteenth Century.* Translated by Albert Wimmer. Edited by Steven Rowan. Notre Dame: University of Notre Dame Press, 1993.

351

Gonthier, Nicole. *Cris de haine et rites d'unité. La violence dans les villes, XIII–XVIe siècle.* Turnhout: Brepols, 1992.

Gottfried, Robert S. *Bury St. Edmunds and the Urban Crisis: 1290–1539.* Princeton: Princeton University Press, 1982.

Goudineau, Christian, Paul-Albert Février, and Michel Fixot, 'Le Reseau urbain'. *HFU* 1: 71–137.

Goudineau, Christian. 'Les villes de la paix romaine'. *HFU* 1: 233–390.

Gouron, André. 'Diffusion des consulats méridionaux et expansion du droit romain aux XIIe et XIIIe siècles'. *Bibliothèque de l'Ecole des Chartres* 121 (1963): 26–76, reprinted with original pagination in Gouron, *Science du droit.*

Gouron, André. *La Réglementation des Métiers en Languedoc au Moyen Age.* Etudes d'histoire économique, politique et sociale, 22. Geneva: E. Droz, 1958.

Gouron, André. *La science du droit dans le Midi de la France au Moyen Age.* London: Variorum Reprints, 1984. Articles are reprinted with pagination of original publication.

Gregory of Tours. *The History of the Franks.* Translated with an Introduction by Lewis Thorpe. Harmondsworth: Penguin Books, 1974.

Guibert of Nogent. *Self and Society in Medieval France. The Memoirs of Abbot Guibert of Nogent (1064?–c. 1125).* Edited with an Introduction and Notes by John F. Benton. New York: Harper and Row, 1970.

Guillerme, André E. *The Age of Water. The Urban Environment in the North of France, A.D. 300–1800.* College Station, Texas: Texas A & M University Press, 1988.

Gutkind, E. A. (ed.). *International History of City Development,* 8 vols. New York: Free Press of Glencoe, 1964–72.

Gysseling, Maurits. *Gent's Vroegste Geschiedenis in de Spiegel van zijn plaatsnamen.* Antwerp: Standaard, 1954.

Haas, Walter, and Johannes Cramer. 'Klosterhöfe in norddeutschen Städten'. In *Stadt im Wandel* 3: 399–440.

Haase, Carl (ed.). *Die Stadt des Mittelalters.* 3 vols. 1: *Begriff, Entstehung und Ausbreitung.* Darmstadt: Wissenschaftliche Buchgesellschaft, 1969. 2: *Recht und Verfassung.* Darmstadt: Wissenschaftliche Buchgesellschaft, 1972. 3: *Wirtschaft und Gesellschaft.* Darmstadt: Wissenschaftliche Buchgesellschaft, 1984.

Hall, R. A. 'York 700–1050'. In Hodges and Hobley, *Rebirth,* 125–32.

Hall, Thomas. *Mittelalterliche Stadtgrundrisse. Versuch einer Übersicht der Entwickhlung in Deutschland und Frankreich.* Stockholm: Almqvist & Wiksell, 1978. Antikvariskt arkiv 66.

Hallam, Elizabeth M. *Capetian France, 987–1328.* London: Longman, 1980.

Hammond, Mason, assisted by Lester J. Bartson. *The City in the Ancient World*. Cambridge, Mass.: Harvard University Press, 1972.

Hanawalt, Barbara A. *Growing up in Medieval London. The Experience of Childhood in History*. New York: Oxford University Press, 1993.

Haverkamp, Alfred. *Medieval Germany, 1056–1273*. Oxford: Oxford University Press, 1988.

Haverkamp, Alfred. 'Die Städte im Herrschafts- und Sozialgefüge Reichsitaliens'. *SH*, 149–245.

Haverkamp, Alfred. 'Topografia e relazioni sociali nelle città tedesche del tardo medioevo'. *SMOE*, 25–54.

Heers, Jacques. 'En Italie centrale: les paysages construits, reflets d'une politique urbaine'. *SMOE*, 279–322.

Heers, Jacques. *Espaces publics, espaces privés dans la ville. Le Liber Terminorum de Bologne (1294)*. Paris: Editions du Centre National de la Recherche Scientifique, 1984.

Heers, Jacques. *Family clans in the Middle Ages. A Study of Political and Social Structures in Urban Areas*. Amsterdam: North Holland, 1977.

Heers, Jacques (ed.). *Fortifications, portes de villes, places publiques dans le monde méditerranéen*. Paris: Université de Paris–Sorbonne, 1985.

Heers, Jacques. *Gênes au XVe siècle. Civilisation méditerranéenne, grand capitalisme, et capitalisme populaire*. Paris: Flammarion, 1971.

Heers, Jacques. *Parties and Political Life in the Medieval West*. Amsterdam: North Holland, 1977.

Heers, Jacques. *La ville au moyen-age en occident: paysages, pouvoirs et conflits*. Paris: Fayard, 1990.

Hellmann, Manfred. 'Probleme früher städtischer Sozialstruktur in Osteuropa'. *UGS*, 379–402.

Herlihy, David. 'Direct and indirect taxation in Tuscan urban finance, ca. 1200–1400'. *FC*, 385–405.

Herlihy, David. *Medieval and Renaissance Pistoia*. New Haven: Yale University Press, 1967.

Herlihy, David. *Medieval Culture and Society*. New York: Harper and Row, 1968.

Herlihy, David. *Medieval Households*. Cambridge, Mass.: Harvard University Press, 1985.

Herlihy, David. *Opera Muliebria. Women and Work in Medieval Europe*. Philadelphia: Temple University Press, 1990.

Herlihy, David. *Pisa in the Early Renaissance. A Study of Urban Growth*. New Haven: Yale University Press, 1958.

Herlihy, David. 'The rulers of Florence, 1282–1530'. In Molho, 'Raaflanb and Emden', *City States*, 197–221.

Herlihy, David. *Women, Family and Society in Medieval Europe. Historical Essays, 1978–1991*. Providence, R. I.: Berghahn Books, 1995.

Herrmann, Joachim. 'Research into the early history of the town in the territory of the German Democratic Republic'. In Barley, *European Towns*, 243–59.

Higounet, Charles. *Bordeaux pendant le Haut Moyen Age. Histoire de Bordeaux*, 2. Bordeaux: Fédération historique du Sud-Ouest, 1963.

Higounet, Charles. 'Die *milites* in den Städten Südwestfrankreichs vom 11. bis zum 13. Jh.'. *BSS*, 94–102.

Hill, David. *An Atlas of Anglo-Saxon England*. Toronto and Buffalo: University of Toronto Press, 1981.

Hill, David. 'The Saxon period'. *UAB*, 46–53.

Hill, Francis. *Medieval Lincoln*. Cambridge: Cambridge University Press, 1965.

Hilton, R. H. *English and French Towns in Feudal Society. A Comparative Study*. Cambridge: Cambridge University Press, 1992.

Hinton, David. *Alfred's Kingdom. Wessex and the South, 800–1500*. London: Dent, 1977.

Hischfelder, Gunther. *Die Kölner Handelsbeziehungen im Spätmittelalter*. Cologne: Veröffentlichungen des Kölnischen Stadtmuseums, 1994.

Historische Stedenatlas van België. Lier. Brussels: Gemeentekrediet van België, 1990.

Hobley, Brian. 'Lundenwic and Lundenburh: two cities rediscovered'. In Hodges and Hobley, *Rebirth*, 59–73.

Hodges, Richard. *Dark Age Economics. The Origins of Towns and Trade, A.D. 600–1000*. New York: St. Martin's Press, 1982.

Hodges, Richard. 'The rebirth of towns in the early Middle Ages'. In Hodges and Hobley, *Rebirth*, 1–7.

Hodges, Richard, and Brian Hobley (eds). *The Rebirth of Towns in the West, A.D. 700–1050*. CBA Research Report 68. London: Council for British Archaeology, 1988.

Hodges, Richard, and David Whitehouse. *Mohammed, Charlemagne & the Origins of Europe. Archaeology and the Pirenne Thesis*. Ithaca, N.Y.: Cornell University Press, 1983.

Hoffmann, Erich. 'Die Schleswiger Knutsgilde als mögliches Bindeglied zwischen West- und mitteleuropäischen und nordischem Gildewesen'. In Friedland, *Gilde*, 51–63.

Hofmann, Hanns Hubert. '*Nobiles Norimbergenses*. Beobachtungen zur Struktur der reichsstädtischen Oberschicht'. *UGS*, 53–92.

Hohenberg, Paul M., and Lynn Hollen Lees. *The Making of Urban Europe, 1000–1950*. Cambridge: Harvard University Press, 1985.

Hollaender, A. E. J., and William Kellaway (eds). *Studies in London History Presented to Philip Edmund Jones*. London: Hodder and Stoughton, 1969.

Holmes, George. *Florence, Rome and the Origins of the Renaissance*. Oxford: Clarendon Press, 1986.

Holt, Richard. 'Gloucester in the century after the Black Death'. Originally in *Transactions of the Bristol and Gloucestershire Archaeological Society* 103 (1985), reprinted *MT*, 141–59.

Holt, Richard, and Gervase Rosser (eds). *The Medieval Town. A Reader in English Urban History, 1200–1540*. London: Longman, 1990.

Honeybourne, Marjorie B. 'The pre-Norman bridge of London'. In Hollaender and Kellaway, *Studies in London History*, 15–39.

Hopkins, Keith. 'Economic growth and towns in classical antiquity'. In Abrams and Wrigley, *Towns in Societies*, 35–77.

Hörby, Kai. 'Königliche Dänische Kaufleute'. In Friedland, *Gilde*, 41–50.

Hourani, Albert. *A History of the Arab Peoples*. Cambridge, Mass.: Harvard University Press, 1991.

Hourani, A. H., and S. M. Stern (eds). *The Islamic City. A Colloquium*. Papers on Islamic History, 1. Philadelphia: University of Pennsylvania Press, 1970.

Hourani, A. H. 'The Islamic city in the light of recent research'. *IC*, 10–24.

Houtte, J. A. van. *Bruges. Essai d'histoire urbaine*. Brussels: La Renaissance du Livre, 1967.

Houtte, J. A. van. *An Economic History of the Low Countries, 800–1800*. New York: St. Martin's Press, 1977.

Howell, Martha C. *Women, Production, and Patriarchy in Late Medieval Cities*. Chicago: University of Chicago Press, 1986.

Hubert, Etienne. *Espace urbain et habitat à Rome du Xe siècle à la fin du XIIIe siècle*. Collection de l'Ecole française de Rome, 135. Rome: Palais Farnese, 1990.

Hubert, Jean. 'Evolution de la topographie et de l'aspect des villes de Gaule du Ve siècle'. *CAM*, 529–58.

Hugh of Poitiers. *The Vézelay Chronicle,* and other documents from MS Auxerre 227 and elsewhere, translated into English with notes, introduction, and accompanying material by John Scott and John O. Ward, and with supplementary essays and notes by Eugene L. Cox. Binghamton, N.Y.: Medieval and Renaissance Texts and Studies, 1992.

Hughes, Diane Owen. 'Urban growth and family structure in medieval Genoa'. *PP* 66 (1975): 3–28.

Huiskes, Manfred (ed.). *Beschlüsse des Rates der Stadt Köln, 1320–1550. 1: Die Ratsmemoriale und ergänzende Überlieferung, 1320–1543*. Düsseldorf: Droste, 1990. Publikationen der Gesellschaft für Rheinische Geschichtskunde, 65.

Hyde, J. K. *Padua in the Age of Dante.* Manchester: Manchester University Press, 1966.

Hyde, J. K. *Society and Politics in Medieval Italy. The Evolution of the Civic Life, 1000–1350.* New York: St. Martin's Press, 1973.

Hyde, J. K. 'Universities and cities in medieval Italy'. In Bender, *University*, 13–21.

Isenmann, Eberhard. *Die deutsche Stadt im Spätmittelalter, 1250–1500. Stadtgestalt, Recht, Stadtregiment, Kirche, Gesellschaft, Wirtschaft.* Stuttgart: Eugen Ulmer, 1988.

The Itinerary of Benjamin of Tudela. Critical text, translation and commentary by Marcus Nathan Adler. New York: Philipp Feldheim, 1907.

Jacques de Vitry. *Historia Occidentalis.* A critical edition by John Frederick Hinnebusch. Fribourg: University Press, 1972.

Jäger, Helmut, Franz Petri and Heinz Quirin (eds). *Civitatum Communitas. Studien zum europäischen Städtewesen. Festschrift Heinz Stoob zum 65. Geburtstag.* Cologne and Vienna: Böhlau, 1984. 2 vols. Städteforschung 19, 21.

Jakob, Volker, and Gerhard Köhn. 'Wege zum Modell einer mittelalterlichen Stadtsozialtopographische Ermittlungen am Beispiel Soest'. *Stoob FS*, 296–308.

Jakobs, Hermann. 'Stadtgemeinde und Bürgertum um 1100'. *BHS*, 14–54.

James, Edward. *The Origins of France. From Clovis to the Capetians, 500–1000.* London: Macmillan, 1982.

Jansen, Henrik. 'Early urbanization in Denmark'. *CHUO*, 183–216.

Jansen, H. P. H. 'Handel en Nijverheid 1000–1300'. *AGN*, 148–86.

Janssen, Walter. 'The origins of the non-Roman town in Germany'. *CHUO*, 217–35.

Janssen, Walter. 'The rebirth of towns in the Rhineland'. In Hodges and Hobley, *Rebirth*, 47–61.

Johnstone, Hilda (ed. and trans.). *Annals of Ghent.* London: Thomas Nelson and Sons, 1951.

Jones, A. H. M. *The Decline of the Ancient World.* New York: Holt, Rinehart and Winston, 1966.

Jones, A. H. M. *The Greek City, from Alexander to Justinian.* Oxford: Clarendon Press, 1940.

Jones, A. H. M. *The Later Roman Empire, 284–602.* 2 vols. Norman: University of Oklahoma Press, 1964.

Jones, M. J. and J. S. Wacher. 'The Roman period'. *UAB*, 27–45.

Jordan, William C. 'Supplying Aigues-Mortes for the Crusade of 1248: the problem of restructuring trade'. *Strayer FS*, 165–72.

Joris, André. *Huy, ville médiévale.* Brussels: La Renaissance du Livre, 1965.

Joris, André. 'On the edge of two worlds in the heart of the new empire: the romance regions of northern Gaul during the Merovingian period'. *Studies in Medieval and Renaissance History* 3: 1–52.

Joris, André. A propos de 'burgus' à Huy et à Namur'. *FSE*, 192–9.

Joris, André. *La ville de Huy au Moyen Age, des origines à la fin du XIVe siècle.* Paris: Université de Liège, 1959.

Keene, Derek. 'Continuity and development in urban trades: problems of concepts and the evidence'. In Corfield and Keene, *Work in Towns*, 1–16.

Keene, Derek. 'The property market in English towns, A.D. 1100–1600'. *SMOE*, 201–26.

Keene, Derek. 'Small towns and the metropolis: the experience of medieval England'. *PTME*, 223–38.

Keene, Derek. 'Suburban growth'. *PT*, 71–82.

Keene, Derek. *Survey of Medieval Winchester.* 2 vols. Oxford: Clarendon Press, 1985. Winchester Studies, 2.

Kejr, Jiri. 'Les privileges des villes de Bohême depuis les origines jusqu'aux guerres hussites (1419). *LUR*, 126–60.

Kejr, Jiri. 'Zur Entstehung des städtischen Stände im hussitischen Böhmen'. *SSt*, 195–213.

Keller, Hagen. *Adelsherrschaft und städtische Gesellschaft in Oberitalien, 9. bis 12. Jahrhundert.* Bibliothek des deutschen historischen Instituts in Rom, 52. Tübingen: Max Niemeyer, 1979.

Keller, Hagen. 'Gli inizi del comune in Lombardia: limiti della documentazione e metodi di ricerca'. *ECI*, 45–70.

Keller, Hagen. 'Mehrheitsentscheidung und Majorisierungsproblem im Verband der Landgemeinden Chiavenna und Piuro (1151–1155)'. *Stoob FS*, 2–41.

Keller, Hagen. 'Die soziale und politische Verfassung Mailands in den Anfängen des kommunalen Lebens'. *HZ* 211 (1970): 34–64.

Keller, Hagen. 'Über den Charakter Freiburgs in der Frühzeit der Stadt. *Festschrift für Berent Schwineköper.* Sigmaringen: Jan Thorbecke, 1982, 249–82.

Keller, Hagen. 'Der Übergang zur Commune: zur Entwicklung der italienischen Stadtverfassung im 11. Jahrhundert'. In Diesteklkamp, *Beiträge* 1: 55–72.

Keutgen, Friedrich (ed.). *Urkunden zur städtischen Verfassungsgeschichte.* Berlin: Emil Felber, 1901.

Kieft, Co van de. 'Das Reich in die Städte im niederländischen Raum zur Zeit des Investiturstreits'. *BHS*, 149–69.

Bibliography

Kirchgässner, B. 'Studien zur Geschichte des kommunalen Rechnungswesens der Reichsstädte Südwestdeutschlands vom 13. bis zum 16. Jahrhundert'. *FC*, 237–52.

Klebel, Ernst. 'Regensburg'. *SAES*, 84–104.

Klein, Herbert. '*Juravum*-Salzburg'. *SAES*, 77–85.

Knoll, Paul W. 'The urban development of medieval Poland, with particular reference to Krakow'. *USEE*, 63–137.

Köbler, Gerhard. 'Mitteleuropäisches Städtewesen in salischer Zeit. Die Ausgliederung exemter Rechtsbezirke in Mittel- und Niederrheinischen Städte'. *BHS*, 1–13.

Kolb, Frank. *Die Stadt im Altertum*. Munich: C. H. Beck, 1984.

Köln, das Reich und Europa. Abhandlungen über weiträumige Verflechtungen der Stadt Köln in Politik, Recht und Wirtschaft im Mittelalter. Mitteilungen aus dem Stadtarchiv von Köln, 60. Cologne: Paul Neubner, 1971.

Koller, Heinrich. 'Der Ausbau der Stadt Hallein im hohen und späten Mittelalter'. *Stoob FS*, 181–93.

Konvitz, Josef W. *The Urban Millennium. The City-Building Process from the Early Middle Ages to the Present*. Carbondale: Southern Illinois University Press, 1986.

Krautheimer, Richard. *Rome. Profile of a City, 312–1308*. Princeton: Princeton University Press, 1980.

Krautheimer, Richard. *Three Christian Capitals. Topography and Politics*. Berkeley: University of California Press, 1983.

Krekic, Barisa. 'Developed autonomy: the patricians in Dubrovnik and Dalmatian cities'. *USEE*, 185–215.

Krekic, Barisa (ed.). *Urban Society of Eastern Europe in Premodern Times*. Berkeley and Los Angeles: University of California Press, 1987.

Ladero Quesada, Miguel Angel. *La Ciudad medieval (1248–1492)*. 2nd ed. In Francisco Morales Padron (ed.), *Historia de Sevilla*. Seville: University, 1980.

Ladero Quesnada, Miguel Angel. 'Les fortifications urbaines en Castille aux XIe–XVe siècles: Problématique, financement, aspects sociaux'. In Heers, *Fortifications*, 145–76.

Lane, Frederic C. *Venice. A Maritime Republic*. Baltimore: The Johns Hopkins University Press, 1973.

Lane, Frederic C. *Venice and History. The Collected Papers of Frederic C. Lane*. Baltimore: The Johns Hopkins University Press, 1966.

Langer, Lawrence M. 'The medieval Russian town'. In Michael F. Hamm (ed.), *The City in Russian History*. Lexington: University Press of Kentucky, 1976, 11–33.

Lansing, Carol. *The Florentine Magnates. Lineage and Faction in a Medieval Commune*. Princeton: Princeton University Press, 1991.

Lapidus, Ira M. *Muslim Cities in the Later Middle Ages.* Cambridge: Cambridge University Press. 1984.

Lapidus, Ira M. 'Muslim urban society in Mamluk Syria'. *IC*, 195–205.

Larner, John. *Italy in the Age of Dante and Petrarch, 1216–1380.* London: Longman, 1980.

Lassner, J. 'The Caliph's personal domain. The city plan of Baghdad reexamined'. *IC*, 103–18.

Latouche, R. 'The commune of Mans (1070 AD)', trans. by Katie Ward in Hugh of Poitiers, *The Vézelay Chronicle.*

Latreille, André (ed.). *Histoire de Lyon et du Lyonnais.* Toulouse: Privat, 1975.

Lavedan, Pierre. *French Architecture.* London: Scolar Press, 1979.

Lavedan, Pierre, and Jeanne Hugueney. *L'Urbanisme au Moyen Age.* Geneva: Droz, 1974. Bibliothèque de la Société française d'archéologie, 5.

Law, Custom, and the Social Fabric in Medieval Europe. Essays in Honor of Bryce Lyon. Edited by Bernard S. Bachrach and David Nicholas. Kalamazoo, Michigan: Medieval Institute Publications, 1990.

Le Goff, Jacques. 'L'apogée de la France urbaine médiévale'. *HFU* 2: 183–405.

Le Goff, Jacques. 'The town as an agent of civilisation'. *Fontana Economic History of Europe* 1. London: Fontana, 1972, 71–106.

Leroy, Béatrice. 'Tudela, une ville de la vallée de l'Ebre, aux XIIIe–XIVe siècles'. *PU*, 187–212.

Lesage, Georges. *Marseille angevine. Recherches sur son évolution administrative, économique et urbaine, de la victoire de Charles d'Anjou et l'arrivée de Jeanne Ire (1264–1348).* Paris: E. de Boccard, 1950.

Lestocquoy, Jean. *Aux Origines de la Bourgeoisie: les villes de Flandre et d'Italie sous le gouvernement des patriciens.* Paris: Presses Universitaires de France, 1952.

Lestocquoy, Jean. *Patriciens du Moyen-Age. Les Dynasties bourgeoises d'Arras du XIe au XVe siècle.* Arras: Mémoires de la Commission Départementale des Monuments Historiques du Pas-de-Calais, V, 1. 1945.

Lévi-Provençal, E. (ed.). *Séville musulmane au début du XIIe siècle. La traité d'Ibn 'Abdun sur la vie urbaine et les corps de métiers.* Paris: G.P. Maisonneuve, 1947.

Lewald, Ursula. 'Zum Verhältnis von Köln und Deutz im Mittelalter'. *FSE*, 378–90.

Les Libertés urbaines et rurales du XIe au XIVe siècle. Vrijheden in de stad en op het plattland van de XIe tot de XIVe eeuw. Colloque International, Spa 5–8 IX 1966. *Actes. Handelingen.* Brussels: Pro Civitate, 1968.

Lloyd, T. H. *England and the German Hanse, 1157–1611. A Study of*

Their Trade and Commercial Diplomacy. Cambridge: Cambridge University Press, 1991.

Lobbedey, Uwe. 'Northern Germany'. In Barley, *European Towns*, 127–57.

Lobel, M. D. (ed.). *The Atlas of Historic Towns*. *2: Bristol: Cambridge: Coventry: Norwich*. Baltimore: The Johns Hopkins University Press, 1975.

Lobel, M. D. (ed.). *Historic Towns. Maps and Plans of Towns and Cities in the British Isles, with Historical Commentaries, from Earliest Times to 1800*. Baltimore: The Johns Hopkins University Press, [1969].

Lodge, Eleanor C. *Gascony Under English Rule*. London: Kennikat Press, 1926, 1971.

Lopez, Robert S., and Irving W. Raymond (eds). *Medieval Trade in the Mediterranean World*. New York: W.W. Norton, 1955.

Loyn, Henry. 'Towns in late Anglo-Saxon England: the evidence and some possible lines of enquiry'. In Peter Clemoes and Kathleen Hughes (eds), *England Before the Conquest. Studies in Primary Sources Presented to Dorothy Whitelock*. Cambridge: Cambridge University Press, 1971, 115–28.

Luzzatto, Gino. *An Economic History of Italy from the Fall of the Roman Empire to the Beginning of the Sixteenth Century*. Translated by Philip Jones. London: Routledge and Kegan Paul, 1961.

Lynch, Michael, Michael Spearman and Geoffrey Stell (eds). *The Scottish Medieval Town*. Edinburgh: John Donald, 1988.

Lyon, Bryce. 'What role did communes have in the feudal system?' *Revue Belge de philologie et d'histoire* 72 (1994): 241–53.

MacKay, Angus. *Spain in the Middle Ages. From Frontier to Empire, 1000–1500*. London: Macmillan, 1977.

MacKenney, Richard. *Tradesmen and Traders. The World of the Guilds in Venice and Europe, c. 1250–c. 1650*. Totowa, N.J.: Barnes and Noble, 1987.

MacMullen, Ramsay. *Roman Social Relations, 50 B.C. to A.D. 284*. New Haven: Yale University Press, 1974.

Maddicott, J. R. 'Trade, industry and the wealth of King Alfred', *PP*, 123 (May, 1989): 3–51.

Mägdefrau, Werner. 'Patrizische Ratsherrschaft, Bürgeropposition und städtische Volksbewegungen in Erfurt. Von der Herausbildung des ersten bürgerlichen Rates um die Mitte des 13. Jahrhunderts bis zu den innerstädtischen Auseinandersetzungen von 1309 bis 1310'. *SS*, 324–71.

Maire Vigueur, Jean-Claude (ed.). *D'une ville à l'autre: Structures matérielles et organisation de l'espace dans les villes européennes (XIIIe–XVIe siècle)*. Actes du Colloque organisé par l'Ecole française de Rome avec le concours de l'Université de Rome (Rome 1er–4 décembre 1986). Rome: Ecole Française de Rome, 1989.

Martens, Mina (ed.). *Histoire de Bruxelles*. Toulouse: Privat, 1976.

Martin, G. H. 'Domesday Book and the boroughs'. In Peter Sawyer (ed.), *Domesday Book. A Reassessment*. London: Edward Arnold, 1985, 143–63.

Martin, G. H. 'New beginnings in north-western Europe'. In Barley, *European Towns*, 406–15.

Martin, G. H. 'The English borough in the thirteenth century'. *TRHS*, 13 (1963), reprinted *MT*, 29–48.

Martin, G. H. (ed.). *The Ipswich Recognizance Rolls, 1294–1327. A Calendar*. Ipswich: Suffolk Record Society, 1973.

Martin, Jean-Marie. 'Les communes en Italie méridionale aux XIIe et XIIIe siècles'. In Bourin, *Villes, bon villes, cités et capitales*, 201–10.

Martines, Lauro (ed.). *Violence and Civil Disorder in Italian Cities, 1200–1500*. Berkeley and Los Angeles: University of California Press, 1972.

Maschke, Erich. *Städte und Menschen. Beiträge zur Geschichte der Stadt, der Wirtschaft und Gesellschaft 1959–1977*. Vierteljahrschrift für Sozial- und Wirtschaftsgeschichte, Beiheft 68. Wiesbaden: Franz Steiner, 1980.

Matheus, Michael. *Trier am Ende des Mittelalters. Studien zur Sozial-, Wirtschafts- und Verfassungsgeschichte der Stadt Trier vom 14. bis 16. Jahrhunderte*. Trierer Historische Forschungen, 5. Trier: Verlag Trierer Historische Forschungen, 1984.

Mazzi, Maria Serena. 'Milano dei secoli IX–XII in contributi dell 'ultimo trentennio'. *Archivio Storico Italiano* 132 (1974): 371–415.

Meckseper, Cord (ed.). *Stadt im Wandel. Kunst und Kultur des Bürgertums in Norddeutschland, 1150–1650*. 4 vols. Stuttgart-Bad Cannstadt: Edition Cantz, 1985.

Menant, François. 'Aspetti delle relazioni feudo-vassallatiche nelle città lombarde dell'XI secolo: l'esempio cremonese'. *ECI*, 223–39.

Mengozzi, Guido. *La Città italiana nell'alto medioevo. Il periodo langobardo-franco*. Florence: La Nuova Italia, 1973.

Merrifield, Ralph. *London. City of the Romans*. Berkeley: University of California Press, 1983.

Meynen, Emil. 'Der Grundriss der Stadt Köln als geschichtliches Erbe'. *Stoob FS*, 281–94.

Mickwitz, Gunnar. *Die Kartellfunktionen der Zünfte und ihre Bedeutung bei der Entstehung des Zunftwesens. Eine Studie in spätantiker und mittelalterlicher Wirtschaftsgeschichte*. Helsinki: Societas Scientiarum Fennica. Commentationes Humanarum Litterarum, VIII, 8. 1936.

Miller, Edward, and John Hatcher. *Medieval England. Towns, Commerce and Crafts*. London: Longman, 1995.

Mitteis, Heinrich. 'Über den Rechtsgrund des Satzes "Stadtluft macht frei"'. In Haase, *Stadt des Mittelalters* 2: 182–202.

Mitterauer, Michael. *Markt und Stadt im Mittelalter. Beiträge zur historischen Zentralitätsforschung*. Stuttgart: Anton Hiersemann, 1980.

Molho, Anthony, Kurt Raaflaub and Julia Emden (eds). *City States in Classical Antiquity and Medieval Italy*. Ann Arbor: University of Michigan Press, 1991.

Mollat, Michel (ed.). *Histoire de Rouen*. Toulouse: Privat, 1979.

Mollat, Michel. *The Poor in the Middle Ages. An Essay in Social History*. Translated by Arthur Goldhammer. New Haven and London: Yale University Press, 1986.

Mollat, Michel, and Philippe Wolff. *The Popular Revolutions of the Late Middle Ages*. London: George Allen and Unwin, 1973.

Möncke, Gisela (ed.), *Quellen zur Wirtschafts- und Sozialgeschichte Mittel- und Oberdeutscher Städte im Spätmittelalter*. Darmstadt: Wissenschaftliche Buchgesellschaft, 1982. Ausgewählte Quellen zur deutschen Geschichte des Mittelalers, 37.

Monier, Raymond. *Les institutions judiciaires des villes de Flandre des origines à la rédaction des Coutumes*. Lille: Valentin Bresle, 1924.

Mor, Carlo Guido. 'Topografia giuridica: stato giuridico delle diverse zone urbane'. *TUVC*, 333–50.

Morris, A. E. J. *History of Urban Form From Prehistory to the Renaissance*. London: George Godwin, 1972.

Mulholland, Mary Ambrose (ed.). *Early Gild Records of Toulouse*. New York: Columbia University Press, 1941.

Müller, Wolfgang (ed.). *Freiburg im Mittelalter. Vorträge zum Stadtjubiläum 1970*. Bühl/Baden: Konkordia, 1970.

Mumford, Lewis. *The Culture of Cities*. New York: Harcourt, Brace and Company, 1938.

Mundy, John H. *Liberty and Political Power in Toulouse, 1050–1230*. New York: Columbia University Press, 1954.

Najemy, John M. *Corporatism and Consensus in Florentine Electoral Politics, 1280–1400*. Chapel Hill: University of North Carolina Press, 1982.

Nelson, Lynn H. 'The foundation of Jaca (1076): urban growth in early Aragon'. *Speculum* 53 (1978): 688–708.

Nicholas, David. *The Evolution of the Medieval World. Society, Government and Thought in Europe, 312–1500*. London: Longman, 1992.

Nicholas, David. *Medieval Flanders*. London: Longman, 1992.

Nicholas, David. 'Medieval urban origins in northern continental Europe: state of research and some tentative conclusions', *Studies in Medieval and Renaissance History* 6 (1969): 53–114.

Nicholas, David. *The Metamorphosis of a Medieval City; Ghent in the Age of the Arteveldes, 1302–1390.* Lincoln: University of Nebraska Press, 1987.

Nicholas, David. 'Of poverty and primacy: demand, liquidity, and the Flemish economic miracle, 1050–1200', *American Historical Review* 96 (1991): 17–41.

Nicholas, David. 'Patterns of social mobility'. In R. L. DeMolen (ed.), *One Thousand Years. Western Europe in the Middle Ages.* Boston: Houghton Mifflin (1974), 45–105.

Nicholas, David. 'Structures du peuplement, fonctions urbaines et formation du capital dans la Flandre médiévale'. *AESC* 33 (1978): 501–27. English translation 'Settlement patterns, urban functions, and capital formation in medieval Flanders', in Nicholas, *Trade, Urbanisation and the Family.*

Nicholas, David. *Trade, Urbanisation and the Family. Studies in the History of Medieval Flanders.* Aldershot: Variorum Reprints, 1996.

Nicholas, David. 'Vendetta and civil disorder in late medieval Ghent'. In Richard M. Golden (ed.), *Social History of Western Civilization.* I. *Readings from the Ancient World to the Seventeenth Century,* 2nd ed. (New York: St. Martin's Press, 1992), 179–92.

Nightingale, Pamela. *A Medieval Mercantile Community. The Grocers' Company and the Politics and Trade of London, 1000–1485.* New Haven: Yale University Press, 1995.

Nightingale, Pamela. 'The origin of the court of Husting and Danish influence on London's development into a capital city'. *EHR* 404 (1987): 559–78.

Nürnberger Urkundenbuch. Herausgegeben vom Stadtrat zu Nürnberg. Bearbeitet vom Stadtarchiv Nürnberg. Nürnberg: Selbstverlag des Stadtrats, 1959. Quellen und Forschungen zur Geschichte der Stadt Nürnberg, 1.

Nyberg, Tore. 'Gilden, Kalande, Brüderschaften: der skandinavische Einfluss'. In Friedland, *Gilde,* 29–40.

Obst, Karin. *Der Wandel in den Bezeichnungen für gewerbliche Zusammenschlüsse des Mittelalters. Eine rechtssprach-geographische Analyse.* Frankfurt am Main: Peter Lang, 1983.

O'Callahan, Joseph F. *A History of Medieval Spain.* Ithaca: Cornell University Press, 1975.

Opll, Ferdinand. *Stadt und Reich im 12. Jahrhundert 1125–1190.* Forschungen zur Kaiser- und Papstgeschichte des Mittelalters. Beihefte zu J. F. Böhmer, *Regesta Imperii,* 6. Cologne, Vienna and Graz: Hermann Böhlaus Nachfolger, 1986.

Order and Innovation in the Middle Ages: Essays in Honor of Joseph R. Strayer. Princeton: Princeton University Press, 1976.

Otto of Freising and his continuator Rahewin. *The Deeds of Frederick Barbarossa*. Translated and annotated with an Introduction by Charles Christopher Mierow. New York: W. W. Norton and Company, 1966.

Owen, Dorothy M. (ed.). *The Making of King's Lynn. A Documentary Survey*. Oxford: Oxford University Press, 1984.

Owens, E. J. *The City in the Greek and Roman World*. London: Routledge, 1991.

Paul, Jürgen. 'Rathaus und Markt'. In *Stadt im Wandel* 4: 89–118.

Pavoni, Romeo. 'L'Evoluzione cittadina in Liguria nel secolo XI'. In *ECI*, 241–53.

Pérouas, Louis (ed.). *Histoire de Limoges*. Toulouse: Privat, 1989.

Petit-Dutaillis, Charles. *The French Communes in the Middle Ages*. Translated by Joan Vickers. Amsterdam: North Holland, 1978.

Petri, Franz. 'Die Anfänge des mittelalterlichen Städtewesens in den Niederlanden und dem angrenzenden Frankreich'. *SAES*, 227–95.

Petri, Franz. (ed.). *Bischofs- und Kathedralstädte des Mittelalters und der frühen Neuzeit*. Cologne and Vienna: Böhlau, 1976. Städteforschung, Reihe A, v. 1.

Pfeiffer, Gerhard (ed.). *Nürnberg–Geschichte einer europäischen Stadt*. Munich: C. H. Beck, 1971.

Pinto, Giuliano. '"Honour" and "Profit": landed property and trade in medieval Siena'. *CC*, 81–91.

Pirenne, Henri. *Early Democracies in the Low Countries: Urban Society and Political Conflict in the Middle Ages and the Renaissance*. New York: Harper and Row, reprinted 1963.

Pirenne, Henri. *Medieval Cities. Their Origins and the Revival of Trade*. New York: Doubleday, reprinted 1956.

Planitz, Hans. *Die deutsche Stadt im Mittelalter. Von der Römerzeit bis zu den Zunftkämpfen*. 2nd ed. Cologne and Graz: Böhlau, 1965.

Planitz, Hans. 'Die deutsche Stadtgemeinde'. In Haase, *Stadt des Mittelalters* 2: 55–13.

Platelle, Henri (ed.). *Histoire de Valenciennes*. Lille: Presses Universitaires de Lille, 1982.

Platt, Colin. *The English Mediaeval Town*. London: Paladin, 1979.

Platt, Colin. 'The evolution of towns: natural growth'. *PT*, 48–56.

Platt, Colin. *Medieval Southampton. The Port and Trading Community, A.D. 1000–1600*. London: Routledge and Kegan Paul, 1973.

Plesner, Johan. *L'Emigration de la campagne à la ville libre de Florence au XIIIe siècle*. Copenhagen: Gyldendal, 1934.

Portmann, Urs. *Bürgerschaft im mittelalterlichen Freiburg. Sozialtopographische Auswertungen zum ersten Bürgerbuch 1341–1416*. Freiburg (Switzerland): Universitätsverlag, 1986. Historische Schriften der Universität Freiburg, 11.

Powers, James F. 'The creative interaction between Portuguese and Leonese municipal military law, 1055 to 1279'. *Speculum* 62/1 (1987): 53–80.

Powers, James F. *A Society Organized for War. The Iberian Municipal Militias in the Central Middle Ages.* Berkeley: University of California Press, 1988.

Prevenier, Walter. 'Quelques aspects des comptes communaux en Flandre au Moyen Age'. *FC,* 111–45.

Previté-Orton, C. W. 'The Italian cities till c. 1200'. In *The Cambridge Medieval History,* 5 (Cambridge: Cambridge University Press, 1929): 208–41.

Prinz, Friedrich. 'Die bischöfliche Stadtherrschaft im Frankenreich vom 5. bis zum 7. Jahrhundert'. In Petri, *Bischofs- und Kathedralstädte,* 1–26.

Puhle, Matthias. *Die Politik der Stadt Braunschweig innerhalb des sächsischen Städtebundes und der Hanse im späten Mittelalter.* Brunswick: Waisenhaus, 1985.

Rabe, Horst. 'Frühe Stadien der Ratsverfassung in den Reichslandstädten bzw. Reichsstädten Oberdeutschlands'. *BSS,* 1–17.

Racine, Pierre. 'Città e contado in Emilia e Lombardia nel secolo XI'. *ECI,* 99–136.

Racine, Pierre. 'De la porte, élément de defense à la porte, division administrative: l'exemple de Plaisance'. In Heers, *Fortifications,* 177–96.

Racine, Pierre. 'Évêque et cité dans le royaume d'Italie: aux origines des communes italiennes'. *Cahiers de Civilisation Médiévale,* 27 (1984): 129–39.

Racine, Pierre. 'Naissance de la place civique en Italie'. In Heers, *Fortifications,* 301–21.

Racine, Pierre. 'Les palais publics dans les communes italiennes (XIIe– XIIIe siècles)'. *PU,* 133–53.

Rausch, Wilhelm (ed.). *Stadt und Stadtherr im 14. Jahrhundert. Entwicklungen und Funktionen.* Linz: Osterreichischer Arbeitskreis für Stadtgeschichtsforschung, 1972.

Raveggi, Sergio. 'Gli aristocratici in città: considerazioni sul caso di Firenze'. *SMOE,* 69–86.

Raveggi, Sergio. 'Le famiglie di parte Ghibellina nella classe dirigente Fiorentina del secolo XIII'. *CD,* 279–99.

Reinecke, Heinrich. 'Kölner, Soester, Lübecker und Hamburger Recht in ihrer gegenseitigen Beziehungen'. In Haase, *Stadt des Mittelalters* 2: 135–81.

Renkhoff, Otto. *Wiesbaden im Mittelalter.* Wiesbaden: Franz Steiner, 1980.

Renouard, Yves (ed.). *Bordeaux sous les rois d'Angleterre.* Bordeaux: Fédération historique du Sud-Ouest, 1965.

Reyerson, Kathryn L. *Business, Banking and Finance in Medieval Montpellier.* Toronto: Pontifical Institute of Medieval Studies, 1985.

Bibliography

Reynolds, Susan. *An Introduction to the History of English Medieval Towns.* Oxford: Clarendon Press, 1977.

Reynolds, Susan. *Kingdoms and Communities in Western Europe, 900–1300.* Oxford: Clarendon Press, 1984.

Riesenberg, Peter. *Citizenship in the Western Tradition. Plato to Rousseau.* Chapel Hill, N.C.: University of North Carolina Press, 1992.

Rippe, Gérard. 'Commune urbaine et féodalité en Italie du Nord: l'exemple de Padoue (Xe siècle–1237). *Mélanges de l'Ecole française de Rome. Moyen Age, temps modernes* 91 (1979): 659–97.

Rippe, Gérard. 'Dans le Padouan des Xe–XIe siècles: évêques, vavasseurs, *cives*'. *Cahiers de Civilisation Médiévale* 27 (1984): 141–50.

Rivet, A. L. F. *Town and Country in Roman Britain.* London: Hutchinson University Library, 1958.

Roblin, M. 'Cités ou citadelles? Les enceintes romaines du Bas-Empire d'après l'exemple de Paris'. *Revue des Etudes Anciennes* 53 (1951): 305–27.

Roblin, M. 'Cités ou citadelles? Les enceintes romaines du Bas-Empire d'après l'exemple de Senlis'. *Revue des Etudes Anciennes* 67 (1965): 368–91.

Rogers, J. M. 'Samarra. A study in medieval town-planning'. *IC*, 119–55.

Rogozinski, Jan. *Power, Caste, and Law. Social Conflict in Fourteenth-Century Montpellier.* Cambridge, Mass.: Medieval Academy of America, 1982.

Rolland, Paul. *Les Origines de la commune de Tournai. Histoire interne de la seigneurie épiscopale Tournaisienne.* Brussels: Maurice Lamertin, 1931.

Romano, Dennis. *Patricians and Popolani. The Social Foundations of the Venetian Renaissance State.* Baltimore: The Johns Hopkins University Press, 1987.

Rosser, Gervase. *Medieval Westminster, 1200–1540.* Oxford: Clarendon Press, 1989.

Rosser, Gervase. 'The essence of medieval urban communities: the Vill of Westminster, 1200–1540'. *Transactions of the Royal Historical Society*, ser. 5, vol. 34 (1984): 91–112.

Rossetti, Gabriella. 'Il Comune cittadino: un tema inattuale?'. *ECI*, 25–43.

Rossiand, Jacques. 'Crises et consolidations'. *HFU* 2: 407–613.

Rousseau, Félix. *Namur, ville mosane.* 2nd ed. Brussels: La Renaissance du Livre, 1958.

Rubin, Miri. *Charity and Community in Medieval Cambridge.* Cambridge: Cambridge University Press, 1987.

Ruggiero, Guido. *Violence in Early Renaissance Venice.* New Brunswick, N.J.: Rutgers University Press, 1980.

Ruiz, Teofilo F. *The City and The Realm: Burgos and Castile 1080–1492.* Aldershot: Variorum Reprints, 1992.

Russell, Josiah Cox. *Medieval Regions and Their Cities*. Bloomington, Ind.: Indiana University Press, 1972.

Ryckaert, Marc. 'Les origines et l'histoire ancienne de Bruges: l'état de la question et quelques données nouvelles'. *PTME*, 117–34.

Rykwert, Joseph. *The Idea of a Town. The Anthropology of Urban Form in Rome, Italy and the Ancient World*. Princeton: Princeton University Press, 1976.

Sachar, Abram Leon. *A History of the Jews*. 5th ed. New York: Knopf, 1974.

Salter, H. E. *Medieval Oxford*. Oxford: Clarendon Press, 1936. Publications of the Oxford Historical Society, no. 100.

Santini, Giovanni. *Europa medioevale. Introduzione allo studio delle strutture territoriali di diritto pubblico. Lezioni di storia del diritto italiano*. Milan: A Giuffré, 1996.

Sarfatij, Herbert. 'Archaeology and the town in the Netherlands'. In Barley, *European Towns*, 203–17.

Scarlata, Marina. 'Caratterizzazione dei quartieri e rapporti di vicinato a Palermo fra XIIIe e XV secolo'. *SMOE*, 681–709.

Schevill, Ferdinand. *Medieval and Renaissance Florence*. 2 vols. Revised ed. New York: Harper and Row, 1963.

Schich, Winfried. 'Slavic proto-towns and the German colonial town in Brandenburg'. *CHUO*, 531–45.

Schlesinger, Walter. 'Burg und Stadt'. In *Aus Verfassungs- und Landesgeschichte. Festschrift zum 70. Geburtstag von Theodor Mayer*. Lindau and Constance: Jan Thorbecke, 1955, 2: 97–150.

Schlesinger, Walter. 'Stadt und Burg im Lichte der Wortgeschichte'. *Studium Generale* 16 (1963): 433–44, reprinted in Haase, *Stadt des Mittelalters* 1: 95–121.

Schlesinger, Walter. 'Städtische Frühformen zwischen Rhein und Elbe'. *SAES*, 297–362.

Schmiedt, Giulio. 'Città scomparse e città di nuova formazione in Italia in relazione al sistema di comunicazione'. *TUVC*, 503–607.

Schneider, Jean. 'Toul dans la seconde moitié du XIIe siècle'. *FSE*, 185–91.

Schneider, Jean. *La ville de Metz aux XIIIe et XIVe siècles*. Nancy: Georges Thomas, 1950.

Schofield, John. *The Building of London from the Conquest to the Great Fire*. London: A Colonnade Book published by British Museum Publications Ltd in association with The Museum of London, 1984.

Schofield, John. *Medieval London Houses*. New Haven and London: Yale University Press, 1994.

Schofield, John, and Roger Leech (eds). *Urban Archaeology in Britain*. Research Report 61. London: Council for British Archaeology, 1987.

Schofield, John, and Alan Vince (eds). *Medieval Towns*. Madison: Fairleigh Dickinson University Press, 1994.

Schulz, Juergen. 'Urbanism in medieval Venice'. In Molho *et al.*, *City States*, 419–45.

Schulz, Knut. *Handwerksgesellen und Lohnarbeiter. Untersuchungen zur oberrheinischen und oberdeutschen Stadtgeschichte des 14. bis 17. Jahrhunderts.* Sigmaringen: Jan Thorbecke, 1985.

Schulz, Knut. 'Richerzeche, Meliorat und Ministerialität in Köln'. *KRE*, 194–72.

Schulz, Knut. 'Zensualität und Stadtentwicklung im 11./12. Jahrhundert'. *BHS*, 73–93.

Schumann, Reinhold. 'Decadenza e ascesa di Bologna e le sue chiese prima del 1100'. *ECI*, 175–92.

Schwineköper, Berent. 'Die Anfänge Magdeburgs'. *SAES*, 389–450.

Schwarzmaier, Hansmartin. *Lucca und das Reich bis zum Ende des 11. Jahrhunderts. Studien zur Sozialstruktur einer Herzogstadt in der Toskana.* Tübingen: Max Niemeyer, 1972.

Schwind, Fred. 'Beobachtungen zur Lage der nachstaufischen Reichsministerialität in der Wetterau und am nördlichen Oberrhein'. *BSS*, 72–93.

Shahar, Shulamith. *Childhood in the Middle Ages*. London: Routledge, 1990.

Shahar, Shulamith. *The Fourth Estate. A History of Women in the Middle Ages*. London: Methuen, 1983.

Simmons, Jack. *Leicester, Past and Present*. 1: *Ancient Borough to 1860*. London: Eyre Methuen, 1974.

Sivery, Gérard. 'Histoire économique et sociale'. In Trenard, *Histoire de Lille*, 111–270.

Sjoberg, Gideon. *The Preindustrial City. Past and Present*. New York: Free Press, 1960.

Slater, Terry. 'English medieval town planning'. In Genecke and Shaw, *Urban Historical Geography*, 93–105.

Sortor, Marci. 'Saint-Omer and its textile trades in the late Middle Ages: a contribution to the proto-industrialization debate'. *American Historical Review* 98 (1993): 1475–99.

Sosson, J.-P. 'Die Körperschaften in den Niederländen und Nordfrankreich: neue Forschungsperspektiven'. In Friedland, *Gilde*, 79–90.

Sosson, J.-P. 'Finances communales et dette publique. Le cas de Bruges à la fin du XIIIe siècle'. *PTME*, 239–57.

Sourdel, Dominique. 'L'organisation de l'espace dans les villes du monde islamique'. In Heers, *Fortifications*, 1–12.

Sprandel, Rolf (ed.). *Quellen zur Hanse-Geschichte*. Darmstadt: Wissenschaftliche Buchgesellschaft, 1982.

Stehkämper, Hugo. 'England und die Stadt Köln als Wahlmacher König Ottos IV (1198). *KRE*, 213–44.

Stehkämper, Hugo. 'Über die rechtliche Absicherung der Stadt Köln gegen eine erzbischöfliche Landesherrschaft vor 1288'. *FSE*, 343–77.

Stern, S. M. 'The constitution of the Islamic city'. *IC*, 25–50.

Steuer, Heiko. 'Urban archaeology in Germany and the study of topographic, functional and social structures'. In Genecke and Shaw, *Urban Historical Geography*, 81–92.

Stevenson, Wendy B. 'The monastic presence: Berwick in the twelfth and thirteenth centuries'. In Lynch *et al.*, *Scottish Medieval Town*, 99–115.

Stoob, Heinz. *Forschungen zum Städtewesen in Europa.* 1: *Räume, Formen und Schichten der mitteleuropäischen Städte. Eine Aufsatzfolge.* Cologne and Vienna: Böhlau, 1970.

Stoob, Heinz, Friedrich Bernhard Fahlbusch and Wolfgang Hölscher (eds). *Urkunden zur Geschichte des Städtewesens in Mittel- und Niederdeutschland bis 1350.* Städteforschung, Reihe C: Quellen, vol. 1. Cologne and Vienna: Böhlau, 1985.

Stouff, Louis. *Arles à la fin du Moyen-Age.* 2 vols. Aix-en-Provence: Université de Provence, 1986.

Stow, Kenneth R. *Alienated Minority. The Jews of Medieval Latin Europe.* Cambridge, Mass.: Harvard University Press, 1992.

Strait, Paul. *Cologne in the Twelfth Century.* Gainesville: University Presses of Florida, 1974.

Strobel, Richard. 'Regensburg als Bischofstadt in bauhistorischer und topographischer Sicht'. In Petri, *Bischofs- und Kathedralstädte*, 60–83.

Studien zu den Anfängen des europäischen Städtewesens. Vorträge und Forschungen herausgegeben vom Konstanzer Arbeitskreis für mittelalterliche Geschichte, 4. Constance and Lindau: Jan Thorbecke, 1958.

Swan, Leo. 'Monastic proto-towns in early medieval Ireland: the evidence of aerial photography, plan analysis and survey'. *CHUO*, 77–102.

Sydow, Jürgen. *Geschichte der Stadt Tübingen. I. Teil. Von den Anfängen bis zum Übergang an Württemberg 1342.* Tübingen: H. Laupp, 1974.

Sydow, Jürgen. 'Landesherrliche Städte des deutschen Südwestens in nachstaufischer Zeit'. *BSS*, 18–33.

Sydow, Jürgen. 'Tübingen und seine Stadtherren als Beispiel der Entwicklung in einer süddeutschen Territorialstadt'. In Rausch, *Stadt und Stadtherr*, 283–300.

Sydow, Jürgen. 'Zur verfassungsgeschichtlichen Stellung von Reichsstadt, freier Stadt und Territorialstadt im 13. und 14. Jahrhundert'. In *Les Libertés Urbaines et Rurales du XIe au XIVe siècle. Vrijheden in de Stad en op het Platteland van de XIe tot de XIVe eeuw.* Brussels: Pro Civitate, 1968, 281–309.

Bibliography

Szabo, Thomas. 'Xenodochia, Hospitäler und Herbergen–kirchliche und kommerziele Gastung im mittelalterlichen Italien (7. bis 14. Jahrhundert)'. *GTG*, 61–92.

Sznura, Franek. *L'Espansione urbana di Firenze nel Dugento*. Florence: La Nuova Italia, 1975.

Tabacco, Giovanni. *The Struggle for Power in Medieval Italy. Structures of Political Rule*. Translated by Rosalind Brown Jensen. Cambridge: Cambridge University Press, 1989.

Tait, James. *The Medieval English Borough. Studies on its Origins and Constitutional History*. Manchester: Manchester University Press, 1936.

Tangheroni, Marco. 'Famiglie nobili e ceto dirigente a Pisa nel XIII secolo'. *CD*, 323–46.

Tarassi, Massimo. 'Le famiglie di parte Guelfa nella classe dirigente della città di Firenze durante il XIII secolo'. *CD*, 301–21.

Thompson, E. A. *Romans and Barbarians. The Decline of the Western Empire*. Madison: University of Wisconsin Press, 1982.

Thrupp, Sylvia L. 'The Gilds'. In *The Cambridge Economic History of Europe* 3 (Cambridge, 1963), 230–80.

Tillott, P. M. (ed.). *A History of Yorkshire. The City of York*. London: Institute of Historical Research by Oxford University Press, 1961. Victoria History of the Counties of England.

Tirelli, Vito. 'Lucca nella seconda metà del secolo XII. Società e istituzioni'. *CD*, 157–231.

Tittler, Robert. *Architecture and Power. The Town Hall and the English Urban Community, c. 1500–1640*. Oxford: Clarendon Press, 1991.

Töpfer, Bernhard (ed.). *Stadt und Städtebürgertum in der deutschen Geschichte des 13. Jahrhunderts*. Berlin: Akademie Verlag, 1976.

Töpfer, Bernhard (ed.). *Städte und Ständestaat. Zur Rolle der Städte bei der Entwicklung der Ständesverfassung in europäischen Staaten vom 13. bis zum 15. Jahrhundert*. Berlin: Akademie Verlag, 1980.

Töpfer, Bernhard. 'Stellung und Aktivitäten der Bürgerschaft von Bischofsstädten während des staufisch-welfischen Thronstreits'. In Töpfer, *Stadt und Städtebürgertum*, 13–62.

Topografia urbana e vita cittadina nell'alto medioevo in occidente. 26 aprile– 1 maggio 1973. Settimane di Studio del Centro Italiano di Studi sull' Alto Medioevo, 21. Spoleto: Presso la Sede del Centro, 1973.

Trenard, Louis (ed.) *Histoire de Lille*. 1: *Des origines à l'avènement de Charles-Quint*. Lille: Publications de la Faculté des Lettres et Sciences Humaines de Lille, 1991.

Turner, Hilary L. *Town Defences in England and Wales. An Architectural and Documentary Study, AD 900–1500*. Hamden, Conn.: Archon Books, 1971.

Tweddle, Dominic. 'Craft and industry in Anglo-Scandinavian York'. In Corfield and Keene, *Work in Towns*, 17–41.

Uitz, Erika. 'Der Kampf um kommunale Autonomie in Magdeburg bis zur Stadtverfassung von 1330'. *SS*, 228–323.

Uitz, Erika. *Women in the Medieval Town*. London: Barrie and Jenkins, 1990.

Untersuchungen zur gesellschaftlichen Struktur der mittelalterlichen Städte in Europa. Reichenau-Vorträge 1963–1964. Vorträge und Forschungen herausgegeben vom Konstanzer Arbeitskreis für mittelalterliche Geschichte, 11. Constance and Stuttgart: Jan Thorbecke, 1966.

Urry, William. *Canterbury under the Angevin Kings*. University of London Historical Studies, 19. London: Athlone Press, 1967.

Uytven, R. van. 'Stadsgeschiedenis in het Noorden en Zuiden'. *AGN* 2: 188–253.

Vaccari, Pietro. 'Pavia nell'alto medioevo'. *CAM*, 151–92.

Valous, Guy de. *Le patriciat Lyonnais aux XIIIe et XIVe siècles*. Paris: A. and J. Picard, 1973.

Vance, James E., Jr. *The Continuing City. Urban Morphology in Western Civilization*. Baltimore: The Johns Hopkins University Press, 1990.

Van Dam, Raymond. *Leadership and Community in Late Antique Gaul*. Berkeley: University of California Press, 1985.

Van de Kieft, Co. 'Das Reich in die Städte im niederländischen Raum zur Zeit des Investiturstreits'. *BHS*, 149–69.

Vercauteren, Fernand. *Luttes sociales à Liège (XIIIe et XIVe siècles)*. 2nd ed. Brussels: La Renaissance du Livre, 1946.

Vercauteren, Fernand. 'Die spätantike *civitas* im frühen Mittelalter'. *Blätter für deutsche Landesgeschichte* 98 (1962): 12–25, reprinted Haase, *Stadt des Mittelalters*, 122–38.

Vercauteren, Fernand. 'La vie urbaine entre Meuse et Loire du VIe au IXe siècle'. *CAM*, 453–84.

Verhulst, Adriaan. 'An aspect of continuity between antiquity and Middle Ages: the origin of the Flemish cities between the North Sea and the Scheldt'. *JMH* 3 (1977): 175–206.

Verhulst, Adriaan. 'The origin of towns in the Low Countries and the Pirenne Thesis', *PP* 122 (1989): 3–35.

Verhulst, Adriaan. 'La vie urbaine dans les anciens Pays-Bas avant l'an mil'. *MA* 1986: 186–99.

Verhulst, Adriaan, and Renée Doehaerd. 'Nijverheid en handel'. *AGN* 1: 183–215.

Vermeesch, Albert. *Essai sur les origines et la signification de la commune dans le nord de la France (XIe et XIIe siècles)*. Studies Presented to the International Commission for the History of Representative and Parliamentary Institutions, 30. Heule, Belgium: UGA, 1966.

Verwers, W. J. H. 'Dorestad: a Carolingian town?' In Hodges and Hobley, *Rebirth*, 52–6.

Vetters, Hermann. 'Austria'. In Barley, *European Towns*, 261–90.

Vicens Vivas, Jaime. *An Economic History of Spain*. Princeton: Princeton University Press, 1969.

Villani, Giovanni. *Chronicle*. Being Selections from the First Nine Books of the *Croniche Fiorentine* of Giovanni Villani. Translated by Rose E. Selfe and edited by Philip H. Wicksteed. London: Archibald Constable & Co., 1906.

Violante, Cinzio. *La Società Milanese nell'età precomunale*. 2nd ed. Bari: Laterza, 1974.

Vittinghoff, Friedrich (ed.). *Stadt und Herrschaft. Römische Kaiserzeit und hohes Mittelalter*. Historische Zeitschrift, Beiheft 7 (neue Folge). Munich: R. Oldenbourg, 1982.

Vittinghoff, Friedrich. 'Zur Verfassung der spätantiken Stadt'. *SAES*, 11–39.

Vogel, Walther. 'Wik-Orte und Wikinger. Eine Studie zu den Anfängen des germanischen Städtewesens'. *Hansische Geschichtsblätter* 60 (1935): 5–48, reprinted Haase, *Stadt des Mittelalters* 1: 196–238.

Vogt, Emil, Ernst Meyer, and Hans Conrad Peyer. *Zürich von der Urzeit zum Mittelalter*. Zürich: Berichthaus, 1971.

Volpe, Gioacchino. *Medio Evo Italiano*. 3rd ed. Rome: Editori Laterza, 1992.

Volpe, Gioacchino. *Studi sulle istituzioni comunali a Pisa. Città e contado, consoli e podestà, secolo XII–XIII*. 2nd ed., with introduction by Cinzio Violante. Florence: G. C. Sansoni, 1970.

Wacher, John. *Roman Britain*. London: J. M. Dent & Sons, 1978.

Wade, Keith. 'Ipswich'. In Hodges and Hobley, *Rebirth*, 93–100.

Waley, Daniel. 'A blood feud with a happy ending: Siena 1285–1304'. *CC*, 45–53.

Waley, Daniel. *Mediaeval Orvieto. The Political History of an Italian City-State, 1157–1334*. Cambridge: Cambridge University Press, 1952.

Waley, Daniel. *Siena and the Sienese in the Thirteenth Century*. Cambridge: Cambridge University Press, 1991.

Wallace, Patrick. 'The archaeology of Viking Dublin', *CHUO*, 103–45.

Wallace, Patrick. 'The archaeology of Anglo-Norman Dublin'. *CHUO*, 379–410.

Ward-Perkins, Bryan. *Cities of Ancient Greece and Italy: Planning in Classical Antiquity*. New York: George Braziller, 1974.

Ward-Perkins, Bryan. *From Classical Antiquity to the Middle Ages. Urban Public Building in Northern and Central Italy, AD 300–850*. Oxford: Oxford University Press, 1984.

Ward-Perkins, Bryan. 'The towns of northern Italy: rebirth or renewal?' In Hodges and Hobley, *Rebirth*, 16–27.

Weber, Max. *The City*. Translated and edited by Don Martindale and Gertrud Neuwirth. New York: Free Press, 1958.

Wee, Herman van der. 'Structural changes and specialization in southern Netherlands industry, 1100–1600'. *EcHR*, ser. 2, 28 (1975): 201–22.

Weinbaum, Martin (ed.). *The London Eyre of 1276*. London: London Record Society, 1976.

Werveke, Hans van. 'The rise of the towns'. In *The Cambridge Economic History of Europe*, III (Cambridge: Cambridge University Press, 1965): 3–41.

Wickham, Chris. *Land and Power. Studies in Italian and European Social History*. London: British School at Rome, 1994.

Wickham, C. J. *The Mountains and the City. The Tuscan Appennines in the Early Middle Ages*. Oxford: Clarendon Press, 1988.

Wickham, Chris. *Early Medieval Italy. Central Power and Local Society 400–1000*. Ann Arbor: University of Michigan Press, 1989.

Wickham, Chris. 'Rural communes and the city of Lucca at the beginning of the thirteenth century'. *CC*, 1–12.

Wightman, Edith Mary. *Gallia Belgica*. Berkeley and Los Angeles: University of California Press, 1985.

Williams, Gwyn A. *Medieval London. From Commune to Capital*. Second ed. London: Athlone Press, 1970.

Wolff, Philippe. 'Civitas et burgus. L'exemple de Toulouse'. *FSE*, 200–9.

Wolff, Philippe (ed.). *Histoire de Toulouse*. Toulouse: Privat, 1974.

Wolff, Philippe. 'Structures sociales et morphologies urbaines dans le développement historique des villes (XIIe–XVIIIe siècles)'. *Cahiers Bruxellois* 22 (1977): 5–72.

Wood, Michael. *In Search of the Dark Ages*. New York: Facts on File Publications, 1987.

Wülfing, Inge-Maren. 'Städtische Finanzpolitik im späteren 13. Jahrhundert'. *BSS*, 34–71.

Wyffels, Carlos. 'Hanse, grands marchands et patriciens de Saint-Omer'. *Société Académique des Antiquaires de la Morinie. Mémoires* 38 (1962). Separately paginated.

Young, Charles R. *The English Borough and Royal Administration, 1130–1307*. Durham, N.C.: Duke University Press, 1961.

Zbierski, Andrzej. 'The development of the Gdánsk area from the ninth to the thirteenth century'. *CHUO*, 289–334.

Map 1   Italy

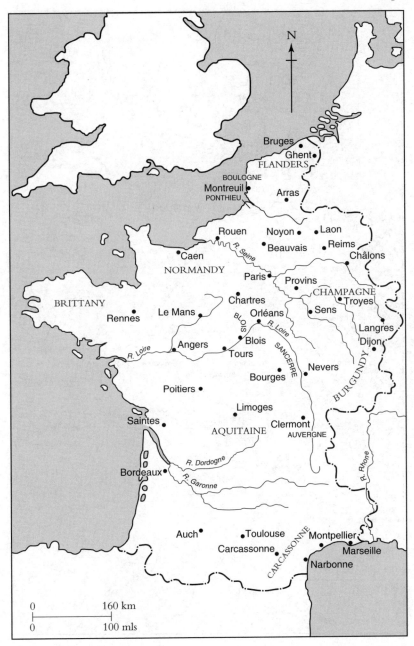

Map 2   France

Map 3   Germany

Map 4   England

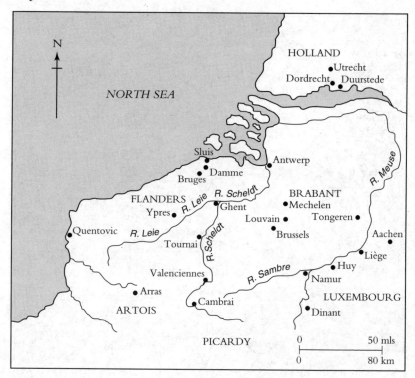

Map 5   Flanders and the Low Countries

City Plans

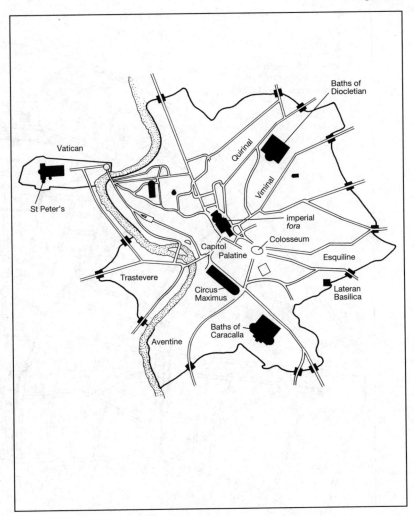

Plan 1   Rome

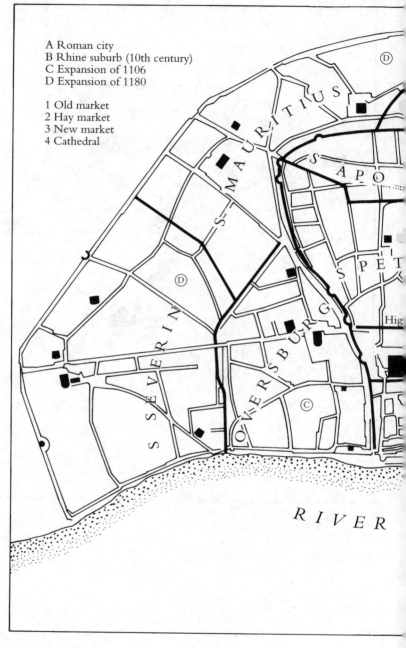

A Roman city
B Rhine suburb (10th century)
C Expansion of 1106
D Expansion of 1180

1 Old market
2 Hay market
3 New market
4 Cathedral

Plan 2   Cologne

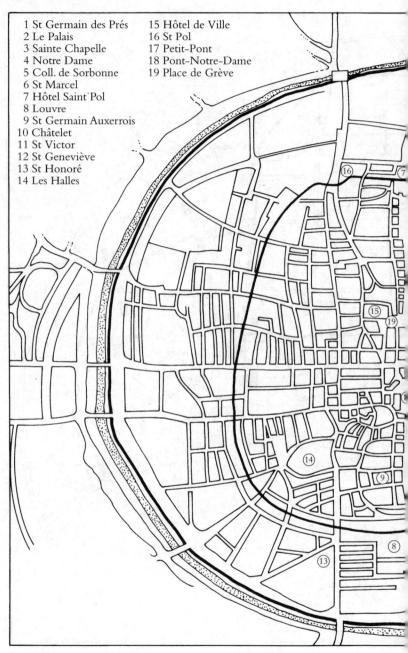

1 St Germain des Prés
2 Le Palais
3 Sainte Chapelle
4 Notre Dame
5 Coll. de Sorbonne
6 St Marcel
7 Hôtel Saint Pol
8 Louvre
9 St Germain Auxerrois
10 Châtelet
11 St Victor
12 St Geneviève
13 St Honoré
14 Les Halles
15 Hôtel de Ville
16 St Pol
17 Petit-Pont
18 Pont-Notre-Dame
19 Place de Grève

Plan 3   Paris

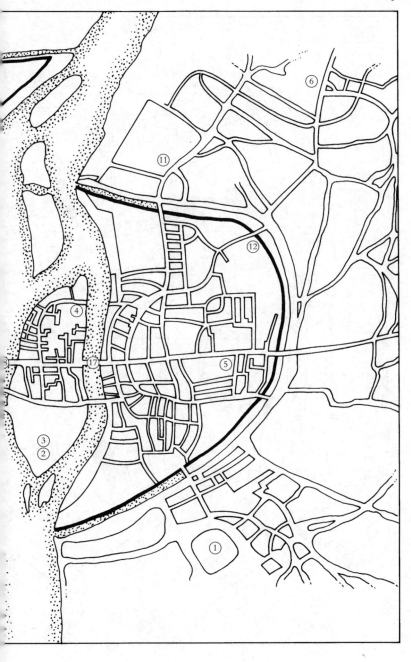

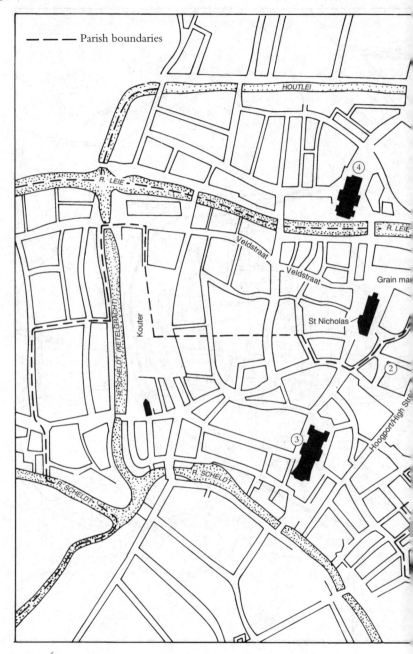

Plan 4   Ghent

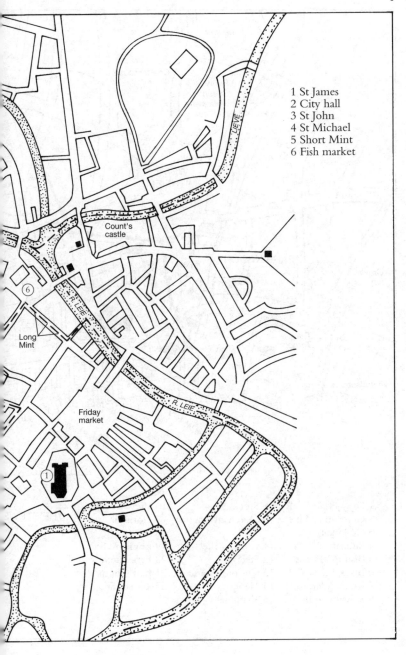

1 St James
2 City hall
3 St John
4 St Michael
5 Short Mint
6 Fish market

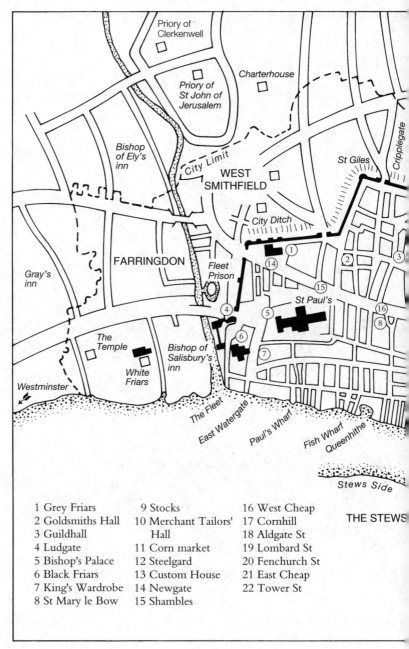

1 Grey Friars
2 Goldsmiths Hall
3 Guildhall
4 Ludgate
5 Bishop's Palace
6 Black Friars
7 King's Wardrobe
8 St Mary le Bow

9 Stocks
10 Merchant Tailors' Hall
11 Corn market
12 Steelgard
13 Custom House
14 Newgate
15 Shambles

16 West Cheap
17 Cornhill
18 Aldgate St
19 Lombard St
20 Fenchurch St
21 East Cheap
22 Tower St

Plan 5   London

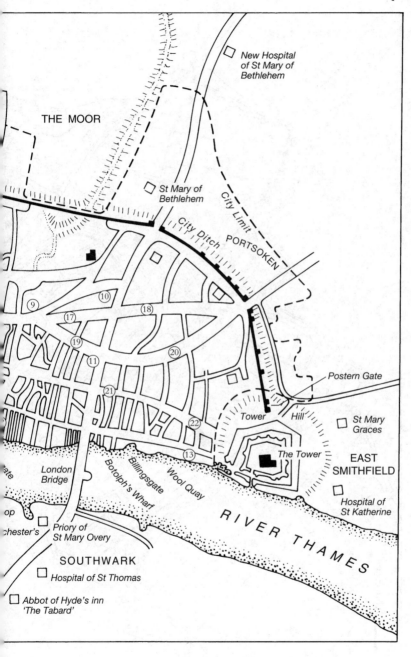

New Hospital
of St Mary of
Bethlehem

THE MOOR

City Limit

St Mary of
Bethlehem

City Ditch

PORTSOKEN

9

10

17

18

19

20

11

21

22

Postern Gate

Tower   Hill

St Mary
Graces

13

Tower

The Tower

EAST
SMITHFIELD

London
Bridge

Billingsgate

Botolph's Wharf

Wool Quay

RIVER   THAMES

Hospital of
St Katherine

op

chester's

Priory of
St Mary Overy

SOUTHWARK

Hospital of St Thomas

Abbot of Hyde's inn
'The Tabard'

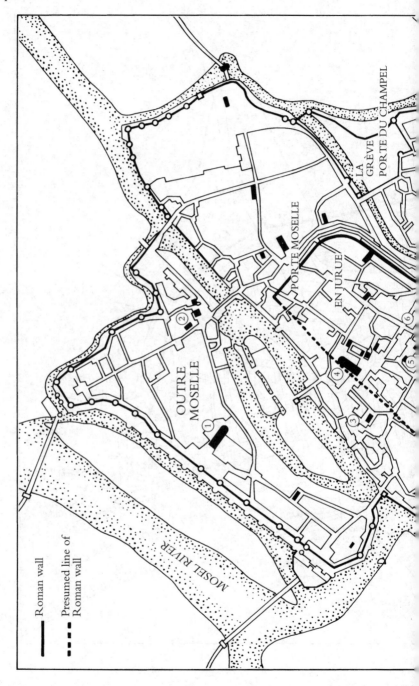

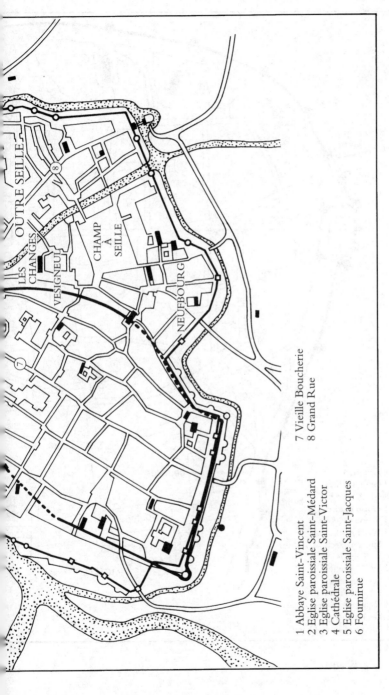

LES OUTRE SEILLE

CHANGES

VESIGNEUL

CHAMP À SEILLE

NEUFBOURG

1 Abbaye Saint-Vincent
2 Eglise paroissiale Saint-Médard
3 Eglise paroissiale Saint-Victor
4 Cathédrale
5 Eglise paroissiale Saint-Jacques
6 Fournirue

7 Vieille Boucherie
8 Grand Rue

Plan 6   Metz

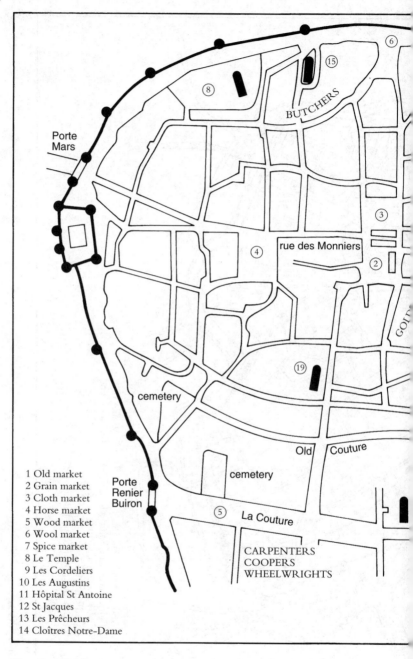

BUTCHERS

rue des Monniers

GOLD

cemetery

cemetery

Old Couture

Porte
Renier
Buiron

La Couture

1 Old market
2 Grain market
3 Cloth market
4 Horse market
5 Wood market
6 Wool market
7 Spice market
8 Le Temple
9 Les Cordeliers
10 Les Augustins
11 Hôpital St Antoine
12 St Jacques
13 Les Prêcheurs
14 Cloîtres Notre-Dame

CARPENTERS
COOPERS
WHEELWRIGHTS

Plan 7   Reims

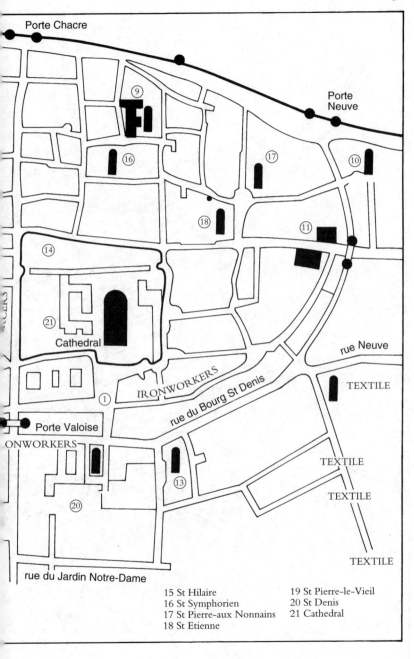

Porte Chacre

Porte Neuve

rue Neuve

TEXTILE

TEXTILE

TEXTILE

TEXTILE

Cathedral

IRONWORKERS

rue du Bourg St Denis

Porte Valoise

ONWORKERS

rue du Jardin Notre-Dame

15 St Hilaire
16 St Symphorien
17 St Pierre-aux Nonnains
18 St Etienne

19 St Pierre-le-Vieil
20 St Denis
21 Cathedral

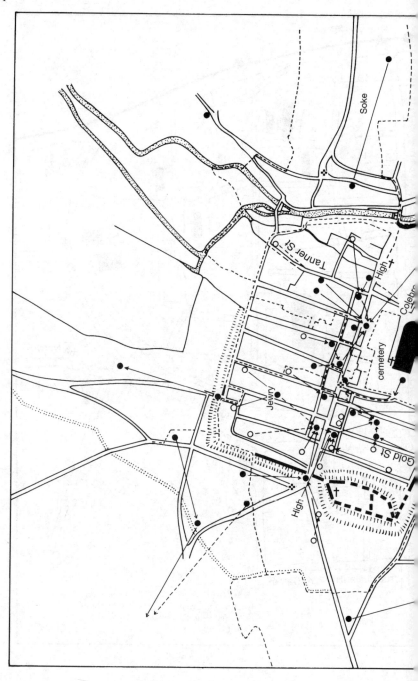

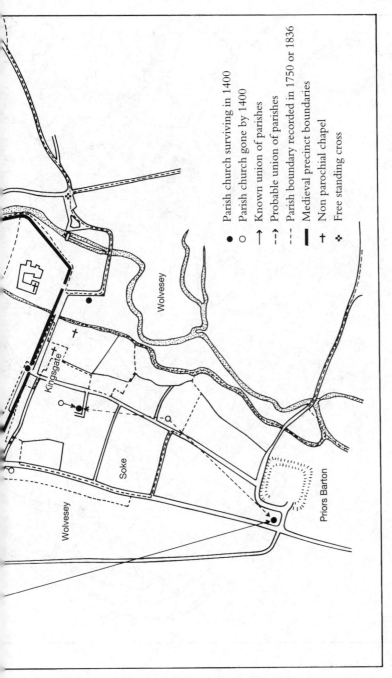

Parish church surviving in 1400 ●

Parish church gone by 1400 ○

Known union of parishes →

Probable union of parishes ⇢

Parish boundary recorded in 1750 or 1836 ┄┄

Medieval precinct boundaries ▌

Non parochial chapel †

Free standing cross ✤

Wolvesey

Kingsgate

Soke

Wolvesey

Priors Barton

Plan 8 Winchester

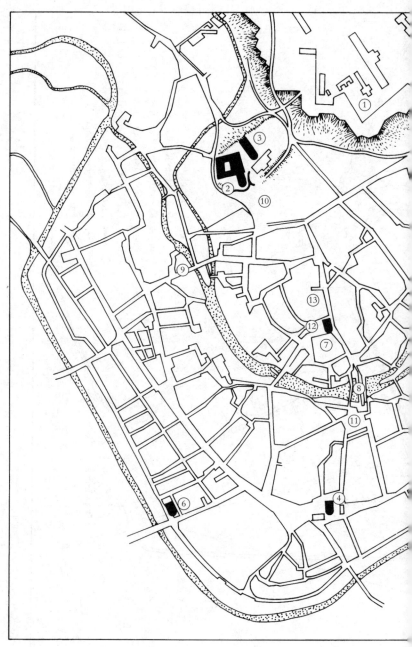

Plan 9   Erfurt

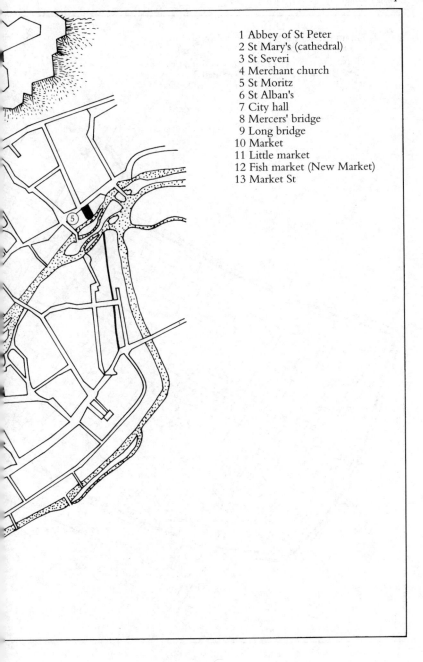

1 Abbey of St Peter
2 St Mary's (cathedral)
3 St Severi
4 Merchant church
5 St Moritz
6 St Alban's
7 City hall
8 Mercers' bridge
9 Long bridge
10 Market
11 Little market
12 Fish market (New Market)
13 Market St

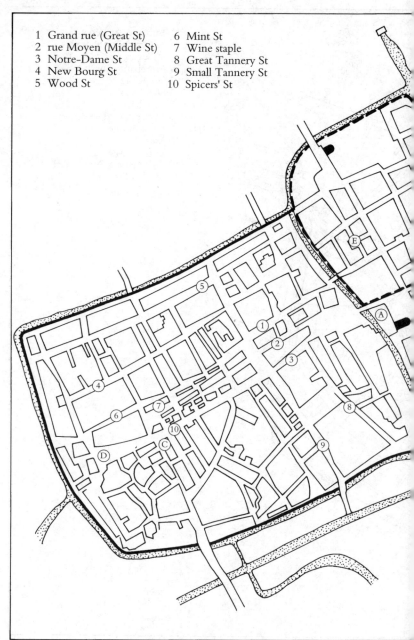

1 Grand rue (Great St)
2 rue Moyen (Middle St)
3 Notre-Dame St
4 New Bourg St
5 Wood St
6 Mint St
7 Wine staple
8 Great Tannery St
9 Small Tannery St
10 Spicers' St

Plan 10 Troyes

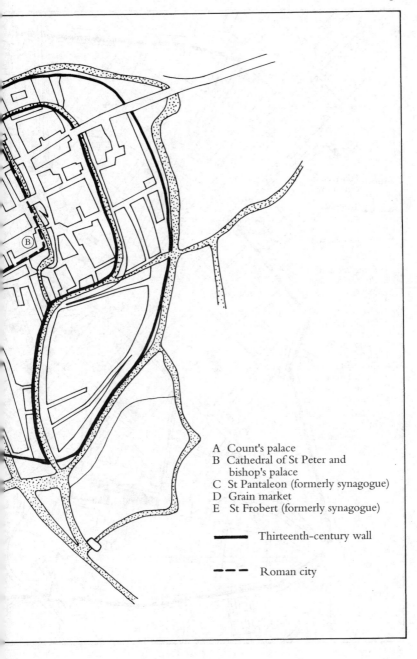

A Count's palace
B Cathedral of St Peter and
   bishop's palace
C St Pantaleon (formerly synagogue)
D Grain market
E St Frobert (formerly synagogue)

——— Thirteenth-century wall

– – – Roman city

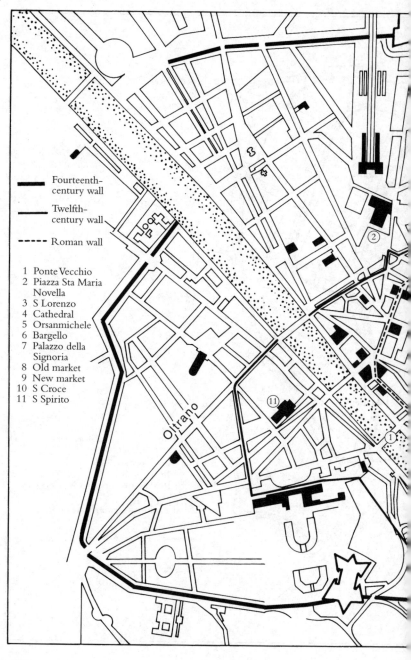

Fourteenth-
century wall

Twelfth-
century wall

---- Roman wall

1 Ponte Vecchio
2 Piazza Sta Maria
  Novella
3 S Lorenzo
4 Cathedral
5 Orsanmichele
6 Bargello
7 Palazzo della
  Signoria
8 Old market
9 New market
10 S Croce
11 S Spirito

Oltrano

Plan 11 Florence

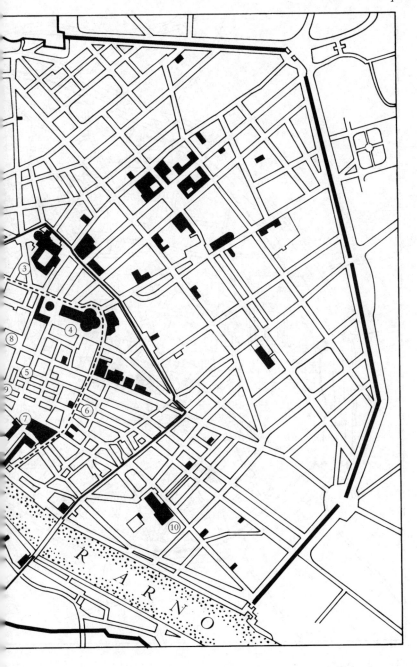

R. ARNO

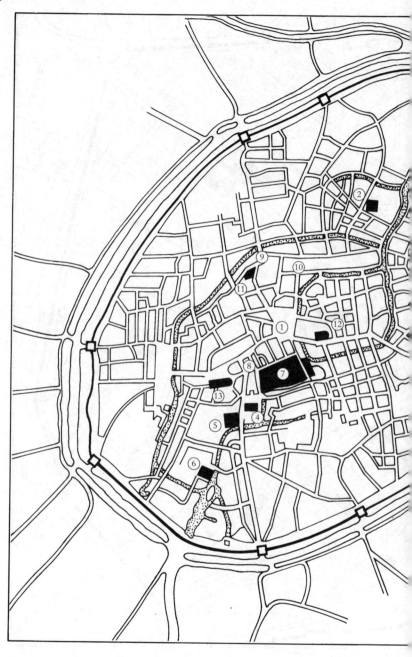

Plan 12   Bruges

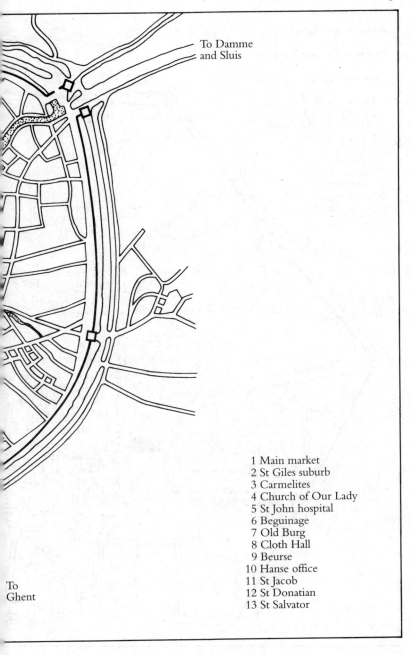

To Damme
and Sluis

To
Ghent

1 Main market
2 St Giles suburb
3 Carmelites
4 Church of Our Lady
5 St John hospital
6 Beguinage
7 Old Burg
8 Cloth Hall
9 Beurse
10 Hanse office
11 St Jacob
12 St Donatian
13 St Salvator

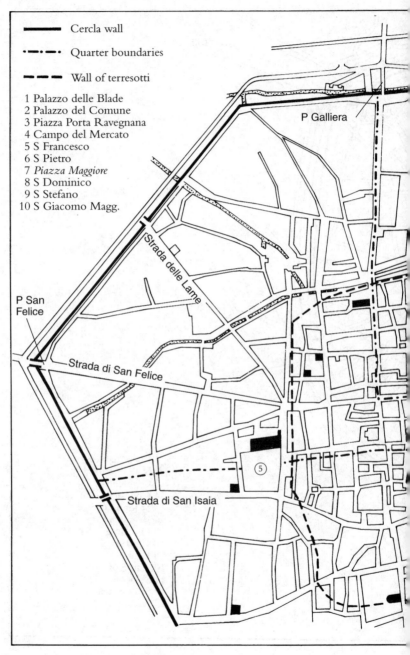

Cercla wall

Quarter boundaries

Wall of terresotti

1 Palazzo delle Blade
2 Palazzo del Comune
3 Piazza Porta Ravegnana
4 Campo del Mercato
5 S Francesco
6 S Pietro
7 *Piazza Maggiore*
8 S Dominico
9 S Stefano
10 S Giacomo Magg.

P Galliera

Strada delle Lame

P San Felice

Strada di San Felice

⑤

Strada di San Isaia

Plan 13   Bologna

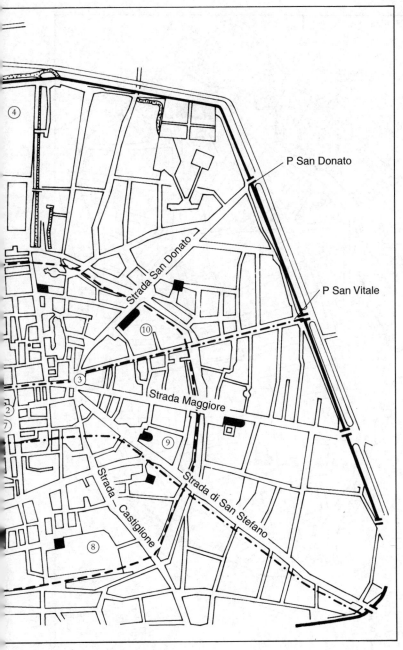

P San Donato

P San Vitale

Strada San Donato

Strada Maggiore

Strada di San Stefano

Strada Castiglione

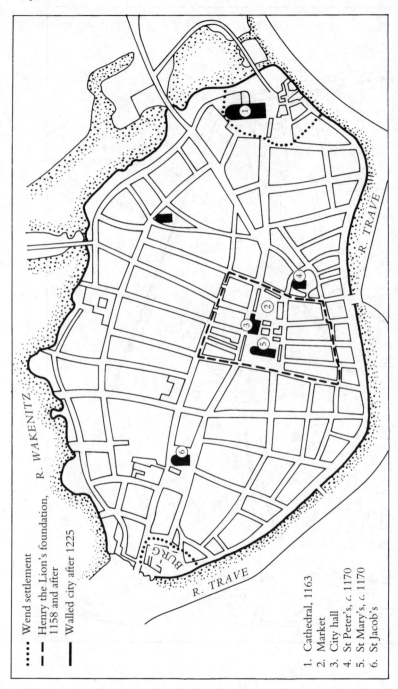

Wend settlement
Henry the Lion's foundation, 1158 and after
Walled city after 1225

1. Cathedral, 1163
2. Market
3. City hall
4. St Peter's, *c.* 1170
5. St Mary's, *c.* 1170
6. St Jacob's

Plan 14 Lübeck

Index